PASSION FOR TRUTH
THE LIFE OF JOHN HENRY NEWMAN

Portrait by Sir William Ross (1845)

PASSION FOR TRUTH
THE LIFE OF JOHN HENRY NEWMAN

FR. JUAN R. VÉLEZ

TAN Books
Charlotte, North Carolina

ISBN: 978-0-89555-871-8

Cover design by Tony Pro.

Cover image: Newman with Oratorian Collar, Engraving
by Henry MacLean, based on Portrait by Richmond, 1845.

Printed and bound in the United States of America.

TAN Books
Charlotte, North Carolina
www.TANBooks.com
2012

DEDICATION

With filial affection and gratitude to my parents, Maria R. Giraldo de Vélez and the late Dr. Rodrigo Vélez-Londoño, And with the same sentiments to my spiritual father and bishop, Bishop Javier Echeverría-Rodríguez, Prelate of Opus Dei.

CONTENTS

Foreword xi

Acknowledgements xv

Introduction xvii

Chronology xx

Abbreviations xxi

Chapter
  1. Newman's England 1
  2. John Henry's Childhood 4
  3. 1816: First Conversion. 11
  4. 1817 to 1822: Undergraduate at Trinity College. . . 20
  5. 1822 to 1845: Fellow at Oriel College. 27
  6. Newman's Religious Development 37
  7. Curate of St. Clement's 55
  8. Death of Newman's Father. 60
  9. Character of the Young Oxford Don 65
 10. 1825: Holy Orders in the Anglican Church 72
 11. Family and Friends. 83
 12. Early Religious Controversies 100
 13. New Anglican Friends 110
 14. Tutor at Oriel. 121
 15. Newman's First Book: *The Arians of the
     Fourth Century* 130
 16. Travel in the Mediterranean 137
 17. Illness in Sicily. 152

18. Origins of the Oxford Movement 158

19. 1833: The Start of the Oxford Movement 169

20. The First Year of the Oxford Movement. 179

21. A Leader at Oxford. 187

22. Seeking a Middle Ground or *Via Media* 201

23. Defending Anglo-Catholic Theology 220

24. Understanding the Holy Eucharist. 245

25. 1839: First Anglican Difficulties. 271

26. Newman's Doubts about His Position in the
    English Church 287

27. The Crisis Over *Tract 90* 316

28. Debate on How to Make Men Moral 348

29. Storm and Calm Over *Tract 90* 361

30. Newman's Resignation from St. Mary's
    University Church 380

31. Reaching Certitude of Conversion to
    Roman Catholicism 404

32. 1845: Last Preparations for Conversion 438

33. Newman's Essay on Development and
    His Final Conversion 470

34. First Years as a Roman Catholic 508

35. Public Defense of Catholics in England 521

36. Founder of the Catholic University of Ireland . . 528

37. Advocate of an Educated Catholic Laity 537

38. *Apologia Pro Vita Sua* 548

39. Newman, the Philosopher 557

40. Papal Infallibility and Letter to the Duke
    of Norfolk 565
41. Cardinal of the Roman Catholic Church 574

About the Author 589

Glossary 590

Bibliography 595

Index 600

LIST OF ILLUSTRATIONS

1. England, Wales and Ireland (ca. 1876)
2. Family Group sketch by Maria Giberne (ca. 1830)
3. Oxford (1901)
4. Trinity College
5. Trinity College Chapel
6. Oriel Quad, Oriel College
7. Mediterranean (1899), Newman's journey during 1832-1833
8. St. Mary, the Virgin, Oxford
9. The pulpit of St. Mary the Virgin
10. Littlemore College (ca. 1950's)
11. Fr. Newman (ca. 1866)
12. St. Mary and St. Nicholas, Littlemore (ca. 1920's)
13. Living Room at Littlemore
14. Newman's Desk at Littlemore
15. Photograph of Cardinal Newman by Louis Barraud (1885)
16. Newman's writing desk, Birmingham Oratory
17. Cardinal Newman Library, Birmingham Oratory
18. Cardinal's Private Chapel, Birmingham Oratory
19. Newman's Tomb at Rednal, Birmingham

FOREWORD

IT is the hope of many that very soon we will be able to appreciate the irony of John Henry Newman's retort to the poor woman who made the mistake of calling him a saint: "Saints are not literary men," he wrote, "they do not love the classics, they do not write 'Tales.'" Literary men do indeed make saints and great leaders too, witness Augustine and Thomas More, but there is so much more to Newman than his own humble estimate. When Pope Benedict raised him to the altars in September, 2010, he extolled Blessed John Henry Newman's extraordinary intellectual contributions, but the focus of his praise was Newman's "lifelong devotion to the priestly ministry" as a "pastor of souls." It is fitting that in the latest "Newman moment"— and there are certainly more to come— the Victorian sage, the master of English prose, and the greatest of modern Catholic thinkers is associated with corporal works of mercy directed at the poor of the Birmingham slums.

The Holy Father, who as a young theologian, was deeply influenced by Newman's seminal thought on conscience, the role of the laity, and the development of doctrine, has the same problem we all have in getting hold of Newman: the sheer largeness as well as the special demands of the project. In the fearless pursuit of truth, Newman's preoccupation with "wholeness," which he defined in contrast to theory, to the "isms" of the day, requires an intense and persistent inquiry rooted in history, doctrine, and the pressing demands of the world. Wholeness requires "consistency," Newman's high ideal in life and thought, but therein lies a paradox for those who insist on traditional categories. Discussing the problem of the Newman biographer, Ian Ker points out that Newman "may be called, without inconsistency, both conservative and liberal, progressive and traditional, cautious and radical, dogmatic yet practical, idealistic but realistic."

It is as a Catholic thinker, not as a theorist, that dubious hero of his time and ours, that Newman's grand mission comes into focus and his discourse becomes lucid. He attempts no less in his vast and varied canon than to understand what he called "the Providential system of the world," whether approached through Church history, apologetics, or philosophy, not to mention poetry, fiction, and the device of satire, all of which tools were at his command; yet throughout he is rooted in here-and-now practical concerns—he wrote only to "calls," he tells us—whether moving the Tractarian argument, attacking the corrosive sources of liberal secularism, or moderating the extremes of Church parties. And always he is the shrewd and penetrating guide to the duties of daily Christian life.

I think of the whole magnificent skein of Newman's discourse spread over his long life as answering to his own argument in the *Essay in Aid of a Grammar of Assent*, where he reasons that "real assent" to religious truth, which we are bound by conscience to seek, according to our gifts, comes only through "the accumulation of probabilities sufficient for certitude," so that the pursuit of truth, or the "real" as he preferred to call it, is instinct with faith. Newman's life, marked by holiness, is a compelling model of the steady, quiet progress of spiritual discernment beneath the stormy events of life—and who in his age was more involved in controversy than Newman?—where we "mount up the heavenly ladder step by step, where transformation is like the unfolding leaves in spring."

Newman, himself among the greatest of autobiographers, is by needs better understood through his life story than a man of theory or system, but the depth and complexity of his life precludes the "definitive biography." Each Newman biography adds some vital perspective, whether it is Wilfred Ward's exposition of Newman's basic theology, Meriol Trevor's invaluable picture of his daily life, or Father Ker's attention to the shape and power of Newman's imagination, a neglected aspect of his genius. When I met Father Juan in 2005 at Mercer House, the Opus Dei residence in Princeton, we talked about, among other things, an article he had just finished, later incorporated in this biography, on Newman's near-fatal illness in Sicily as a young man. This episode brought about a great interior realization and determined Blessed John Henry's course in life. I was struck at the time and then again when I read the manuscript of *Passion for Truth* that Father Juan's worthy pursuit as a biographer has been to search out what was essentially Catholic in the young Newman that moved him inexorably towards that most famous conversion many years later and to recognize that it was that same steady vision in the midst of turmoil, that unflinching cooperation with grace, that was soon to make Blessed John Henry Newman a passionate truth-seeker, the master architect of the Catholic Revival in England, and some day, God-willing, a Doctor of the Church.

Dr. John Hulsman
Delray Beach, Florida
March 31, 2011

Dr. Hulsman is Professor Emeritus of English Literature at Rider University and editor of The Rule of Our Warfare, John Henry Newman and the true Christian Life, A Reader.

ACKNOWLEDGMENTS

THE life of Blessed John Henry Newman has been, for many, a compelling example of Christian holiness and for me, the inspiration for this book. I first came to appreciate Newman's life and ideas when reading *John Henry Newman (1801–1890)* by Fr. José Morales. I was especially attracted by Newman's passion for the truth and his courage to pursue this truth to the end. I soon came to admire Newman's vision of Christian holiness. Like St. Josemaría Escrivá, another priest and an educator, Newman insisted on the laity's call to holiness through the exercise of the virtues in everyday life.

I wish to express my gratitude to the members of Opus Dei and friends for their support during the writing of this book and to Susan Ridlen, Maria Riz Marsella and Anna Gil Exconde for their generous assistance in the preparation of some maps, to Claire O'Leary for her library assistance and to Maria Knox for her help with the "newmanbiography" website. I wish to thank Msgr. James A. Kelly, Professor John Hulsman, Professor William Park, Fr. C. John McCloskey, Carol Buck and Fr. Martin J. Miller, who read the manuscript and offered me valuable advice. Professor Hulsman also graciously wrote the foreword. I also wish to thank Professor John F. Crosby, Dwight Lindley and Janet Madigan, who read the pages on Newman as a philosopher and offered me their advice.

I am grateful to the Princeton Theological Seminary, the University of California in Los Angeles, Fuller Theological Seminary and Christendom College for use of their libraries. My sincere gratitude also extends to Sr. Irene Felder, Sr. Katherine Dietz and Sr. Katy Thomas of The Spiritual Family The Work, the International Centre of Newman Friends, to Fr. Paul Chavasse of the Birmingham Oratory and to Olivia Kirwan for graciously providing me with many photographs of Newman and Oxford.

In particular, I wish to thank Professor Barbara Wyman, Instructor of English and Latin at McNeese State University, and her daughter, Kate Alice Wyman, for their generous editing of the first draft of the manuscript, and Todd Aglialoro, Cecilia Thurlow, Mary Frances Lester, and Lesly Bratt for the final editing and revision. Lastly, I wish to thank Fr. John Ford, C.S.C., for some important corrections which were incorporated in the second printing.

INTRODUCTION

UNLIKE many Newman biographies, the purpose of this one is to highlight Newman's constant search for religious truth and lasting happiness. Newman was drawn by the truth about God, about mankind, and about the Church, like metal is drawn by a magnet. From his early adulthood, he preferred truth to a superficial peace of mind. In a world that offered happiness through material comforts, he chose the lasting happiness that comes from love of God and neighbor. It is primarily a biography of the first half of Newman's life. The subtitle suggests a future second volume, which God willing would appear many years from now.

Each biographer reflects his own perspective. My perspective is that of an American and a Catholic priest who has been enriched spiritually and intellectually by Newman. For me, Newman is an eloquent witness of the healthy relationship between faith and reason, a witness who speaks to contemporary man. In addition to the priesthood, there are a few experiences that I share with Newman. As a young boy I lived and studied for one year in Ealing, and afterward, for another year, at St. John Beaumont, a boarding school outside of London in Windsor. After becoming a priest in Rome, I was stationed for four years at a prestigious university in New Jersey where I engaged the undergraduates in provocative conversations and personal discussions regarding God, mankind, society, and morality. There, amid Princeton's neo-Gothic imitation of Oxford, I preached for some years at the University Chapel. These shared experiences unite me to Newman's childhood education and university life; they afford me some personal insight into the man and priest.

The focus of this biography is to show the spiritual and intellectual path that led Newman from Evangelical Protestantism through Anglicanism to Roman Catholicism. Newman relied on divine Revelation together with logical reasoning and historical facts to reach religious truths and defend religious doctrines. This biography also directs attention to Newman's character and virtues. Newman naturally had personal faults, which he recognized and strove to overcome; this striving, coupled with both human and supernatural qualities, characterizes his greatness as a man. Newman's passion for the truth about God impelled him to live to a great degree the virtues of faith, hope, charity, industriousness, generosity, and magnanimity.

I hope that through these pages the reader will become familiar with Newman: a loyal friend and dedicated priest, a powerful preacher, and an outstanding educator. He was an exceptional writer of English prose and religious poetry. He was a knowledgeable Church historian and a bold reformer. Newman was also the founder of the Oratory of St. Philip Neri in England. Above all, Newman was a man in love with God and His Church. His entire life was aimed at learning and teaching the truth about God and defending His Church, first as an Anglican, and afterward as a Catholic.

The primary source for this biography is Newman's

abundant correspondence, meticulously organized and documented by the Fathers of the Birmingham Oratory. Through many direct quotations, Newman speaks out from the pages. The letters of his correspondents and the biographies and monographs consulted provide the context and add to the narrative.

In an age that presents a mix of rationalism and skepticism, Newman stands out as a wise man who employed reason to reach a deeper understanding of faith and, as a result, a more intelligible way of teaching it to many. He is both a good teacher and an example for contemporary man, who often surrenders to the modern-day disunity between faith and reason. Through his university work at Oxford and Dublin, he showed that faith is not opposed to reason; rather it is an indispensable light for reason. Newman made the convincing argument that faith is essential for the fullness of knowledge.

Chronology of John Henry Newman

1801	Born in London, February 21
1808	Enters school at Ealing
1816	First religious conversion
1817	Begins studies at Trinity College, Oxford
1822	Elected Fellow at Oriel College, Oxford
1824	Ordained a deacon. Becomes curate of St. Clement's. Death of Mr. John Newman
1825	Holy Orders in the Anglican Church
1828–1843	Vicar of St. Mary the Virgin
1831	Resigns Tuition at Oxford
1832–1833	Trip to the Mediterranean
1833	Start of the Oxford Movement
1836	Death of friend R. Hurrell Froude and Mrs. Newman
1841	Publishes Tract 90
1842	Moves from Oxford to Littlemore
1845	Received into the Roman Catholic Church
1847	Ordained a Catholic priest in Rome
1848	Founded English Oratory of St. Philip Neri
1854–1858	Founder and rector of Catholic University of Ireland
1859	Opened Oratory School in Birmingham
1864	Published *Apologia Pro Vita Sua*
1877	Elected first honorary Fellow at Trinity College
1879	Created cardinal by Pope Leo XIII
1889	Last Mass, on Christmas Day
1890	Newman dies on August 11 in Birmingham
2010	Pope Benedict XVI beatifies Newman on September 19

ABBREVIATIONS FOR COMMONLY USED TEXTS OF JOHN HENRY NEWMAN

Apo.	Apologia Pro Vita Sua
Arians	Arians of the Fourth Century
Dev.	An Essay on the Development of Christian Doctrine
DA	Discussions and Arguments
Ess., I	Essays Critical and Historical, Vol. I
Ess., II	Essays Critical and Historical, Vol. II
GA	Grammar of Assent
Idea	The Idea of a University
Jfc	Lectures on Justification
LD	Letters and Diaries
LG	Loss and Gain
MD	Meditations and Devotions
US	Fifteen Sermons Preached Before the University of Oxford (Oxford University Sermons)
PPS	Parochial and Plain Sermons
OS	Sermons Preached on Various Occasions
SD	Sermons Bearing on Subjects of the Day
Tracts	Tracts for the Times
VM, Vol. 1	Lectures on the Prophetic Office of the Church, The Via Media
VM, II	Via Media, Vol. II
VV	Verses on Various Occasions

CHAPTER 1

NEWMAN'S ENGLAND

JOHN Henry Newman was born in London, the financial and intellectual capital of the nineteenth century. During his childhood and early youth, England experienced an extraordinary growth in population and military power. Despite its loss of the American colonies, it enjoyed a period of colonial expansion and a booming economy. Industrialization and new markets would allow the British Empire to retain its power for most of the century.

The English society of Newman's time experienced significant social, political, and religious changes, as the mid-eighteenth-century agrarian economy became an industrial one. Many people were moving to cities looking for work at factories or ports. Working conditions were unhealthy and often dangerous, particularly in the mines and textile mills. Since the wages were low, entire families had to work in these conditions to survive. While a new middle class began to emerge in the cities, consisting of factory owners, shopkeepers, and professionals, the factory workers were almost as poor as the farm workers in the country.

During the 1830s, England barely avoided the revolutions that ravaged Europe, but there was serious social inequality and unrest in the mining and factory cities. In addition to the low wages, child labor, and unsafe work environments, many people lived crowded into buildings without any sewer or lighting systems and with inadequate water supply. In these living conditions, infant mortality was high and crime was common.

England was a monarchy with parliamentary rule and two political parties, the Tories and the Whigs. The Tories supported the Established Church of England and the traditional political and aristocratic structures. During the second quarter of the century the Whig Party carried out important social reforms including the abolition of slavery in the English colonies and the opening up of access to political offices for non-Anglicans.

In 1837, Queen Victoria succeeded to the throne at the age of eighteen. She would have the longest reign of any English monarch, lasting from 1837 until 1901. Her reign was characterized by the expansion of the British Empire together with its customs, its social progress and its literature. Queen Victoria's reign was also marked by liberalism in religion and tragic foreign policies, especially in Ireland.

John Henry Newman descended from a family of small farmers and village tailors in Cambridgeshire who originally came from Holland. Newman's paternal grandfather had moved to London and succeeded as a grocer. He and his wife Elizabeth Good had one son, John Newman, and a daughter, as well as two other children, who died at a young age.

John Newman was an ambitious and enterprising man who, wishing to improve his position, began work for a banking firm. He married Jemima Fourdrinier on October 29, 1799 at St. Mary's church, Lambeth (London). John was thirty-two years old and his wife was twenty-seven. Jemima was the daughter of Henry Fourdrinier, a wealthy papermaker, who had descended from French Huguenots. Jemima received a dowry of £5,000,[1] which at her death was passed on intact to her children. The Fourdrinier ancestry can be traced back as far as 1575 to Henri Fourdrinier, who was from Caen in Normandy and in later life became an Admiral of France and was created Viscount.[2] His family had emigrated to Holland during a time of religious persecution. John Newman rose up the social ladder and in 1812 opened a banking firm, Ramsbottom, Newman and Ramsbottom, with his uncle and cousin, Richard and John Ramsbottom. The firm was located at 72 Lombard Street at the old Fourdrinier residence. As a part of a new wealthy middle class John Newman enjoyed musical entertainment and good meals. He considered himself a man of the world and not very religious.[3] He and his wife were members of the Church of England. Mrs. Newman, inclined to a mild type of Calvinism, was a devoted mother and gave the family life a religious tone.

---

1 At that time a British pound was worth roughly $5.00, and at that time a U.S. dollar was worth many times what it is worth today.

2 See Sieveking, Isabel Giberne, *Memoir and Letters of Francis W. Newman*, Kegan Paul, Trench, Trübner & Co., Ltd., London, 1909, 3; available at: http://www.archive.org/texts/flipbook/flippy.php?id=a608777200sievuoft

3 José Morales Marín, *Newman (1801-1890)*, Ediciones Rialp, Madrid, 1990, 12-13.

CHAPTER 2

JOHN HENRY'S CHILDHOOD

JOHN Henry Newman was born on February 21, 1801, in the city of London to John Newman and his wife Jemima Fourdrinier. His birth was at the family home on Old Broad Street, today the site of London Stock Exchange. John Henry was baptized into the Anglican Church on April 9, at St. Benet Fink Church. He was the first of six children. He had two brothers, Charles Robert and Francis (Frank), and three sisters, Harriet, Jemima and Mary.[1] During the birth of their siblings, John Henry and his brother Charles were taken to live at the family's retreat home in Ham. This Georgian-style home was near Richmond, a London suburb. It was a big house with a garden, located next to the Royal Oak Inn and near the Thames River. Newman was very observant and later could remember the plan of the house, which the family sold before he was five years old. In 1861, in a letter to Jemima, he recalled being at Ham when she was born and having sent his parents the present of a "broom-flower" on the day of her birth.[2] He recalled

---

1 Maisie Ward provides a vivid picture of the Newman's childhood in "Childhood," in *Young Mr. Newman* (New York: Sheed & Ward, 1948), 1-15.

2 Newman, John Henry, *Letters and Diaries,* Edited by Charles Stephen Dessain, Ian Ker, Thomas Gornall, Edward E. Kelly, Gerard Tracey, and Francis J. McGrath (Oxford: Clarendon Press, 1978-2009),Vol. XX,

with great fondness a rocking horse at Ham and a beautiful grove of trees, of which his favorite was a large chestnut.

In 1802, John Newman bought a home on Southampton Street in the residential London district of Bloomsbury, where the family would enjoy a comfortable life. John Henry had many memories from his early childhood. He remembered that, at the age of five, his mother told him that he was a big boy and must behave himself, and that, at the age of six, he recited William Cowper's "Faithful Friend," a tragic story of a goldfinch who, despite achieving his own freedom, returned to be with his still-captive friend. At the age of five Newman could read. His father praised him as a "clever boy" and encouraged him to learn something new every day. He also gave him the assignment to learn the multiplication table by heart, and he would test him. He promised his son that "if I find you improve, I intend after a time to buy a nice Copy Book and teach you to write."[3] This was a fitting present for someone who would spend all of his life writing.

In the first decades of the 1800s, few English children received formal education. Churches offered Sunday school for working-class children. Only in the 1870s did the government establish elementary schools and make education compulsory. Until that time, those who could afford it would pay tutors to educate their children or send them to a private boarding school for an education in the Classics. These privileged children learned to read and

---

JHN to Mrs. John Mozley (September 24, 1861), 46. After this it will be cited *LD*.

3 *LD*, Vol. I, Mr. John Newman to JHN (November 24, 1806), 3.

write Latin and Greek; later they read from important Roman and Greek authors. Some of these children went on afterward to one of the two English universities, Oxford or Cambridge. They were customarily the children of landed gentry, nobles, well-off clergymen, or businessmen.

Although his family amassed only a moderate wealth, John Henry was amongst those privileged children who, at the age of seven, were able to attend a large private boarding school in Ealing, just outside of London. Dr. George Nicholas, a graduate from Oxford, ran this boys' school. He was a kind man and a friend of Mr. Newman. Dr. Nicholas, who perhaps noted a similar kindness in his new charge, took a special liking to young Newman. He must have delighted in John Henry's aptitudes and soon considered him a prize pupil.

Newman soon excelled in studies, learned to play the violin and won prizes for speech competitions. From his diary, we know that at the age of nine, he began to read the Roman poets Ovid and Virgil and to study Greek,[4] and the following year, began writing verses.[5] At the age of eleven, he started reading Homer, whom he would quote the rest of his life, and the following year, Herodotus, the famous Greek historian.

He was a shy and stubborn boy but had a keen eye for observing and narrating events and also possessed an eagerness to learn. From an early age, he began the habit of recording daily entries into a diary,[6] sometimes as short

---

4 *LD*, Vol. I (1810), 6.

5 *Ibid.*, 7.

6 *Ibid.*, 6-8.

as "ill" or "flew kite."[7] Other entries were more interesting, as "did first lesson in Virgil,"[8] "Began music (the violin)," "Began a tune."[9] Still others were just amusing entries, as were those concerning one of the masters at the school: "Laurie turned me last. For what? Ask him."[10] The story ends that he and Mr. Laurie became good friends. Thus, what was missing in conversation skills because of his shyness was surmounted by his writing abilities.

John Henry flew kites, rode on donkeys, and did other things that boys enjoy doing, but instead of playing sports such as cricket, he preferred reading novels. He remembered listening to his mother's reading of Walter Scott's long romantic poem, "The Lay of the Last Minstrel."[11] As he grew older, he relished acting and eagerly sought the opportunity to perform in plays. Every year he took part in the school Latin play. In 1813, he acted in Terence's *Phormio*; in 1814, in *Eunuchus*; in 1815, in *Adelphi*, and in 1816, in *Andria*.[12] He noted in his diary, "Rehearsal in dresses supper,"[13] "Rehearsal before boys,"[14] "First grand night,"[15] and wrote with a friend a poem about their performances with a reference to boys who "glory in the bat and ball" and others who "choose some subject gay or grave

7 *Ibid.*, 7.
8 *Ibid.*, 7.
9 See *LD*, Vol. I (1811), 9.
10 See *LD*, Vol. I (1810), 7.
11 See Ward, *Young Mr. Newman*, 7.
12 *Ibid.*
13 *LD*, Vol. I (1813), 14.
14 *Ibid.*
15 *Ibid.*, 15.

for rhyme." In addition to acting, John Henry delivered speeches at school.

Newman's leadership and writing career began as a young boy at his boarding school with The Spy Club. Interestingly, the sons of John Quincy Adams, Ambassador to Great Britain and later President of the United States, belonged to the group.[16] This confidential boys' club had officers and badges. Newman was the Grand Master. A school classmate made a humorous drawing of Newman in command of a meeting, exaggerating his already prominent nose. The group met to read their own weekly periodical, *The Portfolio,* that ran for twenty numbers and included a contribution by John Adams. At the same time, Newman was writing two periodicals, called *The Spy* and *Anti-Spy,* that were pitted one against the other.[17]

Newman would one day become an avid and gifted letter writer. The beginning of this practice can be traced as far back as the letter that he dictated to a maid for his parents at the age of four. At the age of seven, he began writing short letters; it was the practice at English schools to dictate to students letters for their parents. At the age of fourteen, he began to write longer letters. The letters to his sisters indicate his humorous character. On his fourteenth birthday, he received a heavy birthday package with a note stating: "we all send our love with your affectionate sister."[18] He replied to Jemima that he was led to believe that his "affectionate sister" must be at the bottom of the heavy parcel.

---

16 See *LD,* Vol. I (Memorandum 1812-1817), 10.
17 *Ibid.*
18 *LD,* Vol. I, JHN to Jemima Newman (April 12, 1815), 16.

John Henry had a happy and comfortable childhood with a lot of affection and fun at home. During the holidays, the siblings organized plays, parties, and expeditions. He wrote some plays for his siblings, including a satire on the Prince Regent.[19] In 1815, he composed music for a family opera. This provides an indication of Newman's imagination and creative genius.

The Newman home was also characterized by order, religious piety, and work. Harriet gave a glimpse into the family life in two published stories, *Family Adventures* and *The Fairy Bower*.[20] The latter, which produces a picture of moderate Anglicans, was aimed at inculcating Church Principles and practices, such as attendance at church twice on Sundays, the use of the Prayer Book of the Anglican Church, daily Bible reading and recitation of the Psalms.

Maisie Ward, one of Newman's biographers, notes that, as could well be predicted, John Henry was portrayed by characters in both stories: in the first one as Henry, "a philosophical young gentleman,"[21] and in the second one as a thirteen-year-old boy named George. Ward thinks that George paints a better picture of John Henry as a boy.[22] In *The Fairy Bower,* George is a very bright, overly confident, slightly condescending, wryly humorous yet perfectly proper boy who thought he was clever enough to persuade anyone to do what he chose. He was an insatiable tease, quizzing the young boys and girls and putting up "an odd

---

19 See *LD,* Vol. I (Memorandum 1812-1817), 10.
20 See Ward, *Young Mr. Newman,* 12-15.
21 *Family Adventures,* quoted in *Young Mr. Newman,* 12.
22 Ward, *Young Mr. Newman,* 13.

face" at people who amused him.[23] Through the protago-
nists in these stories we are given a privileged glimpse into
Newman's personality.

During his boyhood, John Henry maintained a special friendship with his sisters, to whom he wrote from
school. Since he was with his brothers at school, the correspondence between them is from later years. In 1845,
his younger brother wrote about their schooldays, telling
John Henry that he did not recall any "cruelties at school"
coming from him. He was sure that if there had been any,
there would have been ten times more acts of protection
and kindness.

Newman's childhood was spent in this close-knit and
morally upright and religious home. In this environment
the affection of his parents and siblings provided him with
a stable emotional background, while the private education under Dr. Nicholas served as an early stimulus for the
development of his exceptional intellectual talents. This
joyful and fruitful period of his life was strongly shaken in
March 1816, when Mr. Newman's bank failed.

23 *Ibid.*, 14.

CHAPTER 3

1816: FIRST CONVERSION

THE end of the Napoleonic Wars brought ruin to many private banks and businesses in England. In March 1816, Mr. Newman's bank failed. The family blamed his father's partner and insisted that all the depositors were paid. The family moved to Alton in Hampshire, where Mr. Newman tried to manage a brewery. Newman was summoned home to be told the bad news and was sent back to Ealing for the summer. At school he fell sick and remained ill and confined to the sickroom throughout the summer holidays. During this illness he had a spiritual conversion from what he later recalled as the sins of intellectual pride and self-sufficiency.

Before this John Henry had grown up in a conventional Anglican family that attended Sunday services in church and held morning and evening prayers at home. As a boy, he prayed and read Sacred Scripture with his grandmother, Elizabeth Good, and his aunt, Elizabeth Newman, to whom he would always remain grateful. These religiously minded women established early spiritual foundations of devotion and biblical reading that would be of utmost importance in Newman's life.

At school, however, Newman was led astray by his readings and the influence of other boys. He became skeptical about religion and fell away from religious practice. In one of his verses addressed to his Guardian Angel, he wrote: "And when, ere boyhood yet was gone, / My rebel spirit fell, / Ah! thou didst see, and shudder too, / Yet bear each deed of Hell."[1] Out of rebelliousness and intellectual curiosity, Newman read Thomas Paine's *Tracts against the Old Testament*, some verses by Voltaire against the immortality of the soul, and Hume's treatise on *Miracles* at the age of fourteen.[2] These texts raised serious religious doubts in the youth. Thus it is no wonder that Newman later spoke of having lived in mortal sin during this time and, in another verse, of having scoffed at sacred things and even of having struck the face of God.

While convalescing at school during the summer months, he came under the religious influence of Walter Mayers, a devout young Calvinist clergyman who had studied at Pembroke College, Oxford. Newman admired Mayers and began to read the Calvinist books recommended by him. As a result he had a decisive religious conversion, of which he later wrote: "When I was fifteen (in the autumn of 1816,) a great change of thought took place in me. I fell under the influences of definite Creed, and received into my intellect impressions of dogma, which through God's mercy have never been effaced or obscured."[3] Newman described Mayers as the one "who was the human means of this beginning of divine faith in me."[4]

---

1 "Guardian Angel," in *VV* (The Oratory, 1853), 300-302.

2 See John Henry Newman, *Apologia Pro Vita Sua,* 1865 edition, available at: http://www.newmanreader.org/works/apologia65/index.html., 3. After this it will be cited *Apo.*

3 *Apo.,* 4.

4 *Apo.,* 4.

A religious conversion is the experience of an overwhelming power outside of a person that leads him to discover a new or deeper worldview that re-directs the purpose of his existence. As a result of his conversion Newman perceived God as a personal Being, not an abstract truth. He came to the belief in God as an all-powerful Being who not only had created the world, but who is present in the world. As he later asserted when explaining the nature of belief, intellectual knowledge of God is more than a summation of truths and logical inference. Belief in God is the result of the coming together of many things in a person's mind. Many years later, in *A Grammar of Assent,* Newman coined the expression "illative sense" to describe the mind's assent to belief in God. Although the word illative derives from *illatum*, the Latin term for inference or logical conclusion, Newman explained that the assent of faith was an unconscious and implicit process rather than a logical, step-by-step, process.

Belief or the illative sense may be compared to seeing a painting. With one look, the viewer takes in what would require many words to describe. The mind brings together all the parts of the painting with one simple glance. In a person's act of faith, childhood experiences, psychological dispositions, and intellectual knowledge coalesce into one act. These elements of faith may only be separated for the sake of analysis, because faith is like that one simple look at the painting. It is the assent of a person as a unified whole to what God has revealed of Himself. This is what happened to John Henry.

Under the light of the Holy Spirit, Newman overcame doubts of earlier years and made religious dogma the foundation of his life. He understood that religious truth, or dogma, must be based on God's self-revelation to mankind. Newman conceived that it was natural that God would communicate Himself to men through the medium of Sacred Scripture. In addition, he concluded that God would make the Church the authoritative interpreter of that Revelation.

This first conversion set Newman on a course of religious devotion and study of Scripture. It also marked the beginning of an Evangelical period of his life. He embraced a sincere religious piety with high moral standards that would have a significant influence in his university years. Charles Dessain describes the year 1816 as a turning point which gave unity to Newman's life: "His unfolding mind was captured by the Christian Revelation, and his heart by the Christian ideal of holiness."[5]

The Evangelical Movement, which influenced Newman, was a religious movement founded on the strong belief in the imminence of Christ's Second Coming that gave impulse to a determined propagation of the Gospel through missionary work, both home and abroad. It was characterized by a renewal in biblical preaching and Christian fervor. In England, a spiritual revival dating back to the mid-eighteenth century gave rise in the 1830s to an Evangelical party within the Established Church. This revival was begun by leaders such as George Whitefield, John Wesley, Thomas Scott, Joseph Milner, John Newton, and Henry Venn. The last-named became the leader of a small group of highly influential families in Clapham, London,

---

5 Charles Dessain, *John Henry Newman* (Oxford: A. and C. Black Ltd., 1966), 5.

known as the Clapham Sect, which became a strong force for moral and social reforms in English society.

In the ensuing Evangelical period of his youth, John Henry adopted a series of Calvinist practices and beliefs. One of the beliefs that he accepted, a belief that was later among the first that he rejected, was the Calvinist doctrine on justification and predestination.[6] Calvin taught that there is a double predestination. People are predestined either to glory or to eternal damnation. According to this doctrine, a person who is justified cannot fall away, while another who is predestined to damnation will be so regardless of the good moral actions that he performs. This doctrine espoused the belief in the total corruption of man's nature owing to original sin and undermined the belief in man's freedom in accepting grace.

At the same time, Newman began to express belief in God's omnipresence. This presence was not that of an impersonal power in creation, but that of an all-powerful and merciful God. Newman later described this belief as the luminously self-evident idea that there are only two beings in the world, himself and the Creator.[7] The human person can be sure of this reality and make it the framework for his beliefs and actions. This vivid realization remained with him as an adult and served as a truth upon which his knowledge of Sacred Scripture and Christian doctrine were built.

In a sermon on the immortality of the soul delivered in July 1833, he described the person's awareness of being

---

6 *Apo.*, 6.
7 *Apo.*, 4.

distinct and independent of the material world and of having an immortal soul.[8] He wrote that misfortunes and the contingency of earthly things lead the human being to be weaned from love for material goods. A person then catches a glimpse of independence from temporal things and of immortality. By degrees, he perceives that there are two beings in the whole universe, one's own soul and God who made it. Along with these realizations, there were further influences on Newman during his adolescence.

Thomas Scott, a famous Evangelical and a biblical commentator, made an even deeper impression on the young man than Mayers had. Newman referred to Scott as the man "to whom (humanly speaking) I almost owe my soul."[9] Newman read Scott's autobiography, *The Force of Truth,* which described his spiritual journey from Unitarianism to belief in the Holy Trinity. Newman embraced the truths of the Incarnation and Redemption as well as the doctrine of the indwelling of the Holy Spirit in the soul, a teaching emphasized by Scott.

With these mentors, the young student became an Evangelical, yet he did not go through a conventional Evangelical conversion, which is typically marked by a sudden and emotional change. His conversion already had an intellectual bent: Newman was reading and searching for the truth about God and religion. He was concerned with the meaning and content of divine Revelation and the truths contained in the Creeds, and not merely an emotional

---

8 John Henry Newman, *Plain and Parochial Sermons,* Vol. I, 14-21; 16-17, available at: http://www.newmanreader.org/works/parochial/volume1/index.html After this it will be cited *PPS.*

9 *Apo.,* 5.

experience. Inspired by Scott's *Essays* and Jones of Nayland's comments on Scripture, he drew up a collection of texts to support each verse of the *Athanasian Creed*.[10]

Newman also adopted the Gospel ideal of holiness explained in William Law's *Serious Call to Holiness and Devotion*.[11] This well-known book on Christian devotion, written in 1728, transmitted the Christian ideal of giving glory to God through one's occupations by practicing prayer and humility throughout the day and by having the proper detachment from material goods. This work had a tone that was different from the Calvinist books that Newman had been reading; its emphasis was on human correspondence to grace and practice of the Christian virtues.

Law's book also convinced Newman of the reality of a spiritual warfare between the city of God and the powers of darkness. The young man accepted Christ's teaching about eternal punishment and eternal reward. He made two of Scott's phrases his own: "Holiness rather than peace" and "Growth the only evidence of life."[12] These maxims would guide Newman's moral and ascetical practices and play a significant role in his sermons. He realized that Christ calls all men to eternal life and that this calling does not allow for moral complacency. Like Scott, Newman had never really accepted the doctrine of predestination to eternal death.

Other important influences on the fifteen-year-old Newman were two contradictory works, namely Joseph Milner's *History of the Church of Christ* and Sir Isaac Newton's

---

10 *Apo.*, 5.

11 *Apo.*, 6.

12 *Apo.*, 5.

Observations on the Prophecies.[13] The first enamored him with the Church Fathers, like St. Augustine and St. Ambrose, while the second rooted in him the conviction that the Pope was the Antichrist, a belief that he held for a long time. Newton's work had a more immediate effect on Newman, whose prejudice against the Pope and the Catholic Church would repeatedly appear in his early writings.

Another influence was William Beveridge's *Private Thoughts Upon Religion,* a gift sent to Newman by Mayers. This book stirred Newman to a greater devotion to God, the practice of daily prayer, reading of Scripture, and self-examination. Its exhortation to a life of self-denial and a vision of Christian life as spiritual warfare also inspired Newman. For some time, Newman even imitated Beveridge's writing style.

In the autumn of the same year, he was gripped by the desire to devote his life to the service of God as an ordained minister in the Anglican Church.[14] He would refer to this as the "deep imagination" of God calling him to a celibate life.[15] This idea that "took possession of him" was associated with the desire of becoming a missionary, which he

---

13 *Apo.*, 7.

14 Historically the Anglican Church has been called the "Church of England," the "Established Church" and the "Anglican Church." In this biography we refer to her thus as a "Church." Over time Newman came to realize that she had separated from the Catholic Church. In recent times Pope Benedict XVI explained that there is only one Bride of Christ, the Catholic Church. Furthermore, he explained that "the ecclesial communities which have not preserved the valid Episcopate and the genuine and integral substance of the Eucharistic mystery, are not Churches in the proper sense." See Declaration *Dominus Iesus,* Vatican, July 16, 2000, n. 17.

15 *Apo.*, 7.

seriously considered once at Oxford. The young man had the remarkable sense that celibacy was a special grace in the church tied to greater responsibility and demand for holiness. Although some clergymen at Oxford and Cambridge remained celibate, most of the rectors of English parishes married. Newman was later happy to discover through his Anglican friend, Richard Hurrell Froude, that this ideal of celibacy had long been held by Roman Catholic tradition.

Newman's spiritual conversion from skepticism to Evangelical Christianity at the age of fifteen and his desire for a complete dedication to God prepared him to face the worldly environment he was to find at Oxford University. Though he had started as a Low Church Anglican, Newman had become a fervent Evangelical Anglican. He had acquired some important basic beliefs, such as that of God's omnipresence and the soul's immortality, and a desire to live a life of piety. At Oxford he would wrestle with the Calvinist doctrines of predestination and the Antichrist.

CHAPTER 4

1817 TO 1822: UNDERGRADUATE AT TRINITY COLLEGE

IN June of 1817, Mr. Newman took his son John Henry, aged sixteen, to Oxford and enrolled him at Trinity College, one of the colleges at Oxford University. Oxford and Cambridge were England's centers of higher education as well as cultural and religious life. Both universities had been founded by Catholics in the twelfth and thirteenth centuries, respectively, for the education of the clergy primarily. Students at Oxford and Cambridge were imparted with a classical education in Latin and Greek.

Oxford began as a town built on the Thames River. In the sixteenth century, it became a city as well as an Episcopal See of the Church of England. After the schism by Henry VIII, Oxford University retained its role in the education of clergy, but from then on, for the Church of England. With the advent of the 1844 Oxford-London railroad line and the construction of the London-Midlands canal, commerce grew. The population increased correspondingly from 12,000 to 49,000 during the nineteenth century.

At the beginning of the same century, Oxford University had over twenty colleges. During Newman's time, the university was open to students from both poor and wealthy families and about four hundred students were admitted each year. Poor students who obtained scholarships were able to attend, but the student body had more students from wealthy families and the nobility. Among the student population there was a growing number of youths from the upper-middle class of landed gentry, clergy, professionals, and businessmen. In 1810, the sons of married clergymen made up 29 percent of the student body.[1] In the following decades, over 40 percent of these men were receiving Holy Orders and many obtained parish livings.

Trinity College had been established in 1555, by Thomas Pope, who had served as Treasurer of the Court of Augmentation, which had dissolved the estates of monasteries for Henry VIII. The college was built on the site of an earlier school founded in the thirteenth century to educate monks at the Cathedral Church of Durham. The original charter of Trinity stipulated that all Fellows must take Holy Orders and remain celibate.

The entire time that Newman was at Oxford, Dissenters from Anglicanism, among them Roman Catholics, were excluded from Oxford. This policy changed with a parliamentary act in 1856. The Oxford Newman entered was a worldly environment that focused on gaining social advantage while maintaining some external appearance of religion. On top of this, Trinity College was at the forefront of liberal-minded theological thinking.

Overly self-conscious, shy and, at the same time, disgusted by the excess drinking of the college students, Newman had a difficult beginning. At Trinity, he dedicated

---

1 *The University in Society: Oxford and Cambridge from the 14th to the Early 19th Century,* Vol. 1, ed. Lawrence Stone (Princeton: Princeton University Press, 1974), 39; 74.

himself to his studies and to practices of piety. Despite his reserved nature and exacting moral character, he managed to make some friends. The closest one was John William Bowden, a youth from a wealthy family, who would remain a loyal friend all his life.

Bowden was a few years Newman's senior and an excellent student. He and John Henry prepared for their Bachelor's exam at the same time. At Trinity, they edited anonymously a periodical, *The Undergraduate,* and they composed a romantic poem, *St. Bartholomew's Eve,* which depicts a Catholic priest leading assassins in search of Protestants. Both of these literary projects are early indicators of Newman's interest in verse and poetry. The theme of *St. Bartholomew's Eve* also reveals his youthful prejudice toward Roman Catholics.

Newman had a weak physical constitution, and before going up to Oxford for the first time, he experienced an eye illness. For some months, he was unable to read for more than a short time every day. At Oxford, he had bouts of poor health, which he recorded in his diaries. While preparing for the exams to obtain the undergraduate degree, he experienced lightheadedness and exhaustion, probably due to excess work, a lack of sleep, and inordinate worry over his achievements at school. He recovered by following his mother's insistence that he rest and exercise. Newman accepted physical ailments and periods of suffering with patience and even good humor. He drew meaningful spiritual lessons from them. For instance, the exhaustion as an undergraduate led him to combat his pride and vanity. On his seventeenth birthday, he composed the following prayer:

No! give to me, Great Lord, the constant soul,
Nor fooled by pleasure nor enslaved by care;
Each rebel-passion (for Thou canst) controul,
And make me know the tempter's every snare.[2]

A few months after Newman's arrival at Oxford, he made his First Communion, and the following year, he was confirmed in the Anglican Church. As was the common practice at the time, his siblings also made their First Communion and received Confirmation in their late adolescence. Starting in August of 1821, Newman began to take Holy Communion every fortnight; this practice set him apart from most Anglicans since frequent Communion was not a custom, and it caused his mother to warn him of becoming overly righteous.[3]

In addition to his earnestness in prayer, Newman was studious and very bright and thus he did well academically. Success, however, came after defeats and humiliations. His Tutor, Thomas Short, soon moved him up to a higher class because of his proficiency in mathematics and encouraged him to enter a scholarship competition newly opened to the University, which Newman won in 1818. Although competing against more qualified and older students, the young undergraduate displayed his abilities and earned the reward of being elected a scholar at Trinity. This position allowed him to remain in residence and to compete for a position as Fellow of one of the colleges; it also afforded him a burse of £60 a year. Informed by Francis, Mrs. Newman sent John Henry a congratulatory letter entitled "My dear

---

2 *VV (February 21, 1819)*, 7.

3 John Henry Newman, *Autobiographical Writings*, ed. Henry Tristram (New York: Sheed and Ward Inc., 1957), 174.

Scholar" that read: "Accept the sincere congratulations of every one of us, that you have so early reaped honour and advantage from your assiduity."[4]

During the summer of 1820, Newman prepared under an incredibly demanding schedule for his final college undergraduate examinations. Detailed diary entries show that from July to November he spent an average of 12 hours a day studying, and on some days, he studied as much as 14 hours a day. In November of that same year, he passed his Bachelor of Arts degree examination, but without obtaining the honors that he greatly desired and for which he had prepared. Thus he wrote in a despondent mood to his parents: "It is all over; and I have *not* succeeded."[5]

The desire of achieving academic honors had haunted him during his undergraduate studies. Although these honors were necessary for advancing in academic life, Newman confessed in his diary and verses to a frequent struggle against the temptation of pride in the outcome of his studies. He explained to his parents that he had studied earnestly and the examiners had been kind to him, yet he had failed out of nervousness during the examination.[6] His parents responded with an affectionate letter conveying their understanding and admiration for him.[7]

Nonetheless John Henry earned a Bachelor's degree and kept his Trinity Scholarship for nine years. For some of these years he was able to remain in the college rooms. This was a difficult period for his family because in the

---

4 *LD,* Vol. I, Mrs. Newman to JHN (May 24, 1818), 52.
5 *LD,* Vol. I, JHN to Mr. Newman (Dec. 1, 1820), 94.
6 *Ibid.*
7 *LD,* Vol. I, Mrs. Newman to JHN (Dec. 2, 1820), 95.

fall of 1821, Mr. Newman's business failed and he was declared bankrupt. In response, John Henry, who always tried to keep his father's failure secret, exchanged a number of loving letters with his parents. Newman assured them of divine assistance in their financial distress, and wrote to his father insisting that he wished to pay for Francis's expenses at Oxford.[8] In 1823, following the advice of his brother's friends, Francis enrolled at Worcester, which was less expensive than Trinity.

As a student, and later as a Tutor at Oxford, Newman took to heart the concerns of his siblings, writing to them and supporting them financially. In their letters, his parents acknowledged the good example of piety, the diligence in study, and the upright moral life that he, as the eldest brother, had given to his siblings. On John Henry's twenty-first birthday, Mrs. Newman called him a "second father" to his sisters and brothers.[9]

In light of the financial circumstances of the family, Mr. Newman, who had entered his son at Lincoln's Inn some years earlier, advised him to become a lawyer, and he asked him to make up his mind about his future plans. John Henry was interested in debating and suggested that the university have a debating society, but he did not seriously consider a career in law. While Bowden made plans to study law in London, Newman wavered about his own future plans. In June, he was turned out of Trinity College and had to take lodgings at a boarding house. Finally, in January 1822, John Henry gave up secular ambitions and

---

8 *LD,* Vol. I, JHN to Mr. Newman (Dec. 5, 1822), 156.
9 *LD,* Vol. I, Mrs. Newman to JHN (Feb. 21, 1822), 122.

decided instead to serve the Church as a clergyman. With this goal in mind, he wished to pursue his studies at Oxford and began to prepare to stand for a Fellowship at Oriel, a more difficult contest than his undergraduate degree. His mother worried because he was overworked and depressed and because he lacked confidence. She advised him to get fresh air and exercise as well as drink some wine. Following her advice, John Henry attended music parties and dined out. He also returned to two hobbies that he had developed as a child: playing violin and horseback riding. He liked to play Beethoven, Mozart, Haydn, and Corelli on the violin, and took frequent and long horseback rides. He would also often walk for an hour and a half.

While Newman enjoyed these activities in the company of friends, he was able to resist the dissipation of many of his fellow undergraduates. His dedication to study and piety paid off. He won the scholarship at Trinity and obtained his Bachelor's degree. Furthermore, he was set on the course to take Holy Orders and to become a Fellow at Oriel College. The demanding years at Trinity had prepared Newman for the challenging time at Oriel.

CHAPTER 5

1822 TO 1845:
FELLOW AT ORIEL COLLEGE

ORIEL College, originally called "House of the Blessed Mary the Virgin in Oxford," had been founded in 1326, by Adam de Brome, a functionary at the Court of Edward II. At the end of the eighteenth century, Oriel was a leading college distinguished for its Fellows and Tutors and its academic reforms that gave new intellectual life to Oxford. Fellows were members of the teaching staff of colleges and the governing bodies who elected the Provost or Master governing each college or house. Oriel prided itself in choosing as Fellows men who were original thinkers. One of the reforms introduced was the method in which Newman was elected Fellow: a competition open to graduates from other colleges and one that placed more importance on capacity to reason over erudition. Thus, Newman, as a Trinity graduate, competed for a Fellowship at Oriel and beat candidates who had read more extensively than he had.

When Newman entered the contest for a Fellowship at Oriel College, he vied with ten candidates for two vacancies. This Fellowship was among the most coveted at the university and the examination to obtain it was very difficult. On the first day of the examination Newman almost repeated the collapse of earlier exams at Trinity, but his

Tutor Mr. Short helped him to regain his composure. Newman expected to have to stand for the Fellowship examination on repeated years, but he was elected on April 12,
after his first attempt. The messenger who brought him the
news found him playing the violin. Newman replied, "very
well" in a seemingly disinterested tone, but as soon as the
messenger left, he flung down his instrument and dashed to
Oriel College.

That same day, Newman wrote with the news to his
father, his aunt, Dr. Nicholas, and Bowden. To Mr. Newman he wrote: "I am just made Fellow of Oriel. Thank God.
Love to all."[1] Newman would spend the next eleven years,
from 1822 until 1833, at Oriel College, where he would
hold two academic appointments, first that of Fellow and
later that of Tutor.

Still today, those who wish to teach at Oxford follow a
similar career path. Having obtained the Bachelor of Arts
degree, a graduate competes for Fellowships at one of the
colleges. Once made a Fellow, he remains a Fellow for life
unless he gives up his position. Usually after twenty-one
terms (seven years) at the university, a Fellow may obtain
his Master of Arts degree. Some Fellows, also known as
Dons, are later offered the post of College Tutor and a few
are elected professors. Undergraduates are assigned to a
Tutor with whom they meet once a week to discuss their
subject of study.

At the time Newman went to Oxford, the Anglican
Church was the official State religion and the clergy was
formed at Oxford and Cambridge. The State imposed

---

1 *LD,* Vol. I, JHN to Mr. Newman (April 12, 1822), 129.

significant interference in Church affairs, including the establishment of dioceses and the naming of bishops and certain university professors. Bishops even held a seat in the House of Lords in Parliament. Membership in the Anglican Church and making an oath of Subscription to the *Thirty-Nine Articles* dating back to Edward VI were requirements for teaching at a university and for holding government posts. Taxes went to pay for part of the financial support of the State Church.

For the greater part of its three-century existence, with each new monarch, the Anglican Church underwent numerous changes in ecclesiastical governance, theology, and liturgical practices. Clergy and theologians, both Catholic and Protestant, vied with one another to exert their influence on the government, doctrine and liturgy of the Established Church. Anglicanism was soon divided into High Church and Low Church, the former resembling Roman Catholicism in its doctrine and liturgy and the latter identifying with Protestantism. High Church Anglicans were also known as Anglo-Catholics.

As will be explained later, many High Church Anglicans in Newman's time subscribed to the Branch Theory, according to which the Anglican Church was one of three branches of the true Catholic Church, the other two branches being the Roman Catholic Church and the Orthodox Church. Newman himself would later embrace this theory for a period of years. With this notion of the Church, he would struggle to recapture the true Catholic understanding and practice of the Holy Eucharist, Confession and the other sacraments, based on his assumption that these rites were valid sacraments within Anglicanism.

Still other Anglicans, such as Newman when he entered Oriel, were Evangelicals. These Anglicans were inspired by John Wesley, a clergyman at Oxford who had begun the Methodist revival, which at first was part of the Evangelical Movement within the Anglican Church. Wesley, initially influenced by the rule and practice of holy living of William Law, fell under Luther's ideas of *sola fide*. Subsequently, he underwent a classical experience of justification by faith alone, which was heavily dependent on a subjective assurance of being saved without reliance on any personal spiritual works. Wesley's Movement led to a schism from the Anglican Church; by 1795, the Methodists had broken away from the Anglican Church.

Unlike the Methodists, most Evangelicals remained within the Anglican Church, but they conceived of Christian life primarily in terms of personal piety and evangelization. They reduced doctrines to a few basic Christian truths and paid little attention to ecclesiastical hierarchy. One aspect of the Evangelical spirit that initially seized Newman was the need for missionary work, and he held membership in various missionary societies while at Oriel. He also entertained the possibility of going abroad to do missionary work, but due to poor health, he desisted from this pursuit.

The ensuing period of life at Oriel was a critical one for Newman's religious growth. During these rich years of his youth, he sought answers to many theological questions concerning Revelation, the sacraments and the nature of the Church. The environment of the Oriel Common Room, the meeting room for the college, was a difficult one because its members, sometimes known as the Noetics, were older than Newman and more interested in philosophy and politics. These men were leading intellectuals at Oxford, noted for liberal ideas in religion. Newman received a wide range of theological influences, although the predominant influence was a liberal one, which placed into doubt and even rejected commonly held religious doctrines. In the Common Room, Newman had many discussions with influential men such as Edward Hawkins, Richard Whately, and Joseph Blanco White. The last-named, a former Roman Catholic priest, was markedly anti-Catholic. Reading the books of these men and having discussions with them helped Newman to think on his own and formulate ideas; this exchange of ideas forced him to defend his conclusions.

Once elected Fellow at Oriel in 1822, Newman learned a great deal from Dr. Hawkins, who was the Provost of Oriel and Vicar of St. Mary's, the University Church. Hawkins challenged Newman's Calvinist notion of Christianity, which Newman exemplified in his first sermon. In that sermon, Newman had divided men into two classes, the one being all darkness and the other all light. Hawkins objected that men were neither saints nor sinners, but somewhere in between. Hawkins was the first who taught him to "weigh his words and to be cautious in his statements,"[2] as well as to anticipate objections.

One of the first friends John Henry made at Oriel was Edward Bouverie Pusey, with whom he would share a life-long friendship. Pusey, who was six months Newman's senior, came from a family of wealthy landowners. Having studied at Christ Church, Oxford, Pusey was elected a

---

2 *Apo.*, 8.

Fellow at Oriel in 1823. Although initially Newman regretted Pusey's lack of sympathy for the Evangelical Movement, he was impressed by his religious gravity. Both took a private class with Charles Lloyd, Regius Professor of Divinity at Christ Church. Lloyd's views differed completely from Whately's; he represented the High Church with its emphasis on authority and tradition. It seems Lloyd liked Newman as a person, but was impatient with his Evangelical doctrines. Pusey, on the other hand, became a disciple of Lloyd and, on the professor's recommendation, went to Germany to pursue theological studies.

Newman credited William James, another Fellow of Oriel, with teaching him in 1823 the doctrine of Apostolic Succession.[3] Although he did not provide details on their conversations, Newman would later refer to this central belief, and to the Antiquity of the Church, as some of the criteria for ascertaining the authenticity of the Catholic Church.

Richard Whately, a former Fellow of Oriel from 1811 to 1821 and Anglican Archbishop of Dublin by 1831, took Newman under his wing. He wanted to see what Newman, often struck dumb among the older Fellows, was made of and to whip him into shape. Whately, just married, was a huge man with an aggressive manner. He soon recognized that Newman had a very clear mind and put him to work writing articles on Aristotelian logic for him; the articles were later turned into a book. In 1824, Whately had Newman commissioned by the *Encyclopedia Metropolitana* to write an article on Cicero. Newman completed the

---

3 *Apo.*, 10.

assignment on short notice and demonstrated his capacity for intense work and his talent for writing.

The following year, urged on by his mentor, Newman worked on two more articles for the *Encyclopedia Metropolitana*. The first was on Apollonius of Tyana, a Pythagorean teacher and mystic, reputed by his biographers to have performed miracles that rivaled those of Christ;[4] the second, *Essay on Miracles*, was almost a sequel to the *Essay on Apollonius of Tyana*.[5] Edward Smedley, the editor of the encyclopedia, was a demanding man, and Newman had to work at a fast pace to meet the deadlines. The week that he sent the article on Apollonius to the publisher, he wrote to Harriet: "I am up to my chin in Apollonius, and very cross, as you may suppose."[6] A month later, he sent Smedley the finished *Essay on Miracles*.

In this early writing, Newman displayed his skill for identifying internal and external errors in a text. As for the former, he noted that Apollonius himself never claimed to perform miracles and that Apollonius's alleged miracles could be explained by his knowledge of events, such as foretelling the death of a tyrant based on the sage's political connections. The refutation from external evidence was based on the date of composition of Apollonius's life, which was over a century after his death, and from the exaggerated style typical of the esoteric and mystical Pythagorean School.

---

4 This article first appeared in *The Encyclopedia Metropolitana.* (1826) and was later published under Newman's *Historical Sketches,* Vol. I, 1910.

5 This article first appeared in *The Encyclopedia Metropolitana.* (1825-1826) and was later published under Newman's *Two Essays on Biblical and Ecclesiastical Miracles,* I, 1910.

6 *LD,* Vol. 1, JHN to Harriet Newman (March 21, 1826), 280.

The article on miracles dealt with the nature of miracles and the criteria for distinguishing authentic miracles from those professed miracles attributed to pagans like Apollonius, Christians of the primitive Church, or Catholic saints. It was a defense for the evidence of the New Testament miracles that Newman described as God's intervention or interposition in the ordinary course of nature. He discounted as true miracles those events explained by known ordinary causes or surrounded by suspicious circumstances.

Before writing the article, Newman read many authors of the preceding centuries who wrote on this subject. They ranged from men like Hume, who denied the existence of miracles, to those like Butler, who established their antecedent probability as proof of Revelation. In the article, Newman refuted Hume's claim that all miracles are based on exaggeration, deception or invalid testimony because of ignorance on the part of the observer. Newman explained that an uneducated person using common sense might be as credible a testimony of the miraculous event of a resurrection as a physician might.

Following Butler, Newman wrote that the intrinsic character of miracles is in accord with man's knowledge of the attributes and government of Almighty God. They are what one would expect from God's works. Furthermore, the purpose of Scripture miracles, the sober manner of their recounting, and their attending circumstances, bear the mark of the divine. "Their grandeur, beauty and consistency; the clear and unequivocal marks they bear of superhuman agency; the importance and desirableness of the object they propose to effect, are in correspondence with the variety and force of the evidence itself."[7]

At the same time, Newman discounted many professed miracles based on invalid testimony, which was motivated by the desire for gain, or power on the part of witnesses or by rivalry between religious parties. He enumerated other reasons to invalidate testimony for professed miracles, such as the previous history of pious frauds by Catholics, inconsistencies in testimony, and a significant distance in time and place from the miraculous event to the telling.

This study reveals the breadth of Newman's analysis of subject matter and the importance that he attributed to miracles as confirmation of divine teaching. It also manifests the anti-Catholic bias that poisoned some of his reasoning. For example, in this first article on the subject of Miracles, Newman distinguished between Scripture miracles and those attributed to Catholic saints. Due to the weak evidence provided, testimony adduced many years after the fact, and superstition, he rejected the miracles attributed to Catholic saints, or "Popish Miracles," as not authentic miracles. In 1843, he wrote a longer essay on Miracles in which he corrected the harsh and incredulous tone toward the Roman Catholic claim to miracles and disavowed his general dismissal of them.[8]

In March of 1825, Whately became Principal of St. Alban's Hall, a small residence for undergraduates unable to enter or to stay at one of the colleges. He offered

---

7 John Henry Newman, *Two Essays on Biblical and Ecclesiastical Miracles*, 93, available at: http://www.newmanreader.org/works/miracles/index.html.

8 "The Miracles of Early Ecclesiastical History" was published under *Two Essays on Biblical and Ecclesiastical Miracles*.

Newman the office of Vice-Principal. Newman, who had been seeking the authority and responsibility of a college office, readily accepted and, overnight, he became "Dean, Tutor, Bursar and all—in his absence indeed, Principal."[9] His relationship with Whately, however, soon grew cold over religious and political differences. Despite this parting of beliefs, Newman later complimented Whately in the *Apologia Pro Vita Sua* as a kind and generous mentor who taught him to reason: "He, emphatically, opened my mind, and taught me to think and to use my reason . . . he taught me to see with my own eyes and to walk with my own feet."[10] Furthermore, Newman credited Whately with having taught him, at least on a theoretical level, that Church and State should be independent of each other. He argued that the Church should not interfere in temporal affairs nor the State in spiritual ones.[11]

Newman matured during his first years at Oriel and acquired understanding about liberalism in religion and about politics. Whately and Hawkins had taught him a great deal. Article writing sharpened his logical reasoning and writing skill. As a result of many discussions in the Oriel Common Room and much personal study, he began to form his own theological opinions and to criticize the opinions of his peers. He thus grew in the necessary self-confidence and social skills that he would later employ as a leader.

---

9 *LD*, Vol. I, JHN to Mrs. Newman (March 29, 1825), 222.
10 *Apo.*, 11.
11 *Apo.*, 13.

CHAPTER 6

NEWMAN'S RELIGIOUS DEVELOPMENT

A T Oriel College, Newman's religious beliefs were forged through continuous study and many conversations with his mentors, peers, and students. From 1824 to 1828, he wrestled with some of the Protestant doctrines that he had previously accepted. Newman studied the scriptural and dogmatic foundations of many Christian doctrines concerning salvation. He focused on various central doctrines over the following years, particularly baptismal regeneration, the means for justification, the nature and office of the Church, Purgatory, and the intercession of the saints.

At the end of 1824 and start of 1825, Newman thought at length about the arguments regarding the Lutheran doctrine of justification known as imputed righteousness. Based on St. Paul's letter to the Romans, Luther had emphasized the need for faith as the source of man's salvation, almost to the exclusion of good works. According to Luther, salvation is a legal declaration through which Christ obtains man's salvation by "covering" over his sins. This view, which looks to salvation from an extrinsic perspective, contrasts with the Roman Catholic teaching of baptismal regeneration whereby the sinner's soul is intrinsically renewed through Baptism. Christ's grace acts on the soul, giving it a new supernatural life-principle. Sanctifying grace is a supernatural quality that inheres in the soul, enabling it to participate in the nature and life of God.

In 1824, Newman was ordained a deacon in the Anglican Church. Visiting the sick and dying the young curate considered the state of their souls and salvation. He realized that although some parishioners had lived estranged from the faith, they were not altogether without grace.[1] Years later he referred to this experience in one of his sermons:

> We know, indeed, that privileges not improved will save no one; but we do not know, we cannot pronounce, whether in souls where there is but a little strength, yet much conflict, and much repentance, their regeneration may not, as in the case with children, avail them hereafter in some secret manner which, with our present knowledge, we cannot speak about or imagine.[2]

Newman believed that the grace of Baptism required growth on the part of the recipient, but even when little growth was evident, there was reason to believe in the soul's regeneration. Newman applied this belief to the consideration of the action of grace in the souls of those who had been ordained deacons with him. He did not think they led the proper life of piety and zeal, yet he realized that he should not judge regarding God's action in their souls.

During his first sermon preached at Mayer's parish in July of 1824, Newman made a sharp division of Christians into two classes of men, corresponding to the Evangelical distinction of "the converted and the unconverted." The claim that only some baptized persons were converted or saved through a tangible experience of conversion was a

---

1 See *AW*, 206.
2 "Infant Baptism," in *PPS*, Vol. III (May 24, 1835), 298.

denial of baptismal regeneration and served as a test of Evangelical orthodoxy. Dr. Hawkins was upset at Newman and told him that pastoral experience argues against a strict line of demarcation between two types of Christians.[3] He loaned him John Bird Sumner's *Apostolic Preaching Considered In An Examination of St. Paul's Epistles* to support the position that St. Paul did not divide Christians into two categories, "the converted and the unconverted."[4]

In August, a month after this rebuff from Dr. Hawkins, Newman noted in his diary that he continued to wrestle with the perplexing subject of baptismal regeneration. Sumner's book argued that the preaching of the Apostles in the New Testament ran counter to the Calvinist doctrines of predestination, but this text also shed doubt on baptismal regeneration. Newman noted that "it threatened to drive him into either Calvinism or the Catholic doctrine of baptismal regeneration."[5] That month he was so distressed by his doubts that he shed tears and even considered that he might have to leave the Church. He wrote, "I do not know what will be the end of it. I think I really desire the truth, and would embrace it wherever I found it."[6] And a week later, after tea with friends who wished him to be more Calvinist, he wrote similarly, "What shall I do? I really *desire* the truth."[7] The search for doctrinal truth was already a

---

3 *AW*, 77.

4 In 1825, Newman recommended to his friend Simeon Lloyd Pope that he read, study, and pray over Sumner's "Apostolical Preaching." See *LD*, Vol. I, JHN to Simeon Lloyd Pope (June 1, 1825), 234-35.

5 *AW*, 202.

6 *Ibid.*

7 *AW*, 202.

clear guiding force in Newman's life.

In January of 1825, Newman finally gave up belief in the doctrine of imputed righteousness. He reasoned that, if God did not grant grace with Baptism, why would He ordain Baptism for infants? A few years later he preached a sermon in which he said, "We need a new birth, because our first birth is a birth unto sin. Who does not see that this reason is equally cogent for infant Baptism as for Baptism at all? Baptism by water and the Spirit is necessary for salvation . . . because man's nature is corrupt; therefore infants must need this regeneration too."[8]

Newman's own conversion had not been a special Evangelical experience verified by religious feelings. He took back his earlier thoughts that sinful acts indicate the absence of regeneration. It was more reasonable to think that in a baptized person, holiness is achieved gradually by countless degrees.

While he prepared sermons he was obliged to organize and complete his ideas on many subjects, including Baptism. He realized that he had accepted in an uncritical manner the doctrine denying baptismal regeneration and the doctrine of predestination of individuals. It was not until eleven years later, as shown in his *Lectures on Justification*, that he fully understood that those doctrines taught by Scott lacked scriptural confirmation.

In July 1825, he read Bishop Joseph Butler's *Analogy of Religion, Natural and Revealed, to the Constitution and Course of Nature*, a book that ascertains the reasonableness of natural religion based on an analogy with human nature.

---

8 *PPS,* Vol. II, "Infant Baptism" (June 15, 1825), 223.

For instance, Butler wrote that a remedy to an illness might serve as an analogy of redemption for man's fall. Butler also compared God's government of the world to the authority exercised by a father in a family and by a governor in a state. These comparisons strengthened the cogency that God exerts a moral government over the world. Butler's book taught Newman, perhaps more than his senior colleagues did, how to show the credibility of Christianity. The book contained various arguments that helped Newman to refute the claims and objections of various moral philosophers.

Butler, who had been a student at Oriel College one century earlier, had lived during an age of rationalism and Deism, which persistently demanded evidence for the truth of Christianity. Butler rejected the demand of proofs for the existence of God and His attributes. He thought that proofs were insufficient and reduced Revelation to that which reason might explain. Instead, Butler sought, by means of inductive thinking, to draw from the moral experience of individuals and of society to reach a firm knowledge of the intelligent Author and Moral Governor of the universe. Richard Church, a contemporary of Newman at Oxford, would later write that Newman had learned from Butler "as a first principle to recognise the limitations of human knowledge, and the unphilosophical folly of trying to round off into finished and pretentious schemes our fragmentary yet certain notices of our own condition and God's dealing with it."[9]

---

9 Richard W. Church, *The Oxford Movement, Twelve Years, 1833-1845*, MacMillan and Co. Ltd, London, 1904, 211.

Butler explained that the observation of the repetition of events in nature leads the mind to expect their future repetition. Through reason, man presumes that God, who is the Author of Nature, acts in a similar way in the supernatural realm. By comparison with the order in nature, in which the probability of an event becomes a prediction of the likelihood of similar future events, man accepts the probability of a divine order in the realm of morality and the probability of God's revelation to men.

In a work entitled *On Development of Christian Doctrine*, which Newman would write in 1845, he explained the concept of antecedent probability and various rules for syllogisms, which are the grounds for the art of reasoning.[10] He wrote that on the basis of observation there are many events in life that we take for granted without seeking a reason or a demonstration. For example, we take for granted, without any special reasoning, that the sun will come out tomorrow. The likelihood that the sun will rise tomorrow is, in logical terms, called the antecedent probability of the sun coming out. In this case, the antecedent probability is very high. He cited as another common example of antecedent probability the high likelihood of the recurrence of the effects of Newton's laws of gravity.

Newman explained that antecedent probability is as necessary in ethics, history, theology, and philosophy as induction is necessary in medicine. The former require authority, tradition, and analogy, whereas the latter (and

---

10 John Henry Newman, *An Essay on the Development of Christian Doctrine*, 99-121, available at: http://www.newmanreader.org/works/development/index.html. After this it will be cited *Dev.*

other experimental sciences) requires facts. Nonetheless, antecedent probability also leads to the truth about things and, for it to bear weight, the truth of the starting premise is very important. Newman remained indebted to Butler's teaching that material realities speak of unseen realities and that faith has a logical cogency.

During 1825, John Henry thought a great deal about the inspiration and canonicity of the books of Sacred Scripture. He wished to answer objections to the truth of Christianity that his brother Charles posed to him. Charles argued that a few books of the New Testament were non-inspired, corrupted, or interpolated. John Henry was cognizant that some scholars had rejected certain books of the New Testament, but thought that this did not invalidate the likelihood of the divine inspiration and commission of the New Testament. He believed that even if the Apostles had made mistakes in their writings, it would not invalidate the inspiration of the New Testament books.[11] In refutation of his brother's idea that the accounts of miracles were later second and third-century additions to the New Testament, John Henry argued that if this were the case, St. Irenaeus and St. Clement would have known about these large additions and would not have attributed to Mark the authorship of the Gospel that bears his name.[12]

Discussions with his younger brother Frank also helped Newman to study doctrine and articulate his beliefs. In February 1827, Newman completed a paper on infant Baptism

11 *LD,* Vol. I, JHN to Charles Robert Newman (August 25, 1825), 254.
12 *LD,* Vol. I, JHN to C.R. Newman (September 26, 1835), 258-60.

that he wrote in refutation of the Evangelical ideas held by Frank.[13] The paper was sent to his sisters, but it was as much Newman's attempt to educate himself concerning the objective nature of the sacrament of Baptism as it was to educate his siblings.

The comments by the Provost and men at Oriel continued to help Newman to correct his understanding of various doctrines. On Easter Sunday, April 15, 1827, Newman preached a sermon in the chapel at Oriel entitled *On the Mediatorial Kingdom of Christ*. Hawkins, Whately, and Joseph Blanco White criticized him for the content of the sermon. Whately accused it of Arianism, the fourth-century heresy that denied the divine nature of Jesus Christ. In a personal note to himself, Newman explained that his incorrect expressions were the result of trying to account for perplexing Scripture texts. He wrote: "I do not even like the words Trinity, Person, Procession etc etc—indeed any systematic exposition of the doctrine but what is *relative to us and practical*." [14] Newman disliked discussions about the nature of God and shunned any systematic exposition of doctrine. In this regard he would later criticize excesses that he found in Scholasticism.

Although Newman was struggling with these doctrinal questions, he greatly enjoyed the company of Joseph Blanco White, an Anglican clergyman, formerly a Roman Catholic priest, who, after publishing a work entitled *Evidences Against Catholicism*, was awarded a Master of Arts

---

13 *LD*, Vol. II, 4-5.

14 *LD*, Vol. II, Memorandum: Sermon "On the Mediatorial Kingdom of Christ" (May 13, 1827), 15-16.

degree at Oxford and was made a Tutor by Oriel College. Newman admired Blanco White's life experiences and critical opinions of Catholicism. In addition to White's quiet and sensitive character, his kindness must have struck a chord with the young Fellow. In January 1829, Newman published an article on Aristotle's poetry in a new publication, the *London Review,* begun by White, who was keen on Newman's future collaboration. The journal died, however, after only two editions.

For some years, under the influence of the Oriel Common Room, Newman went through a period of intellectual criticism of religion that he later called "a drift towards liberalism."[15] By this, he was referring to his critical approach to Church doctrine and tradition exemplified by his ideas on the subject of the Holy Trinity, the Athanasian Creed, and miracles of the first age of Christianity. Newman awoke from this drift following an illness in 1827 and the death of his sister Mary in 1828. The latter marked the beginning of Newman's appreciation for the High Church Anglican tradition due to the close friendship forged with two Oxford men: John Keble and Keble's former student, Richard Hurrell Froude. Both men had an extensive knowledge on the Anglican tradition, and embodied its true character and piety.

When Newman entered Trinity, Keble had already earned a name for himself at Oxford. John Keble had studied at Corpus Christi College, where he graduated with two first-class honors; he had become a Fellow of Oriel in 1811, and a Tutor in 1817. He was the son of an Anglican

---

15 *Apo.,* 14.

clergyman, who had raised him in a country parsonage in Gloucestershire, in the best of the old English family life. He grew up with the Anglo-Catholic tradition and the theology of the seventeenth-century Anglican. In 1827, Keble published the *Christian Year*, a book of poems based on the Sunday and Feast Day services of the *Book of Common Prayer*. The poems conveyed the symbolic and sacramental character of Christian doctrine and worship. Newman praised the beauty and depth of the book's religious teaching, which he said, "struck an original note and woke up in the hearts of thousands a new music, the music of a school, long un-known in England."[16] After reading it, he sent a copy off to his mother and sisters. Newman would later say that the *Christian Year* impressed on him two truths similar to the ones that he learned from Butler.[17] The first was the belief in a sacramental system whereby material phenomena are types and instruments of real things that are unseen. According to this there is much more to reality than what man can perceive with his senses, namely, the purely spiritual beings, but the material realities point to them and can serve as a medium to them.

The second truth was an improvement on Butler's idea that probability is the guide of life. In the *Apologia,* Newman would write that, for Keble, faith and love gave a firmness of assent that probability did not have. Faith and love are directed to an Object, and this Object renders it reasonable to take probability as sufficient for internal evidence. Newman wrote about Keble, "In matters of religion, he

---

16 *Apo.,* 18.
17 *Apo.,* 18-19.

seemed to say, it is not merely probability which makes us intellectually certain, but probability as it is put to account by faith and love."[18] An illustration can make this clear: a child knows that a burning forge causes damage, so that it is probable the forge will harm him if he touches it. The child, however, reaches certainty about this by faith and love for his father, who tells him not to touch the forge because it will harm him.

Newman admired Keble's view on probability, but attempted to complete it. For Newman, absolute certitude regarding the truths of natural theology and the existence of Revelation arose from the result of concurring and converging probabilities. This altered his thinking about miracles following those recorded in the New Testament. He arrived at the conclusion that, since laws of nature have been suspended in great miracles, such as the Resurrection, there is a probability for future miraculous interventions.[19]

Despite his respect for Keble, when Edward Copleston became bishop in December 1827 and vacated the position of Provost at Oriel, Newman joined Pusey and other Fellows in support of Hawkins's candidacy against Keble. At that time, Newman preferred the practical notions and religious opinions of Hawkins and thought that he would carry out necessary college reforms. Newman candidly admitted this in a letter to Keble, who responded in an understanding and gracious manner.[20] Hurrell Froude and Robert Isaac Wilberforce instead supported Keble, their teacher and

---

18 *Apo.*, 19.

19 *Dev.*, 99-121.

20 *LD*, Vol. II, JHN to John Keble (December 19, 1827), 44-45; J. Keble to JHN, *ibid.*, 46.

friend, but the latter withdrew his candidacy before the election. Hawkins became Provost and occupied the post for forty-six years and, ironically, later strongly opposed Newman's ideas for educational reform.

In August 1828, Newman visited Keble at his parents' home. He was liked at once by the Keble family, and the men grew to be close friends. Over the next years, they corresponded often and sought regular advice from one another. When, on one occasion, Newman read Keble's translation and adaptation of the Psalms to popular tunes and offered some criticism, Keble replied expressing his trust in Newman's honesty.[21]

The other close friendship that Newman developed as a Tutor was with Richard Hurrell Froude, an undergraduate at Oriel, also from a noble family who belonged to the High Church tradition. Richard's father, Robert Hurrell Froude, had studied at Oriel and held a high ecclesiastical office (Archdeacon of Totnes and Rector of Dartington). Richard Hurrell was a gifted youth with a bold character and a cheerful disposition. He had been a student under John Keble at Oriel, and was the one responsible for bringing Keble and Newman together.

In March 1826, Richard Hurrell Froude and Robert Isaac Wilberforce were elected Fellows at Oriel. Newman, who had participated in the deliberations, was delighted. He wrote to his mother: "We were in grave deliberation till near *two* this morning, and then went to bed. Froude is one

---

21 *LD,* Vol. II, JHN to John Keble (August 30, 1831), 354-56; J. Keble to JHN, *ibid.,* 357.

of the acutest and clearest and deepest men in the memory of man."[22] At first, Froude looked with suspicion at Newman's Evangelical habits and liberal views on religion and declined an invitation by Newman to spend Christmas with his family in Brighton. When Newman later changed religious views, they became best friends. Froude taught him to admire Tradition and Roman Catholicism as well as the ideal of celibacy and its role model, the Virgin Mary. Froude, who had a firm faith in the Real Presence, the belief in Christ's sacramental presence in the Eucharist, also awakened Newman's belief in this doctrine.[23]

During the summer and in the fall term of 1827, Newman spent many hours a day preparing for "the Examination Schools," a prestigious university appointment that consisted in examining students for Bachelor's degrees. In November, he fell ill just one day before the Schools began. After the first day, he was obliged to retire.[24] The cause of the illness, whose symptoms were a crippling fatigue with an inability to concentrate, was most likely extreme physical and mental exhaustion. Various causes came together to tax his health: a serious financial debt incurred by his Aunt Elizabeth,[25] concern over the election of a new Provost for Oriel, and long hours of study in preparation for his role as

22 *LD,* Vol. II, JHN to Mrs. Newman (March 31, 1826), 282.

23 In this book we capitalize the term "Real Presence," "the Sacrament" and the names of particular Sacraments as proper nouns, whether referring to Catholic or Anglican, but without implying identity between Catholic and Anglican rites.

24 *LD,* Vol. II (entries for November 25 and 26), 37.

25 Newman recorded that he and his brother Frank paid £500 to £700 for their aunt's debt. *AW,* 213.

examiner had taxed his health. After a few weeks of rest at his family home in Brighton, he recovered.

Newman remarked later that it was a second conversion; as before, he briefly confessed that he had preferred intellectual excellence over moral excellence. His primary concern had been success at Oriel and "the Schools." As a consequence of this mental collapse, Newman began to realize that he had placed too much reliance on his own mental faculties and strength. He saw the need to turn more to God and away from the concerns of the world. In the following months, Newman's bereavement over the death of family members would complete this conversion.

The liberal intellectual environment of the Oriel Common Room and the High Anglican influence of his friends had acted as a catalyst for Newman's departure from Evangelical ideas. He replaced these ideas with the traditional liturgy, sacramental practice, and doctrine. Years later, while still an Anglican, he described in various sermons "the danger" to which he thought Evangelicals are exposed; that is, to make themselves the object of contemplation rather than contemplating God Himself, and the temptation to dwell on their religious feelings rather than on the mystery of God. In one of the *Parochial and Plain Sermons,* entitled "Self-Contemplation," he indicated how this attitude leads to rigid views of predestination and raises the individual's importance above that of the Church.[26]

Newman was not disparaging the important contribution to public morality and missionary activity that Evangelicals made to society. Out of concern, however, for truth and

---

26 "Self-Contemplation," in *PPS,* Vol. II, 163-74.

sound doctrine, he objected to the weakness of doctrinal claims made by Evangelicals. At times, he disputed their indifference toward doctrine, as in the case of Hannah More, a very popular writer of plays, novels, and tracts.[27] More employed her wealth and her influence to open many schools and to generously assist the poor. As the title of one of More's books, *Practical Piety*, describes, she was concerned with prayer and reading of the Bible to encourage the service of one's neighbor and the attack on vice. She thought that speaking of doctrines was unprofitable and divisive, and thus she favored the practice of private judgment in religious matters. She believed in focusing on the subjective awareness of one's own salvation. A few years later, Newman commented that some of More's letters criticizing Church Creeds only strengthened Unitarianism, the epitome of liberalism in religion.

Newman feared this path from liberalism to Unitarianism, which his friend Blanco White had followed. Unitarians not only denied the doctrine of the Trinity but also the divinity of Jesus Christ; in addition, they believed in universal salvation of all men. For Newman, Evangelicals' emphasis on moral teaching and disregard for doctrine unwittingly set the stage for the absence of doctrine, or all-inclusiveness of doctrine.

When his Evangelical mentor, Walter Mayers, died on April 2, 1828, Newman had already given up the majority of his Evangelical views. Naturally, he preached at the funeral of his good friend and teacher, but by this time,

---

27 Ward, "We Must Look Back a Little" in *Young Mr. Newman*, 78-92; 86-92.

he had adopted many Anglican doctrines concerning Apostolic Succession, Tradition, Revelation, liturgy, and church architecture. He did not yet understand devotion to Mary, the intercession of the saints, and the belief in Purgatory, nor, of course, the papacy.

In 1826, Newman told his sister Jemima that he was planning to read the Church Fathers. These early writers, distinguished for holiness of life and orthodox teaching, wrote during the first nine centuries of Christianity. He had told her that it would take him from ten to twenty years to read the more than two hundred volumes of the Fathers. Pusey bought him an edition while in Germany and sent the books to Oxford in the fall of 1827. In a letter to his mother, Newman wrote: "My 'Fathers' are arrived all safe—huge Fellows they are, but very cheap—one folio costs a shilling!"[28]

With a systematic approach, Newman began to read them over the summer or "Long Vacation" of 1828. He started with the Apostolic Fathers, those succeeding the Apostles. He studied Barnabas, St. Clement of Rome, St. Ignatius of Antioch, St. Polycarp, and St. Justin. Intent on tracing the deviations or corruption of the Roman Church, he made slower progress than he desired. A year later he wrote, "I am so hungry for Irenaeus and Cyprian—I long for the Vacation."[29] But by the end of summer 1829, he had made little progress and considered the need to give up his tuition or position as Tutor to be able to advance his plans.

---

28 *LD,* Vol. II, JHN to Mrs. Newman (October 18, 1827), 30.
29 *LD,* Vol. II, JHN to Harriet Newman (June 25, 1829), 150.

The general outcome of Newman's first reading of the Fathers was disappointing because he read them from a Protestant point of view. He cataloged them according to Protestant principles such as justification by faith alone and looked for Protestant doctrines. He reached the rash conclusion that they did not say much, but he later realized the error of the method he had followed in his reading of them.

One exception to his overall poor impression of the Fathers was the doctrine of the Episcopal office that he found in them. They showed the episcopate to be a divine institution, a belief that lay in sharp contrast to Erastianism, a doctrine named for Thomas Erastus (1524–1583). Erastus was a Swiss Protestant who defended the subordination of ecclesial government to civil jurisdiction. Based on his reading of the Fathers, as well as his knowledge of Sacred Scripture and of ecclesiastical history, Newman asserted instead that the Church should have independence from civil government. As he read the Fathers, the book *Letters on the Church by an Episcopalian*, attributed to Whateley, resonated in Newman's mind. The book advocated protesting against the interference of the Church in temporal matters and of the State in spiritual matters. At the same time the author also held that although the clergy are not hired servants, they should support the State and receive State revenues.[30]

Newman read the Fathers of the Church in the wake of his second spiritual conversion at Oriel College. The first one had been a conversion from skepticism. This time he turned from an incipient religious liberalism to a Christianity founded on doctrines that were based on Sacred

---

30 *Apo.*, 13.

Scripture and transmitted by Tradition. The two principal doctrinal truths that he embraced during these years were Apostolic Succession and baptismal regeneration. Both marked his passage from Protestant Evangelicalism to High Church Anglicanism. He reached these beliefs with the help of his Anglican friends but also with the experience of the real-life pastoral situations of the parishioners of St. Clement's Church where he served as curate. During these years at Oriel College Newman's religious beliefs changed significantly. While the intellectual environment at Oriel contributed to Newman's departure from Evangelical beliefs, Newman was able to reject the pure rationalism of the Oriel Common Room.

CHAPTER 7

CURATE OF ST. CLEMENT'S

WHEN Newman turned twenty-three in 1824, he reached the age for ordination as a deacon, and in preparation, he began to fast every week. With the advice and encouragement of Mayers and Pusey, he accepted the offer to be curate at St. Clement's Church, whose rector was in his eighties and suffering from poor health. The church was in a working-class parish in East Oxford over the Magdalen Bridge. Since Newman had lived ten years in residence at Oxford University he felt awkward among poor and uneducated people.

Newman wrote to his father, telling him about the parish and his salary. The parish had approximately 2000 inhabitants, but the capacity of the church was limited to 300 people. He would earn £45 each year. Mrs. Newman wrote to him, "Your Father and I are much gratified to hear of your offer and acceptance of the Curacy of St. Clement's. It appears, my dear, quite providential."[1]

The young graduate did not feel equal to the task, and he was fearful when he considered the ordination vows and his future responsibility for souls. At the same time, he struggled against pride and an excessive desire for academic recognition at Oriel. Conscious of this flaw, he prayed

---

1 *LD*, Vol. I, Mrs. Newman to JHN (May 22, 1824), 174.

for humility and fortitude. When his friend Pusey won an essay prize, Newman wrote in his diary, "I am small and of no reputation—and I thank my God for it most heartily. But are my affections in the same direction?"[2]

As the weeks for ordination approached, Newman prayed with greater joy, offering his whole life: fortune and misfortune, joy and sadness, health and sickness, honor and dishonor, to God. His prayer must have been heard because Newman had no lack of successes and trials in his life. After overcoming one last doubt regarding the decisive step that he was to take, he was ordained a deacon in Christ Church Cathedral by the Bishop of Oxford on June 13, 1824.

Newman felt a big relief from his interior trepidation. It was as if a battle with God was over, and he wrote the following prayer: "It is over. I am thine, O Lord."[3] He felt as a man thrown into deep water, but Newman was a good swimmer. For the long remainder of his life, he would swim in rough seas and with little respite.

Newman preached the first sermon at his mentor's parish. The power he lacked in his voice was made up by the power of his words. From the start of his preaching, he spent long hours preparing sermons and, after the first few, felt almost without anything left to say. Although some complimented him for his sermons, others complained that they were severe. He was unperturbed by the latter and made the Christian vocation to holiness the focus of the homilies. He wrote, "Those who make comfort the great subject of their preaching seem to mistake the end of their ministry.

---

2 *AW*, 199.
3 *AW*, 200.

Holiness is the great end. There must be a struggle and trial here. Comfort is a cordial, but no one drinks cordials from morning to night."[4]

In this new phase of his life, Newman's time was occupied with baptisms, morning and afternoon Sunday services, preaching, marriage ceremonies, and burials for the dead. He devoted a lot of time and effort to visit parishioners who were ill—sometimes the same one more than once a day—and to pray with them until they recovered or died. In his diary, there are many stories of the sufferings, spiritual circumstances, and trials of those who were sick.

He urged many of the sick to repentance for their sins and took "the Sacrament" (short for the sacrament of the Holy Eucharist) to those who were prepared. A forty-year-old woman who suffered extreme pain from a dreadful ulcer in her leg told him that she found great peace in receiving Holy Communion. On February 7, 1825, he recorded in his diary: "Just before she died she told him 'Jesus Christ is there, (pointing) no, He is here, here' (putting her hand on her breast)."[5]

At a young age, this new curate already had a deep and genuine compassion for others. He prayed for them and, on his visits, recited prayers with them. He was concerned for their physical and spiritual suffering and, above all, for the salvation of their souls. Some who had not thought much of religion, when they fell ill, responded to God's graces, repenting of their sins. In May, one parishioner told her

---

4 *AW*, 172.
5 *LD*, Vol. I, 208.

mother that, when the curate would enter the bedroom, she thought of Jesus Christ as depicted in pictures.[6]

In less than two months, he visited all of his parishioners, house by house, and all were pleasantly surprised and tremendously thankful to see a clergyman. He also raised money for constructing a new church and for establishing a Sunday school through monetary pledges commonly known as subscriptions. Not all was good, though. One day the new curate had a dispute with the parish choir and the choir members became indignant and left the church. In support of their neighbors, some parishioners met with Newman or sent letters of protest with threatening remarks, but in the end, nothing came of it.

During the visits, the *Treatise on Apostolical Preaching* recommended to him by Hawkins helped Newman to give up his remaining Calvinism and accept the doctrine of baptismal regeneration. Hawkins conveyed to Newman the importance of Tradition for Anglicans and foretold that, before long, the books and canon of Scripture would come under attack. According to Hawkins, the formulas of the Church set forth in the Catechism and Creeds are intended to teach the faith, whereas Sacred Scripture serves as a proof for these formulas and Creeds. The Scriptures are not an organized and complete exposition of the religious truths that should be believed. On his twenty-fourth birthday, Newman concluded, "I have taken many doctrines almost on trust from Scott etc and on serious examination hardly find them confirmed by Scripture."[7]

---

6 *LD,* Vol. I, 232.
7 *AW,* 205.

In addition to carrying out this demanding pastoral work as a deacon, Newman was involved in college life, administrative work at St. Alban's, and in writing essays for the *Encyclopedia Metropolitana*. In November of 1825, while recovering from an illness, Newman wrote to his mother saying, "Parish, Hall, College and Encyclopedia go on together in perfect harmony."[8] He exaggerated to relieve his mother's worries. He wanted to study and write more, but he realized that he could not continue working at the same pace with all the obligations of the parish and the Hall. In February of 1826, with the prospect of succeeding his friend Richard Jelf as Tutor at Oriel College, Newman resigned from the curacy at St. Clement's Parish and from his offices at St. Alban's Hall. He had worked tirelessly for the poor parishioners, caring for their souls with dedication and zeal. The parishioners, especially the sick, had gladly welcomed him and also taught him a great deal. Many accepted illness as a purification for their sins and a preparation for death. In this period Newman also experienced the sorrow brought by the death of a loved one, his own father.

---

8 *LD*, Vol. I, JHN to Mrs. Newman, 268.

CHAPTER 8

DEATH OF NEWMAN'S FATHER

JOHN Henry had a good relationship with his father, characterized by the respect and the restrained affection proper to English custom. John Henry admired his father's hard work and honesty and the care for his family. From school, he wrote almost forty letters to his father. These were usually short, versing on specific details about studies or finances. In general, the letters to his parents were like a dutiful report of activities, almost indicating a certain emotional distance; yet he did have affection for his parents. Naturally, both parents were proud of their son's responsibility and accomplishments at Oxford. On his twenty-first birthday, Mrs. Newman wrote "I thank God, it is a day of rejoicing to us all; to your Father and me, that it has given us a Son who has uniformly persevered in improving the talents given to him, and in forming his character both morally and religiously to virtue. And now that we have no more the dear child, we may boast instead, a companion, counselor and friend."[1]

Mr. Newman, who followed closely his son's progress, also wrote him, although much fewer letters than Mrs. Newman. He always encouraged John Henry in his studies and trusted in the plans that the older brother made for

---

1 *LD*, Vol. II, Mrs. Newman to JHN (February 21, 1822), 122.

Frank at Oxford. Mr. Newman's letters express gratitude toward God and trust in Divine Providence. In October 1821, while experiencing serious financial concerns, Mr. Newman conveyed to John Henry his serene acceptance of God's assistance gained through prayer and attendance to church services.

Mr. Newman observed religious practices, but disliked excess in religious fervor and worried about the path that John Henry and Frank were following. One Sunday he corrected them for intransigence in their Evangelical practices. He rightly chided them for holding a rigid interpretation of moral norms, when they refused to write a business letter that he asked them to write, claiming that it would be a violation of the Third Commandment. He warned John Henry of excesses in religion and, interestingly, foretold his departure from the Evangelical religion.

Mr. Newman sought the best education for his oldest son and wished to prepare him for a future livelihood. With this end in mind, when the brewery business failed, he encouraged his son to take up law. When John Henry refused his father's plans, Mr. Newman did not oppose him. He recognized that John Henry's talents would serve a higher cause and sensed the futility of trying to change his son's plans. After this second failure of his father's businesses, the young Newman did everything possible to earn money and pay for his own expenses and Francis's schooling by teaching pupils and writing articles. Newman did not wish for his father to worry about the cost of Francis's education. In December of 1822, he wrote to his father, "As to Francis, you will very much distress me, if you think at all of the money about him. He is in no want of it; he has paid his entrance money etc and he will have plenty when he comes up to reside."[2]

Despite his hard work, Mr. Newman had been beset by repeated business failures that affected his health and from which he never recovered. Years later, John Henry wrote a long note defending the actions and good name of his father throughout these failures. It became typical of Newman to write summaries of past events, in part for future reference and the sake of justice but also in part out of an excessive sensibility for others' opinions.

In July of 1824, Mrs. Newman sent her son a message from his father: "Your Father desires his love [sic]. He talked of writing to you, but, when the time comes, he generally declines, knowing you will accept his love through me."[3] Then on September 19, Newman heard from his mother the unexpected news that his father was ill and was being attended by a physician. Mr. Newman was dying. John Henry immediately traveled to London and remained next to his father during the last days of his life. Upon seeing him, Mr. Newman put out his hand to greet his son and said, "God bless you."[4] He was calm and composed and, shortly before dying, asked his son to read aloud the 33rd chapter of Isaiah. Mr. Newman died on September 29; he was only fifty-nine years of age.

Newman grieved at his father's death, yet was supported by his faith in eternal life. The scene of his father's lifeless corpse gripped Newman with a sense of the soul's immaterial and immortal nature, leading him to a philosophical consideration which he jotted down in his *Autobiographical Writings*: "Can a man be a materialist who sees a dead body?"[5] It was a perceptive insight into the separation of soul and body at the moment of death, especially for a young man who had not yet witnessed the death of many.

On October 6, with three uncles and other family members in attendance, the remains of Mr. Newman were buried. The young Newman was now the head of the family. Two weeks later, John Henry, back at Oxford, sent a consoling letter to his mother in which he wrote: "The days will come, when one after another, we shall drop away like leaves from the tree. But, being, as we trust, in Christ, we shall meet one and all in Heaven to part no more . . . we shall meet, as our hope is, him, whom we have just lost."[6] This was the first death of a loved one for John Henry, and it brought him to consider the promise of Heaven in a real and personal manner.

In these circumstances, Mrs. Newman, who still had a small family fortune from her parents, considered the uncertain future of her children and expressed the desire to see John Henry married before her death. He replied that he had chosen to live a celibate life, and to teach at a college or to go as a missionary to a foreign land. Since his adolescence, he had had a sense that his mission in life called for the sacrifice of celibacy. At his father's death, the thought of the finitude of earthly life and the eternity of Heaven only increased his resolve to live a celibate life. Newman

---

5 *AW*, 203.

6 *LD*, Vol. I, JHN to Mrs. Newman (October 18, 1824), 195.

envisioned celibacy as way of dedication, or a way to be fully devoted to his responsibilities, without the tug of a home life. He continued his course to receive Holy Orders in the Anglican Church.

Newman was only twenty-three when all the family responsibility fell upon his shoulders. From Oxford, where he continued at Oriel College, and until 1826 at St. Clement's Parish, he provided financial assistance, moral support, and guidance to his mother and siblings. His sense of responsibility for the family and his generosity were among the many virtues that animated his entire life, beginning at Oxford.

CHAPTER 9

CHARACTER OF THE YOUNG OXFORD DON

YOUNG Newman was a thin and wiry man. From sketches we know he had a prominent nose and a wide mouth. He wore small spectacles with a metal frame. The color of his eyes was gray-blue; the color of his hair light brown. He walked fast and wrote just as fast. He was shy in large company but talkative and humorous among friends.

Newman's *Autobiographical Writings* gives a good picture of his spiritual character, his weaknesses, and earnest desire for Christian holiness. This candid confession confirms that Newman's life, like that of most men, was a mix of good and bad inclinations and actions, a complex fusion of noble and selfish human and spiritual motives. His diary entries indicate that Newman strove to acquire and grow in human and supernatural virtues, desiring to become a man of proven character. He gave generously of his time and money to family, friends, and parishioners. One entry reads: "gave sacrament money to poor women."[1] His diaries record frequent letter writing and many appointments and meals with friends.

As a Fellow, he earned money by giving private classes to students, which was a common practice at Oxford, but

---

1 *LD,* Vol. II (Dec. 21, 1829), 179.

the students were often late to pay for his services. On one such occasion a diary entry reads: "I have but a few shillings left in my pocket, and owe many bills."[2] In November, he prayed more earnestly for relief, and the post brought him a letter with an enclosed payment of £25 from one of his students.[3] By December 1823, pupils still owed him nearly £100.[4]

The young Oxford don also earned some money for articles that he wrote for the *Encyclopedia Metropolitana* and from different administrative positions he held at Oxford. In October of 1824, he was elected Junior Treasurer at Oriel, which provided him £60 per year, and in March of 1825, he was appointed Vice-Principal of St. Alban's, which provided him with an additional £50 per year.

Newman enjoyed a modest living within his means. At Oriel he had a servant, as was the custom in the colleges. He paid for the keep of a horse that he liked to ride, for exercise and for the pleasure of riding. As a Fellow he did not travel much, and when he did, it was by coach (like most people) or on horseback. He ate meals in the College Hall, and sometimes in the Common Room except for the occasional entertainment of friends in his own rooms.

In addition to his own expenses, Newman's early financial burdens included the support given to his brothers, Francis and Charles. When Mr. Newman died in 1824, his wife was left with a small income of £150 from £5000 invested in funds at three percent. She and her three daughters lived

---

2 *AW* (October 10, 1823), 194. He had £2 in the bank and was expecting £50 or part thereof from a student.

3 *AW* (November 4, 1823), 194.

4 *AW*, 195.

almost "in trunks," traveling from relatives to friends when they did not stay at an establishment at Strand-on-the-Green in London, which their aunt operated as a boarding home. This business ran a deficit, which John Henry also supported with sums of money. When he became Tutor at Oriel in 1826 his financial situation changed since he began to earn between £600 and £700 each year.

Newman was meticulous about recording expenses and debts. He acquired this experience while acting as Bursar for St. Alban's Hall and as Junior Treasurer at Oriel. In 1825, he was able to boast to his mother: "I have balanced my [Junior Treasurer's accounts], (between £4000 and £5000) to a few shillings!"[5] He would promptly send payments to creditors and ask Fellows at Oriel to send in payments corresponding to their lodgings and other expenses. He was good at acknowledging and thanking people for monetary contributions to the projects he organized.

The young don was very focused with his studies, recording the books he read, the subjects he researched, and the sermons or essays that he wrote. Due to his ambitions, Newman was sometimes excessively saddened by academic setbacks, but he persevered in his objectives. Determination and perseverance were among his lifelong traits, exhibited first at Oxford, and then later at the Catholic University of Ireland and the Birmingham Oratory.

Newman was punctual in keeping his religious obligations. He read the Bible daily, and with time knew it very well. In the year 1823, he recorded memorizing the Epistle to the Ephesians and chapters of Isaiah. During the Long

---

5 *LD,* Vol. II, JHN to Mrs. Newman (July 16, 1825), 242-43.

Vacation of 1826, he began to learn Hebrew in order to read some of the books of Scripture in their original language. That vacation he made it through Genesis and continued with Exodus.

Early on, the Oriel Fellow accepted all the Christian doctrines taught by the Creeds. He relied on the Creeds as the sure guide for correctly understanding the Sacred Scriptures, and he exerted himself in examining and weighing theological doctrines to distinguish error from truth. Passion for the truth in religious matters kept him from easy compromises or fast solutions to intellectual difficulties. He had a strong faith in God's goodness and justice that he tried to foster in his parishioners. From an early age, he had a deep sense of hope in Divine Providence at work in his life and that of all individuals.

Nonetheless, Newman was often impatient with correspondents, and at times imprudent and harsh with parishioners. He recorded how he severely reprimanded a coachman who had been a heavy drinker.[6] His personal annotations convey sorrow for failures in charity toward others, especially family members, and the resolve to be more charitable in his dealings with them. But the Achilles' heel of the young Newman was pride. The Oxford don had to fight a great deal against the inclination to vanity and pride, which, given his intellectual talent and his pursuit of an academic career, were more pronounced in him than in the average man. Newman must have experienced repeated temptations in this area because his diary records a per-

---

6 See *LD,* Vol. I (August 1824), 187-88.

sistent petition to God for Him to take away the desire for praise and his excessive concern for a good name.

When Newman's brother Francis obtained two first-class honors that he himself had not achieved, Newman saw this as a divine lesson in humility and, with good humor, alluded to the Greek play *Electra,* calling his brother "avenger of his father." John Henry, whose pride was mixed with a noble sense of family honor, felt that Francis had obtained, for their father, the honors that he had failed to win.

"Snapdragon," a poem Newman wrote in 1827, on the eleventh year of his academic life, reflects an ongoing desire and struggle to be humble. He wished to be like a simple snapdragon that covers the walls of the Oxford towers and halls: "Humble—I can bear to dwell / Near the pale recluse's cell, / And I spread my crimson bloom."[7] In the final verses, the young writer recognized his God-given talents by comparing himself to the simple flower that, in addition to its crimson blooms, emits a pleasant fragrance. Newman did not have a false humility; while he chastised himself for vanity, he admitted his talents and considered his academic successes as Heaven's response to his prayers. In the last verse of "Snapdragon," he repeated his desire to live and die dedicated to university life. Although Newman would always remain a university man and an educator at heart, this wish would not be granted to him.

In diary entries, Newman accused himself of exaggerating matters and of being worldly. By the latter, he was referring to the wholesome comfort enjoyed in the company of many of his peers, hardly a worldliness in the sense

---

7 "Snapdragon," in *VV* (October 2, 1827), 17-19; 18.

of sinful revelry. Once he wrote to his mother: "I dined out once, and was three times out in the evening; to two music parties, and one dance."[8] This, however, was innocent fun; from his youth Newman practiced temperance and lived a chaste life. As expected for a young man, Newman was tempted by impure thoughts, but he did not fall into improper behavior with women or indulge, as did most of his peers, in excessive drinking.

For a few years after having read William Wilberforce's *Practical Christianity* in 1821, he considered it improper for a Christian to attend a play and gave this advice to some friends, such as Simeon Lloyd Pope, a clergyman friend of Trinity days. He thought it was a frivolity to be avoided by a clergyman. He soon came to understand, however, that attending decent plays posed no contradiction with Christian piety.

Newman admitted having many defects, including anger (in particular toward his brother Frank), contentiousness, and ill temper. He would have to fight against these defects all his life. His contentiousness was shown in controversies, in which he was quick to draw out the consequence of arguments and reach conclusions regarding their cogency and truthfulness. Although he was often correct, he lacked a charitable tone, as was often the case in discussions over religion with his brothers, especially Charles.

His sharp wit in response to slights or disagreements would sometimes get the worst of him in confidential letters to friends. Still it displayed his talent as a controversialist, and in the course of some controversies while at the

---

8 *LD*, Vol. I, JHN to Mrs. Newman (March 12, 1822), 124.

university, he made efforts to forgive his opponents and pray for them. With some, he would correspond even if only to acknowledge having received their letters.

As a result of daily self-examination, Newman had a good self-knowledge and formulated firm desires to overcome defects and grow in specific virtues. In one of his sermons, he wrote what could be a summary of his own battle for virtues: "a fight is the very token of a Christian."[9] Newman's defects were evident in his dealings and correspondence with others, but equally evident was his determination in fighting sin and striving for virtue.

It would be incomplete to paint a picture of Newman's character with an eye only to his pride, vanity, and contentiousness. He was a very bright, quick-witted, generous, and determined person with a passion for the truth. He was a kind and loyal friend devoted to the service of others. His sensitive and serious nature was complemented by his capacity to forgive and by good humor. He had sincere interest in people, a keen knowledge of their traits, and the ability to inspire them. These qualities were only enriched by his love for classical music and literature. With these qualities and many virtues, the Oriel Fellow and deacon was well prepared for Holy Orders.

---

9 John Henry Newman, *Discourses Addressed to Mixed Congregations,* 120, available at: http://www.newmanreader.org/works/discourses/index.html.

CHAPTER 10

1825: HOLY ORDERS IN THE ANGLICAN CHURCH[1]

O N May 29, 1825, Newman received Holy Orders at Christ Church Cathedral from Edward Legge, the Bishop of Oxford. For most Anglican clergy, marriage was a common path. Newman, however, chose to remain celibate. Maisie Ward, a biographer of Newman, writes that Newman was "by nature a bachelor, by grace a celibate."[2] It is true that by nature he enjoyed being single and immersed in extensive reading, studying, writing, playing music, and conversations with friends. From his early youth, however, he had felt a divine call to celibacy, which he believed was both an ideal state for serving the Church as well as an ascetical means of spiritual development. Observing his austerity, his sisters jokingly called him a monk.

Newman realized that a parish needed dedicated women, like his mother and sisters, to offer services such as teaching

---

1 Pope Leo XIII, In Apostolicae Curae (1896) reaffirmed the judgment of the invalidity of Anglican Orders due to a defect in the intention and form of the sacrament. Since then, due to some Anglican Episcopal ordinations by bishops of the Old Catholic Churches some argue that in rare cases there is a "prudent doubt" about the invalidity of a minister ordained in this line of succession. The judgment and practice of the Catholic Church, however, remains the same: unconditional absolution of former Anglican ministers who become Roman Catholic priests.

2 Ward, *Young Mr. Newman,* 272.

children, setting example to parents and helping young women find employment.[3] Frank complained when Newman hired a maid for his mother and sisters, suggesting that it was a matter of pride on their part. Newman replied explaining that a maid would free his mother and sisters to exercise works of charity in the parish. These works were actually like those that deacons traditionally performed in the first-century Church. Mrs. Newman jokingly told her son that she and her daughters would be his deacons.

Pusey's opinion regarding a feminine presence in the parish rectory was that the revival of sisterhoods in the Church of England would solve the problem of the necessity of having other women help in a parish. Many of Newman's friends believed that married clergy was the obvious and time-honored solution for providing parishes with women to carry out work to which they were more naturally suited. Newman was initially sad when his close friends, who were clergymen, Henry Wilberforce, John Keble and Thomas Mozley, married. Newman envisioned an inner circle of celibate clergymen who would be leaders in the Church in a time of dire need. For this very reason, in 1834, Henry Wilberforce was afraid to tell Newman the news of his future marriage to Mary Sargent, daughter of John Sargent, a clergymen whose four daughters all married friends of Newman. Newman became very upset at Henry for withholding this news from him, but Henry had been afraid that Newman would cut him from his circle of friends. From the human perspective, Newman also felt the loss of intimacy with his closest friends who married.

---

3 Ward, *Young Mr. Newman,* 268-86.

Among these early friends, only Froude remained celibate. Robert Wilberforce, writing later to Newman, noted that an "old bachelor" becomes despondent when his friends marry, and old friendships seem closed. Aside from his feelings, Newman was not objecting to married Anglican clergy, but was, instead, advocating a system of married country clergy and unmarried clergy. The unmarried clergy would live an ascetical life, like the Orthodox clergy in Greek monasteries. He once wrote to his friend George Ryder, who was anticipating marriage:

> It is quite absurd to suppose that you are not *at liberty* both to marry and to go into the Church—indeed I think that country parsons ought as a general rule, to be married—and I am sure the generality of men ought, whether parsons or not. The celibate is a high state of life, to which the multitude of men cannot aspire. I do not say that they who adopt it are necessarily better than others, though the noblest ηθοσ (ethos) is situated in that state.[4]

Newman realized that the celibate state required a specific vocation, God's assistance, and the support of intimate friendships. He relied on the human affection of his mother, sisters and a number of male friends. With these persons, he shared confidences, intellectual endeavors, and spiritual ideals. As is common with celibate persons, these very close friendships with family members and friends made it possible to forego a spouse's love and companionship.

Meriol Trevor, another female biographer of Newman, explains that Newman had a very positive idea of Christian virginity, which consisted in a self-dedication out of love for God analogous to the dedication of spouses within

---

4 *LD*, Vol. III, JHN to George Ryder (July 22, 1832), 70.

marriage. In no way did Newman depreciate the dignity and goodness of marriage, nor did he disregard the pleasures of human love and the attractiveness of domestic life. He, too, felt the charm of female company and understood the power of feelings.[5] He wrote that these natural feelings did not constitute sin; in themselves, they were good and innocent.[6] He relinquished them for a supernatural motive—for the sake of the kingdom of Heaven. In addition to the female friendship of his mother and sisters, Newman shared a lifetime spiritual friendship with Maria Giberne. Maria, sister of Walter Mayer's wife, was an attractive young woman who initially became friends with Frank, an Evangelical like her. At first, she found Newman to be proud, distant, and too High Church. She befriended the Newman sisters and finally John Henry, whom she soon came to admire for his sincerity and intelligence. Maria eventually became Roman Catholic and a nun of the Visitation of Mary Order.

Newman also shared a chaste friendship with other women: Elizabeth Bowden, her daughter Marianne Bowden, and Anne Mozley. Marianne, whom Newman had baptized, was the daughter of his dear friend John William Bowden. After her father's death, Marianne became Roman Catholic and a contemplative nun with the Visitation Order. In 1854, Newman gave the homily at the ceremony in which, dressed as a bride, she received the habit that signified her complete dedication to Christ. In notes for

---

5 Trevor, *Newman, The Pillar of the Cloud*, "The Idea of Virginity," 88-96.

6 *Ibid.*, 93-94.

his homily, Newman wrote that the idea of Matrimony is possession. In marriage, the husband is the wife's and no other's and vice versa. Likewise, virginity for a Christian is the soul's marriage with Christ.[7]

In 1829, when Tom Mozley, Newman's student, was elected Fellow and his brother James was an undergraduate, the Mozley family visited the Newmans at Oxford. The Mozley sisters made friends with the Newman girls. The Mozley sisters had heard a lot about Tom's Tutor. Anne remembered the striking impression that Newman and Froude made when the two walked into breakfast one Saturday morning. She remembered their "marked individuality" and "unconscious dignity of aspect."[8] Newman liked Anne Mozley the day they met, and they became friends. Toward the end of his life, Newman asked Anne to edit his letters for publication. She outlived Newman and prepared the first publication of his letters in two volumes.

Celibacy was a high ideal that Newman embraced for love of God and His Church. He lived by this ideal and yet, at times, admitted his attraction to the intimate friendship of marriage. Trevor points out that in our age the attraction of marriage has been confused with the need to satisfy physical pleasure and that since Newman did not confess to the latter, his confession about the need for marriage has been regarded as meaningless.[9] She correctly argues that we have no right to assume what he felt on a physical plane. What we can say is that Newman knew how to love and

---

7 Trevor, *Newman, The Pillar of the Cloud*, 90.
8 *Ibid*, 109.
9 *Ibid*, 95.

that his capacity to love increased as he grew older. Moreover, because this was true, at times he found the sacrifice of celibacy hard.

Newman thus began the life of an Anglican clergyman with a serious commitment to a celibate life and a clear sense of his spiritual mission. At St. Clement's, he officiated Sunday services and delivered two sermons weekly. In August of the same year—1825, he celebrated his first Communion Service and administered Holy Communion to Jemima and Mary, who had been confirmed shortly before.[10] He continued as a Fellow at Oriel College, but also became Vice-Principal of St. Alban's Hall, attached to Merton College, that same year.

In January 1826, Newman was asked to be Tutor at Oriel beginning with the Easter Term. This step would mark the start of his public life at the university. He was obliged to interact with students and his peers, and he began to exert his moral and intellectual influence on many. In 1828, when Hawkins was elected Provost of Oriel, he vacated St. Mary's Church, and Newman was appointed vicar. As a Tutor at Oriel and Vicar of St. Mary's, Newman came out of his shell and rose to new heights at Oxford. It would be a period of his life that he described as springtime following winter. The seeds that had germinated in the rich soil of Oriel and Trinity were now ready to sprout up from the earth.

The University Church of St. Mary the Virgin, where Newman was appointed vicar, had begun as the parish

---

10 *LD,* Vol. I, JHN to Mrs. Newman (July 1825), 244. It was the first time Mrs. Newman saw her son perform his clerical duty.

church around which the university was built. Its tower dates back to the middle of the thirteenth century. Since students lived nearby and classes were conducted in the vicinity, the church became the seat of the university government, academic disputations, and conferral of degrees until the seventeenth century, but formal university worship continued. Over the centuries, the architecture and interior decoration of the church were enriched.

St. Mary's association with the university and its use as the place of worship gained for it the name of University Church. Every Sunday of the term, a formal University Sermon was delivered there before the Vice-Chancellor and other university authorities. William Laud, Archbishop of Canterbury in the seventeenth century, and later on John Wesley, founder of Methodism, were other noteworthy men tied to the history of the church. Wesley, a Fellow from Lincoln College, preached a famous sermon titled "Almost Christian" at St. Mary's in 1741. After an equally controversial sermon in 1744, he was forbidden to preach there again. Almost a century later, Newman preached at St. Mary's and, thereafter, became part of the history of this Oxford church. And one day he too would be censured at Oxford for his religious views.

Men like Cardinal Manning and Prime Minister Gladstone, who had heard Newman's sermons in their youth, could not forget them. As was the custom, Newman read his sermons. His delivery was poor, yet his choice of words, the arguments, and the figure of the man himself combined as a whole to form a lasting impression. According to James Anthony Froude, Newman's sermons described real persons, with their experiences and temptations, their mix of good and evil, and their strengths and weaknesses. Other notable men who counted themselves fortunate to have heard these remarkable sermons were Lord John Taylor Coleridge and Principal J. C. Shairp.

Newman's Sunday sermons, preached at four in the afternoon, had a noticeable intellectual and spiritual influence at the University of Oxford. They served as a catalyst for the beginning of the Oxford Movement that formally began in 1833, and later as an inspiration for its members. Newman spoke in a simple and direct manner with perfect command of the English language, a keen knowledge of human character, and a lively faith. He constantly referred to God's greatness, goodness, and eternal glory and exhorted his listeners to full submission to God's designs.[11] The sermons had abundant references to Sacred Scripture, and the first published edition contained some references to the Church Fathers.

William Lockhart, one of Newman's friends and later a curate under him, compared the sermons with those of other good preachers at St. Mary's. He commented that many of these other preachers were impressive, but they did not reach the soul. According to Lockhart, they were good actors who played on the senses and the imagination, but they did not forget themselves in order to help those in the congregation focus on God.[12] With Newman, however, people felt that he was a seer of God and of invisible realities. Lockhart wrote: "Newman had the power of so

---

11 José Morales Marín, *John Henry Newman (1801-1890)* (Madrid: Rialp, 1990), 48.

12 William Lockhart, *Cardinal Newman* (London: Burns & Oates), 1891, 5.

impressing the soul as to efface himself; you thought only of the majestic soul that saw God. It was God speaking to you as He speaks to you through creation; but in a deeper way, by the articulate voice of a man made to the image of God and raised to His likeness by grace . . ."[13]

Newman tried to develop a single idea in each sermon and criticized attempts to develop a complete subject in one sermon. He quoted often from the pages of Sacred Scripture and insisted particularly on two patristic themes, the Incarnation and the Redemption. Although the sermons contained much doctrine, they were primarily moral in content. Newman concluded that the basic obstacles to faith were of an ethical rather than intellectual nature; instead of objecting to faith, people often simply lacked the proper disposition. His sermons were therefore designed to move people to correspond to God's grace in their lives.

Newman's sermons conveyed religious truth with courage and charity. While the content was strong, he refrained from employing the sarcasm often used in his letters. He would identify the essence of the argument that he wished to refute and would expose its fallacy or erroneous consequences.

The content of an early sermon from August 1826, *Holiness Necessary for Future Blessedness*, exemplifies the general tone of Newman's preaching. It was a demanding invitation to Christian holiness in preparation for life after death and communion with the Only Holy One. When he began publishing his sermons, he chose this one to open the

---

13 Edwin A. Abbott, *The Anglican Career of Cardinal Newman,* Vol. II (London: Macmillan and Co., 1892), 7.

first volume. It was indicative of the whole tone and goal of his preaching.

Newman later corrected some of his sermons for publication. The first volume of sermons, which appeared in March of 1834, met with immediate success. He dedicated this volume to his friend, Edward Pusey. The collection of sermons was first published as *Parochial Sermons*; later, when added to another collection, *Plain Sermons*, it was titled *Parochial and Plain Sermons*. In total, they comprised eight volumes, even though Newman only published just over a third of the sermons that he wrote as an Anglican. In recent years, the notes of Newman's unpublished Anglican sermons have appeared in five volumes.

While at St. Mary's, since it was a smaller parish than St. Clement's, Newman was obliged to preach only once on Sundays. He was glad about this because he thought that parish life was more than the Sunday sermon, which, according to him, should not be the focus of Sunday worship. He missed the frequent parish visitations to the sick that he had made at his former parish. Therefore, he soon began to visit the sick of St. Mary's and of Littlemore, a part of the parish outside of Oxford. He started Confirmation classes for the parish children. He also married couples, "churched mothers" after childbirth (a liturgical blessing for mothers), baptized their children, and performed the burial rites for deceased parishioners.

Thus, although after ordination there was a short period in which Newman dedicated himself primarily to college work at Oriel, soon afterward, upon becoming rector of St. Mary's, he returned to a demanding amount of pastoral work. His decision to live as a celibate clergyman did not originate in the absence of female friendships; it was an ascetical and spiritual vocation, part of a higher calling for the sake of the service of God in the Church. In his new condition, he managed to combine a life of intense pastoral duties with one of study and writing, and, given his new assignment as Vicar of the University Church, from its pulpit he became a powerful voice for renewal within the Anglican Church.

CHAPTER 11

FAMILY AND FRIENDS

A S the head of the family, Newman was concerned about the family's living arrangements. In August of 1826, he told his mother that she should have a home and argued that he and Frank also needed one. He also wished for his sisters not to have to live where they lived, in a damp little house on the river's edge. One day during the summer vacation, he looked for a home in Brighton, by the sea, but Mrs. Newman and her oldest son did not agree on a house. In 1827, after one year of hesitation, Mrs. Newman took a house at Marine Square, No. 11, Brighton, but with the agreement that she would sublet it every summer to earn some money. During the summers, mother and daughters stayed scattered about with relatives and friends, and Newman spent part of the Long Vacation with them.

In the summer of 1827, Newman spent six weeks with his mother and sisters in Hampstead, a few miles northwest of London, where he took the duty of a clergyman named Marsh. Charles Golightly and Henry Wilberforce went as Newman's pupils. Newman also spent some time at Samuel Rickards's home in Ulcombe. Unlike his friends, during this time Newman did not have a family house that he could call home and to where he could invite his friends.

Newman had a close relationship with his mother and sisters, sharing in their common domestic interests and religious piety. The abundant correspondence between Newman and his family reveals their tender affection, good humor and common everyday concerns. There was frank and lively correspondence between the family members. A letter addressed to Mrs. Newman conveys the affectionate and humorous tone of his relationship with his sisters. Newman sent his sisters the following greeting: "Love to all to *s*aucy H, *s*ly J, and *s*illy M."[1] Whether out of pure affection or with concern for having hurt their feelings, he wrote a few days later: "Love to H, J and M, sensible H, sober J and sprightly M, (this by way of making amends)."[2]

Mary, the youngest sister, respected the authority and learning of her older brother, nine years her senior, but teased him all the same. She was a lighthearted and very bright young woman, adored by the family. Although, like her sisters, she had not had any formal education, at fifteen, she was able to write letters in French and had read a lot for her age. She resembled John in her philosophical mind, her quick wit, and vivid writing style. To Jemima, for instance, she replied in a letter: "I was very right to begin on a sheet of foolscap, for the ideas of the thermometer of my brain are rising rapidly, and I expect that if they have not room to expand they will overflow and make terrible havoc; besides the name of the paper has something congenial with their nature."[3]

Because of their similarities Mary enjoyed the visits of Newman's friends. During the stay at Hampstead in

---

1 *LD,* Vol. II, JHN to Mrs. Newman (Feb. 1, 1827), 3-4.

2 *LD,* Vol. II, JHN to Mrs. Newman (March 8, 1827), 7.

3 Ward, *Young Mr. Newman,* Letter from Mary Newman to Jemima Newman, 119.

the summer of 1827, Henry William Wilberforce often went on horseback rides with Newman and ate meals with his family. The Wilberforce family would have, in time, three sons attending Oriel: Robert Isaac, Henry William, and Samuel. The family had strong ties to the Evangelical party, but when the sons attended the university, Robert and Henry were moving toward the High Church party in the Anglican Church.

Mary Newman captured the character of Henry William and his brother Robert Isaac, the one talkative and the other very shy, and she taunted their innocent compliments. She wrote John:

That nice little Henry W. what a nice fellow he is! Has Mamma told you of his absurd impudence last Friday? I like them all better and better; and R.W. with all his quietness and gentleness, he is as bad as H.W. and worse, because he is not so honest. H.W. says, "I am impudent, I am a torment"—and he is so. R.W. says, "I am gentlemanly and timid" and he is—impudent and tormenting.[4]

In early November of 1827, Mary wrote to Newman twice, expressing her desire to have him visit. With an almost childlike expression, she said, "Oh John . . . How I long to see you, nice creature! I can fancy your face—there it is looking at me:—how silly I am."[5] In December, she wrote to him with similar words, longing to see him.

Scarcely four weeks later, on January 4, 1828, Mary unexpectedly became ill during a family dinner. She

---

4 Ward, *Young Mr. Newman,* Mary Newman to John Henry Newman, 129.

5 *Ibid.*

developed a strange chest pain and went sick to her room.
Enduring the pain, she repeated some verses from Keble's
Christian Year that she had committed to memory. The
next day, after more violent spasms, she had a few hours
without pain in which she was told of the severity of her
condition. Mary reviewed her short life and asked pardon
for her sins. She received medical assistance but to no avail
and died at 9 p.m. on January 5. Maria Giberne, who was
visiting at Brighton, described Mary's death and the intense
grief experienced by her brother, John. This sudden and
premature family death affected him even more profoundly
than his father's death.

To Robert I. Wilberforce, who had written Newman
to convey his sorrow, Newman replied that he had had a
presentiment of Mary's future death because he could not
conceive of such beauty, goodness, and innocence on earth.
Reflecting on her premature death, he concluded that,
through her death, God was teaching him to desire Heaven
and preparing him for future trials. The loss of his young
sister had a lasting spiritual effect on Newman; he began
to ponder the transitory nature of goodness and beauty in
the visible world, which points to the invisible world that is
hidden behind an earthly veil.

This was the second close death in the family and a
painful one for all. Newman grieved the death of his young
sister for a long time. While riding on horseback in the
countryside, he thought about her and about life after death.
He wrote to Jemima how the beautiful countryside was but
a veil to an invisible world: "I never felt so intensely the
transitory nature of this world as when most delighted with
these country scenes . . . Dear Mary seems embodied in

every tree and hid behind every hill. What a veil and curtain this world of sense is! beautiful but still a veil—."[6] Many of his sermons subsequently referred to this invisible world of which faith affords us only a dim glance.

As a young clergyman, he had assisted his parishioners to prepare for death and God's judgment, but now he was obliged to experience, in his own flesh, the sorrow produced by the loss of a loved one. Mary's premature death forced him to think of eternal life in a new light. His thoughts and feelings were expressed in a succession of poems. Three months after Mary's death, he wrote in a poem entitled "Consolations in Bereavement" that Mary's swift death was a divine consolation because it had spared her, as well as the family, greater suffering. A few months later, in another poem entitled "A Picture," Newman reflected on Mary's spiritual presence among her loved ones: "She is not gone;—still in our sight / that dearest maid shall live . . ."[7] He portrayed Mary's love for her Maker, which was manifested in a serene and hope-filled response to His call. The poem ends, evoking the blessedness of glory where God will "knit in love souls parted here, / where cloud is none, nor change."[8] In addition to acceptance of God's Providence, Mary's death was made bearable for John by his family's love and friendship.

Almost a year after Mary's death, his sentiments alternated between prayerful submission to God's will and prolonged grief. The overall tone of his feeling was, however,

6 *LD*, Vol. II, JHN to Jemima Newman (May 10, 1828), 69.
7 "A Picture," in *VV*, (Oxford, August 1828) 29-32; 29.
8 *Ibid.,* 32.

one of acceptance of that which he considered the Providence of a loving and wise God. He knew that Mary had been prepared for Heaven and expressed this thought in verse: "All warning spared, / for none He gives where hearts are for prompt change / prepared."[9]

With the death of Mary as a reminder of the finitude of life, John determined to remain close to the rest of his family, something that came easily because he shared intellectual and religious interests with his mother, Harriet, and Jemima. The three women read and commented on his sermons and read religious books by authors such as Bishop Warburton and Thomas Arnold. Mrs. Newman and Jemima studied Greek and used this knowledge to read St. John's Gospel in its original language. Mrs. Newman shared her son's fondness for Walter Scott and read this author's *History of Scotland* and his novel, *Ivanhoe.* Harriet and Jemima's interests extended also to history and politics. In 1828, both studied Euclid; Harriet worked on learning German. Many of their interests were related to those of their older brother. They liked to discuss his verses and papers and to be kept abreast of news from the different colleges.

Newman's mother and sisters did not like Brighton, for the cold winters at Brighton affected Mrs. Newman's health. They longed to be together, especially after the loss of Mary. John Henry needed help in the parish at Littlemore, and Mrs. Newman wished to reduce John's contribution to their income. For all these reasons, the family moved closer to John, first to Nuneham and Horspath and

---

9 "Consolations In Bereavement," in *VV* (Oxford, April 1828), 26-28; 27.

then to Iffley, just outside of Oxford. At John Henry's urging, in August 1828, Newman's mother and sisters subleased the Brighton home and rented a cottage in Nuneham, a few miles south of Oxford. Newman wrote in his diary: "Thank God, my Mother and Sisters came safe."[10] He moved in with them, and they often dined and went on walks together. They stayed in Nuneham until the end of October, during which time Newman rode back and forth to Oxford on Oriel business.

During the Long Vacation of 1829, Mrs. Newman and her two daughters moved again to the vicinity of her oldest son. They leased a cottage in Horspath, a few miles to the east of Oxford. As had been the case during the previous summer, Newman moved in with his family and traveled back and forth to Oxford as needed. During the times together at home, one of the family activities was reading out loud from Volume I of David Hume's *History of England* on King James I. Once more Henry Wilberforce lodged near the Newmans and was tutored by Newman. Thanks to Newman's guidance and teaching, the following year Wilberforce obtained first-class honors in Classics and second-class honors in Mathematics.

From October 1829 to March of the following year, the Newman family leased the same cottage in Nuneham once more. Newman moved back to Oriel College and, when his busy schedule permitted, visited his family, but the visits were often short. Jemima later recalled that he "used to come ramping over hedge and ditch now and then." At Oxford, he received daily letters from Nuneham, and

---

10 *LD*, Vol. II (August 26, 1828), 93.

in one of them, Harriet complained: "I hope you can give us a decent-lengthened call—I should like a quarter of an hour's quiet time with you."[11]

In 1828, Newman had introduced his mother and sisters to Edward B. Pusey, whom they immediately admired. A friendship arose between them and soon afterward with Maria Pusey, his wife. In August 1830, Pusey and his wife went with Newman to see some houses for lease in Iffley, a town just east of Oxford. They had the hope of having Newman's family close by, and offered their home to the Newmans until their house was ready.

Many letters went back and forth between John and his mother about the endless details needed to prepare the house. Mrs. Newman wanted his opinion about many things such as furniture, carpeting, glass, and crockery. She also asked him for money for moving expenses. Newman had someone go to sales looking for furniture and found a carpenter to make some repairs. In October, Mrs. Newman, Jemima, and Harriet moved to Rose Hill, their new place of residence in Iffley. The mother and sisters promised to make the house neat and beautiful. They soon prepared a comfortable and charming room and study for John.

In the various homes, the family entertained occasional visitors from nearby Oxford. Family life was captured in *The Lost Brooch*, a short story by Harriet. In this story, she depicted a group of girls sewing while duets were sung and verses recited; the attitudes toward their brothers and life in general were discussed. In addition to this story, Maria Giberne sketched an image of the home circle with

---

11 *LD,* Vol. II, Harriet Newman to JHN (November 3, 1829), 172.

humorous conversations alternating with serious ones on history, religion, and church affairs. According to Maria, the charm, good humor, and wit of the sisters were coupled to their physical attractiveness and pretty apparel. John acquired some of his good taste in this family setting and sharpened his wit and good humor in the daily exchange with his sisters.

It was a happy family scene in these years despite the loss of father and youngest daughter. The family unity, though, was slowly becoming unraveled. Frank and Charles were going their own ways, the former traveling far from home and the latter separating himself from the family. In many letters prior to the move to Iffley, Mrs. Newman expressed to John her concern with the sons. For his part, John spent less time with the family, and gradually his diverging religious views would meet with resistance from his mother and his sisters.

Newman did not write down much about his brother Frank, with whom he attended Oxford. After obtaining double first-class honors at Worcester College in 1826, Frank was elected a Fellow of Balliol College. In the following years, the two brothers would sometimes dine together or meet to talk. They differed greatly in religious views. Whereas John was becoming more Catholic, Frank was becoming more Evangelical. Also, in contrast to his brother, Frank advocated Catholic Emancipation. He was convinced that justice demanded the admission of Roman Catholics to Parliament.

In 1827, while working as a tutor to a family in Ireland, Frank met John Nelson Darby, the founder of a branch of the Plymouth Brethren, a fundamentalist Christian denomination that had arisen at the start of the 1800s. This encounter revived Frank's earlier desire to be a missionary, and in May 1830, he decided to go as such to Persia (Iran). Before his departure and after his return, Frank proposed marriage to Maria Giberne; she refused twice.

John was disappointed that his brother did not consult him before making final plans for missionary work in Persia and, even more, that he was not going there as a part of an established Christian church. Nonetheless, he wished Frank well and prayed for the success of his plans. The expedition turned out to be a failure, and Frank was very ill on two occasions; he almost died during the second illness. He returned from Persia in 1833.

Frank never took his M.A. degree at Oxford because religious objections kept him from signing the *Thirty-Nine Articles*. Sacrificing a career at Oxford, he went to Bristol, where he joined a Baptist sect. Later he would move to London and go through other religious affiliations. He had an eccentric personality and seemed to substitute faith with a large number of causes, such as anti-vaccination, anti-vivisection, anti-tobacco, and so forth.[12] In 1834 he married Maria Kennaway, a Plymouth Sister. (After the death of his wife in 1876, he married a second time.) In 1840 he became professor of Latin at New College in Manchester and, in 1846, at University College in London. He was a scholar also in Greek, Arabic, Berber, Numidian, and other North African tongues. Despite their diverging religious beliefs, academic pursuits and personal interests, Frank and John respected each other and remained in occasional contact.

---

12 Ward, *Young Mr. Newman,* 166.

Charles Robert, who was older than Frank, rebelled early in life against the religious beliefs of his brothers and against the family as a whole. Although intelligent, he was, according to John, both proud and ungrateful. In 1825, he began to argue with his older brother on the credibility of Christianity and started an intense exchange of long letters on the subject. John reproved him for making precipitous changes in his beliefs, for faulty reasoning based on *a priori* objections to Christian doctrines, and for drawing conclusions from partial facts. Against wavering opinions he counseled him that "Truth is to be preferred to comfort."[13]

A few days later, John wrote his brother: "I do not assert that the Christian evidences are *overpowering,* but they are *unanswerable . . .*"[14] He wished to prove to his brother the rational nature of Christianity. Then, attempting to frame the discussion, he sent Charles a long list of questions on Sacred Scriptures and on miracles for him to answer. John wrote to Charles that he should contend with the idea of man's need for revelation and the external evidence for that revelation rather than judge its contents. He explained that the very notion of revelation implies that certain truths are not discoverable by human reason.[15] These important religious and moral truths require revelation. Charles needed first to begin by examining the external evidence for revelation, rather than start at the wrong end by examining the

---

13 *LD,* Vol. I, JHN to Charles Robert Newman (March 3, 1825), 212-15; 215.

14 *LD,* Vol. I, JHN to C. R. Newman (March 24, 1825), 219-21; 219.

15 *LD,* Vol. I, JHN to C. R. Newman (July 7, 1825), 240-41.

contents.[16] Since there are revealed truths that are beyond the reach of one's present reason, it would be a mistake to judge the truth of a revelation on its content, unless there were flagrant immoralities or falsehoods.[17]

Charles sought moral or ethical proof of the truth of Christian Revelation. According to his older brother, he was acting with pride by rejecting without due consideration the arguments of wiser men. He chastised him for his pride: "you're rejecting the *credentials* of Christianity *because* you dislike the *contents*."[18] By "credentials" John was referring to miracles, prophecies, the establishment of Christianity, and other events that are considered a preparation for faith.[19]

John, who was busy as a Fellow and a curate, was annoyed by his brother's careless manner of debating in letters. Before continuing further epistolary discussions, he insisted that Charles reply to the entire list of questions and keep to one subject. Charles, who had begun by refuting the inspiration of the New Testament, wanted to move on to the refutation of miracles.

After this, Charles sent his brother a long paper on Judaism and introduced an argument against one of Ezekiel's prophecies. John replied to his brother that the validity of the New Testament does not depend on a book of the Old Testament. In addition, John argued that neither the lack of

---

16 *LD,* Vol. I, JHN to Charles Robert Newman (April 14, 1825), 224-28.

17 *Ibid.,* 226.

18 *Ibid.,* 224-28; 228.

19 *LD,* Vol. I, JHN to C. R. Newman (July 7, 1825), 240-41.

inspiration of an Old Testament book, an error in copying a text, nor an interpolation of a passage would be proof that the Christian religion is false.[20] Although John was upset with his brother, he sent him a paper on the authenticity of the Gospels. By means of this paper, he wished to show Charles that "there are no reasonable grounds for doubting, and good grounds for believing the genuineness of the Gospels."[21] After a few months, the lengthy correspondence was closed.

In October 1828, Charles wrote to John wishing to continue the debate, but John replied: "I will *not* get into an unprofitable correspondence with you."[22] In May 1830, Charles demanded again that his older brother re-commence their discussion, but John refused to do so, considering it pointless. In August of the same year, however, John replied to his brother in a twenty-four-page letter, in which he recounted all of their correspondence of 1825.[23] It took John over a week to write this long and painful epistle.

Although the letter exposed Charles's rambling, faulty reasoning and false accusations that John had not answered his objections, the letter also conveyed John's impatience and harshness with an opponent. In the letter, John's reply did not leave a stone unturned in showing the false assumptions and inconsistencies of his brother's reasoning. The tone of his reaction was, however, excessive.

---

20 *LD,* Vol. I, JHN to Charles Robert Newman (August 25, 1825), 253-55.

21 *Ibid.,* 255.

22 *LD,* Vol. II, JHN to C. R. Newman (October 10, 1828), 101.

23 *LD,* Vol. II, JHN to C. R. Newman (August 19, 1830), 266-81.

John refuted his brother's assertion that demonstration alone is certain proof and that certainty arising from probability does not provide sufficient certainty for action.[24] He explained that practical matters are not decided from demonstrative proof, which is only found in pure mathematics. For example, if a man were roused by a cry of fire, he would not go back to sleep waiting for some demonstration, because he could well be burned. He concluded that, likewise, the testimony of the Apostles should not be rejected because it is not demonstrative proof.

It was not only in religious matters that Charles annoyed his brothers. John and Frank found various employments for Charles that he lost after a relatively short time, often with embarrassment to them. To a clergyman by the name of Mullins, whom he disliked, Charles went so far as to address a package, "Parson Mullins, Pharisee Cottage."[25] He always incurred debts that his brothers would forbearingly pay for him; Charles felt entitled to their financial support. All the while, Mrs. Newman suffered greatly and prayed a lot for her second son, advising him when he would listen and writing to John about him.

Meanwhile, in his professional life, throughout the years of 1828 to 1831, Newman was consumed with both treasurer's duties at Oriel and parochial duties at his new vicarage. However, he managed to spend time with his friends, sharing meals, long conversations, walks, and rides on

---

24 *LD,* Vol. II, JHN to Charles Robert Newman (August 19, 1830), 266-81; 280.

25 Ward, *Young Mr. Newman,* JHN to Jemima Newman, 169.

horseback with them. With those who were away, he kept in touch by writing.

One such friend who was away from Oxford for most of these years was Blanco White. When he stopped to visit at the university, he and John Henry would often eat dinner and meet to play music together, improvising a quartet. These musical soirées provided solace for Blanco White, who felt humiliated as an outsider at Oxford. He sometimes assisted Newman with the sacrament of the Lord's Supper, but before long, recurring doubts of faith made him incapable of carrying out any religious duties.

Besides these old friends, there was also Frederic Rogers, one of Newman's pupils at Oriel. He was one of the students to whom Newman dedicated most attention. The Tutor and pupil became close friends through their hours of study, meals together, and walks. One day in August 1831, Newman took tea with Rogers to meet William Ewart Gladstone, the future Prime Minister. In preparation for Rogers's undergraduate examination, Newman actually read to him for weeks because Rogers was afflicted by an illness affecting his vision. The clever and shrewd student, who would later become a politician, honored his Tutor by gaining first-class honors at Oriel in 1832.

While lodging at Iffley in 1831, Rogers visited the Newmans and played violin with John Henry. Beethoven, then recently deceased, was Newman's favorite composer. Many years later, Newman recalled Rogers, then Lord Blachford, as one of his intimate friends at Oriel and dedicated the work, *Two Essays on Biblical and on Ecclesiastical Miracles,* to him.

Thomas Mozley was another of Newman's pupils at Oriel. He obtained a B.A. degree in 1828, and, urged on by Newman, stood for a Fellowship, to which he was elected the following year. Beginning at this time, he entered into close terms with Newman's mother, sisters, and circle of friends. Newman tried to obtain support from the Archdeacon of Oxford in procuring the election of Mozley as curate for a parish, but the Bishop of Oxford naturally declined because Mozley was not a clergyman. Newman then encouraged Mozley to take Orders, and in 1831, Mozley was ordained a deacon and took up parochial duties. Thomas Mozley married Harriet Newman in 1836. It is no surprise that Newman would figure prominently in Mozley's *Reminiscences Chiefly of Oriel College and the Oxford Movement,* published while Newman was still alive.

While at Oriel, Newman also maintained correspondence with earlier friends, such as William Bowden, Simeon Lloyd Pope, and Samuel Rickards; Newman had a standing invitation from them and from John Keble and Richard Hurrell Froude to visit their homes. When Newman traveled to London in order to go to the dentist or to a bank, he visited Bowden, a close friend from his undergraduate years at Trinity, and his family. In 1831, he was honored to baptize Bowden's second child, Julia Marianne. The ties between Newman and the Bowdens continued to grow and became lifelong.

Newman knew how to love his friends. He was loved and admired by them. He had many good friends from among his peers, students, and some of his teachers. They were drawn to friendship with him by his genuine concern for their families, their endeavors and difficulties, his sincere advice to them, his good humor, and high moral standards. He managed to stay close to his family and to maintain the ties of friendship with each one of its members, except with Charles, with whom it was increasingly difficult to get along. Although the years between 1827 and 1831 were marked for Newman by university conflicts and a significant controversy over the tutoring system at Oriel, he continued to act as the head of the family and, at last, brought his mother and sisters to live close to him and to assist him in the parish duties at Littlemore. All the while, he felt the spiritual company of his sister Mary and continued to write about her.

CHAPTER 12

EARLY RELIGIOUS CONTROVERSIES

IN the year 1829, Newman became involved in two religious controversies: the independence of the Church of England from the State and the orientation of the Christian Missionary Society. The first altered Newman's position at Oriel and began his exodus from the college. Both would consolidate his separation from the Evangelical party.

During the age of the Tudor and Stuart kings, relations between Church and State consisted of an alliance that was more than an external policy. It was a deep-seated relationship based on a religious (and cultural) understanding of the sacred character of kingship with its corresponding customs and piety. Royal authority was not limited to purely temporal matters. This notion of society and government had been shaken by Cromwell's dictatorship, but the long reign of George III had renewed the relationship between Church and State and restored the influence of the High Church Party in the Establishment.[1]

The marriage between Church and State known as Erastianism was replaced in the nineteenth century with a new Erastianism based on the Liberal and Unitarian concept of progress as the new secular religion. Lord Brougham and Lord John Russell, who espoused these ideas, led the

---

1 Dawson, *The Spirit of the Oxford Movement,* 6-11.

Whig Party to advance Catholic Emancipation and pass the Reform Bill. The Whigs wanted to break the united front of the traditional allies: High Church, the Crown, the Bishops, and the Tory Ministry. High Church Anglicans tried in vain to maintain ecclesiastical autonomy, while Broad Church Anglicans, inspired by Thomas Arnold, headmaster of Rugby and Stanley, sought Latitudinarian inclusiveness. Despite their divergent positions, these men were prepared to make any sacrifice to preserve the national character of the Established Church.[2]

In 1828, under the threat of a civil uprising in Ireland, the Tory government, led by Prime Minister Arthur Wellesley, and Home Secretary Robert Peel, radically changed its policy toward Ireland in favor of Catholic Emancipation. Peel was a graduate from Christ Church at Oxford and represented the University in Parliament. In light of his constituency he resigned in February 1829.

The same day that Peel's resignation was read, the Convocation of Fellows at Oxford once more petitioned Parliament against Catholic Emancipation. The previous year, Newman had voted in Convocation against Emancipation, but this year, he abstained from voting.[3] Before he had acted on the ideas of ecclesiastical independence taken from Whately's *Letters of an Episcopalian,* Newman wrote years later that although he did not vote and was ambivalent about Catholic Emancipation, he opposed Peel for academic motives, under the influence of Keble

---

2 *Ibid.,* 10.

3 *LD,* Vol. II, Diary entry (February 5, 1829), 117.

and Froude, not ecclesiastical or political ones.[4] On the other hand, Newman saw the Irish Temporalities Bill for Catholic Emancipation as the beginning of the disestablishment of the Church of Ireland (the Anglican Church), but he was not hostile to Catholic Emancipation.[5] The day following Convocation he confided to Rickards: "I was not for the Petition, but should like much to turn P. out." And then he commented: "The clamours of the Catholics are but the accidental developments of the jealousy Ireland must feel towards a country which has stolen her Parliament and independence. It is not a religious question."[6]

Although the Oxford Fellows differed on their view of the "Catholic question," the majority opposed the emancipation bill. They were unified only in opposing Peel's reelection. By this, they hoped to assert the independence of the Church and of Oxford University from Parliament. Newman led the opposition to Peel at Oxford. Provost Hawkins and Whately rallied in support of Peel without consulting, as was customary, the Oriel Common Room. Sir Robert Inglis was elected with a majority of 146 as representative for the university. Inglis had been an undergraduate at Christ Church and in 1825 had strongly opposed Catholic Emancipation.

Newman was jubilant about this victory, but it angered Hawkins and Whately, who remonstrated with Newman for his important role in Peel's defeat. Although Hawkins and Newman remained on civil terms, from this point on

---

4 *Apo.*, 14.

5 Dawson, *Spirit of the Oxford Movement,* 36.

6 *LD,* Vol. II, JHN to Samuel Rickards (February 6, 1829), 117-19; 118.

Hawkins would use his authority as Provost at Oriel to successfully oppose Newman.

In 1830, the Whigs returned to power after a period of seventy years. Lord Grey formed a Whig government and made Brougham Lord Chancellor of the new Ministry. Brougham, a Scottish lawyer who had argued for parliamentary reform for years, played an important role in persuading the House of Lords to pass the 1832 Reform Act and the 1833 Anti-Slavery Act. In July 1833, the Whig Ministry passed the Irish Temporalities Act that would reduce the Episcopal sees of the Irish Church from 22 to 10. Although many of these sees were small Anglican dioceses supported by tithes imposed on Irish-Catholics, Newman feared a State reform of the Church. He thought that Evangelicals within the Whig Government did not have "much use for the Church or the Creeds" and thus played into the hands of Liberals and secularists. According to Newman, Blomfield, the Bishop of London, had promoted Evangelicals to positions of influence and had lost the simplicity and unworldliness of men such as Milner and Scott; the new Evangelical party played into the hands of the Liberals.[7]

Another case of civil government interfering in ecclesiastical matters was the establishment of a joint Anglican–Lutheran Episcopal See in Jerusalem. Since the turn of the century, English missionary societies had desired to establish a mission in Jerusalem for the conversion of Jews, and in 1833, Anglican services began in Jerusalem. In 1841, however, for the sake of political expediency among the English, Prussian, and Turkish governments, a mixed

---

7 *Apo.,* 31.

diocese was established without regard for religious truths and practices.

Newman could not bear the religious liberalism or doctrinal indifference of the ruling party that carried this out. He opposed Parliament's control over the Anglican Church, and, at the same time, he considered the loss of Church prerogatives as an abuse. In some sense, he held an inconsistent position that favored government patronage of the Anglican or Established Church while objecting to State interference. Newman hung on to some of the High Church and Tory beliefs in a national church, espousing the Divine Right of Kings and Passive Obedience, but his sympathy for the Tories was short-lived. Neither they nor the Whigs respected the Church.

In 1833, Newman wrote to Walter John Trower, a Fellow at Oriel:

> . . . I am become neither Whig nor Tory. In proportion as a Government disconnects itself with the Church, so does it cease to be the duty of a Churchman to be a Politician, and both the Tories and the pious Whigs are disconnected since the Reform Bill, and other political measures have been passed.[8]

While acknowledging the importance of the emancipation of slaves, Newman told him that he would press for more effective Church discipline, independence of bishops from the Crown, and restoration of the power of excommunication.

Contrary to Newman's view, the Irish ecclesiastical reforms were moderate and reasonable measures.[9] None-

---

8 *LD,* Vol. III, JHN to Walter John Trower (April 16, 1833), 290-93; 292.

9 Dawson, *The Spirit of the Oxford Movement,* 9-15.

theless, like Keble and Froude, Newman did not accept older Church-State models, such as the Tudor Settlement, the Church-State envisioned by Hooker, nor the theocracy advocated by Laud and Stafford. Historian Christopher Dawson describes Newman's ideal as "the spiritual freedom of the Apostolic Church and the Catholic inheritance of the Church of the Fathers."[10]

The greatest threat that Newman perceived was the Liberal and Utilitarian philosophy, which he refuted in a sermon that he delivered in 1832. To the self-satisfaction and superficial optimism of Deism he presented the Christian doctrine, which recognized the dark reality of evil and suffering. He opposed the true natural religion of fallen man to the sham natural religion of some philosophers. Socinians, also known as Unitarians, and some Deists based their beliefs on a mistaken notion of God and a shallow optimism about man. Newman described the tenets of these systems thus:

> [T]hat the rule of Divine government is one of benevolence, and nothing but benevolence; that evil is but remedial and temporary; that sin is of a venial nature; that repentance is a sufficient atonement for it; that the moral sense is substantially but an instinct of benevolence; and that doctrinal opinions do not influence our character or prospects, nor deserve our serious attention.[11]

Newman opposed another sort of liberalism that was taking place among deeply religious people who organized

---

10 *Ibid.,* 10.

11 "On Justice as a Principle of Divine Governance," in John Henry Newman, *Oxford University Sermons* (April 8, 1832), 104, available at: http://www.newmanreader.org/works/oxford/sermon6.html. After this it will be cited *US*.

societies for propagating the Christian faith in far-off lands. Two of these societies were The Society for Promoting Christian Knowledge and The Society for the Propagation of the Gospel, established in 1689 and 1701, respectively. These societies wished to preach Christianity in parts of Africa that had never heard of the Gospel. The first of these new missionaries to Africa were neither English nor Anglican; they were Lutherans from Germany.

The Christian Missionary Society was another association of Evangelical Anglicans established for the same laudable purpose in 1799, but which, unlike the other two, sought Episcopal supervision after it was founded. At its founding, the Society's first resolution was that every Christian, not only the church as a body, had the obligation to propagate the Christian faith. Furthermore, the first resolution stated, "if the church did not move, individual Christians must move."[12] Its first missionaries were also German Lutherans.

In spite of the praiseworthy goal of these societies, they disregarded the importance of doctrine by seeking membership from any Christian even if he espoused heterodox beliefs. Aware of the doctrinal indifference that resulted, Newman, who had by then left Evangelical doctrines behind, remained in the Christian Missionary Society, hoping to exert a positive influence. In March of 1829, he was elected as joint-secretary for the Oxford Branch of the Society.

Before the end of the year, however, he debated with

---

12 Eugene Stock, *The History of the Church Missionary Society,* Vol. I (London: Gilbert & Rivington, 1899), 68.

John Hill, his joint-secretary and a well-known Evangelical from St. Edmund Hall, over the doctrinal content of two sermons given in support of the Society.[13] Newman followed this disagreement with the circulation of a letter by which he aimed to increase subscription to the Society with members of the university. He wished to increase the influence of the university clergymen and the Anglican hierarchy in the Society. His authorship of the letter soon became public news.[14]

In the letter addressed to the clergymen residing at Oxford University, Newman outlined the evils of the Society.[15] He criticized the espousal of Calvinist doctrine by some of its central directors, and pointed out the confusion caused by large public meetings that rivaled the parochial system. He objected to the prominence given to preaching over church services and the usurpation of the Church's prerogative to ordain ministers and send them as missionaries. Newman urged his peers to act in favor of the doctrine and authority of the Anglican Church: "Things cannot remain as they are. This Society must approach the Church, or recede from her. If with an unwise timidity we let things take their course, it will insensibly be familiarized to the principles and practices of schism, and be lost to us with its resources, actual success, prospects for the future, its piety and activity . . ."[16]

---

13 *LD,* Vol. III, JHN to John Hill (December 11, 1829), 178.

14 *LD,* Vol. III, Diary entry and footnote (March 8, 1830),198.

15 Newman, *VM,* Suggestions Respectfully Offered to Individual Resident Clergymen of the University in behalf of the Church Missionary Society by a Master of Arts (February 1, 1830), Vol. II, 9-16.

16 *Ibid.,* 15.

In 1830, Newman was not reelected as secretary. Instead, an extreme Evangelical was elected. Newman complained that the Society did not recognize any doctrinal principles and that its inclusion of all types of Christians undermined Christian doctrine. Such inclusion conciliated all Christians at the expense of the truth.

It was at about this same period, in 1830, that Frank Newman set off on a missionary enterprise in Persia. John Henry Newman realized the importance of missions and wished to support their work, yet he considered that the risk of losing legitimate authority and a definitive creed in the Church was too great. The Methodists had already separated themselves from the Anglican Church over the question of ordination and commission of missionaries to North America.

During this period, even as he was embroiled in these controversies, Newman continued to serve his parishioners. At the outset of 1830, he obtained permission from the bishop to have a curate for Littlemore, a village at one end of his parish. He contracted Mr. Gower, the chaplain of Magdalen College, for a proposed sum of £50.[17] The curate had the care of approximately 200 people living in Littlemore. Gower was an Evangelical and expressed disagreement with Pusey's teaching of baptismal regeneration and therefore was a poor choice. In September, Newman replaced him with his friend Isaac Williams, who was elected Fellow of Trinity College the following year.

---

17 *LD,* Vol. II, JHN to Richard Bagot, Bishop of Oxford (February 1, 1830), 194-95; Bishop's reply, *ibid.,* 195.

A year earlier at Littlemore, Newman had hired a room for weekly services and catechetical lectures. He realized the village needed its own church and anticipated it ultimately becoming a parish separate from St. Mary's. The people were poor and unable to support a pastor, and the neighboring parishes were hostile to having another parish because these parishes could charge double fees for non-parishioners. Newman obtained support for his scheme of building a church at Littlemore from Froude and Robert Wilberforce, but Provost Hawkins rejected the proposal. Newman would have to wait seven years to build the church.

Newman faced the party politics at Oxford, but on a greater scale he was introduced into national politics. The controversy over Catholic Emancipation of Ireland heightened his concern for State-Church relations that would respect ecclesiastical government. During the period of 1829 to 1830, he also understood more keenly the need for doctrinal orthodoxy and episcopal oversight of the missionary societies.

CHAPTER 13

NEW ANGLICAN FRIENDS

A FTER the uproar caused by the Peel controversy of 1829, Newman rose as a visible leader at Oxford. Whately blamed him for a selfish desire to gain power by becoming the leader of a party. Newman had, instead, acted out of ideas and convictions. He had become a leader by his intelligence, determination, and capacity for persuasion. The days of shyness and lack of self-confidence in the Oriel Common Room were now very distant.[1] Interested by past and current events and their causes, he had read a great deal for his young age. He was gifted with an excellent capacity for synthesis, reasoning, and clarity of expression.

Newman sought the truth in theology, history, and philosophy without intimidation by others' opinions. He was willing to labor over an intellectual difficulty and to correct his mistakes and views. He was well disposed to seek advice from his seniors and peers. Newman's breadth of knowledge and his passion for the truth drew others to him. Whately was correct: Newman was the center of a party, but his motives were not power. Once he became a Fellow, and even more when he became a Tutor, Newman entered into new friendships with other men of varying ages from whom he would learn and with whom he would share his own ideas and beliefs.

---

1 *Apo.*, 16.

In addition to Edward Pusey, at Oriel College Newman became friends with other High Church Anglicans. In particular, John Keble and Richard Hurrell Froude occupied a special place in this stage of Newman's spiritual and religious development. They came from social and religious backgrounds that were very different from Newman's Protestant middle-class London. Both played a key role in shaping Newman's theological and religious ideas and, ultimately, the beginnings of the Oxford Movement.

John Keble was the son of a Gloucestershire clergyman who had educated both his sons at home and then sent them to Oxford. John won the highest distinctions at the university: a double-first at Corpus Christi, the Prizes for the Bachelor's Latin and English Essays, and a coveted Fellowship at Oriel. This promising star carried his honors without ostentation and surprised all when, in 1823, he left the university to become a curate in his father's country parish and work among the poor.

Just like his father, Keble adhered closely to the doctrines and devotions prescribed in the *Book of Common Prayer* and disliked the teaching and practices of the Evangelicals. Like most wealthy families, he held an intense loyalty to the Church of England and to the Tory Party in government.

Keble was not ambitious for material gain and was content with being a good country parson while caring for his elderly father. He was a humble man with disdain for outward displays of emotions. As a curate, he maintained his literary interests in Greek and Roman literature and wrote poetry that, for a long time, he kept to himself and closest friends. His reserved manner prevented him from being a leader, but he was a loyal friend and adviser to Newman, the rising party leader.

Keble and Newman met at Oxford. Keble, although still a young man, was nine years older than Newman and already highly respected. For a short time, they coincided as Fellows at Oriel, but it took almost a decade for them to become friends. Keble and Froude harbored a superficial dislike for Newman because of his Evangelical and liberal background.

Upon leaving Oriel, Keble invited some of his students to study under him during the Long Vacation. He took Froude along with two other talented students, Robert Wilberforce and Isaac Williams. In 1824, Froude obtained a double-second-class in Classics and Mathematics and, in 1826, he was elected a Fellow at Oriel. The following year, Froude became a Tutor along with Robert Wilberforce. There, at Oriel, in close proximity with Newman, Froude saw beyond his earlier prejudice and quickly established a friendship with Newman. Soon afterward, Froude acted as a catalyst for the friendship between his teacher and his new friend. Froude later wrote that facilitating this friendship was the greatest deed that he had ever done.

Richard Hurrell Froude was two years younger than Newman and the eldest son of Archdeacon Robert Hurrell Froude, the wealthy rector of a parish in Dartington, Devonshire. Keble and Froude had opposite, yet congenial temperaments. The first was serene and scholarly; the latter restless, pugnacious, and playful. Although Froude also hated any sign of pretense, he was mischievous and arrogant, and Newman later described him as "an Englishman to the backbone." His conversations were full of wit and irony; he was persistent and impertinent in his arguments, unsatisfied with evasions. He had a youthful zest for life, characterized by a passion for sailing and horseback riding. His English love for the concrete was expressed in a keen interest for details of mechanics, hydrostatics, and astronomy.

The character and interests of Newman and Froude were also quite different but somewhat more compatible than those of Keble and Froude. The former two were controversialist and energetic by nature. Froude seems to have stirred the fighting trait in Newman, a contentious spirit evident even in his childhood days at home. Froude moved him to speak out and take action. He tested Newman's arguments and further sharpened Newman's wit.

Although playful and seemingly inconsiderate, Froude was also a deeply spiritual and prayerful Anglican. Charles Lloyd, later Bishop of Oxford, taught Froude that the *Book of Common Prayer* embodied the medieval and primitive devotion still found in the Roman service books. Lloyd set on the minds of his pupils, including Newman, the historical connection between the pre-Reformation and the modern.

Froude's beliefs and religious practices are disclosed in his journal notes and letters published under the title *Remains of the Late Rev. Richard Hurrell Froude*. These writings were published after his premature death in 1836. *The Remains* are a two-volume set of journal entries, occasional thoughts, and sermons. Through the journal entries that span the years 1826 to 1827, the seriousness and sincerity with which Froude pursued virtue and piety shine.

Many of the journal entries were detailed notes on personal faults with specific resolutions for progressing in virtue. For instance, some record his inattentiveness at the chapel services, quickness to criticize the follies of others, vanity, pride, and oversensitivity to small injuries. Froude determined to avoid idleness, useless conversations, and any ostentation. With the goal of having purity of intention in his actions, he fought the desire to make a good impression on others and to act out of selfish motives.

Concerning his practice of daily attendance to morning and evening prayers, he wrote in October of 1826: "Somehow I feel that I go to chapel more to pass away the time than from love of God; and the little that I do is attributable to the same motive."[2] For that reason, he resolved to try to be indifferent to others' praise or censure of his actions.

Only upon reading Froude's diaries did Newman and other friends discover that he had practiced many unnoticed acts of self-denial by which he sought to master himself and, above all, to please God. In addition to fighting against his faults, he set for himself other ascetical goals, such as waking up at six in the morning, sleeping on the floor, keeping rigorous fasts, reducing expenses in order to increase almsgiving and assisting in the Church's worship. While keeping these religious practices and pursuing such high moral standards, Froude also fought the accompanying temptation to spiritual pride. Years later, Newman

---

2 Richard Hurrell Froude, *Remains of the Late Reverend Richard Hurrell Froude*, Vol. I, ed. John Henry Newman (London: J, G & F Rivington, 1838), 28.

and his friends imitated some of Froude's same practices at Littlemore, a hamlet just outside Oxford.

With his religious mind and high moral standards, it is understandable that Froude supported the position of Newman, his friend and Senior Tutor, on the reform of the tutoring system at Oriel. Froude and Robert Wilberforce agreed with Newman that Tutors should form the character and religious temper of the undergraduates, instead of having a purely academic role. In 1828, both junior Tutors stood by Newman in a drawn-out battle against Hawkins, Provost at Oriel. That same year, Froude left Oriel and, the following year, was ordained an Anglican clergyman.

Just as in the development of spiritual matters, so too did Froude's political and ecclesiastical views have a gradual influence on Newman. In the early 1830s, Froude expressed great indignation for the reforming parties in England—the Whigs, the Radicals, and liberal religionists—but when the Tory Party's authority failed, he condemned the government's betrayal of the Established Church and labeled himself a "radical." Froude was very vocal with his friend in both religious and political matters, but he did not know how to persuade and attract the following of a larger group. In the end, however, his genuine friendship and conversations had the effect of inciting others, especially Newman, into action.

Although Froude was accused of Romanizing or supporting the Roman Catholic Church, he, in fact, was a loyal supporter of the Church of England. He maintained the teaching of seventeenth- and eighteenth-century bishops, known as the Caroline Divines and the Non-Jurors.

The latter were a group of bishops and noblemen who did not accept the succession of William of Orange and his wife Mary to the throne of England after the Glorious Revolution of 1688. Froude accepted Whately's idea of the Church of England as the one, historic, and uninterrupted Church, which was a great sacred corporate body, separate from the State. Froude filled in the internal elements that Whately had left undefined: the liturgy prescribed by the *Book of Common Prayer* and the theology of the Caroline Divines.

Froude decried some serious faults in the Anglican Church at the start of the nineteenth century. He lamented the acceptance of the State's control over the Church and its clergy, low standard of spiritual life, weak discipline, and poor religious instruction. These complaints were coupled with praise of the good principles and practices of the Roman Church, such as Episcopal authority, worship of the Real Presence of Christ in the Eucharist, and frequent celebration of the Lord's Supper with Holy Communion. These doctrines and practices were either ignored, or looked at with prejudice by the majority of Englishmen, who had accepted a thoroughly Protestant Church.

Froude's sharp criticism of the Church of England was an important lesson for Newman, who was gradually beginning to understand Anglicanism's Catholic heritage. Over some years' time, Newman came to accept Froude's view of the Roman Church as being neither the one true Church nor the Antichrist. Eventually, however, Newman's logical reasoning led him to go further than his friend to conclude that Roman Catholicism alone was able to safeguard the truths that they sought to defend.

Richard Church, who met Newman in 1836, the year Froude died, compared Froude to Blaise Pascal for the great mental qualities of both men. They shared a great love for the Church and moral self-discipline, and both sadly died at an early age. Richard Church, later a Fellow of Oriel and a devoted friend to Newman, commented many years afterward that Froude, drawing from all he had learned from Keble, had a significant influence on Newman at a critical point. Thus, according to Church, it might well be said that Keble was at the origin of the Oxford Movement (1833)—a truth that Newman admitted in his *Apologia*. Church explained that Froude resolved to make Keble's ideas active, public, and aggressive.[3] Church offered the following summary: "Keble had given the inspiration, Froude had given the impulse; then Newman took up the work, and the impulse henceforth, and the direction, were his."[4] Despite the truth in this statement, it should be noted that Froude was more than a receptacle for Keble's ideas. Froude had a deep sense of the historical continuity in the Catholic Church and the richness of its medieval practices. He had an active and independent mind, which led him to doctrinal conclusions that Keble did not accept.

Besides these two new Anglican friends, there was another, Isaac Williams, who was born in Wales in 1802. Williams attended Harrow, where he mastered Latin composition and literature, and, from there, went to Trinity College. Upon winning a Latin prize at Oxford, Williams

---

3 Richard William Church, *The Oxford Movement* (London: Macmillan & Co., 1894) 28.

4 *Ibid.*, 29.

gained Keble's attention and accepted an invitation to study under him during the Long Vacation of 1823. Like Froude, Williams learned from Keble's spiritual traits and orthodoxy. He became a clergyman and began his pastoral work under John Keble's brother, Thomas Keble, vicar of the parish of Bisley, a town in Gloucestershire. After two years Williams returned to Oxford to be a Tutor at his college. It was then that Froude, who had become an intimate friend of Newman, introduced them to each other.

Williams was pleased to meet Newman and recognized his genuine benevolence, but he did not accept the emphasis that Newman gave to the intellect as the guide for life. At this time, Newman was no longer an Evangelical and was distancing himself from Whately's rationalism; he was looking with admiration to the religious ideals of Keble and Froude. In 1830, Newman offered Williams the curacy of St. Mary's, and, despite his misgivings toward Newman, the Trinity Fellow accepted. He was a loyal curate and rendered a great service by taking care of Newman's parish during an extended trip in Europe that Newman took with Froude at the start of December 1832.

Unlike Keble and Froude, Williams was not an influence on Newman's religious ideas. Williams differed greatly from Newman in his desire to avoid public controversy. He wished to limit himself to doing his duty and practicing greater self-discipline and religious piety. Despite these differences Williams was still a collaborator at the initial stages of the Oxford Movement. Williams later criticized the stir made by the *Tracts of the Times*, the initial vehicle for the Oxford Movement. In 1839, he proposed a plan for a series of *Plain Sermons* that would include contributions by the Kebles, Copeland, Pusey, Newman, and himself. By publishing the teachings of other members of the Oxford Movement, he wanted to provide some counterweight to Newman's approach to the religious condition of the Church.

Ironically, Williams wrote the *Tract* that first stirred popular indignation, *Tract 80*, on *Reserve in Communicating Religious Knowledge*. Sometime after its publication, a battle ensued at the university over Williams's contest for the professorship in Poetry. This was, in the words of Church, "the first decisive and open trial of strength and the first Tractarians defeat."[5]

Williams, a moderate Anglican, was distrustful of the intellectual focus of the Movement and its leanings toward Rome. Under this strain, his ties with Newman soon broke. In 1842, Williams moved to the parish of his brother-in-law and spent his life writing devotional commentaries. He suffered from chronic and debilitating asthma and died in 1865. Before he died, Newman traveled to visit him and the two friends met once again.

Newman's new Anglican friendships, especially those with Keble and Froude, signaled a new period in his religious life. Keble and Froude introduced Newman into a deeper understanding of the spiritual nature of the Church. They made him aware of its history and its ecclesial authority. Froude was instrumental in breaking Newman's prejudice and opposition to the Roman Catholic Church. Both men, but especially Froude, moved Newman to denounce abuses committed by the government against the Roman

---

5 Church, *The Oxford Movement,* 57.

Catholic Church. Newman shared with both men a deep friendship that originated with their common desire for renewal in the Anglican Church, and they grew in mutual respect, affection, and concern for each other. As would be expected, not all of Newman's friendships with other Anglicans connected with Oxford had a major influence on him, or them. This was the case with Williams, Samuel Rickards, and Simeon Lloyd Pope. These clergymen did not have Newman's urgency for reform. With the help of his friends, Froude and Robert Wilberforce, both Fellows at Oriel, Newman began a spiritual and doctrinal renewal of the undergraduates at his college.

CHAPTER 14

TUTOR AT ORIEL

O N January 20, 1826, ten years after entering Trinity College, Newman agreed to be a Tutor at Oriel. He had been a Fellow at Oriel for four years and the promotion was the natural advancement in academic life that he pursued as a part of a larger spiritual calling. He wished to reform the moral and spiritual climate of his college.

The tutorial system was, as it is now, an integral part of the Oxford education. Prior to Newman's time, college Tutors were supposed to oversee the expenditures of young scholars and their moral conduct and, at times, to discipline them. When Newman was appointed Tutor, ordination to the clerical life was still a qualification for this office, but things were beginning to change. While Mayers advised Newman to be ordained at once, others discouraged any haste with such a decision. Hawkins even pointed to some incompatibility with activities of college life, such as hunting, shooting, and theater. Hawkins held a disciplinarian view of the Tutor while Newman held a pastoral one. For Newman, the ordination vow was not incompatible with, but rather intrinsic to, the mission of a Tutor. He believed that the ordination vow made him a minister of Christ, who was responsible for souls. He resisted Hawkins's view because he was convinced that a Tutor should be more than a college lecturer and disciplinarian. Newman wrote his sister, Harriet:

> I have a great undertaking before me in the Tutorship here. I trust God may give me grace to undertake it in a proper spirit, and to keep steadily in view that I have set myself apart for His service for ever. There is always the danger of literary pursuits assuming too prominent a place in the thoughts of a College Tutor, or his viewing his situation merely as a secular office, a means of future provision when he leaves College. [1]

On a larger scale, the culture of Victorian England had brought a considerable change to university education. At the start of the nineteenth century, gentry and nobility wanted their sons to return home as gentlemen with social skills like dancing and fencing; they did not want them to return home as monks or deacons.[2] Victorian society no longer appreciated a rigorous education in the Classics, and instead preferred social polish, good manners, and knowledge of foreign countries. The nobility regarded a classical university education as useful only for the training of future clergymen. Furthermore, modern employment called for the practical knowledge of science, law, and other professions. The ideal of the Christian gentleman and scholar was replaced by the new ideal of the "virtuoso," a person skilled in arts and science.

Many Oxford students who proceeded from noble families lived an idle lifestyle and were commonly called "smarts." By extension, the name was used to denote the

---

1 LD, *Vol. I,* JHN to Harriet Newman (March 21, 1826), 280-81.
2 Stone, *The University and Society,* 48-52.

increasing numbers of idle students from other social classes. Excessive drinking, extravagant lifestyles, and idleness were common aspects of student life. The university was equated with a place of moral corruption, and respected men, like the First Earl of Clarendon, lamented the excessive drinking and how little he had learned at Oxford. The English philosopher Thomas Hobbes called Oxford a breeding place for left-wing Radicals. In the mid-nineteenth century, society complained of the aristocratic lifestyle and education forced upon middle-class students who needed training to become attorneys, engineers, and merchants.

Years later, in a series of lectures titled *The Tamworth Reading Room,* Newman opposed this rejection of classical education at Oxford for an education aimed at science and practical knowledge. In these lectures Newman argued that physical science does not make men moral. He wrote:

> I consider, then, that intrinsically excellent and noble as are scientific pursuits, and worthy of a place in a liberal education, and fruitful in temporal benefits to the community, still they are not, and cannot be, *the instrument* of an ethical training; that physics do not supply a basis, but only materials for religious sentiment; that knowledge does but occupy, does not form the mind; that apprehension of the unseen is the only known principle capable of subduing moral evil, educating the multitude, and organizing society . . .[3]

---

3 John Henry Newman, "The Tamworth Reading Room," in *Discussions and Arguments* (February 1841), 304. Available at: http://www.newmanreader.org/works/arguments/tamworth/section7.html. After this it will be cited *DA.*

In 1826, however, Newman's main concern was the moral reform of the college and the individual attention given to students by Tutors, not the threat of practical education which came later. He fought the decadence of the "Gentlemen-Commoners" who were the "scandal and the ruin of the place." He tried to check their haughtiness and their custom of gaining influence from authorities at the university.

Newman thought that theology and the practice of religion make men moral, and advocated the Tutors' responsibility for the religious formation of their pupils. He lamented the practice of compulsory Communion at the opening of the School Year because he considered that undergraduates' drinking habits and other sinful revelry were tantamount to profanation of a sacred rite. The authorities, including Hawkins, turned a blind eye and did not want to hear about this. Newman, on the other hand, wanted the Tutors to fight such evils.

In 1832, when Joseph Dornford retired as Dean of Oriel to a living in Devonshire, Newman was next in line for the position. The office was to be decided by election, but Henry Jenkyns, one of the Fellows close to the Provost, asked Newman to withdraw from the contest due to his differences with Hawkins and his interpretation of college rules. Newman explained to Jenkyns: "I am against the present rule of obliging undergraduates to receive the Sacrament."[4] Newman believed that in certain cases he could deny the Sacrament to a student, over the veto of

---

4 *LD,* Vol. III, JHN to Henry Jenkyns (before July 4, 1832), 62-63; 63.

the Provost.[5] Soon, though, the election was not an issue because a long trip to the Mediterranean on which he was about to embark made it no longer possible for him to be Dean of Oriel that academic year. A few years later he held the office.

Newman's complaints did not end there. The new Tutor also opposed the practice of obtaining Private Tutors, Bachelors or Masters, who prepared undergraduates to obtain honors at the Schools. As an undergraduate, Newman had been tutored by James Ogle for the exams and, as a Fellow, had tutored students himself. His experience with this system led him to object to the additional costs for students and its unfair advantage over those who could not afford Private Tutors. He also thought that the Private Tutors interfered in the relationship between the College Tutor and the pupil.

The custom at Oriel was for Tutors to give lectures to many students without much direct contact with them. Through his own more personal manner of treating his students, Newman began to reform the tutorial system on his own when he was appointed a Tutor. In 1828, Hurrell Froude and Robert I. Wilberforce, newly elected Tutors at Oriel, joined Newman in his reform effort. They agreed on the preeminence of the Tutor's role in the moral and religious education of students by means of personal influence and friendship.

Acting with the "discretion" afforded him under university statutes, Newman introduced modifications that

---

5 *LD*, Vol. III, JHN to Henry Jenkyns (on or after June 29, 1832), 60-61.

provided Froude, Wilberforce, and himself an opportunity for a more personal connection with the students and influence over them. This did away with the need for Private Tutors. Dornford, Dean and Senior Tutor, agreed to the changes on a trial basis. The modifications gave the Tutor the intended role of Tutor, not of a mere lecturer. Each Tutor was first responsible for his pupils, not for all of the undergraduates. He would choose the subject matter for the lectures his pupils should attend, and have first choice on giving those lectures himself.

Newman began to focus his attention on his assigned pupils that were most methodical and promising. He helped them in their college work and cultivated a mutual friendship. This relationship went beyond the appearance of a mere friendship. It was in no way condescending. Newman exercised with his pupils, spent evenings in their company, and vacationed with them. His goal was a spiritual one, to gain souls for God, and these friendships allowed him to exert the requisite spiritual and moral influence. Many of the students attended his sermons at St. Mary's and thus received his religious instruction.

In light of his conflict with Hawkins, Newman did not formally inform him of his plans for the tutorial system. When Hawkins noticed the changes, he allowed them at first because he was new as Provost and the standards at the college began to improve, but he did not agree with Newman's philosophy. Later, the differences of opinion were mixed up with other academic and ecclesiastical differences, and collision was unavoidable. In the aftermath of the reelection affair with Peel, the Provost ordered a return to the old tutorial system.

The controversy came to a head when, in April of 1830, the Provost asked Newman for a short sketch of the new system, arguing that the old one worked perfectly well. Newman replied that the alleged "new system" was, in fact, a modification of the old system that only worked when students, at their own request and at great expense, sought extra Private Tutors. Newman argued that since 1823, when idle students were admitted to Oriel and Tutors ceased to take private pupils, men had ceased to obtain high honors. Newman summed up his case on honors to Hawkins thus: "Nature (so to say) forces us into the private-tutor system— why not recognize it, control it, and make it economical?"[6]

Hawkins argued that others with more experience had established the present system in which the students had contact with all the Tutors and not an almost-exclusive contact with one. Hawkins made it clear to Newman that there was only one Tutor in Oriel; the others were Assistant Tutors and Lecturers. Newman replied that under this arrangement he felt obliged to resign, but he would wait for the Provost's decision; until then, he would continue to consider himself as the real Tutor of the men to whom, upon their admission, he was committed.

A number of letters ensued between Provost Hawkins and Tutor Newman. Hawkins gave the appearance of being conciliatory and urged Newman to return gradually to the college system. Hawkins, however, did not seem to assess the merits of Newman's proposed plans and attributed some of Newman's views to being overworked and depressed; all of this controversy and especially the latter

6 *LD*, Vol. II, JHN to Edward Hawkins (April 29, 1830), 212.

remarks annoyed Newman. Despite Newman's arguments and support from junior Fellows, the Provost prevailed. In June 1830, Hawkins stopped assigning students to Newman as well as to Wilberforce and Froude. In doing so, Hawkins eventually eliminated Newman from his Tutorship, save for the few students he had already been assigned. Newman informed his mother of Hawkins's arrangement to have Wilberforce, Froude, and himself "die off gradually with our existing pupils."[7] After this drawn-out controversy, Newman remarked with an air of relief that he welcomed having more time on his hands with the same financial resources.

The last students that Newman prepared for examinations at Oriel honored him well when they took their exams in the spring of 1831. Samuel Francis Wood and Robert Francis Wilson obtained first class in Classics; Algernon Perkins obtained first class in Mathematics, and Wilson second class. Frederic Rogers, one of Newman's favorite pupils, obtained a "double first," two first-class honors, when he graduated in 1832. On June 11, 1831, Newman wrote in his journal: "second day of Collections—finished *my* men—and so ends my Tutors-work!"[8] Newman had had a beneficial influence on his students, but the overall attempt at reform of the college had failed. While he resigned from his position as Tutor, he would retain his Fellowship at Oriel until October 3, 1845.

The end of the controversy over the tutorial system was a blessing in disguise. Newman wrote to his mother about

---

7 *LD,* Vol. II, JHN to Mrs. Newman (June 18, 1830), 244.

8 *LD,* Vol. II, Diary entry (June 11, 1831), 334.

his intentions: "Now that I shall have more time, I am full of projects what I shall do [sic]. The Fathers arise up again full before me."[9] The following year he received, as a present from friends and pupils, the valuable gift of thirty-six volumes of Church Fathers.[10] Newman began to study the Fathers of the Church and to write on the history of the Arian Heresy, which would have a significant impact on his life. A new and rich period in his intellectual and spiritual life was beginning. In addition to the study of the Fathers and of the Arian Heresy, he applied his teaching energy to sermons that he preached at St. Mary's.[11] Years later, he would acknowledge to a friend that, had his work at Oriel not terminated, he would not have studied the Fathers, and the Oxford Movement would not have begun.[12]

---

9 *LD,* Vol. II, JHN to Mrs. Newman (June 25, 1830), 245.

10 *LD,* Vol. II, JHN to Mrs. Newman (October 24, 1831), 368-69.

11 Trevor, *Newman, The Pillar of the Cloud,* 99. According to Trevor, when Newman published his sermons, he took more from 1831 than from any other year.

12 *LD,* Vol. II, 245. Footnote refers to a letter to Henry James Coleridge.

CHAPTER 15

NEWMAN'S FIRST BOOK: *THE ARIANS OF THE FOURTH CENTURY*

W ITH his attention freed from the obligations of Tutor, Newman accepted an invitation from Hugh James Rose, a Cambridge scholar and founder of the *British Magazine*, to contribute a book to a new series of theological works, *The Theological Library*. Newman suggested studying the *Thirty-Nine Articles*, but Rose, co-editor with Archdeacon William R. Lyall, asked him instead to write a history of the Church councils that included the content of the *Articles*. After a few months of reading, Newman explained to Rose that the Eastern Councils required a volume of their own that should be prefaced by an account and history of Arianism.[1] The rest of the year, he worked on and off on this project, as his occupations allowed. In June of 1832, Newman worked intensely on the book for a month, and by July, he had finished it. He sent the manuscript to Rose, and, exhausted from many long days of work and nights of poor sleep, he went to Brighton for some rest.

During August, Newman met a few times with Rose, who helped to edit the manuscript. Rose liked the manuscript and sent it to Archdeacon Lyall, who thought that

---

1 *LD*, Vol. II, JHN to Hugh James Rose (August 24, 1831), 352-53. Initially Newman thought that his work on the councils could be divided by subject matter into three volumes.

it was excellent but too specialized for a general audience and unsuitable for a collection on Church councils.[2] The Archdeacon thought that it favored Roman Catholic views of Tradition. For these reasons the book was not accepted for the series, but Rose and Lyall encouraged Newman to revise some parts of the manuscript and to publish the book as a work on its own.[3] The publication of this work was delayed until October 1833, after Newman's long journey to the Mediterranean.

The Arians of the Fourth Century, Newman's first book, was a history of theology and a short treatise on Trinitarian theology. In it, he dealt with the complicated doctrinal errors of the Arians, semi-Arians, and Sabellians that indirectly contributed to the correct formulation of doctrine on the Trinity. Newman employed many of the available sources, especially the writings of Church Fathers, early Church historians, like Sozomen and Socrates, and modern authors like Tillemont and Gibbon. He relied heavily on John Bull's comprehensive work, *Defensio Fidei Nicenae*, published in 1703.

In addition to its historical and doctrinal character, this book was remarkable for its opening chapter on the subject of biblical hermeneutics. In this long chapter, Newman explained and defended the Church's authority in interpreting Scripture and the role of Apostolic Tradition and Creeds for a proper understanding of biblical truths.

---

2 *LD*, Vol. III, William R. Lyall to Hugh James Rose (October 19, 1832), 104-5.

3 *LD*, Vol. III, H. J. Rose to JHN (October 21, 1832), 104.

Newman argued that the Church Creeds were a chief source of instruction on the faith and a guardian of the correct interpretation of Sacred Scripture. He reasoned that the Sacred Scriptures cannot be interpreted with the Scriptures alone. The Scriptures must be interpreted by those who lived under the same Divine Influence that inspired them.[4] The Creeds provide an organized presentation of the doctrine that Christians must believe. Newman wrote:

"Scripture being unsystematic, and the faith which it propounds being scattered through its documents, and understood only when they are viewed as a whole, the Creeds aim at concentrating its general spirit, so as to give security to the Church, as far as may be, that its members take that definite view of that faith which alone is the true one."[5]

As a necessary introduction to the Arian Heresy, Newman explained the literal and allegorical interpretations of Sacred Scripture, which were prevalent in the Churches of Antioch and Alexandria. Chapter One of *The Arians* presents Tradition and Church teaching as the authoritative interpreters of Scripture. According to Newman, the Apostolic Tradition is contained both in the Sacred Scriptures and in the Church Creeds; the Creeds were a safeguard to the truths revealed in Scripture. He had earlier expressed some of these ideas in letters to his brother Charles, and later wrote some sermons and lectures on these same subjects. Newman went as far as to consider a type of divine revelation the "inspirations" of ancient poets and philosophers; these inspirations served as a preparation for the Gospel.[6]

---

4 *Arians,* 148.

5 *Ibid.,* 147.

6 *Ibid.,* 79-83; 82; *Apo.,* 27.

The first part of *The Arians* explains the *"Disciplina Arcani,"* which was a custom practiced in early Christian churches. According to this custom, Alexandrian converts to the Catholic faith were introduced progressively to the truths of Christianity after having first learned those of natural theology and the precepts of natural law. Related to this was the principle of "economy," which involved withholding a truth, or using it to one's advantage, as St. Paul did at the Aeropagus when he spoke of the unknown God instead of Yahweh. Newman wrote that:

> Instead of uttering any invective against their Polytheism, he began a discourse upon the Unity of the Divine Nature; and then proceeded to claim the altar, consecrated in the neighbourhood to the unknown God, as the property of Him whom he preached to them, and to enforce his doctrine of the Divine Immateriality, not by miracles, but by argument, and that founded on the words of a heathen poet.[7]

Economy adapted an explanation to the needs of the listener and to his philosophical notions, while it recognized the inadequacy of human language to fully convey dogmas. Newman further noted that:

It is thus we lead forward children by degrees, influencing and impressing their minds by means of their own confined conceptions of things, before we attempt to introduce them to our own; yet at the same time modelling their thoughts according to the analogy of those to which we mean ultimately to bring them.[8]

---

7 *Arians,* 65-66.
8 *Ibid.,* 72.

The central part of *The Arians* focuses on Arius's biblical arguments and their refutation. Newman presented the historical setting for the controversy about Christ's Divinity and the counter-arguments made to Arius, who denied that the Father and Son have the same being, or substance. Arius held that the Son of God was a creature, separate from the Godhead, and created in time. Newman indicated that the Church Fathers referred to Christ with two names: the eternal begotten Son and the Word of God. The latter corrected any reduction of the first to a being inferior to the Father. In the words of Newman:

> The title of the *Son* marks His derivation and distinction from the Father, that of the *Word* (i.e. Reason) denotes His inseparable inherence in the Divine Unity; and while the former taken by itself, might lead the mind to conceive of Him as a second being, and the latter as no real being at all, both together witness to the mystery, that He is at once *from*, and yet *in*, the Immaterial, Incomprehensible God.[9]

In other sections of the book, Newman traced the origin of the Arian Heresy and other heresies that followed in its wake and listed numerous local Church councils that met to examine Christological doctrines and condemn erroneous ones. Although raised in Alexandria, Arius had studied in Antioch, where the school of biblical interpretation, at odds with the heavily allegorical school of Alexandria, fell into the error of an exaggerated literal interpretation of biblical texts.

In a hurry to meet his initial deadline, Newman ended with a short section on the Ecumenical Council of

---

9 *Arians,* 156-57.

Constantinople held in the year A.D. 381. This section traced the historical background of the Council of Constantinople beginning in the year A.D. 325, when Emperor Constantine, who sought religious cohesion for his empire, convoked the first ecumenical council, which was held at Nicaea in Bithynia, not far from Constantinople. At Nicaea, the vast majority of the three hundred bishops in attendance ratified the orthodox doctrine on the consubstantial nature of the Father and the Son, giving rise to the Nicene Creed. This Creed defended the biblical truth of the unity of the Father and the Son with the celebrated expression: "begotten, not made, consubstantial to the Father."

Athanasius, Deacon at the Church of Alexandria and assistant to Patriarch Alexander at the Council of Nicaea, appears throughout this history as the champion of orthodoxy. After the death of Alexander, he became Patriarch of the Alexandria. Athanasius, an intelligent and courageous bishop, was exiled five times by various imperial courts at the instigation of his theological opponents. At Alexandria, Athanasius exercised the power of excommunication to fight heretical views held by bishops and clergy; yet, according to Newman, he maintained a forgiving and conciliatory attitude toward them. Newman was struck by the noble and valiant character of St. Athanasius and referred to him many times as "champion of the truth"[10] and an inspiring figure for Christians facing doctrinal liberalism. In 1842, he translated *De Incarnatione*, one of Athanasius's works. For Newman, the English Church needed more men like St. Athanasius and St. Basil the Great, another bishop

---

10 *Apo.*, 26.

of the same period, to remedy the disease of doctrinal dissent, which was decimating the faith.

Published in 1833, *The Arians* was Newman's first book. It was the theological history of a complex subject. The young author considered his work imperfect from the start, both in its content and language; nevertheless, he always agreed with the substance of the work, and believed that through it he had made some original contributions to the study of exegesis and the Arian Heresy. Many years later he added a short preface, some footnotes, and an appendix with longer notes as well as chronological charts.

Most important, however, was the effect that the study of this early heresy had on Newman's religious ideas. Newman had begun a chronological reading of the Ancient Fathers in 1828, but only in the years after Hawkins stopped assigning him new students at Oriel was he finally able to dedicate the necessary time to study the Church Fathers in depth and learn their Christology and other doctrine.

CHAPTER 16

TRAVEL IN THE MEDITERRANEAN

IN the spring of 1832, Archdeacon Froude invited New man to accompany him and his son, Richard Hurrell Froude, to Europe, hoping that a stay in Southern Europe would be of benefit to his son's ailing health. By the fall, Newman agreed to this trip and thought that the journey would expand his mind. He wrote Froude that he would never again have the opportunity of traveling abroad in the company of such a good friend and of Froude's father, an older person of proven character. The three men began their travel on December 8 aboard a steamship named *Hermes,* sailing toward Malta and the Greek Isles.

Before leaving England, Newman suggested to Rose that he send a regular contribution of poetry to the *British Magazine*. The magazine had been founded the year before in response to the influx of liberal theological speculation coming from Germany and to the Whig reform plans. In November, he wrote to Rose: "Our object is, to bring out certain truths and facts, moral and ecclesiastical, and religious, simply and forcibly, with greater freedom, and clearness than in Keble's Christian Year. I will not go on to say, with greater poetry."[1] In the same letter, he suggested the

---

1 *LD,* Vol. III, JHN to Hugh James Rose (November 26, 1832), 119-20; 120.

title *Lyra Apostolica.* The poems first appeared in the *British Magazine,* but in 1836, the collection was published in one volume under the proposed title. Keble, Froude, and others contributed to the volume, but the major contribution was Newman's.

One of the first verses composed on the trip was "The Saint and the Hero," in which the author addresses a saint unknown to the reader:

> O aged Saint! far off I heard
> The praises of thy name;—
> Thy deed of power, thy prudent word,
> Thy zeal's triumphant flame.[2]

In the following stanza, the author admits his weakness of heart before this saint and, in the third stanza, expresses his desire to serve Heaven in the "humblest ways" without spurning any extraordinary blessings. "Humblest ways" may refer to Newman's uncertain future at Oriel.

"Private Judgment," the next poem he wrote, was addressed to "Poor wanderers," or the current Church of England. Newman said that these wanderers trusted their own weak will and languished as a blind idol. To the Church, God had granted prophets and a Creed that had been cast aside. He ended this short poem with a summons, which foreshadowed the Oxford Movement:

> Wand'rers! come home! obey the call!
> A Mother pleads, who ne'er let fall
> One grain of Holy Truth;
> Warn you and win she shall and must,

---

2 "The Saint and the Hero," in *VV* (Bay of Biscay, December 10, 1832), 77.

For now she lifts her from the dust,
To reign as in her youth.[3]

By the end of his travels, Newman had written at least 107 poems. This collection is a unique spiritual record of his desires and prayers for the renewal of the Church of England. The tone of the verses, unlike Keble's gentle verse, was forceful and, at times, tormented. Despite the sadness of some of the verses, overall they express Newman's firm trust in Divine Providence and his growing sense of a personal vocation at the service of the Anglican Church. For example, in "The Patient Church," Newman wrote about the sin of schism foreshadowed in the Old Testament by the revolt of ten tribes from the House of David. Newman entreats the Church: "Bide thou thy time!"[4] while she waits for "the bright Advent that shall loose thy chain."[5] This was as much an entreaty to himself as to the Church. The young Oxford don was like a compressed spring ready to uncoil; the question was when and how.

In effect, the poems convey the spiritual and doctrinal vision underpinning the Oxford Movement. The poems were soon followed by tracts, written essays in booklet form that stated and developed the theological principles underlying this vision. In a letter to his sisters, Newman explained that, through his verses, he tried to attend to ideas more than to language. He wished to avoid the obscurity of much contemporary poetry. Even though Newman

---

3 "Private Judgment," in *VV* (Off Cape Ortegal, December 11, 1832), 78-79.

4 "The Patient Church," in *VV* (Off Algiers, December 20, 1832), 92-93; 92.

5 *Ibid.*

was not pleased with his sonnets, he accomplished his goal of presenting key ideas with rich language, good cadence, and clear expression. Some of these poems were published in the *British Magazine* and were later compiled with other texts under the title of *Verses on Various Occasions*.

The scenery along the voyage afforded Newman imagery for his poems. The *Hermes* crossed the English Channel and sailed around the coast of Portugal and Spain to Gibraltar, where the group was welcomed by English officers stationed there. Newman was impressed by the heavy military fortifications of the English stronghold.[6] Struck by the powerful image of English military might, Newman reflected in verse on the character of his country and on its contrasting and precarious spiritual condition. Thus at Gibraltar, he penned "England," a warning and a plea to his country that, to be spared, it must, like Sodom, show ten good men. It should not vaunt, as Babel did in its high towers, nor find comfort in its military power:

> Tyre of the West, and glorying in the name
> More than in Faith's pure fame!
> O trust not crafty fort nor rock renown'd
> Earn'd upon hostile ground;
> Wielding Trade's master-keys, at thy proud will
> To lock or loose its waters, England! trust not still.[7]

After a short stay in the English territory, the three continued on the steam packet to Malta, and along the way, they were able to see at a distance the imposing mountain

---

6 *LD,* Vol. III, JHN to Jemima Newman (December 18, 1832), 151-54.

7 "England," in *VV* (At Sea, December 18, 1832), 89-90.

range of Northern Africa. In Malta, they were confined under quarantine at a Lazaret and were obliged to spend Christmas Day isolated.[8] Nevertheless, they were treated well and soon continued their journey to the Greek Isles. As they journeyed on, Newman read Homer's *Odyssey*.

From the start of the voyage Newman had given full reign to his descriptive narrative and poetic verses, but the beauty of Corfu (Corcyra) and Sicily stirred his imagination the most and led him to praise these above all other places. Newman's youthful romanticism, combined with his reading of classical epics and modern novels, elicited his marvel at mountain ranges, harbors and countryside about which he had read.

His imagination was particularly vivid when the *Hermes* passed the island Ithaca. Upon first seeing the island, he must have remembered patient Penelope, faithful at her loom, waiting for the great Odysseus to punish the cruel suitors. Soon his thoughts returned to his earliest memories as a schoolboy, when he first began to read the Classics, and to Ham and other places associated with his childhood.

Continuing by the Greek Isles, the party stopped in Patras on the coast of the Peloponnesus and then continued to Corfu. The travelers spent a week at Corfu, and with great detail, Newman narrated to his family everything that he saw. He was taken by the sight of the picturesque town, the dress of the population, and local commerce. He described with interest the numerous churches and the piety of the people and clergy. It is no surprise that his thoughts went to theologians of the early Church, in particular the

---

8 *LD*, Vol. III (Entries for December 24 and 25, 1832), 162.

fourth-century Greek Fathers. In a short poem, he praised the attributes of Clement, Dionysius, Origen, Basil, Gregory Nazianzen, Athanasius, and the Apostle Paul. Another poem composed later in Palermo was dedicated exclusively to Nazianzen, the "PEACE-LOVING man, of humble heart and true."[9]

Newman was awestruck with the beauty of Corfu's harbor and the island's landscape, composed of tall cypress trees and countless olive and orange trees in full fruit. Most of all, he was struck with the thought of the ancient Greeks whose land he was treading. During this part of the journey, he reread *The History of the Peloponnesian Wars*; the musings of Thucydides and Homer would not leave his mind.

In a flight of literary enthusiasm, he told Harriet:

> If Thucydides were to rise from the dead, he would recognize the spot—he would point at the mountains which dressed in the old fashion; thus I have something in common with him—and knowing his lines, seeing the change, I am in his place, as it were, and see the vision for him. I am Thucydides with the gift of second sight.[10]

For a scholar of Classics, this visit would hold extraordinary significance; for Newman, it was enrapturing.

Besides his awe at Greek history, Newman found similarities between himself and a biblical figure. Newman compared himself with Melchizedec in the poem titled with this name and penned while at Corfu. It was like a miniature spiritual biography of Newman who, fatherless, and

---

9 "St. Gregory Nazianzen," in *VV* (Palermo, June 12, 1833), 151-52; 151.

10 *LD,* Vol. X, JHN to Harriet Newman (January 2, 1833), 176-85; 177.

experiencing loneliness far from home and friends, sought God's presence and will. The beauty of the island made his sorrow keener, yet Newman felt richly blessed by God, of Whom he wrote:

> He moulds the vessel of His vast design;
> Fatherless, homeless, reft of age and place,
> Sever'd from earth, and careless of its wreck,
> Born through long woe His rare Melchizedec.[11]

These verses, which may at first suggest presumption on Newman's part, are better understood in light of his distress over the situation of the Church in England and his growing awareness of a divine vocation. His deep spiritual sense was, at the same time, mixed with his love for the magnanimous elements of Greek heroes.

Naturally, Newman desired to go on to Athens, which was within a day's travel, but the fear of bandits kept the group from going farther. Greece was in political turmoil and unsafe for travel; it was awaiting the arrival of its future king, Prince Otto of Bavaria, with his army. Therefore, after an overnight stop at Patras, the party returned to Malta.

Upon reaching Malta, a port of entry to Europe, they were obliged to undergo quarantine for ten days owing to an alarm concerning cholera. On various nights, Newman was awakened by strange noises that he could only explain by attributing them to a visitation by a spirit.[12] Though mildly amusing, this incident kept Newman awake and

---

11 "Melchizedec," in *VV* (Corfu, January 5, 1833), 108.

12 *LD*, Vol. III, JHN to Jemima Newman (January 15, 1833), 187-92; 191.

exposed him to cold weather. In such conditions, he developed an upper respiratory infection that confined him to bed for a week after the quarantine. Despite illness, his letters mention a number of times the satisfaction of being on the island where St. Paul had stopped on the way to Rome, and before departing from Malta, he managed to visit by boat the Bay of St. Paul where Paul was once shipwrecked.

Throughout his trip, Newman wrote many detailed letters to his mother and sisters, which serve as a colorful description of the journey. Next to the elaborate narration of events, he playfully summed up the small group's activity at the Lazaret: "The F.s draw and paint. I have hired a violin and it sounds grand (bad as it is) in such spacious halls."[13] Of course, he did more than play the violin; in addition to prayer and taking Italian lessons, he wrote several long letters to his family, Isaac Williams, and John W. Bowden. In one letter he explained how Catholic clergy were tried in their own courts, and commented: "I mention all this at length, because it exemplifies the admirable system of the Papacy as *an instrument of power*."[14]

After Malta, the group made a short stop in Sicily. They planned to visit the island at length during warmer weather after first traveling to Rome. Newman narrated the quite amusing arrival at Palermo. He and Froude raced a countess and her party from aboard ship to secure the best lodging in the city. After jumping from the ship and trying to outdo the other party that was rowing ashore, they ran

---

13 *LD,* Vol. III, JHN to Jemima Newman (January 15, 1833), 187-92; 188-89.

14 *Ibid.,* 190.

through streets thronged with people to the best lodging. The countess, however, arrived before them and "took the whole inn."[15] On top of this, she instantly set off by coach to procure two other inns, sent a servant to a third, and "[t]hus in fact she took the whole town."[16]

From Palermo, they traveled by mule to the ancient town of Egesta. There they visited the remains of a Greek temple. For Newman, Sicily represented the repository of Greek culture. Enamored by the past, he wrote to Jemima: "Such was the genius of early Greek worship, grand in the midst of error; simple and unadorned in its architecture, it chose some elevated spot, and fixed its faith as a solitary witness on heights where it could not be hid."[17] After four days, they traveled from Palermo to Naples by ship and from Naples to Rome by land, but Newman was determined to return to Sicily.

The contrast between Newman's impressions of Naples and Rome could not be more distinct. The former had miserable weather, dirty streets, a frivolous and profligate populace, and, worst of all, a post office that devoured a person's correspondence. He wrote Thomas Mozley: "wretched Naples keeps all the letters you direct to it—you might as well direct to its bay as to its poste restante."[18] Newman also criticized the clergy of Naples and described the religious worship as pagan. Newman's humorous yet

---

15 *Ibid.,* 190.

16 *Ibid.,* 190.

17 *LD,* Vol. III, JHN to Jemima Newman (February 19, 1833), 215-21; 219.

18 *LD,* Vol. III, JHN to Thomas Mozley (Rome, March 9, 1833), 241-44; 243.

candid caricature of Naples reflects his frustration with not having received news from home for over two months because of the inefficiency of the post office and, even more, his sensitive nature that would sometimes lead him to harsh and hasty judgments of people.

Newman wrote this biting account of Naples despite a kind welcome by Mr. Bennett, the Anglican chaplain at the English consulate, an evening at the opera, and a trip to the ruins of Pompeii. He did acknowledge that the cathedral and the museum were both worth visiting and noted the beauty of the surrounding town and cleanliness of the people. On his return trip to Sicily, an obliged stay in Naples made him reconsider and soften his earlier description of the city. He even admitted that Naples' bay was larger than that of Palermo or Corfu and almost as beautiful. Still, he referred to the post office with contempt.

At last came Rome, which was described by Newman as the most beautiful city that he had visited. Rome had large streets with beautiful churches. By comparison to Malta and Naples, he found the clergy moral, methodical, and pious. Newman and the Froudes spent five weeks in Rome visiting different sites every day, with the exception of St. Peter's Basilica and Square, which they revisited many times despite Newman's disdain for "popery." In particular, he was impressed with the dimensions of the basilica, especially from within the dome. He was most struck by the mosaics and the fountains in Rome, including the mosaics of the Transfiguration in St. Peter's and the two fountains in its square. But the sight of St. Peter's Basilica on Easter night, with the dome illuminated and men tied by ropes streaming from it, was a most memorable one.

During this long stay, made pleasant by good weather, they visited many churches, the catacombs, the city walls, picture galleries in the Vatican and on Capitoline Hill, the Roman palazzi, and surrounding sites in Frascati, Marino, and Albano. On Good Friday, they attended the service at the English Chapel and, in the afternoon, visited the Sistine Chapel, where they heard the *Miserere,* or Psalm 50, beautifully sung. On the previous day they had heard a version of the *Miserere* by another composer. Newman was able to write to his Oxford friend, Robert F. Wilson: "Rome is one of the most delightful residences imaginable."[19] The remains of classical and Christian history, the performance of sacred and profane music and the sight of beautiful statues and paintings blended together with devout religious practice and interesting conversations with friends that delighted his mind and gave him ample material for his letters.

In Rome, the travelers met with various friends including Edward Neale, a former student of Newman at Oriel, William Wilberforce, Jr. and his wife, who were living in Rome at the time, as well as Charles Anderson, also from Oriel, and his family. They called twice on Nicholas Wiseman, Rector of the English College in Rome, and had a long conversation with him. They met with Joseph Severn, a painter and later British Consul in Rome. Newman also had several meetings with Abbot Santini, a musicologist, as well as Baron Christian Bunsen, a Prussian diplomat to the Vatican.

---

19 *LD,* Vol. III, JHN to R. F. Wilson (March 18, 1833), 255-58; 258.

Newman's youthful fascination with Rome was mixed with the difficulty of reconciling the fact that the Roman Church was established at the site of Pagan Rome. His fundamentalist reading of the fourth kingdom mentioned in the Book of Revelation made an appearance in the letters to his friends. For him, it was useless to distinguish between imperial Rome and Christian Rome:

> [Y]ou have to view Rome as a place of religion; and here what mingled feelings come upon one—you are in the place of martyrdom and burial of apostles and saints; you have about you the buildings and the sights they saw, and you are in the city to which England owes the blessing of the Gospel. But then, on the other hand, the superstitions, or rather, what is far worse, the solemn reception of them as an essential part of Christianity.[20]

Newman imagined that there must be good Christians among the Catholics in Rome and observed the appearance of piety in its clergy and churches, yet he insisted that the overall system was corrupt and that Rome was under a curse.[21] To Rickards he explained that the city and State were the heirs of Pagan Rome and were still accursed, and that this curse affected God's Church there. He tried, however, to exonerate the Church by speaking of "a sort of Genius Loci which enthralls the Church which happens to be there." [22] The Church was the instrument and slave of Rome, and one day it would be set free.

---

20 *LD,* Vol. III, JHN to J. F. Christie (March 7, 1833), 240.

21 *LD,* Vol. III, JHN to R. F. Wilson (March 18, 1833), 255-58; 258; *LD,* Vol. III, JHN to Jemima Newman (March 20, 1833), 262-66; 265.

22 *LD,* Vol. III, JHN to Samuel Rickards (April 14, 1833), 287-90; 288.

Though he had many misgivings about the Roman Church, he felt different about its ancient counterpart. He thought that the Greek Church had less corruption and could move more easily toward the English Church. He wrote to Jemima about the Greek Church: "It does not teach purgatory or the Mass, two chief practical delusions of Romanism."[23] Newman wrote that the Mass and Purgatory were inventions, and "Saint worship," which he considered polytheism, was a corruption of the faith. He admitted, however, that popular devotion to saints was only sanctioned, not taught by the Church. This popular devotion ran into excesses such as fabulous miraculous tales and superstitions.

Newman judged the Roman Catholic Church harshly on the subject of the Sacrifice of the Mass. However, at Zante, he had entered a Greek Church "at the time the priests were consecrating the elements" and found it to be "most imposing," even though he believed that Greeks do not hold it to be a sacrifice.[24] Even though the Orthodox consider worship as entering into the mystery of Divine life and emphasize the action of the Holy Spirit in the Eucharistic liturgy, they believe that Christ becomes present when the Holy Spirit descends upon the congregation and Eucharistic bread and wine; this was the consequence of Christ's sacrifice on the Cross.

---

23 *LD*, Vol. III, JHN to Jemima Newman (March 20, 1833), 262-66; 265.

24 *LD*, Vol. III, JHN to Jemima Newman (January 15, 1833), 187-92; 192.

Newman was also mistaken in the claim that Rome had the custom of "forced celibacy" for its clergy.[25] Since the early Middle Ages men in the West who wished to be ordained to the priesthood freely chose celibacy as a requirement for ordination. In the East, the practice remained that married men could be ordained to the priesthood, but men, once ordained, could not seek marriage.

In Rome, Newman and his friends parted company. The Froudes traveled to France, wishing to visit religious sites in Southern France associated with the life of St. Thomas Becket, Archbishop of Canterbury, who was martyred by King Henry II in 1170. From Rome, Newman set off for Naples, planning to travel from there by steamer to Messina in Sicily. Bad sailing weather delayed him in Naples for a few days, and as a result, he had time to go on a very difficult excursion up Vesuvius and down into its steep crater that emanated sulfur fumes and was lined with hot ashes. On other days during this stay, Newman visited Virgil's tomb, St. Elmo Castle on a hill overlooking the beautiful Bay of Naples, a library, and a museum.

This young, adventurous thirty-two-year-old Newman made fast judgments about people and institutions that resulted in harsh comments or trite generalizations. Nevertheless, he sometimes later changed his mind or qualified earlier statements. Regarding Naples, for example, he wrote his mother: "I think the popular and exoteric religion as nearly pagan as you can fancy—but I really have found the people very civil and good-natured, tho knaves; and very

---

25 *LD,* Vol. III, JHN to Samuel Rickards (April 14, 1833), 287-90; 289.

clever and humorous. They are complete punches."[26] He also described the tricks of boys who played a tune when unsuccessful at begging, and concluded: "so altogether I think we were hard on this poor place, which I begin to like if it were only out of remorse at having been so violent against it."[27]

Newman's Mediterranean voyage had two memorable high points: the visits to Corfu and to Rome. In Corfu and the other Greek Isles the young traveler recalled Homer's heroes and thought often about the Greek Church Fathers. In Rome he was impressed by the grandeur of the monuments of Ancient Rome, and the beauty of Christian churches, especially the Vatican Basilica of Saints Peter and Paul. The visit to the Eternal City mitigated his bias against Roman Catholicism. From Naples, Newman embarked on the last leg of his trip, which was an extended stay in Sicily. This was to prove decisive for the years immediately following.

---

26 *LD,* Vol. III, JHN to Mrs. Newman (April 17, 1833), 293-97; 294.
27 *Ibid.,* 295.

CHAPTER 17

ILLNESS IN SICILY

THE beauty of the countryside in his native England delighted Newman, and so it is no wonder that the scenery of the Greek Islands and Sicily likewise moved him. He wrote to his friend, Frederic Rogers: "I can only say that I did not know before nature could be so beautiful . . . It passes belief. It is like a garden of Eden, and though it ran in the line of my anticipations (as I say), it far exceeded them."[1] Anyone who has seen the wild flowers of the hillsides of Sicily would share Newman's rapture and see in these landscapes the goodness and beauty of the Creator. The young Oxford Fellow anticipated the second visit to this ancient Greek colony because of its association with ancient civilization. However, as it turned out, all of this would take second place to a life-threatening illness, which became a powerful source of spiritual direction for his changing life.

After a delay at Naples occasioned by bad weather, Newman journeyed to Messina by a sailing ship and arrived on April 21. From there, he set off to climb Mt. Etna, traveling with a servant, two mules, and several muleteers. He dressed in gray trousers, a straw hat, and a flannel jacket with a black neck cloth, which was the only black he wore.

---

1 *LD,* Vol. III, JHN to Frederic Rogers (June 5, 1833), 312-15; 315.

He felt embarrassed by his external appearance and by such a poor cavalcade. The first day's twenty-mile journey, without the companionship of a friend, was rewarded by a visit to the ruins of Taormina, ancient Tauromenion.

Taormina was a place that enchanted Newman. From the site of an ancient theater, he took in the beautiful scenery. He wrote:

> The theatre is situated in a hollow hill, and the scena forms a screen—through it you see magnificent steeps, falling down and down—and above all, Etna towers —at the bottom you see the sea, and the coast circling into a bay and then jutting out into a point, where formerly stood Naxos, the first Greek settlement.[2]

Later, some miles from Taormina he was able to see Mt. Etna, which was "magnificent beyond description."[3] The following day he traveled to a grove of chestnuts at Mt. Etna's base, hoping to climb it, but since the mountain was covered with snow, he gave up his plans.

Newman then traveled on a 35-foot sailing vessel from Catania to Syracuse, carrying with him Virgil's *Aeneid* and reading Thucydides. Aside from some beautiful sights along the way and a visit to the ruins of a Temple to Minerva, once off the coast of Syracuse pouring rain vexed the travelers, who had almost no food provisions and slept poorly on board.

These dangerous sailing conditions forced Newman to make a portion of the return trip to Catania over land with

---

2 *LD,* Vol. III, JHN to Harriet Newman (April 25, 1833), 301-05, 303.

3 *Ibid.,* 304.

mules. Following an exhausting trek in which the guide
lost his way, they made it to their destination close to midnight. After a day's rest in Catania, and after seeing the
amphitheater, Newman set off on a rainy day for Aderno,
a town located twenty miles away on the road to Palermo.
The next day, May 2, a very ill Newman reached the town
of Leonforte. After a few days of bed rest there, he set off
again, but he became so weak that he collapsed along the
road. As he lay in a roadside cabin, a physician who passed
by attended to him. Newman was taken to Castro San
Giovanni, a nearby town, where he was bled as a treatment.

Newman had developed a debilitating febrile illness,
possibly typhoid fever. He suffered with high fevers and
delirium for eleven days and came close to death.[4] When
the crisis of the fever passed, Newman still remained in bed
for a week. His subsequent letters described many details
of the illness and the diligent care of a local physician at
Castro San Giovanni. He also wrote about the honesty of
his hosts and the thoughts of his future that had crossed his
mind while he lay sick.

For Newman, who bore illness well, this would be his
only life-threatening illness, and through it, he saw the
hand of God's Providence. As when he succumbed to mental exhaustion while examiner at Oriel, he understood that
everything is part of God's plan and an indication of God's
care. Newman earnestly believed that God guides the lives
of men, in sickness and in health; he thought God was spar-
ing him for a mission.

---

4 *LD,* Vol. III, Diary entries, 311; *AW,* 121-38.

In all, he spent seven weeks in Sicily; the last two weeks were spent in Palermo, where he continued his convalescence while awaiting a sailing vessel for Marseilles, on which he finally set sail on June 13th. Even more than the memory of the beautiful landscape and churches, the dangerous fever and the nearness to death remained etched in his mind. This illness marked a decisive moment in Newman's life, comparable to the Crossing of the Rubicon for Julius Caesar. Heading home to England, Newman knew that he must fight in defense of the Anglican Church's doctrinal, spiritual, and ecclesiastical prerogatives. In his mind, Newman had declared a war against what he termed "liberalism in religion."

Prior to this watershed experience, Newman had been speaking with his friends at Oxford for some years about the Church's urgent need for good leaders, especially celibate men from the university. On his voyage, he had put into writing many of the ideals that he and his friends had about the renewal of the English Church. Newman's poems inspired adherence to doctrinal truths, holiness of life, devout sacramental practice, and continuity with the Church's Tradition. His recovery made it clear to him the leading role that he would play in this renewal. He did not conceive a specific plan of action, but he felt God protecting him and preserving him for this important mission. He wrote to Rogers that, though he had given his servant instructions of how to convey news of his death to England, he had had the firm conviction of recovery: "I thought God had work for me."[5]

---

5 *LD,* Vol. III, JHN to Frederic Rogers (June 5, 1833), 312-15; 314.

In Palermo, he at last received news from home. With great joy, he read in a newspaper about Rogers's election as Oriel Fellow. Newman had been worried about being away from Oxford for that election of his pupil and friend and at once wrote to him a congratulatory letter.

Homesick and awaiting a ship for the return home, Newman continued to pour his spiritual convictions into verse. At this point, the principal subject of the verses was the attack on the Church, which he calls by the reverent and pious name of Mother. In "Day-Labourers," he urges the Christian warrior to rid his mother of her present chain. In "Liberalism," he disdains the comforts of tranquility and the doubting character of statesmen and Churchmen.

In this frame of mind, and finally at sea on his way home, Newman wrote the now celebrated poem "Lead Kindly Light" on June 16, 1833, almost seven months after the departure from England. The poem was more like a prayer, a recapitulation of the state of his soul:

> LEAD, Kindly Light, amid the encircling gloom
> Lead Thou me on!
> The night is dark, and I am far from home—
> Lead Thou me on![6]

Amid the darkness of the moment, the poem was a prayer of faith in God's power and hope in His goodness. In this poem, Newman admitted to a prideful way of life and overconfidence in his youth. Now with humility he was determined to pursue the doctrinal and spiritual renewal of the Church of England, even though he did not

---

6 "The Pillar of the Cloud," in *VV* (At Sea, June 16, 1833), 156-58; 156.

know the specific path to follow. Only a few weeks from the "beginning" of the Oxford Movement, he entrusted the future of this daunting work to God's power.

CHAPTER 18

ORIGINS OF THE OXFORD MOVEMENT

NEWMAN grew up in a fragmented Anglican Church whose origins can be traced to legal and theological developments dating as far back as the thirteenth century. The origin of the Anglican Church had three major influences: anti-papal legislation by the English Crown in the later Middle Ages, Lollardy, and the Lutheran Reformation.[1] These influences and the political events of the Anglican Reformation explain why Newman sought a "second reformation." In his *Apologia*, Newman wrote: "That ancient religion had well nigh faded away out of the land, through the political changes of the last 150 years, and it must be restored. It would be in fact a second Reformation: a better reformation, for it would return not to the sixteenth century, but to the seventeenth."[2]

Between 1351 and 1389, anti-papal legislation, which curtailed papal nominations for vacant benefices, was enacted. In 1353, other statutes known as *Praemunire* established a punishment for any appeal of legal cases to courts outside England, especially to Rome, and for the publication of papal bulls of excommunication.

---

1 Nichols, *Panther and the Hind*, 1-36.
2 *Apo.*, 43-44.

Lollardy, the second influence, was a popular movement that followed the teaching of John Wycliffe (1330–1384), a secular priest and Oxford theologian who anticipated much of Luther's doctrines, except for *sola fide*.[3] The Lollards (from the Dutch word for "mumblers of prayers") formed congregations of Christians who dissented from various Church doctrines. The Lollards used vernacular translations of the Bible to disseminate Wycliffe's ideas. This led the English Crown to ban the translation of the Bible into English and to enact capital punishment for heretics. A century later, this popular movement provided an existing base for Lutheranism, the third of the influences leading up to the separation of the Church of England from the Roman Catholic Church.

The Lutheran Reform was the immediate precedent for the English Schism. This reform brought significant ecclesial, doctrinal, and religious changes, notably the rejection of papal authority and the sacrament of Holy Orders, abolition of the Mass, reliance on *sola scriptura* and *sola fide* and wholesale rejection of Catholic practices of piety.

In 1533, Henry VIII established himself as Head of the Church of England when the Pope refused to declare invalid King Henry's first marriage, that to Catherine of Aragon. Catherine had borne Henry a daughter, Mary, but she had no surviving male child. The previous year Henry cut off the financial subsidy to the Roman See with the Act in Restraint of Annates. By another law, the Act in Restraint of Appeals, he established that the ecclesiastical jurisdiction of courts was subject to the king. In that same

---

3 Nichols, *The Panther and the Hind*, 6-7.

year, Henry secured the consecration of Thomas Cranmer, a Fellow from Jesus College, Cambridge, as Archbishop of Canterbury. Cranmer declared Henry's first marriage invalid and celebrated the wedding of Henry to his second wife, Anne Boleyn. Anne bore him Elizabeth, who would be Queen after Mary, Catherine's daughter. Cranmer became the chief architect of the nascent Anglican Church and strove to remove "popery" from the new worship. By forcing worshipers to receive Communion in the hand, he hoped that he could destroy belief in the Real Presence in one generation.

Earlier, Henry had expressed his opposition to Luther's ideas in the treatise, *Assertio Septem Sacramentorum*, but after his divorce, the Holy See excommunicated him and declared null his marriage with Anne Boleyn. This and the breakdown of relations with Catherine's nephew, Emperor Charles V, resulted in a Lutheranizing influence on the new Anglican Church. There was much bloodshed and martyrdom over this splitting of the Church. In 1534, the Act of Supremacy declared the king as the supreme head of the Church in England. The following year, the Treasons Act made it high treason to refuse to acknowledge the king as supreme head of the Church. Sir Thomas More, Bishop John Fisher, and some Carthusian monks were executed for refusing to do so.

In 1536, a profession of faith known as the *Ten Articles* was drawn up by Thomas Cranmer and approved by Convocation, the general assembly of the clergy. The intent of the *Articles* was to conciliate both Catholics and Lutherans; later in 1539, another profession, the *Six Articles*, which was more explicitly Catholic, was promulgated. *The*

Bishop's Book, a book dictating liturgical reforms, was issued in 1537. This liturgical book was soon replaced by one that was less Lutheran, but despite Henry's intention to maintain the traditional medieval liturgy, his appointee and chief minister, Thomas Cromwell, led the stripping away of popular devotions, religious holidays, and the dismantling of shrines. These changes produced religious confusion among the common people, and led to religious persecution under successive monarchs.

In the succeeding reigns of Henry's children (Edward, Mary, and Elizabeth), both High Anglicans ("Anglo-Catholics") and Calvinist groups vied to assert the beliefs, texts, rituals, and practices that they thought to be authentically Christian. Under Edward VI (1547–1553), Henry's son by his third wife, Jane Seymour, England was ruled by a council of regency. During this period Archbishop Cranmer was able to establish Protestantism in England by altering the liturgy through the publication of the *Book of Common Prayer,* which together with a series of sermons known as the *Homilies,* introduced significant doctrinal reforms. He was aided by Continental reformers to whom he gave refuge in England.

Edward was succeeded by his half-sister Queen Mary I (1553–1558), who attempted to return England to Catholicism and reconciled her country with Rome through Cardinal Reginald Pole. Queen Mary had Cranmer tried for treason and heresy. He was imprisoned for two years and afterward executed. Queen Mary named Pole, her close adviser, Archbishop of Canterbury, and her first Parliament repealed Protestant religious laws passed by Henry VIII and Edward VI. She authorized the execution of close to three hundred Protestant leaders who threatened the re-establishment of Roman Catholicism in England. A larger number chose exile to Europe.

After an early death from cancer, Mary was succeeded by her half-sister, Elizabeth I. The new Queen began her reign (1558–1603) with a liking for pomp and ritual bereft of principal Catholic beliefs such as the Real Presence of Christ in the Eucharist. Then in 1559, she reached a religious settlement with Parliament, which had proposed a Reformation Bill that banned images from churches, forbade the use of the surplice or Catholic vestments, allowed ministers to marry, and called for abuse of the Pope in the liturgy. The settlement consisted in two acts of Parliament, the Act of Uniformity and the Act of Supremacy. The Act of Uniformity replaced the Latin Mass with the *Book of Common Prayer* and Communion Service. The Act of Supremacy declared the Queen to be the supreme governor of the Church of England. A royal commission administered an Oath of Supremacy; all the bishops except for one refused to take the Oath and were removed from their dioceses. This so-called Elizabethan Settlement thus resulted in the elimination of the Catholic hierarchy in England. The settlement was enshrined in three important texts: the *Thirty-Nine Articles* of 1571, the *Book of Common Prayer* of 1559, and the *Ordinal* for consecrating bishops, priests, and deacons.

Elizabeth I chose England's new bishops from the English exiles of Mary's reign who had returned from Geneva with Calvinist ideas and practices. She adopted confessional articles that were acceptable to Calvinists. During the decade of 1580, Elizabeth faced serious political threats, both internal and foreign. Under pressure from Puritan merchants and gentry, she allowed Calvinist principles to take a firm hold of the Anglican Church.

At this time Catholic priests were considered a threat and were executed for celebrating the Mass. Some priests bravely continued to do so in people's homes at great risk of being found out by spies. St. Edmund Campion was one of these priests. In 1581, he was captured and accused of sedition. Campion was sentenced to death, tortured, and executed for this supposed crime and his writings against the Anglican Church.

While Roman Catholics were persecuted under Elizabeth's reign, no one party in the Anglican Church enjoyed full favor with the Crown. The Queen's ecclesiastical appointments continued to favor Calvinists, but at the end of her reign she took vigorous measures against Puritans. The Stuart Successors to Elizabeth aligned themselves wholeheartedly with the High Church party.[4] They held the doctrines of the divine right of kings and of hierarchy in church government.

Under the rule of King Charles I (1625–1649) and the interregnum before Charles II (1660–1685), a school of preachers and theologians developed which was later collectively called the Caroline Divines. These men tried to defend the early Anglican Church prior to the Protestant Reformation, based on their extensive patristic and scriptural learning. In particular, these Divines upheld the Episcopal form of church government against the Calvinist claims; they taught the Real Presence, the use of auricular

---

4 Nichols, *The Panther and the Hind*, 52.

Confession, and the observance of fast and feast days of the Church year.

William Laud was one of the most notable Caroline Divines. In 1633, Laud, who was Chancellor of the University of Oxford, was made Archbishop of Canterbury. He attempted to impose liturgical uniformity with a modest revival of Catholic liturgy and traditions within the Anglican Church and instituted new canons that proclaimed the divine right of kings and defended the Episcopal order of the Church. These changes angered the Puritans, and in 1640, the Parliament issued an order for the arrest of Laud and twelve other Anglican bishops. Laud was tried on the charge of secret "popery" and executed in 1645. This triggered the outbreak of a civil war and the abolition of Anglicanism by Oliver Cromwell.

The seventeenth century was considered by some a sort of golden age for the Church of England, as reflected in its theology, devotional literature, and Church music. Other well-known Caroline Divines were Lancelot Andrewes, Jeremy Taylor, and Thomas Wilson. The members of the Oxford Movement referred often to these theologians and began an Anglo-Catholic Library to reprint their works. During this golden period, however, there was a simultaneous growth in Low Church practice in English society, which was followed by an eighteenth-century Evangelical Revival.

The religious climate of the age in which Newman went to Oxford was one of rising agnosticism, doctrinal relativism, and growing religious indifference. In the face of vast social changes and political unrest, a growing sector of society turned toward Jeremy Bentham's Utilitarianism, placing faith in regulations, institutions, new laws, and "useful knowledge." Still the Established Church had a significant place in society. In the early 1830s, the Church of England consisted of two circumscriptions: the Province of Canterbury and the Province of York, which was composed of 27 dioceses with approximately 11,077 parishes and 11,825 churches and chapels.[5] In 1851, Anglican churches at Oxford numbered 19 with seating capacity for 11,300, compared to 13 other places of worship with seating capacity for 4200.[6]

After the violent political and religious upheavals of the sixteenth and seventeenth century, two peaceful reform movements issued from within the Anglican Church, one in the eighteenth century and another in the nineteenth century. The first was the Evangelical Movement, which was closely associated with the Methodist revival, and the second was the Oxford Movement. According to Dean Church, a member of the Oxford Movement, it was "a determined revolt . . . (although) not the only one, nor the first" against the state of religion in England.[7] It was a renewal of doctrinal principles regarding the nature of the Church, Episcopal authority, the sacraments, and the role of Tradition, which were all exemplified in the liturgy, and practices of piety.

Together with a small group of clergymen, primarily from Oxford University, Newman founded the Oxford

---

5 Hermann Ferdinand Uhden, *The Anglican Church in the Nineteenth Century* (London: Hatchard, 1844), 60-63.

6 *History of the County of Oxford*, Vol. 4, ed. Alan Crossley and C. L. Elrington (Oxford: Oxford University Press, 1979), 254.

7 Church, *The Oxford Movement,* 5.

Movement, which bears the name of the university where it began. Oxford was virtually a medieval town rich in beauty and tradition that held fast to the religious ideal of an old order being overturned in England. Oxford University was still closed to Dissenters and Papists (Roman Catholics); along with Cambridge, it continued to be the place for the education of English clergy. The threat of liberalism in religion was naturally felt much more at Oxford than in the rest of England. Newman wrote that Oxford, as a center for theological learning and the training of clergy, should be won over to the anti-modern and anti-Liberal reforms and thus become the Geneva of the second Reformation. He thought that "living movements" must arise from universities, which are the natural center for intellectual ideas where there is a connection between personal minds.[8] These connections, rather than associations and committees, were the path for renewal.

Evangelical Anglicanism, which antedated the Oxford Movement, was the other reform movement, started in the late eighteenth century under men such as Thomas Scott, whose writings inspired Newman. At the start of the nineteenth century the first generation of Evangelical leaders were a layman, William Wilberforce, and three clergymen: Charles Simeon, Daniel Wilson, Bishop of Calcutta, and C. R. Sumner, Bishop of Winchester. They were followed by a second generation of Evangelical Anglicans, men such as Wilberforce's sons and George Ryder, an Oriel graduate who eventually became Catholic. This second generation was succeeded by a younger rank of men such as Edward

---

8 Dawson, *The Spirit of the Oxford Movement*, 78.

Irving and Henry Drummond, who sustained the premillen-nialist doctrine that Christ would establish a political reign of a thousand years before His Second Coming.

Some Evangelical preachers and authors were strongly anti-Catholic in their preaching and explicitly considered the Roman Catholic Church to be the harlot described by the Book of Revelation. Even during his first journey to Rome, Newman held these ideas that he had learned from Evangelical writers. Nevertheless, other Evangelical lead-ers were moderate in their views toward Roman Catholi-cism, and some backed the Whig Reforms that brought political and economic relief to Irish-Catholics.

William Wilberforce (1759–1833), whose family held strong ties of friendship with Newman, was a wealthy mer-chant and Member of Parliament. He lived with his friend, Henry Thornton, in Battersea Rise, a mansion located in the Clapham section of London. This home became a meeting point for pious and wealthy Evangelical families, often connected by family ties. The Wilberforces and their friends formed the so-called Clapham Sect, known for the name of the neighborhood in London where they resided. The group consisted mostly of Tories and included vari-ous members of Parliament and men with administrative posts. This influential group of families began a renewal of the moral customs and piety of English society. They com-prised the Evangelical party within the Anglican Church.

A few of the early members of the Oxford Movement came from the Clapham families. Aside from this fact, the influence of the Evangelicals on the origins of the Oxford Movement was negligible. In fact, Newman claimed that Evangelical beliefs and practices prepared the ground for liberalism in religion. Many Oxford men and the leaders of the Oxford Movement were adamantly opposed to the Evangelicals' impoverished notion of Church authority and Apostolic Tradition.

The Oxford Movement, which Newman began, was a revival of the seventeenth- century Anglican ecclesiastical practices, doctrine and piety. The Movement was wholly distinct from the Evangelical renewal even though it shared with Evangelicals a sincere devotion and concern for moral life. The primary belief that the Movement sought to defend was the doctrine of Apostolic Succession and Episcopal authority in the Church. Although a few of its members, including young Newman, had once been Evangelical, these members soon left Evangelical Anglicanism and strongly contested its very tenets and practices. The founders of the Oxford Movement were either Anglo-Catholics or inclined to this party of the Anglican Church.

CHAPTER 19

1833: THE START OF THE OXFORD MOVEMENT

SINCE 1826 or earlier, the principles behind the Oxford Movement had been developing and gathering strength in the minds of its founders. Newman, however, ascribed the start of the movement to a famous sermon by Keble on National Apostasy delivered from the university pulpit on Sunday, July 14, 1833, a week after Newman's return from Europe. Newman gave credit to Keble and, indirectly, to Froude, his former student, for igniting the religious renewal. In his sermon, Keble argued that the English nation had broken its covenant with God by the abolition of the Test Act and the suppression of Irish sees; the latter was an act of National Apostasy, which rejected the divine theocracy that in England had been accepted for centuries. The rejection of divine authority over the State obliged Christians to submit to the tyranny of the State.

The birthday of the Movement might also be considered as January 22, 1832, the day on which Newman, as one of the Select Preachers for the university that year, delivered a sermon titled "Personal Influence, the Means for Propagating the Truth," which was an appeal to Christian holiness. Newman pointed out how doctrinal truths are easily questioned and apparently defeated by secular reason because "Truth is vast and far-stretching, viewed as a system; and, viewed in its separate doctrines, it depends on the combination of a number of various, delicate, and scattered evidences; hence it can scarcely be exhibited in a given number of sentences."[1]

However, Truth prevails because it is not a system upheld in the world by books, arguments, or temporal power, but by the personal influence of men who are teachers of it and at the same time, examples of it.[2] Newman praised these men for their "unconscious holiness," simple, honest devotion to God, moral excellence, and consistency in the practice of virtue. These men are the "hidden saints" chosen by God in every age, who are His noiseless instruments carrying the flame of Truth from one generation to another.

Newman's University Sermon titled "Willfulness, the Sin of Saul," preached on December 2, 1832, also contained seminal ideas that would be central to the Movement. In that sermon, Newman denounced those who wish to rid themselves of the shackles of Revelation and constitute themselves as self-appointed prophets. He likened Saul's sinfulness to the modern indifference to the Catholic Creed, wanton violation of the Church's commands, irreverence toward Antiquity, "craving for change in all things," and the transgression of ecclesial unity.[3]

The foundational meeting was held at the end of July 1833, at Hugh James Rose's parsonage in Hadleigh, Suffolk. Rose gathered a group of Churchmen who shared the

---

1 "Personal Influence, the Means of Propagating the Truth," in *US*, 90.
2 *Ibid.,* 91-92.
3 "Willfulness, the Sin of Saul," in *US*, 174.

serious concerns voiced by Keble. Rose, William Palmer of Worcester College, and Arthur Perceval, the older men at the meeting, were judicious persons already established in society; in comparison to these, Keble, Newman and Froude, all from Oriel College, were young men. Newman and Froude were just beginning their careers. The Oriel men were more adamant in their response to the attacks against the Church of England and had much less to lose in case of defeat. They spoke plainly and preached forcefully. They entered into a sort of religious "warfare" with the liberal political establishment and its designs on religion. Newman even spoke of the need for a second Reformation, but one better than the first. Keble and Newman did not actually attend the meeting, but they actively corresponded with those who did.

Despite the differences in their character and circumstances these men were bound by a common belief in the sacred nature of the Church. They recognized that the government was attacking the Church's authority, doctrine, and liturgy, and they wished to lessen the number of liberal-minded preachers and theologians, and their influence on the Church. Rose was the most prominent man in the group. He was a widely respected theologian, loyal to the English Church. In addition to great learning, he possessed the character of a statesman. He commanded authority and courageously insisted that soon, "something must be done" about the situation in the Church.[4]

---

4 According to Church, Rose said: "That *something must be done* is certain. The only thing is, that whatever is done ought to be *quickly* done." Church, *The Oxford Movement*, 93.

From the onset, Rose and especially Palmer wanted to form an association that would prepare addresses and petitions to fight the government's abandonment of the Anglican Church. They were cautious men who moved slowly and wished London to be the center of the Movement. Newman resisted Palmer's idea of establishing an association—he felt it would bog down efforts and water down the individual temper of people's responses. Newman explained that an association would require the sanction of the local bishop, one that they did not have. He was not opposed, however, to an association formed in the future; he only objected to one at the start.

Instead of the plan for an association rejected at Hadleigh, Newman agreed to present an address to the Archbishop of Canterbury and wrote the initial draft. The signatures of 7000 clergy were obtained, and the address was delivered to the Archbishop in February of 1834. It included the signatures of the Masters of Trinity and Brasenose colleges. A Lay Address followed; it was signed by 230,000 heads of families and presented to the Archbishop in May of 1835.

Within months of the meeting at Hadleigh, under Newman's organization, the group began to publish pamphlets soon called *Tracts of the Times*. As the *Tracts* spread throughout England, the Movement was dubbed "the Tractarian Movement." Newman wrote about one third of the *Tracts*; other contributors were Perceval, Froude, John Keble, Thomas Keble, Bowden, Harrison, Mezies, Pusey, J. Miller, Copeland, and Williams also contributed some. The first *Tracts* were short, direct, and strong statements aimed at rousing people from fear or inaction. Newman argued against having a committee review the *Tracts* for publication because he thought that this would limit the spontaneity of the authors and make them overcautious.

The first three *Tracts*, written by Newman, appeared in the autumn and winter of 1833. They defended the authority of bishops and priests on the basis of its Apostolic origin. Newman made it clear that the sure foundation for the authority of priests could not be popular agreement or financial support, as it was in the Protestant churches, but rather Apostolic descent or succession. Christ's ministers in the Church were ordained by the power of the Holy Spirit through uninterrupted succession since the Apostles. Government should protect this sacred appointment. Newman challenged church ministers to act: "CHOOSE YOUR SIDE. To remain neuter [sic] much longer will be itself to take a part."[5]

Froude's ideas influenced Newman. On the one hand, Newman decried, as Froude did, the Erastian position of State control of the Church and, on the other, the religious Liberalism that threatened the Church from within. Palmer wrote *Tract* no. 15, titled "On the Apostolic Succession in the English Church," but fearing the strong tone of the *Tracts,* he wrote a letter to friends in which he disassociated himself from them. With some hesitation, Newman consented to suppressing the *Tracts*, but soon afterward, Froude convinced him of the need to continue publication

---

5 John Henry Newman and others, *Tracts for the Times* (London: J.G.F. & J. Rivington, 1833-34), No. 1, 4, available at: http://www.newmanreader. org/works/times/index.html. After this they will be cited *Tracts.*

and not to take part in the association proposed by Palmer.

At first the authorship of the *Tracts* and membership in the Movement was anonymous. Later on, the *Tracts* were printed with the initials of the author. Some of the *Tracts* were extracts from respected ecclesiastical writers or theologians such as Bishop William Beveridge, Bishop Thomas Wilson and Bishop John Cosin. Other *Tracts* were translations from early Church Fathers—Ignatius of Antioch, Justin, and Irenaeus.

Initially, collaborators such as Thomas Mozley, Bowden, or Archdeacon Froude distributed the *Tracts*. Other friends and Newman himself called upon clergy and traveled to their meetings to distribute the *Tracts*. Soon, in December, Newman consigned the distribution of the *Tracts* to Rivington's, a London bookseller. Newman also wrote to many friends and acquaintances to ask them to buy and distribute the *Tracts*.

The *Tracts* soon raised interest and gained support for the Movement, but Newman's four o'clock Sunday sermons at St. Mary's Church became the real voice and soul of the new movement. Through these sermons Newman drew out the moral and spiritual consequences derived from the doctrinal principles he put forth in writing. He created a spiritual atmosphere of renewal that naturally attracted men around himself and the Movement. Newman, a talented organizer, was also capable of getting into people's ways of thinking and enlisting their help. He inspired his young colleagues with high ideals and roused them from their comfortable and indulgent college lives to think about the Church's doctrine and mission.

From the outset, people objected that the *Tracts* favored

"Romanism," but the *Tracts* in fact maintained the Anglican teaching and tradition embodied in the official *Book of Common Prayer*. The advertisement or preface of a volume with the first forty-six *Tracts* expressed the intention of reviving the basic doctrines held by the English Divines of the seventeenth century regarding Apostolic Succession and the nature of the Holy Catholic Church.

Apostolic Succession was an important doctrine to defend, for it affirmed the uninterrupted link of bishops in the Church that began with the Apostles and thus Christ Himself. This link provided certainty that the Church's beliefs and practices were handed down by Jesus Christ Himself. The doctrine of Apostolic Succession holds that Christ gave authority to the Apostles to organize the Church and to sanction its practices. Newman found that the teaching of the visible Church, with its sacraments and rites as the channels of invisible grace, was present in Scripture, the early Christian Church and the Anglican Church.

The preface of the first volume of *Tracts* asserted that sinful men need to be taught "that the Sacraments, not preaching, are the sources of Divine Grace; that the Apostolic ministry had virtue in it which went out over the whole Church, when sought by the prayer of faith; that fellowship with it was a gift and privilege, as well as a duty . . ."[6] With a desire to stimulate renewal in the Anglican Church, he admitted that both Catholicism and Methodism served as "the foster mother of abandoned children."[7] Anglicans were deprived of sacramental grace in the Church. In this

---

6 *Tracts,* Vol. I, Advertisement, iv.
7 *Ibid.*

preface to the *Tracts*, Newman cataloged the abuses and grievances that the Movement sought to redress: "the neglect of daily service, the desecration of festivals, the Eucharist scantily administered, insubordination permitted in all ranks of the Church, orders and offices improperly developed . . ."[8]

Newman's criticism of the Roman Catholic Church voiced earlier during his Mediterranean travels continued on his return to Oxford. He seldom explained the reasons for his criticism other than to enumerate stereotypical complaints related to devotion to saints and Purgatory. Newman erred in his rash judgments of Catholicism and the harshness of his expressions. Part of these mistakes can be attributed to his youthful zeal for the Anglican Church.

For the most part, clergy and educated men welcomed the *Tracts*' call for religious and ecclesiastical renewal. Surprisingly, the Evangelical party's *Christian Observer* and later *The Record* criticized the *Tracts*. But this seemingly bad publicity actually provided the Movement with the attention of a wider public. Newman considered it a blessing, and the sale of the *Tracts* increased.

Perceval, one of those present at the Hadleigh meeting, wrote a systematic exposition of the nature and claims of the Anglican Church titled *The Churchman's Manual*. Unlike the *Tracts* it was a rather dry summary of Anglican teaching and of the English Church's position toward Roman Catholics and Dissenters. Its emphasis was on Apostolic Succession and the integrity of Christian doctrine found in the *Book of Common Prayer*. Perceval was

---

8 *Ibid.*

alarmed and angry that some of the persons in government who nominated the bishops, the successors of the Apostles, were schismatic, or non-Christian. As expected, the manuscript was well received by his High Church friends, but the Archbishop did not give it his endorsement.

At the end of 1834, Edward Pusey added strength to the Movement by fully adhering to it. Already from the start, he had shown favor toward the Movement and he had contributed a paper on the practice of fasting, which became *Tract 18*. Pusey was Regius Professor of Hebrew and Canon of Christ Church. He was a man of extensive theological learning, of whom Newman later wrote: "Dr. Pusey gave us at once a position and a name. Without him, we would have had no chance, especially at the early date of 1834, of making any serious resistance to the Liberal aggression."[9]

Rose had an untimely death in 1839. Newman wrote that Pusey became to the Movement all that Rose would have been had he lived longer, but unlike Rose, he had the indispensable close friendship with those who had begun the Movement. According to Newman, Pusey became the head and center of the Movement for people in different parts of England and gained recognition from other parties at the University. In effect, Pusey became the Movement's second head in close friendship with its original leader.

One of Pusey's notable contributions was the change in the character of the *Tracts*. Initially they lacked the proper form and completeness in the exposition of doctrine. In 1835, Pusey wrote three *Tracts* (67, 68, and 69) that formed

---

9 *Apo.*, 61.

a treatise on Baptism. After this treatise, the *Tracts* were either serious theological papers or a re-edition of *catenae* from Church Fathers or Anglican Divines. Pusey wished to give the Movement the theological foundations that it needed and made plans to promote college Fellows, prepare serious publications, and start a library of the writings of Church Fathers and English Divines. Shortly afterward in 1836, "The Library of Fathers of the Holy Catholic Church Anterior to the Division of the East and West" was announced with a dedication to the Archbishop of Canterbury; Pusey, Keble and Newman were the editors.

By 1834, the Oxford Movement had spread quickly in Oxford and parts of England. Through his *Tracts* and sermons at St. Mary's as well as his charismatic personality, Newman had become the primary leader. By 1835, Pusey became a second leader, giving the movement the weight of his prestige and scholarship. Thus Newman and Pusey each contributed his own gifts and strengths to the Movement. With the ability and determination of these leaders and their collaborators, the first years of the Movement would prove to be very successful.

CHAPTER 20

THE FIRST YEAR OF THE OXFORD MOVEMENT

THE twelve months after July 1834 were busy and productive ones for the new movement, even though the men who had assembled at Hadleigh never solidified as a group because of differences in their personal backgrounds and their views on the course of action to follow. In contrast to the overcautious nature of the older men, Froude and, in some degree, Keble agreed with Newman that "the field is before us," and we must "stir up the church."[1] In addition to writing tracts and editing those written by others, Newman helped to draft the clergy's address to the Archbishop. Newman also led the opposition to two bills: one bill would repeal Subscription to the Thirty-Nine Articles upon matriculation at Oxford, and another would oblige Anglican clergymen to be witnesses of non-Anglican marriages.

The Church suffered not only from its own internal disputes and from the ruling Whig Party but also from the Crown. Henry Phillpotts, the Bishop of Exeter, told the Lords that the king had broken his Coronation oath in which he pledged to defend the Church. Years later, the same bishop denied a clergyman, George Cornelius Gorham, appointment to a rectory because of the clergyman's

---

1 *LD,* Vol. IV, John Keble to JHN, (Aug. 5, 1833), 20.

unorthodox doctrine on baptismal regeneration. The Crown Court, instead of supporting the Church's doctrinal author- ity and discipline, decided against the bishop. In doing so, the Crown not only erred in doctrinal matters, but it also undermined the Church's legitimate authority.

In letters to friends, Newman pointed out the king's fail- ure to live up to his oath, and he asked them to stand up in defense of the Church. In an 1834 letter to the Editor of the *British Magazine*, he compared the usurpation of the power of the Church of England by the State with that of the Pope in the sixteenth century.[2] Just as the Act of Settlement secured people's liberties, the Coronation oath was meant to secure the Church's liberties. He went on to criticize the State's control of the Church and its disregard for her pro- tection. As examples, he referred to Henry VIII's creation of various dioceses and Elizabeth I's elimination of others. In 1833, another egregious action was mandated under the Irish Church Temporalities Act: the English Crown elimi- nated two archbishoprics and reduced eighteen Anglican dioceses in Ireland to ten.

In a letter to an Oxford graduate, Newman wrote that the Movement sought to rouse the clergy and assist the bishops in defending these principles: Apostolic Succes- sion and the proper relationship between Church and State. Newman wrote that only bishops and priests should conse- crate the Bread and Wine; he believed the *Book of Common Prayer* should not suffer heretical alterations nor should

---

2 *LD*, Vol. IV, JHN to the Editor of the *British Magazine* (January 3, 1834), 163.

the Church suffer the appointment of heretical bishops.[3] He wrote to Rose: "The Bishops must come forward; else it is intolerable that all sort of nonsense should be thrown out by Churchmen on the side of innovation, without the bishops saying a word, and yet it should not be allowed to us to agitate on the other side."[4]

Newman corresponded often in the first months of the Movement with his Trinity classmate John Bowden, by then a London resident. This trusted friend would fill, in many ways, the void left by Hurrell Froude, who remained for a very short time at Oxford. Bowden gave Newman personal encouragement, an open ear, advice, and the warmth of his family. Newman dedicated his second volume of published sermons to Bowden. This volume, prepared for publication at the end of 1835, consisted of sermons on saints' feast days. The tone of the correspondence between these two friends was spontaneous and confidential. In a letter to Bowden, Newman wrote that the Church should use the power of excommunication. "If I were a Bishop, the first thing I should do would be to excommunicate Lord Grey and half a dozen more, whose names it is almost a shame and a pollution for a Christian to mention."[5]

Newman grasped the weakness of the bishops and their need for assistance; for him, the Church was worse off than at the time of the Arian Heresy because it lacked bishops of the moral stature of Athanasius and Basil. However,

---

3 *LD* IV, JHN to Charles Portales Golightly (August 11, 1833), 28-29.
4 *LD*, Vol. IV, JHN to Hugh James Rose (January 1, 1834), 155-59; 156.
5 *LD*, Vol. IV, JHN to John William Bowden (August 20, 1833), 32.

out of reverence for the Episcopal office, he was determined not to act against the bishops or to offend them.
One of his friends warned him of the appearance of possible schism. Newman understood this concern and now
thought that their objectives should be presented as those
of a committee at Oxford rather than a national body, and
thus would not pose a challenge to the overall authority of
the bishops.

Newman told his friend Frederic Rogers that he was
still a Tory in favor of the monarchy and in favor of the
marriage between Church and State, but that if Thomas
Arnold, a Broad Church Anglican, were made a bishop,
he might reconsider his position. He was beginning to feel
like a radical and to see precedents in the exercise of popular acclaim, as at the time of St. Ambrose and St. Thomas
Becket.

The addresses by the clergy and by the laity were bold
and controversial measures that ran the risk of undermining the Episcopal discipline that the Tractarians sought
to uphold. Archdeacon Froude's friends told him that the
address was the most radical step ever taken by the clergy
of the Church of England. The clergy were bypassing
their bishops. Another friend who claimed to voice the
opinion of the clergy of his diocese wrote that the address
should have been made through the bishops of several
dioceses.

In November, Newman commented to Rose: "Palmer's Address is milk and water—however it affects three
points—it teaches the Clergy to reflect and combine—it
strengthens the Archbishop against his opponents; and it
brings out the Church as a body and power distinct from the

State."[6] The milk and water referred to Palmer's watering down of the draft that Newman had made.

Newman's emphasis on the failure of the Whig Party and Crown, and his deference for bishops, left a large part of the problem unaddressed, namely the hierarchy's failure to grasp and defend the true nature of the Church. The bishops were so identified with the Tories and associated with the temporal power of the State that they did not see themselves as successors of the Apostles. They were afraid to teach and to govern. For the most part, Newman was quiet about the bishops' errors and ignored the originating cause, the break with Apostolic Succession. Ironically, he grasped this principle, but he failed to recognize that the English Church's hierarchy had broken away from the Church when it had accepted the model of a church dominated by the king.

In a January 1834 letter to the Editor of the *British Magazine,* Newman actually criticized the position of the Bishop of Ferns who advocated submission of the English Church to the Pope.[7] Newman objected that the tyrannical acts of King Henry VIII and Queen Elizabeth I constituted neither precedents for posterity nor a denial of their religious authority. Returning to the king's Coronation oath, he claimed that the king of England was still, or should still be, Defender of the Faith and Protector of the Church. Despite this theory or desire, Newman was aware that reality was different. In a series of papers, "The Church of the Fathers," also

---

6 *LD,* Vol. IV, JHN to James Hugh Rose (November 23, 1833), 120-122; 122.

7 *LD,* Vol. IV, JHN to the Editor of the *British Magazine* (January 3, 1834), 163-66; 163.

published in the *British Magazine*, Newman pointed out that the early Church "threw itself on the people." That is, the power of the Church did not depend on the ruling class. It was now apparent that the English Crown and aristocracy had deserted the Church, so the Church must depend on the people. Interestingly, this situation of the English Church forced Newman to consider the role of the laity in the first centuries of Christianity and begin to understand that role. Years later, he vindicated the laity's role as witnesses of Apostolic Doctrine, giving rise to the "sensus fidelium," a concept which he would explain in an essay entitled "On Consulting the Faithful in Matters of Doctrine."[8] Nonetheless, Newman objected to a strict separation of Church and State.

Aspiring to have greater influence through a university post, Newman thought of standing for the Moral Philosophy professorship, vacant every five years. He believed that he had a good chance of gaining it, but in the end, Renn D. Hampden was elected. Newman, however, was elected Dean for Oriel College and continued closely engaged in university life and politics. He had to face these challenges without Froude, his closest friend and aide. In November of 1833, Froude had traveled to Barbados seeking to recover from pulmonary tuberculosis. In 1834, after the death of the university chancellor, Newman attempted to have the Archbishop of Canterbury nominated for the position,

---

8 John Henry Newman, "On Consulting the Faithful in Matters of Doctrine," in *The Rambler*, July 1859, 189-230, available at: http://www.newmanreader.org/works/rambler/index.html.

but the Duke of Wellington was chosen instead and was appointed by the Crown.

In letters to his supporters, Newman encouraged them to be temperate in their language and to unite the clergy in their common cause, but always to be supportive of the bishops. He was the first to follow his own advice with respect to the clergy and the bishops. With the government, on the other hand, his patience and respect were spent. To a potential supporter he wrote: "We groan under the heterogeneous un-ecclesiastical Parliament, and we will not submit to its dictation."[9] Among those endorsing the Movement were some Archdeacons, the Vice-Chancellor of Cambridge, many rectors, and a few nobles. He hoped to garner the backing of at least one bishop, but this did not happen.

During this period, Newman wrote a total of six letters to *The Record* signed "*A Churchman.*" In the second one, he wrote that Rome is the "pillar and ground of error."[10] He argued that the increase in Papists in England was due to the laxity in Church discipline. The Church, which, according to St. Paul, is the "pillar and ground of truth," should retain the good elements of the Roman Catholic system and remove the errors. He urged that "popery" should be driven out through a war of living holy lives and teaching the truth. Newman's severe attack was as sincere as it was mistaken. Only the first five letters were published because *The Record* began to attack the *Tracts* and the teaching of Apostolic Succession as the Church's foundation.

---

9 *LD,* Vol. IV, JHN to Charles Girdlestone (November 1, 1833), 79-80; 79.

10 *LD* IV, JHN to the Editor of *The Record* (November 14, 1833), 102.

While directing the Movement, Newman managed to give attention to other related projects. The *Lyra* came out in September; the *Church Fathers* series started in October; and his first book, *The Arians of the Fourth Century,* completed in 1832, was finally published on November 5, 1834. Still, Newman's primary preoccupation was to rouse the clergy and bishops, especially the Archbishop of Canterbury. Considering the bishops' apparent indifference in the face of abuses by the Crown and the ruling Whig Party, he wrote Rose that the members of the Church were "as sheep without shepherds."[11]

In the essays that he published in the *British Magazine* and *The Record,* he showed respect to the bishops, but exposed the laxity of Church discipline and the inaction of the Crown. In these essays, Newman also encouraged the educated laity to protest against disregard for early Christian doctrines. Newman was very concerned by the Church's situation, yet he was confident in God's Providence. In January 1834, the young Anglican clergyman concluded a letter to the Editor of the *British Magazine* with the conviction that the Church would overcome her enemies; the gates of Hell would not prevail against her. He ventured to say that the fight was not one to be decided in 1834, or even in one century; it was for their posterity 500 years from then: "We are fighting the battle of 2334."[12]

---

11 *LD,* Vol. IV, JHN to Hugh James Rose (January 1, 1834), 155-59; 155-56.

12 *LD,* Vol. IV, JHN to the Editor of the *British Magazine* (January 3, 1834), 163-66; 166.

CHAPTER 21

A LEADER AT OXFORD

IN the year 1834, the government discussed bills concerning two controversial subjects: university degrees
and marriages of Dissenters. The events that took place
led to heated debates in a society that was still a confessional state. In both cases, Newman voiced his opinions
firmly and became a leading figure in the debates at Oxford
University.

Religious pluralism had been a cause of social and
political tension and violence since the sixteenth-century
breakdown of religious cohesion in England. A rise in the
numbers of Christians belonging to churches other than
the Anglican Church now presented a growing problem in
admission to higher education and a serious problem for
the marriage of Nonconformists and Catholics. Persons
who were not Anglicans were deprived of obtaining university degrees and were obliged to marry before an Anglican clergyman.

In a state in which the Establishment involved a strong
alliance between State and Church, higher education had
been the domain of the religious and political institutions.
Oxford and Cambridge had originated as schools of Roman
Catholic theology, dating back to the twelfth and thirteenth
centuries. Nevertheless, since the English Reformation,
they had become the realm of the Anglican Church and

the locus of the religious and intellectual formation of its clergy.

Members of religious bodies other than the Anglican Church were not admitted for studies at Oxford. At Cambridge, they were allowed to study, but the university did not confer degrees on them unless they subscribed to the *Thirty-Nine Articles* of the Anglican Church. These injustices led to the formulation of the Dissenters University Relief Bill. This proposed legislation came on the heels of the 1828 repeal of the Test and Corporation Acts, laws that had excluded Dissenters from municipal offices, and of the Catholic Emancipation Act of 1829.

Religious tests or Subscription to the *Thirty-Nine Articles* for matriculation at Oxford would constitute reprehensible religious discrimination today. It is important, however, to note the historical context in which these religious tests were administered and the reason for their existence. Newman opposed a change in the statutes that would allow admission to Nonconformists and Catholics to Oxford because he considered that this change would harm an Anglican institution with legitimate rights.

Newman argued that non-Anglican students would not participate in prescribed chapel worship and would therefore give a bad example to others. In addition, he thought that Dissenting students would demand Dissenting Tutors to fill the ranks of the university and thus alter the composition of the faculty. The university and its Tutors would not be able to fulfill their role in the religious formation of their students.

Newman's position seems unjust in today's pluralist society that all too readily sacrifices religion to other goals or that seeks religious ecumenism by accepting the least common denominator. Newman contended that Oxford had the prerogative of a private religious institution, which seeks the intellectual and religious training of its members, and even more, its future leaders. Newman conceived the role of the Tutor as both a religious and an intellectual one. Thus, admission of religious pluralism would mean the abrogation of one of the university's primary missions.

Agitation over the admission of Dissenters to Oxford became strong in March of 1834. In April, Newman prepared and circulated a declaration against the admission of Dissenters. By May 2, the number of supporters had risen to 1800, and Heads of Houses and Proctors also added their names. Newman wrote to Bowden that recusants among the Tutors came around to their side, and all but two signed, increasing the number of Tutors to 90 or 92.

Newman first took a legal approach to the debate. In a letter to the editor of *The Standard,* he argued that the Vice-Chancellor, the Heads, and each Tutor had an oath to keep the university statutes, which forbade Dissenters. The repeal of the oath would be a violation of the university statutes. Only Convocation could alter the statutes, but Convocation would not alter it because the Masters of Arts would not agree to such a change; if they did, the university would lose its moral influence over the students. To repeal its statutes would be to abrogate its corporate privileges and its power of self-legislation. Alternatively, the government might try to repeal its charter, but the country would not stand for this. In a second letter to *The Standard,* dated May 1, Newman inquired: "Does Parliament have the power to legislate over this university?"[1] He continued that, even if the statutes were repealed, the officers of the university had received a trust from its members. Parliament could not absolve the oath that they had made. The declaration objected to the separation of religion from the university and the relinquishing of the idea of Christian education. Newman asserted that religion should not be reduced to the vague acceptance of many religious creeds. In effect, the declaration reaffirmed the belief that the faculty of the University of Oxford had the duty of providing Christian education, and this was only possible by holding uniformity of faith. Newman realized the injustice caused to other Christians outside of the Anglican Church who were excluded from the universities, yet he did not see how Oxford University could yield in this matter to the detriment of the Anglican Church. Mandatory Subscription seemed safe until August of 1834 when Renn Dickson Hampden, Principal of St. Mary's Hall at Oxford, came out with a pamphlet titled "Observations on Religious Dissent," advocating the removal of religious tests at the university.

For a few weeks, there was growing tension in expectation of the examination of this question by the Heads of Houses. In November, the Heads decided, by a majority of one vote, to send a measure to Convocation of Masters of Arts at Oxford regarding the removal of Mandatory Subscription to the *Articles* at matriculation. Then, at Hampden's prompting, the idea of replacing the oath with a declaration of conformity began to circulate at Oxford.

---

1 *LD*, Vol. IV, JHN to the Editor of *The Standard* (May 1, 1834), 245-47; 246.

By this declaration, students would manifest their conformity with the worship and discipline of Oxford. Keble and Pusey, in part stirred by their friend, strongly opposed this proposal and wrote against it. William Sewell of Exeter College was another adamant opponent. On Saturday, November 15, 1834, Pusey printed an essay, "Twenty-three questions, without title, addressed to Members of Convocation," signed "A Bachelor of Divinity," in which he argued against Hampden's proposal. Only two days later, upon further consideration, the Board of Heads gave up the proposed measure.

The controversy raged on with pamphlets from both sides. Edward Hawkins, Provost of Oriel, published anonymously a pamphlet in support of Hampden while Henry Wilberforce, coached by Newman, wrote a pamphlet which was a stinging attack on Hampden. Wilberforce's pamphlet was also published anonymously, but Hampden, who was greatly annoyed by its claims, discovered the identity of the intellectual author. When Newman edited a collection of the pamphlets against Hampden, the latter wrote an enraged letter to Newman accusing him of "dissimulation, falsehood and dark malignity."[2] Newman wrote to his friend Rickards that Hampden was "like a red hot iron" and asked Rickards's help in showing that Hampden was one of the main troublemakers.

Given the overtly secularized present-day universities, it is hard for the modern mind to make sense of this struggle at Oxford. Nevertheless, Oxford was not the equivalent of

---

2 *LD*, Vol. V, Renn Dickson Hampden to JHN (June 23, 1835), 83-85; 84.

a contemporary State university; it was a private corporation with a religious origin and a strong religious affiliation
(first Roman Catholic, then Anglican). As with other institutions, it was under the Crown, which appointed the chancellor and some of its professors. At that time, the English
Church and State were still closely intertwined, as was evident by the appointment of bishops by the Cabinet and by
the standing membership of some bishops in the House of
Lords. In sum, the university was a confessional university
belonging to the Established State-Church. In this context,
the religious tests were not an injustice, but a prerogative or
right of a religious institution that wished to ensure adherence to a creed and moral code.

During this period of time, those in favor of the bill
sought to secularize the university by an act of law, but
the secularization was a process that would happen over a
period of many years before a law would actually sanction
it.[3] In fact, the conservatives at the university did not wish
to admit Dissenters, precisely in order to avoid the secularization of the university. If passed, the bill would disestab-
lish the Anglican Church from the center where its leaders
were formed, thus endorsing the conclusion that doctrinal
truths could not be known with certainty among Christians.
Sewell summarized the goal of the bill: "Education without Religion; and Religion without distinction. In plain and
simple words, No Christianity."[4] Newman could not toler-
ate this liberal view of truth.

---

3 *The Imperial Intellect: A Study of Newman's Educational Ideal*,
Dwight Culler (New Haven: Yale University Press, 1955), 101-15.
    4 *Ibid.*, 108.

In May of 1835, Convocation of the Masters in Arts at Oxford heavily defeated Hampden's proposition by a vote of 459 to 57. From Oriel, of the 38 nonresidents to come, 37 sided with the *Tractarians*. Despite this opposition at Oxford University, in July 1835 the House of Commons passed a bill removing the religious tests by a vote of 164 to 75. However, later that same month, the House of Lords threw out the new bill. Students continued to subscribe to the *Thirty-Nine Articles* for matriculation and a Bachelor of Arts degree until the Oxford University Bill of 1854. Nonetheless, even then Subscription to the *Articles* continued to be a requirement for obtaining a Master of Arts degree, voting in Convocation, and being admitted to Fellowships, until the 1871 University Tests Acts.

Newman's role in the Oxford controversy revealed his capacity for leadership and commitment to the mission of the university, and it exemplified his position on the proper relationship of the Church and State. The English State had severed ties with the Roman papacy and established a national Church. Newman thought that the State's role should be the protection of this Church, not its domination. The Church was not subservient to the State in doctrinal, liturgical, or disciplinary matters, which were received through Apostolic Succession. However, a large part of both medieval and modern English history records the same usurpation of Church rights and property by the State.

In the first year of the Movement, its members engaged in a second major battle: opposition to a Dissenter's Marriage Bill proposed by Lord John Russell in the House of Commons in March 1834. Lord Russell, a champion against many social injustices, was one of the men responsible for the repeal of the Tests and Corporation Act, and for the Reform Act of 1832. The Marriage Bill sought to redress domestic and religious grievances against Roman Catholics and Protestants outside the Anglican Church. For everyone, Anglican and non-Anglican alike, marriage required the publication of banns to be posted outside of an Anglican church. The non-Anglicans had to agree to a religious ritual that they did not accept.

At this time in England, there was no civil registry for marriages or a system of civil magistrates to act as witnesses. Neither was there a civil registry for recording births. People were bound to the Anglican Church's registry for wedding and baptismal records. Since there was no civil registry for births, the recognition of a birth required Baptism by Anglican clergymen, to which some parents objected. The Anglican Church also regulated Christian burial in cemeteries. The situation presented anomalies and imposed difficulties for Dissenters and Anglicans. For Nonconformists and Catholics, it was a religious imposition and a denial of religious freedom. For Anglican clergymen, it meant turning religious ceremonies into a sort of legal transaction. It also obliged clergymen to act against their conscience by sometimes administering sacraments to unbelievers.

Nonetheless, Newman drafted a declaration against the bill in which he argued that such a bill would oblige clergymen to become mere instruments for the State to prevent clandestine marriages. Clergymen would be forced to degrade their office by going against the Church's discipline. Upon request, Dissenters would have the right to be married by any clergyman. Bishops would therefore have to approve Dissenting clergymen. The declaration petitioned the House of Commons that Anglican clergy not be required to sanction directly or indirectly the union of Dissenters.

Newman held that the bill would force a clergyman to act against his own conscience. He confided to his friend Henry Wilberforce:

> To my mind it is not a point for the Bishop to determine, but of conscience. The Bishop cannot give me license to derogate from his authority—he has not self-destructive power—to uphold him and the Church is a plain and Christian duty. Again I will not call that Holy Matrimony which may be but a licensed concubinage.[5]

In the midst of this debate, Newman was providentially drawn into a difficult and unexpected pastoral situation that would turn out to be a sort of test case for the Marriage Relief Bill. Miss Jubber, a young unbaptized woman, asked Newman to officiate at her marriage. Because she was not baptized, Newman refused to officiate at her wedding. All the same, another clergyman married the young woman that very day. The Jubber Affair soon made it to the newspapers, and based on accounts by Miss Jubber's father, Newman was criticized for rudeness and condescension. In a characteristic manner, he wrote to the papers in his own defense.

A long time before this event, both Isaac Williams, Newman's curate, and Newman himself had spoken with the Jubber family about the children's Baptism. Nothing came of it because they were Baptists who defer Baptism to a later age. A year later, when Miss Jubber appeared asking to be married, the issue resurfaced. After Newman's

---

5 *LD,* Vol. IV, JHN to H. Wilberforce (March 29, 1834), 221-22.

refusal to officiate for doctrinal reasons, Mr. Copley, her Baptist minister, complained to the Bishop of Oxford, who sent a message to Newman reprimanding him for not having "solemnized" the marriage of the unbaptized woman and instructing him to do so in any future case.

Although Newman had not done anything to bring the question of marriage of Dissenters by Anglican clergymen to a crisis, this case epitomized his concern. The Marriage Bill forced men's consciences to act against the formularies of the Church. Many, including his mother, Keble, and Pusey supported Newman. He wrote to his sister Harriet that he was happy to have acted as he did. He hoped that the Jubber Affair would underscore the necessity of Baptism, showing that a clergyman could act against the law for a proper reason. To Henry Wilberforce, he put it in other terms; the case was a reminder of two principles: Baptism is essential, and the Church is above unjust civil laws.

In the same letter to Wilberforce, he tried to defend his actions from another point of view by appealing to English law. From his perspective of a moderate theocracy he argued that only those who were baptized members of the Established Anglican Church were British subjects, and therefore Miss Jubber was not truly a British subject. Despite Newman's reasoning and faithfulness to religious principles, he was out of touch with the *de facto* religious plurality of England. His theory of Church and State was no longer practical without producing significant injustice to Dissenters and Roman Catholics. He was justified in not acting against conscience in the Jubber case, but he was wrong in opposing measures to ensure equal freedom of conscience for others.

The opposition to the Marriage Bill by Newman and the Tractarians was unable to stop the civil recognition of marriages by non-Anglicans. In 1836, Lord Russell proposed two bills: one establishing a general registry for all births, marriages, and deaths, and another advancing comprehensive legislation on marriage. The Marriage Bill was passed into act. It did not alter the marriage ceremony for a member of the Anglican Church except for the addition of civil registry. The practice of marriage banns would continue unless a party wished to notify a registrar instead of the parish clerk. For Dissenters, after the proper notification of the marriage to a registrar, marriage would be "solemnized" in the chapel of the couple's choice. The few Dissenters who did not want a religious ceremony would be allowed to enter into a civil marriage contract before a registrar. This comprehensive act thus met the varied needs of the population, while still respecting the religious nature and rights of various Christian denominations.

Newman's defense of ecclesiastical practice and sacramental life was not in vain. Although the legislation that he opposed passed into law, the defense that he had led encouraged Anglicans to consider the sacramental nature of marriage and the Church's sacramental discipline. In addition to this political activity, he was occupied with pastoral work and writing. The young Oxford vicar also supported societies that worked in mission countries to spread the Christian faith by providing for the endowment of clergy, publication of Bibles, and religious instruction.

Various societies for the promotion of the Christian faith were founded in England at the end of the seventeenth century and throughout the eighteenth century. Among these were the Society for the Promotion of the Gospel (SPG) and the Christian Missionary Society (CMS) for Africa and the East. John Venn, rector of Clapham, and a number of laymen founded the CMS in 1779. Almost a century earlier, in 1698, four Anglican laymen and one clergyman founded the Society for the Promotion of Christian Knowledge (SPCK) to combat religious ignorance, especially through the publication and distribution of Christian literature.

In the 1830s, the SPCK lost its orthodox religious identity and leadership. Newman was worried by the disregard of many of its members for Episcopal authority and Creeds, in particular the belief in baptismal regeneration. Newman did not like the views of the Society's chairman, Christopher Bethell, Bishop of Bangor, and he disagreed with another of its influential figures, Charles J. Blomfield, Bishop of London. During the years 1834 and 1835, Newman voiced concern to his friends about the eclectic doctrinal positions held by the SPCK. He wrote to his friend R. F. Wilson that the SPCK is "the most miserable of our miseries . . . the Evangelicals have taken advantage of the difficulties of the Church to push; but we do not mean to be beaten."[6] At an April 1834 meeting in London, he and his friends in vain tried to replace some board members, including Bishop Blomfield and James E. Tyler, Rector of St. Giles and once Dean of Oriel College.

Newman also belonged to another society, The British and Foreign Bible Society, commonly known as the Bible Society, which was founded in 1804. He had subscribed to it in May 1824, and attended its meetings, but he withdrew

---

6 *LD,* Vol. IV, JHN to R. F. Wilson (March 31, 1834), 257.

from it in June of 1830. He explained to Simeon Lloyd Pope:

> The Society recognizes no *Church principles* on which the
> friends of the Church who join can fall back . . . On the
> contrary, *as a fact*, I do believe it MAKES CHURCHMEN
> LIBERALS—it makes them undervalue the guilt of schism—
> it makes them feel a wish to conciliate Dissenters at the
> expense of truth.[7]

Newman thought that, by joining the Society, he would
act against its tendency and evils, but he later concluded
that men were instead drawn to them.

During the summer months, Newman maintained a significant amount of activity. In August of 1835, he spent a
week of his vacation visiting various friends: the Kebles at
Bisley, the Bowdens in London, and Rogers in Blackheath.
During this time, he read a great deal about the history of
Convocation of the Province of Canterbury and wrote three
articles on the subject for the *British Magazine*. Convocation was the meeting of all the bishops and representatives
from the clergy with the purpose of discussing religious
matters or presenting grievances to the king or Parliament.
At the time Newman wrote, Convocation had not convened
for about one hundred and twenty years.

On vacation, Newman included a visit to the home of his
youth at Alton in Hampshire. He recalled family incidents
and remembered his father's pride when he gained a scholarship at Trinity. He also read various books, including
Charles Butler's *The Book of the Roman Catholic Church*,
Herbert Marsh's *A Comparative View of the Churches of*

---

7 *LD,* Vol. II, JHN to Simeon Lloyd Pope (August 15, 1830), 264-65,
265.

England and Rome, and George S. Faber's *Difficulties of Romanism.* After reading these books, Newman thought that it would be impossible to unite with Rome, but he confided to Jemima that he was willing to go a long way with Catholics and Evangelicals. Newman told his sister that he was developing a comprehensive system. During July and August, at the suggestion of Bowden that he forestall the accusation of "popery," he published two *Tracts* on the Anglican *Via Media.*

After almost a year and half since the start of the Movement, a great deal had been accomplished to delineate its purpose and to influence clergymen and others throughout the country. The defeat of the University Dissenter's Bill was, in part, a reflection of the Movement's capacity to unite and rally the university community at Oxford in defense of the Anglican Church and its mission. Newman had united a core group of Tutors and Fellows at Oxford, who, together with friends in various cities, were fully committed to continue the work begun in July 1833. Newman had gained admiration for his preaching and exercised moral leadership in university life and politics. Although his religious views and prejudices toward Roman Catholicism remained overall the same during this period, he finally began to study the doctrinal claims of the Roman Church. Newman believed that the Anglican Church was a *Via Media* between Protestantism and Roman Catholicism, but he continued to search for religious truth concerning the nature of the Church and its relation with the State.

CHAPTER 22

SEEKING A MIDDLE GROUND OR *VIA MEDIA*

FOR Newman, the Oxford Movement was a war against the government and various Church parties over Church Principles. After an initial declaration of principles, Newman tried to clarify in his mind what the Anglican Church was, or should be. In order to do so, he was forced to distinguish the Anglican Church from what he called the abuses of the Church of Rome and the Protestant churches. In this new stage of the war, he unwittingly began to examine some of the claims made by Rome more seriously and to adopt some Catholic practices. At the end of June 1834, Newman began daily morning services at St. Mary's and expressed his desire to start observing saints' feasts. By doing so, he was putting into effect the liturgical practice of the Church before the English Reformation. He was, however, conscious of the charge of Romanism. His friends, especially Bowden, warned him of this Catholic appearance and encouraged him to write in his own defense. Newman held three main objections to the Roman Catholic Church: his perception of its doctrine of Transubstantiation, devotion to saints, and Purgatory.

In July and August 1834, Newman wrote two *Tracts* on the *Via Media* in which he justified the *Thirty-Nine Articles* as a defense against doctrinal and liturgical additions and other abuses by Rome. Newman then tried to delineate and justify a system that he thought lay between the Roman Catholic and Protestant excesses. Newman believed that the Church of England constituted a *Via Media,* which was based on Scripture and the teaching of Antiquity, between the corrupt Roman Church, which appealed to its own infallibility, and Protestantism, which appealed to private judgment.

In 1835, Newman continued correspondence that he had begun late in 1834 with Abbé Jean-Nicholas Jager, a French priest. Jager was a professor of theology and chair of Ecclesiastical History in the Faculty of Theology at the University of Paris. This exchange of letters started in 1834 as a debate between Benjamin Harrison and Jager in the periodical *L'Univers.* Harrison was a Hebrew scholar and author of some of the *Tracts of the Times.* The debate initially centered on the application of the canon of Vincent of Lerins as a rule of faith by Anglicans and Roman Catholics. In the fifth century, Vincent had proposed Tradition as a rule of faith, with Tradition understood as that which was held always, everywhere, and by everyone *(quod semper, quod ubique, ab omnibus).*

After some correspondence between Jager and Harrison, the latter pressed Newman to take up the debate. Newman wrote two letters; the first was printed in various installments in *L'Univers:* on December 25, 1834, and on January 28 and 29, 1835. In the first one, Newman explained his understanding of the relationship between Scripture and Tradition.[1] According to him, Anglicans hold Scripture as

---

1 *John Henry Newman and the Abbé Jager: A Controversy on Scripture*

the ultimate basis of proof and appeal for fundamental doctrines (those necessary for Church communion).[2]

Newman claimed that Roman Catholics allow for a certain use of Tradition that did not appeal to Scripture. He wrote that Robert Bellarmine, the sixteenth-century Roman Catholic theologian, held that Scripture does not measure everything. The Council of Trent spoke of the Tradition by which the Church receives the doctrine of Transubstantiation. Newman pointed out two other examples from Trent: the offering of Mass for the souls in Purgatory, and the decree concerning indulgences. All these doctrines are explained in terms of Tradition divinely handed down, not in terms of Scripture texts.

At the root of the debate were various questions: What are the fundamental doctrines one must believe for salvation? What are the fundamental doctrines one must believe for communion with the Church? Moreover, what are the criteria used to ascertain which doctrine is fundamental? He claimed Anglicans believe that fundamental doctrines must be found in Scripture, the only exception being the doctrine about the canon, or the list of the New Testament books.[3] For him, this doctrine was the only one legitimately established by the Church's Tradition. Thus with one sweep of the pen, Newman was granting a major exception to his theory yet denying any further role to the Church in establishing fundamental doctrines.

Newman underestimated the intellectual capacity of the

---

and Tradition, 1834-1835, ed. Louis Allen (London: Oxford University Press, 1975), 33-52.

2 *Ibid.*, 35.

3 *Ibid.,* 48.

French priest. He had entered the controversy to dispel any suggestion of weakness on the part of Anglicans. In addition, he saw this correspondence as a beneficial opportunity to work out his own beliefs and especially to show that he was not a papist. In the course of the debate, and during the lectures, Newman began to reach an important understanding of the development of doctrine, which would lead to his eventual acceptance of Roman Catholic belief in Tradition.

In his first reply to Jager, he wrote that Anglican and Roman Catholics agree that the Church is the keeper and teacher of doctrine, but they disagree about the Church's authority over doctrine. "We believe that the fundamentals admit of no increase. Christ's doctrine is the foundation: Christ, the Trinity as confessed in the baptismal form."[4] Newman wrote that Anglicans believe that the Church has the power to develop its fundamental Creed into *Articles* of religion according to times and circumstances. These *Articles* are necessary for communion only, not for salvation. He argued that, at Trent, the Church of Rome imposed belief in some doctrines as necessary for salvation; it was "adding to the fundamentals of faith."[5]

Concerning ecclesiastical practice, Newman wrote that he accepted the doctrine and practice of infant Baptism handed down by ecclesiastical tradition, but not as a doctrine necessary for salvation because this teaching was not found in Scripture. In writing this, he contradicted himself because the Baptism of children was precisely for the sake of their salvation.

---

4 *Ibid.*, 39.
5 *Ibid.*, 41.

An example that he offered of legitimate development of doctrine is the early Church's reasoning about the Procession of the Holy Spirit, which was based on Scripture. He affirmed that when the whole Church had made these declarations in early times, they held great weight. Newman wrote to Jager that Anglicans give particular weight to the first four General councils; these are the rule of orthodoxy against heresy.[6] As the distance in time from the Apostles becomes greater and there are more external circumstances, such as political ones, the subjects debated have a less fundamental character and should not be imposed on any as terms of communion. According to Newman, only the contents of the Apostles' Creed are fundamental for Church communion.

Jager replied with three long letters to Newman's first letter. He asked Newman where he found the principle that Scripture contains all things necessary for salvation, and denied his claim that this principle was supported by Vincent's rule. In fact, in his famous work, the *Commonitorium,* Vincent had held that Scripture is insufficient for judging and putting an end to a dispute about the faith, because it can be mutilated.[7] For Vincent, the Tradition of the Church, comprised by the teaching of the Fathers and Church doctrine contained in Creeds and councils, is essential.

Jager placed into question the Protestant's certainty of faith, and he defended the infallibility of that of Roman

---

6 *Ibid.,* 40.

7 Vincent of Lerins, *Commonitorium,* XXVIII, available at: http://www.fordham.edu/halsall/ancient/434lerins-canon.html.

Catholics. He did this by indicating how Church councils saw themselves as teaching what had always been
professed. He adduced Scripture's promise of assistance
to Peter and to the Church. In addition, the French priest
pointed out how the Fathers calmly affirm the Church's
authority, although they do not refer explicitly to it as a
dogma. According to Jager, the Fathers of the first centuries declared Catholic doctrine necessary for salvation.

Jager argued that Tradition and Catholic doctrine are
necessary for the correct interpretation of Scripture.[8] He
explained that Christ gave us a body of teaching necessary
for our salvation, but since disputes of faith are inevitable,
an infallible voice is needed: the voice of the Church's
authority. Scripture alone is insufficient because it is subject to so many interpretations. The interpretation of the
Fathers is inadequate because it requires a vast amount of
reading.

In the last of a series of replies to Newman, Jager
refuted the Reformation's distinction between fundamental and nonfundamental doctrine.[9] This notion of a system
of nonfundamental doctrines was, in itself, an innovation
that even heretics had not used in the past. The Scriptures
require accepting all of Christ's commands and maintaining the unity of faith. Jager asked if anything could be more
exclusive of the idea of nonfundamental errors than Christ's
commands. He argued that the system of nonfundamentals
implies that the Church before the sixteenth century was
mistaken in excluding heretics, and did not understand the

---

8 *John Henry Newman and the Abbé Jager,* 58.
9 *Ibid.,* 54.

Creed because it expelled people who did not hold to so-called nonfundamental doctrines. Jager pointed out that, in France, sects have reduced the fundamental doctrines to Redemption only, considering all other doctrines to be non-fundamental doctrines.

Lastly, in refutation of assertions by Blanco White, Jager explained that Roman Catholics believe that Tradition and Scripture are in perfect harmony, even though apparent contradictions exist. Furthermore, the Church of Rome never claimed Tradition to be superior.

Newman spent a long time writing a draft of a second letter to Jager, and discussed it with Froude, who pointed out various mistakes. Writing as if he were Jager, Froude told Newman: "The Fathers say that the Holy Eucharist is a tradition; that it is fundamental."[10] He challenged Newman to "prove that I misrepresent them, and prove that they state doctrines, not in Scripture, as authoritative."[11] Part of Newman's letter was published in two sections by *Le Moniteur de la religion*, between December 1835 and February 1836.

The debate with Jager forced Newman to think seriously about the nature of Tradition and the Church's authority and to discuss this with Froude. Newman later admitted that the correspondence with Jager resulted in a series of lectures that he gave during 1836 at St. Mary's. As the lectures progressed, some young adherents to the Movement were made; one of these was William George Ward, whose

---

10 *LD*, Vol. V, Richard Hurrell Froude to JHN (July 30, 1835), 116-18; 116.

11 *Ibid.*, 116.

son, Wilfred Philip Ward, and granddaughter, Maisie Ward, later became biographers of Newman. The lectures on Romanism, as Newman called them, were published in 1837 under the title of *Lectures on the Prophetical Office of the Church Viewed Relatively to Romanism and Popular Protestantism*. He dedicated the volume to Martin Routh of Magdalen College, who was a patristic scholar and representative of the Anglo-Catholic Tradition of the English Church. Routh, who lived to his hundredth year, referred to Newman as "that clever young gentleman of Oriel."

In December 1835, Nicholas Wiseman gave a series of well-attended public lectures in London on the Catholic Church. In these, he referred to Newman's book on the Arians to argue that the Christian faith was taught in the Church by oral Tradition, not by the Bible.[12] Newman reviewed these lectures in the October 1836 issue of the *British Critic.* Years later, Newman wrote that Wiseman's lectures had been another impetus for the publication of his own *Lectures on the Prophetical Office*, in which he indirectly answers Wiseman.[13]

Newman considered that the Anglican Church respected the Antiquity without sacrificing the authority of Sacred Scripture. It was a *Via Media* between Roman Catholicism and Protestantism. Thomas Sharkey, who worked for Thomas Cromwell under Henry VIII, had used the term *Via Media* already in 1533. In the midst of the early struggle between Roman Catholic and Lutheran parties in

---

12 Ian Ker, *John Henry Newman* (Oxford: Oxford University Press, 1988), 129, 135.

13 *Apo.,* 64.

the Anglican Church, Sharkey made a plea for a middle ground in the observance of religious rites and traditions. A middle ground was not reached, although some advocated giving up liturgical and ascetical practices in order to reach a peaceful coexistence. Over the next three centuries, religious bodies would seek the support of the government to extend their own practices.

In the introduction to the lectures, Newman presented the most likely objections to his affirmation of a *Via Media*. The first objection was that a *Via Media* was unreal, an illusion; second, that the Church of England, despite its episcopacy, was essentially Protestant; third, that the Church of England did not have an intellectual basis and was, in fact, a department of the State.

Newman held Antiquity as the measure of orthodoxy and considered that it was represented by the Anglo-Catholic doctrine and the practices of the Anglican Church. At that time, he thought that the Anglican Church was the nearest approximation to the primitive Church of Ignatius and Polycarp, both disciples of the Apostle John. In the first lecture, Newman claimed that Rome retains the principle of true Catholicism, but perverted, while popular Protestantism lacked the principle. He considered the errors of both positions. In the next lectures, he argued that the Roman Church must be held accountable for many instances of abuse of political power. An example of perceived abuse was Catholic support for Irish politicians like O'Connell.

Newman was aware of problems in the appeal to Antiquity. The voluminous nature of the Fathers' writings made them an impracticable guide for ordinary men who wished to know Christian doctrine. Newman recognized the problem of sorting out what was essential in the large mass of patristic teaching, and he thought the answer lay in the Creeds, the *Book of Common Prayer*, and Church formularies.[14] In other words, Antiquity, as a test of orthodoxy, was contained in the Church's Creeds and liturgy. The Latitudinarians, or Broad Churchmen, instead had given up historical tradition as a truth-bearer and had retained a vague allegiance to the Bible as conferring a Christian mind.

These lectures marked an important point in Newman's life because in them, he examined Catholic claims in a more serious manner. He identified objections that he saw in Roman Catholicism and began to notice the weakness of his own position. In the years that followed he realized that his interpretation of the Church Fathers was tainted by the Anglican theologians, Laud, Taylor, and Leslie. In an 1877 re-edition of the lectures he admitted, with a certain shame, his derogatory use of the word "Romanists" and his vague charges and scornful name-calling. Newman granted that two objections made by Anglican Divines were worthy of consideration: one being the difference in teaching, liturgy, and ecclesiastical government between the Primitive Church and the Roman Catholic Church, and the other being the difference in the Roman Catholic Church between its formal teaching and popular manifestations, such as sermons and addresses by ecclesiastics. Newman addressed at length the first set of difficulties in his book *On the Development of Christian Doctrine*, which he finished within days before entering into full communion with the Roman Catholic Church.

---

14 Ward, *Young Mr. Newman,* 264-65.

In the years that preceded the lectures, Newman had been disturbed by what he thought were inconsistencies between doctrinal, liturgical, and ecclesiastical matters. In the lectures, he focused on only one of the three offices of the Church, namely that of teaching doctrine, which he called the prophetical. The other two, sanctification through the liturgy and ecclesiastical governance, were not addressed. Over the years, Newman arrived at the conclusion that the Roman Catholic Church was gifted with infallibility in doctrinal matters, but not with impeccability in liturgical or ecclesiastical matters.[15]

Richard Hurrell Froude played a key role in helping Newman examine more critically his positions. Froude finally returned from a prolonged stay in Barbados since October 1833. His health had not improved, but he wished to see his family and friends. In May, after a short visit to Oxford he went to his family home in Devonshire. Froude arrived at the end of a few months of heated debate in Oxford over the proposal by Renn D. Hampden, Principal of St. Mary's House, for the repeal of the oath of Subscription by undergraduates upon admission to Oxford.

Hampden, already holding a university chair, would now be promoted to the highest rank of professorship at Oxford: Regius Professor. In January 1836, the Archbishop of Canterbury submitted six names to the government as candidates for one of the two university professorships of theology. Newman, Pusey, Keble, and Hampden were among these names. Archbishop Whately and Bishop Copleston of Llandaff recommended Hampden. Newman

---

15 *VM,* Vol. I, Preface to the 3rd ed., xliii-xliv.

held little hope of Pusey or his own appointment and urged Keble to accept the position if he were chosen.

In February 1836, Lord Melbourne, then Prime Minister, appointed Hampden as Regius Professor of Divinity at Oxford. The appointment shocked everyone, including heads of colleges, because of Hampden's views on Revelation and his recent support of discarding religious tests at the university. Newman wrote a pamphlet titled "Elucidations of Dr. Hampden's theological statements" in which he objected to Hampden's theological views. Newman sent the pamphlet to Hampden, and they exchanged acrimonious letters. On February 19, 1836, despite the opposition at Oxford, the king confirmed Hampden's appointment.

Richard William Church, then at Oxford, explained that Hampden did not wish to be unorthodox or unevangelical and actually claimed to be orthodox. He wished to give greater weight to Scripture over dogma and to be anti-scholastic and anti-Roman. In the end, however, the Creeds and dogmas were minimized and he "left nothing standing but the authority of the letter of Scripture." [16]

Newman and Pusey sought to censure Hampden's works and prepared a declaration against him, which was signed by 385 Members of Convocation.[17] In May, a meeting of Convocation passed a public vote of no confidence against Hampden by a majority of five to one that curtailed Hampden's powers. Newman, who played a significant role along

---

16 Church, *The Oxford Movement,* 166.

17 *LD,* Vol. V, 264-66. This Convocation was the Convocation of Masters of Arts at Oxford University, not the Convocation of the Province of Canterbury.

with Pusey in articulating Hampden's errors, considered it a victory. Later, the responsibility for the university's reaction to Hampden's appointment, the so-called "persecution of Dr. Hampden," was blamed on the Tractarians, even though almost all of the university had felt seriously threatened by Hampden's unguarded speculations.[18]

Since Hampden was about to vacate the head of St. Mary's Hall, Newman sought Keble's appointment as head. Through James Hugh Rose, he obtained the support of the Archbishop, but the Duke of Wellington, Chancellor of the University, had already chosen someone else.[19]

When Hampden resigned from White's chair of Moral Philosophy to take the chair of Regius Professor of Theology, Martin Routh, President of Magdalen College, expressed his desire that Newman be appointed. Newman declined upon knowledge of Sewell's interest in the position, and Sewell became Professor of Moral Philosophy.[20] The great irony in the course of events was that in order for Newman to obtain his B.D. degree, he was obliged to read the *Thirty-Nine Articles* to Hampden, the new Regius Professor of Divinity.[21]

The resistance to Hampden's position at Oxford was based on the general acceptance of the *Thirty-Nine Articles* as religious truths essential to Christian belief. In addition, there was a sense that a theology professor had the

---

18 Church, *The Oxford Movement,* 171-72.

19 *LD,* Vol. V, JHN to Hugh James Rose (February 21, 1836), 241; JHN to John Keble (February 28, 1836), 243-44.

20 *LD,* Vol. V, JHN to Martin Joseph Routh (March 12, 1836), 256.

21 *LD,* Vol. V, Diary entry (October 26, 1836), 375.

obligation to adhere to the Church's doctrine as understood by the general consensus of Tradition embodied in Church Creeds and liturgy. Hampden was departing from Christian orthodoxy by undermining fundamental points of Christian Revelation. His position could be compared to the so-called academic freedom sought by many contemporary theologians to teach whatever they please.

Lord Melbourne not only failed to understand the outcry at Oxford over Hampden's writings, but he did not do anything to correct his mistaken appointment once he had made it. Similar disregard for doctrine by the government and various usurpations of ecclesiastical power created a growing resistance on the part of Churchmen. The close alliance between Church and government could only possibly work if the government respected ecclesiastical decisions and did not exert undue control over the Church. After some years of tolerating this abuse of power by the State, many clergymen and some laymen were determined to fight for the Church's rights.

Newman held a prudent position regarding the *Thirty-Nine Articles*. He was aware that many of the *Articles* had a Protestant origin, but he thought that they should nonetheless be upheld for the sake of maintaining authority in the Church. He told his friend R. F. Wilson that he did not tell others his reason lest they should scoff at authority. He would submit and obey. On January 11, 1836, Newman wrote to Perceval that Subscription to the *Articles* was important because they impart the notion that religion is the submission of reason to faith. He wrote: "[T]he great lesson of the Gospel is faith, an obeying prior to reason, and *proving* its reasonableness by making experiment of it—a casting of heart and mind into a system, and investigating the truth by practice."[22]

He told Perceval that he would prefer the Creeds and certificates of Baptism and Confirmation to the *Articles*, but these would not exclude Roman Catholics. He also told his friend that he thought the "Romanists" had an advantage over the Anglicans by professing, at the Council of Trent, their belief in Tradition as that which is received from the Apostles. Nevertheless, he thought they erred by making this profession necessary for salvation and for Church communion.[23]

In the year 1836, one of intense controversy at Oxford, Newman endured two of the greatest losses of his life: the deaths of his friend Hurrell Froude and, later, of his mother. By the start of the year, he was thinking of the impending death of Froude. He wrote his sister Jemima expressing his desire to work for God's glory and confiding in her that God was teaching him to depend solely on Him. He told her that Froude's death would be the greatest loss that he could have for his work in the next 25 years. Archdeacon Froude kept Newman informed of his son's failing health. On February 28, Hurrell Froude died at the age of 33.

Archdeacon Froude wrote Newman asking him to distribute £100 to five of Hurrell's friends.[24] Newman was also to take whatever he wished of Hurrell's possessions.

---

22 *LD,* Vol. V, JHN to Arthur Philip Perceval (Jan. 11, 1836), 196-98; 196.

23 *Ibid,* 196-98; 197.

24 *Ibid,* 246.

On Roger's suggestion, he kept a copy of the Roman Breviary that once had belonged to Froude. Newman later asked for the theological work of Petavius, his *Dogmata theologica,* which cost £20. Among Hurrell's greatest spiritual gifts to Newman were his love for the sacrament of the Eucharist and an understanding of Tradition in the Church. With these, he had opened for Newman the door to Roman Catholicism.

Hurrell had been like a dear brother to Newman, one of the closest friends that he would have in his life. In a beautiful letter to Bowden, another of his close friends, Newman wrote of his debt to Froude in intellectual principles, religion, and morals. Despite the earnest friendship and support of Bowden and his family, as well as that of Keble and Pusey, nobody would be able to fill the void left by Hurrell. His spontaneity and vigor, his independent spirit and love for the Church's Tradition, his honesty and zeal for the truth in religion had inspired Newman.

After the death of his friend came another strong blow, the death of his own mother. On May 17, Mrs. Newman died at the age of 63. Newman wrote his Aunt Elizabeth Newman: "Every thing is strange in this world—every thing is mysterious. Nothing but sure faith can bring us through."[25] The previous year, Mrs. Newman had laid the first stone of the new church at Littlemore and continued to follow the activity of her son. At Littlemore, Mrs. Newman and her daughters had helped Newman by carrying out a great deal of charitable work. They had played an

---

25 *LD,* Vol. V, JHN to Elizabeth Newman (May 17, 1836), 299.

important feminine role in the life of this small Christian community.

Newman was saddened by not having been able to share more of his mother's company when she had moved from Brighton to be close to him. What made him even sadder was the absence of a shared religious understanding of Christianity. He wrote that, from the start, his mother and sisters had not understood the Oxford Movement; as it had developed, so had their differences. Charles wrote, lamenting his ungratefulness to his mother and expressing remorse for his behavior: "I feel deeply indebted to my brothers and sisters for having so amply filled the office, in which either from my fault or misfortune I have failed, of good children towards my Mother."[26] In a second letter, he remarked on the unfortunate difference of opinions in religious matters that existed between the three brothers.

Mrs. Newman had been a pious and upright woman and had given her son a great deal of affection and moral support. She had taught him many virtues such as piety, order, service to others, and courtesy. Sadly, she had failed to appreciate his pursuit of doctrinal orthodoxy. In the relationship with his mother, we have a glimpse of one of Newman's personal difficulties, namely that of expressing his sentiments outside of writing. He wrote the following shortly after her death: "I know in my own heart how much I ever loved her, and I know too how much she loved me—

---

26 *LD,* Vol. V, JHN to Newman from Charles Robert Newman (May 18, 1836), 300.

and often, when I had no means of showing it, I was overpowered from the feeling of her kindness."[27]

Newman's two sisters married that same year: Jemima to John Mozley in April 1836, and Harriet to Thomas Mozley in September. Newman was happy to have introduced his sisters to their future spouses. He did, however, lament that Harriet would marry so soon after their mother's death and tried to dissuade her, but to no avail. He gave Harriet a gift of £30 and regretted not having been able to do the same with Jemima. Frank had married in December 1835.

In the midst of these busy years, Newman attended to the pastoral care of his parishioners with the help of Isaac Williams, his curate at Littlemore. He recorded, as usual, his many visits to the sick and the sermons that he preached. In January 1836, the third volume of *Parochial Sermons* was published; it was dedicated to Archdeacon Robert Hurrell Froude, the father of his dying friend. Rickards wrote to Newman, telling him that he and his wife liked the sermons and found them gentler than the earlier ones.[28] The volume contains sermons on important topics, such as baptismal regeneration, intercessory prayer, the invisible church, daily service, and the intermediate state.

Newman's mind was also occupied in raising money for the construction of the new church at Littlemore and in overseeing the construction itself, which was carried out in less than fourteen months. The Bishop of Oxford consecrated the church and the churchyard on September 22,

---

27 *LD,* Vol. V, JHN to Mrs. John (Jemima) Mozley (June 26, 1836), 313-14; 314.

28 *LD,* Vol. V, JHN to Newman from Samuel Rickards (February 18, 1836), 248-49; JHN to Samuel Rickards (March 1, 1836), 247.

1836. The small church was dedicated to St. Mary and to St. Nicholas, for whom a former monastery at Littlemore was named. Newman's detailed description of the windows, altar, and floor plan, which he relayed to his Aunt Elizabeth and friends, gives a sense of the beauty of the church. It was only 60 feet long by 25 broad and 40 high. It had an altar rail, a pulpit, and the old baptismal font of St. Mary's, which had been badly damaged by a mob during the Reformation. The three lancet-shaped windows in the east cast light upon the stone sculptings of the Commandments, the Creed, and the Lord's Prayer beneath them. The stone altar also had some handsome carving.

The simple elegance of the church at Littlemore and Newman's care for the spiritual life exemplified the Christian ideals of the Oxford Movement. The intense debate with Abbé Jager on the relationship between the Scriptures and Tradition, which had occupied Newman's attention and inspired his *Lectures on the Prophetic Office of the Church*, was also emblematic of the Movement's attempt to defend the Anglican Church. Yet despite Newman's efforts to portray the Anglican Church as a *Via Media,* he confided to close friends his hopes and fears for the Anglican Church. Newman's views on the *Thirty-Nine Articles* and the Creed, his laboring over the meaning of Tradition, and his introduction of daily service and saints' days, indicated a movement toward Roman Catholicism. In 1836, he listed the discovery of the Roman Breviary as one of the turning points for that year. The Breviary was, in some sense, Froude's parting gift to help his friend delve into the spiritual heritage of Roman Catholicism.

CHAPTER 23

DEFENDING ANGLO-CATHOLIC THEOLOGY

D URING 1837 and 1838, Newman tried to build upon the Anglican theology of well-known and respected Anglican Divines. A primary concern of Newman during these two years of study and writing was the publication of *The Prophetical Office* and the preparation of the *Essay on Justification*. In the same period he devoted a great deal of time and effort to preparing the edition of the papers of his friend Richard Hurrell Froude.

Newman began a weekly Monday evening tea party held in the Oriel Common Room. He called these parties *soirées,* and eight or nine men attended the first one. The conversation included a wide variety of subjects; an undergraduate reported that Newman talked about everything except Tractarianism. In addition to the *soirées*, he organized a Theological Society that met on Fridays. In November 1836, Newman read a paper at the Theological Society entitled, "Ignatius a witness for Catholic doctrine," and in February of 1837, he read another under the heading "Ignatius." Later he incorporated this material into an article for the *British Critic.* In July an article of his on Augustus Herman Franke appeared in the *British Critic,* and in October his review of Lamennais's work entitled "Affairs of Rome" appeared in the same journal.

That same month, Rivington's asked permission to print a second edition of the *Lyra Apostolica*. The poems comprising the *Lyra Apostolica* had been written by several men in response to the loss of faith and doctrine in the Anglican Church and the accompanying lack of ecclesiastical discipline. The *Lyra Apostolica* became an important milestone in the Oxford Movement. The response to these publications by Newman and his friends was varied. Newman told Manning that the writing of both Keble and Pusey was being criticized and he expected his turn would come. He commented that Evangelicals, pejoratively labeled Peculiars, were "attacked on so many sides at once that they are quite out of breath with having run about to defend their walls—Tradition, Baptism, Apostolical Succession, Faith and works, etc. etc. No sooner do they recover their breath after one blow, but they receive another in their stomach."[1]

Newman candidly admitted his satisfaction to Maria Giberne at the confusion the Tractarians were creating among the Evangelicals: "They have been sailing along with all things their own way, and I wish to take them in the flank. It is remarkable how plans for altering the Liturgy have died away ever since our movement began. We have given them other things to think about."[2] The Tractarians' emphasis on the place of beauty in the liturgy was based on their own rediscovery of this important aspect of worship befitting the Church, which is a divine institution, deserving of the most beautiful of everything that man has

---

1 *LD*, Vol. VI, JHN to H. E. Manning (February 24, 1837), 34.

2 *LD*, Vol. VI, JHN to Maria R. Giberne (July 24, 1837), 103-04; 104.

to offer. At the same time, Newman continued his attempts to justify the divisions within the Church, with the Anglican Church as one branch.

Newman's *Lectures on the Prophetical Office* were sent to the press at the beginning of 1837. In these lectures, Newman wished to show that there was one visible Church, a claim denied by Protestants and (he thought at the time) perverted by Catholics. For Newman, this truth was found in Sacred Scripture and corroborated by Antiquity and the Church Fathers. Six years would pass before he understood it insufficient to accept the Fathers of the Church alone as witnesses of Antiquity. The testimony of the Church divinely instituted and its teaching authority were also necessary.

Newman had reason to concern himself with the nature of the visible Church, for during his time Anglicans held the Branch Theory, according to which the Church had three branches: Roman, Greek, and Anglican. The English Church, considered the middle road or *Via Media,* had resulted from the schism by Henry VIII. The Protestants, with their emphasis on private judgment, rejected the idea of authority. The Roman Catholics justified their beliefs and practices by appeal to the Church's teaching authority. The Anglican Church fell in the middle. In his lectures, Newman wrote that the Anglican Church considered Antiquity and catholicity the real guides and the Church their organ. Newman found a major objection to this explanation of the Anglican Church: there was no counterpart to the *Via Media* in earlier times. It was this objection that Newman and his friends struggled to remove.

In March, *The Prophetic Office of the Church* was published, and the following month Newman reported to Jemima that he was satisfied because the book was selling well. He thought that this book would show the absurdity of the notion that he was a papist. Despite his disavowal of affection for Roman Catholicism, he admitted in the same letter: "However, I frankly own that in some important points our Anglican ετηοσ [ethos] differs from Popery, in others it is like it—and on the whole far more like it than like Protestantism."[3] Newman asked Dr. Martin Joseph Routh, President of Magdalen College, if he could dedicate the book to him. Dr. Routh, who seldom accepted this type of request, agreed to Newman's request.

Newman hoped this latest book would not only dispel concerns about his alleged leanings toward popery, but also serve as a critique of Protestantism. However, to the people of London, the *Lyra,* the *Tracts,* and the editorials from the *Christian Observer* all combined to cast the shadow of popery on Newman and his friends. One London voice denouncing High Church Principles as heretical was Daniel Wilson, a leading London Evangelical. Writing to Bowden, Newman reported this and boasted: "Earthen jars should not swing with iron ones, or the crockery will suffer. The Fathers are a match for many Daniel Wilsons."[4] Similar accusations continued, and in June 1837, Peter Maurice, Chaplain of New College and All Souls, came out with the book, "The Popery of Oxford confronted, disavowed, and

---

3 *LD,* Vol. VI, JHN to Mrs. John Mozley (April 25, 1837), 61.

4 *LD,* Vol. VI, JHN to John William Bowden (January 13, 1837), 11-12; 12.

repudiated."[5] The result of these accusations was to prompt Newman's subsequent defense of the Anglican theology on Justification.

The controversies continued unabated. In December of 1836, the Evangelical *Christian Observer* denounced the *Tracts* as being contrary to the *Thirty-Nine Articles* and official Anglican *Homilies* and claimed that the *Tracts* were based upon the authority of the darkest ages of popery. The newspaper challenged any Tractarian to show his belief in the *Articles* and *Homilies*. Newman replied to the editor with two letters which were published in the *Christian Observer*. Roger and Wood, who were worried about alienating the moderate Evangelicals, discouraged Newman from continuing the correspondence. As a result, Newman decided instead to publish the letters as *Tract* 82 and to prepare lectures on the subject of Baptism and the Protestant doctrine of Justification by faith alone. He delivered the lectures twice a week, between April 13 and June 1, at the Adam de Brome Chapel. Years later he wrote, "As my Lectures on the Prophetical Office of the Church rose out of my correspondence with the Abbé Jager, so those on Justification rose out of controversy with the Christian Observer."[6] Although time-consuming, the lectures did not interfere with either his attendance to the theological meetings or his pastoral duties.

In the first lecture, Newman outlined the Lutheran view of Justification, and in the second, he outlined the Anglican and Roman Catholic view. Newman explained that for

---

5 *LD,* Vol. VI, footnote, 82.

6 *LD,* Vol. VI, footnote inserted by Newman to a copy of a letter to J. W. Bowden (April 12, 1837), 52-54; 53.

Lutherans, Justification is God's declaration or imputation of righteousness to a sinner; the instrument of this is faith. For Anglicans and Catholics, Newman explained that Justification is the spiritual renewal of the soul brought about by the Holy Spirit. This spiritual renewal capacitates the soul for acts of love and obedience. Newman quoted the Epistle to the Romans: "By the obedience of One shall many be made righteous," the One referring to Christ. He then explained that to be made righteous is more than being accounted righteous. Being made righteous means taking on a whole new nature from Christ who is Righteousness.[7] For Newman, God's infinite perfections and holiness are His righteousness, and man's righteousness is man's participation in God's holiness. This participation is synonymous with man doing what is acceptable to God. Newman asserted that to be justified is both a declaration by God's word and the action resulting from that declaration. He wrote that "justification is an announcement or fiat of Almighty God, which breaks into the gloom of our natural state as the Creative Word upon Chaos; that it *declares* the soul righteous, and in that declaration, on the one hand, conveys *pardon* for its past sins, and on the other *makes* it actually *righteous.*"[8]

At the end of the second lecture, Newman wrote a long list of characteristics describing the views of Luther and St. Augustine on the matter:

---

7 John Henry Newman, "Faith Considered as the Instrumental Cause of Justification," in *Lectures on Justification,* John Henry Newman, 26, available at: http://www.newmanreader.org/works/justification/index.html. After this it will be cited *Jfc.*

8 "Primary Sense of the Term Justification," in *Jfc,* 83.

Luther says that a man is made a Christian not by working but by hearing; Augustine excludes those works only which are done before grace is given;—Luther, that our best deeds are sins; Augustine, that they are pleasing to God. Luther says, that faith is taken instead of righteousness; Augustine, in earnest of righteousness;—Luther, that faith is essential, because it is a substitute for holiness; Augustine, because it is the commencement of holiness;—Luther says, that faith, as such renews the heart; Augustine says, a loving faith . . .[9]

Newman summarizes the disparity between the two views by stating, "Augustine contemplates the whole of Scripture and harmonizes it into one consistent doctrine while Protestants entrench themselves in a few texts."

Throughout the lectures Newman contended with Luther's dictum of Justification by faith alone, referring to texts by the German reformer as well as Melanchthon, Luther's coreligionist. Newman showed that doctrinal misunderstandings arise when one or a few passages of Sacred Scripture are privileged and taken out of the whole context of God's Revelation. He criticized Luther's notion that faith exists by itself, or at least separate from charity. Newman countered with the belief that faith, as with the other virtues, is informed by charity; in other words, all virtues are enlivened and perfected by charity.

Newman's writing on this important concept of Justification anticipates by nearly a century some of the joint Lutheran–Roman Catholic agreement on the role of faith in man's Justification. He dispelled the purported contradic-

9 "Love Considered as the Formal Cause of Justification," in *Jfc,* 59.

tion between St. Paul's teaching on "Justification by faith" and St. James's teaching on "Justification by good works." Newman stressed that St. Paul does not exclude the importance of good works; instead, he emphasizes that these corporal works are not the cause of man's Justification. On the contrary, man is justified by God's grace through faith which is manifested in good works. As an illustration, Newman noted that St. James and St. Paul both refer to Abraham and Rahab. St. Paul refers to Abraham's faith while St. James refers to Abraham's works, which justified him. St. Paul speaks of Rahab's faith while St. James of her good works, which justified her. These parallels show that faith is practically identical with the works of faith, "and that *when* it justifies, it is as existing in works." Newman advanced the idea that St. James was "alluding to St. Paul's words, and fixing their sense by an inspired comment [on them]."[10]

In the same lectures, Newman quoted the Anglican Articles and *Homilies*. He pointed out that the eleventh Article states, "we are justified by Faith only" and the *Homily* on the Passion asserts that faith is the "one mean and instrument" of Justification.[11] Newman explained that one can speak of faith as the sole instrument of Justification and Baptism also as the sole instrument whereby faith is an inward instrument and Baptism is an outward instrument. Baptism, however, is the primary instrument of Justification; it confers a faith enlivened by hope and charity. Since

---

10 "Faith Viewed Relatively to Rites and Works," in *Jfc*, 274-303; 297.
11 "The Office of Justifying Faith," in *Jfc*, 223-51; 223.

the Anglican *Homilies* were addressed to those already baptized, they spoke of faith as the sole instrument of Justification.[12] Newman stressed that it is from Baptism that faith derives its authority and virtue. Since the *Homily* on Salvation states that Baptism effects the first Justification, Newman concluded that faith should be considered an instrument, secondary to the sacraments. Later, as a Roman Catholic, he annotated his lectures and included a passage from the Council of Trent affirming that not only faith, but faith, hope, and charity are the cause of Justification.[13]

In the ninth lecture, Newman articulated the role of the Holy Spirit in man's Justification. Earlier, Pusey had been attacked by Evangelicals for asserting in his *Tracts* on Baptism that the grace of the Old Testament differed from that of the New Testament. Newman indicated that the indwelling of the Holy Spirit had been promised in the Old Testament as the distinguishing grace of the Gospel. Newman wrote that the Apostles insisted on Christ's Resurrection and Ascension as the necessary condition for the indwelling of the Holy Spirit, the source of Justification.[14] Newman wrote that Christ "atones by the offering of Himself on the Cross; and as certainly (which is the point before us) He justifies by the mission of the Holy Spirit . . . The Holy Spirit realizes and completes the redemption which Christ has wrought in essence and virtue."[15]

---

12 *Ibid.,* 227-28.

13 "The Office of Justifying Faith," in *Jfc,* 223-51; 226, footnote n. 1.

14 "The Righteousness the Fruit of Our Lord's Resurrection," in *Jfc,* 202-22.

15 *Ibid.,* 203-04.

Throughout the lectures, while still an Anglican, Newman referenced the Council of Trent. For example, in one passage, the Council of Trent is his source for the teaching on the continuous nature of Justification. It is "not the mere remission of sins, but the *sanctification* and the *renovation* of the inner man by the voluntary acceptance of grace and gifts."[16] He noted that according to St. Thomas Aquinas the soul is changed from one state to another. Newman also studied the seventeenth-century Catholic theologian St. Robert Bellarmine. After much work, the lectures were published at the end of March 1838.

The *Lectures on Justification* drew criticism, including from those who wrote that the book was unintelligible. However, Johann J. Döllinger, a contemporary German historian, praised the lectures by declaring them to be the greatest masterpiece in theology produced in England in a hundred years. Two decades later, Newman confided in his *Apologia Pro Vita Sua* that the absence of a sound theological understanding of Justification in harmony with the Anglican formularies was one of the greatest deficiencies of the English Church.

While attempting to develop a theological system for his *Via Media,* he was, in fact, studying and beginning to understand Roman Catholic theology and magisterial teaching, and thus his bias against Roman theology was lessening. At the same time he was learning about the Roman practices of piety.

Within months of the 1836 death of his close friend, Newman began to adopt some practices, which in fact

---

16 *LD,* Quote from Council of Trent, in *Jfc,* 3rd ed., 1874, 96.

seemed natural to him since he held the Anglican Church to be Catholic. A diary entry dated January 9, 1837, records his intention to "use the breviary daily."[17] The Breviary, an integral part of the daily devotional life of Roman Catholic priests in Newman's time, as well as now, is a systematic arrangement of the Catholic Church's prayer, consisting of the Psalms, short prayers, biblical readings, and lessons that have their origin in the Jewish prayer adopted by the Apostles. Since Apostolic times Christians have recited these prayers and readings at set times of the day called hours, hence the alternate name, "Liturgy of the Hours." Most of the hours of the day correspond to times that Scriptures tell us that Jesus and the Apostles prayed.

Studying Froude's copy of the Roman Breviary inspired Newman to write *Tract 75* on the subject of the Breviary. He wished to "re-appropriate" what Roman Catholics had supposedly appropriated as their own and to "illustrate and explain our own prayer-book." The tract, which sold well, included an explanation of the history of the Breviary. Newman criticized the thirteenth- and fifteenth-century changes that had not only decreased the amount of Scripture reading, but also had included legends of saints and hymns plus invocations to the Blessed Virgin Mary. He considered the latter innovations, ratified by the Council of Trent and Pope Pius V, to be grievous.

Despite his censure of innovations in the Roman Breviary, he chose to use the Roman Breviary for daily prayer instead of the Parisian or Ambrosian editions. He would jot down his recitation of the different hours that he prayed.

---

17 *LD,* Vol. VI, Diary entry (Monday, January 9, 1837), 10.

For example, when he prayed Morning Prayer and Evening Prayer he would write down in his diary, "MP" and "EP" respectively. In March, he responded to questions about the Breviary that a woman had sent to Henry Wilberforce. He wrote, "The Psalms should be the basis of all devotion . . ."[18] In a praising tone, different from that of the tract, he noted that the short prayers (responses and collects) of the Breviary required less effort of the mind in comparison with the "long prayers" composed after the Reformation. He felt that the Latin devotions were majestic and austere. Newman also noted the embellishments added on festive days and how shorter biblical readings helped to keep one's attention. He remarked that the answer "*Deo gratias*" was more religious than the English "Here endeth etc."[19]

Another Roman Catholic discipline adopted by Newman was fasting. Beginning in January, he made diary entries that recorded his fasting at meals, using initials such as f.d. for fast day, f.b. for fast breakfast or ½ f.b. for half breakfast, and so forth for other meals. Undoubtedly, he had in mind Froude's example, and just as his friend had done, Newman refrained from speaking about this personal practice. The entries probably served as a record for personal spiritual accountability.

Another practice most likely inspired by Froude was the weekly Communion Service. On April 9, 1837, the second Sunday of Easter, Newman initiated an early-morning

---

18 *LD*, Vol. VI, JHN to Henry Wilberforce (March 25, 1837), 46-49; 47.
19 *Ibid.*, 48.

Eucharist at St. Mary's. The Eucharist was a Communion Service on Sundays, and according to usage, he referred to it as the "Sacrament." The custom at the university was to have the Sacrament for the university on the first day of each term. Each service included a collection of money, which Newman gave to various charities, especially to assist curates in financial need. Pusey and other friends assisted him at the Communion Service, although on occasion, he had no assistance.

During the course of the year a few Roman Catholic priests passed by Oxford. One was an Irish priest, Fr. Maguire, who, according to Newman, "came and bullied me last year."[20] Another priest, whose name he did not record, evidently won the admiration of all at Trinity College. These contacts and the correspondence with Abbé Jager were the entirety of his dealings with Catholics because he did not have any Roman Catholic friends.

Rather than to Roman Catholicism, Newman turned to Anglican Divines who had tried to maintain the rubrics and dignity of liturgical worship. In 1837, Newman and his friends published a selection of William Beveridge's sermons, and the following year an edition of the private devotions by Bishop John Cosin. Newman esteemed the sermons and prayers of these early Anglicans.

Newman's rapprochement to Catholics and Roman Catholicism should be attributed to those whom he correctly called the Catholic Fathers, the eminent writers of the first nine centuries of Christendom, renowned for

---

20 *LD,* Vol. VI, JHN to Mrs. John Mozley (October 6, 1837), 148-49; 149.

their holiness. In January of 1837, Newman and his close friends finally began working in earnest on a desired project of translating into English the writings of the Church Fathers, a project Newman had begun in March of 1836. This was an important task because the Church Fathers' writings were only available in their original languages, mainly Greek and Latin, except for a translation into German.

This translation project was an ambitious and unique literary and theological endeavor. The plans for this project occupied the mind of the Tractarians, but especially that of Newman and Pusey, who were to be the editors. Newman in particular embarked on the time-consuming enterprise of looking for good translators and of choosing the works for translation. Soon the project was underway. The publication of the first translations, however, was delayed until the following year. Keble's posthumously published translation of St. Irenaeus's *Adversus haereses* did not appear until 1872.

Even though Newman dedicated much time and effort to the *Library of the Church Fathers,* he allotted more attention to the posthumous publication of Froude's writings. The month after the February 1836 death of Richard Hurrell Froude, Newman received a collection of his papers to be published as he and Keble saw fit. Newman had some initial fears about their publication, but Keble, Rogers, Pusey, Copeland, and Wood advised immediate publication. With this impetus, Newman decided to publish Froude's papers without delay. Newman ascertained that Froude's "Private Thoughts" were the best introduction to Froude and kept clear of his political essays. Newman explained that Froude's "Private Thoughts" illustrated how his friend has countered the temptation to rationalism.[21]

For Newman, the diaries revealed Froude's sincere recognition of his own faults and his struggle to improve; they indicated how Froude combined metaphysical speculation with the concerns of a practical man. Newman thought that Froude's diaries exemplified how a man between the ages of 18 and 30 formed his views. It was Newman's hope that Froude's thoughts would kindle enthusiasm in the reader. Newman was careful in the use of names and omitted them in Froude's letters in an effort to avoid upsetting the people to whom Froude referred. Newman wrote Bowden, "What a marvel it is! But I really do think that a fresh instrument of influence is being opened to us in these Papers. They do certainly portray a saint."[22] In December he wrote again to Bowden on the same subject, but this time with concern that Froude's *Remains* "will scandalize and I fear throw back some persons by their uncompromising Anti-protestantism—and they do tend to make people disloyal toward the Establishment—I *hope* not, to make them Romanists. He is very severe on the Romanists."[23]

The first two volumes were published in February 1838, following intense editorial work; the exact title was *Remains of the Late Rev. Hurrell Richard Froude.* In these volumes Froude's views on the Church were expressed; he lamented

---

21 *LD,* Vol. VI, JHN to John Keble (June 30, 1837), 86-88; 87.

22 *LD,* Vol. VI, JHN to J. W. Bowden (October 6, 1837), 145-46; 145.

23 *LD,* Vol. VI, JHN to J. W. Bowden (December 12, 1837), 178-77; 176.

that the Church's synodal powers and the power of excommunication were suspended, and she was thus in bondage to the State. Although in the Preface, Newman indicated that Froude criticized Roman Catholics as idolaters, publication of Froude's writing caused a scandal to both Anglicans and Protestants—who were outraged, accusing the Tractarians of popery. The risk taken by the Tractarians in publishing *The Remains* brought mixed results as exemplified by the public response of Lord Morpeth in Parliament, who used the Catholic tone of *The Remains* to oppose allocation of funds for the education of Irish Catholic clergy.

Even while working on Froude's papers, Newman followed his practice of frequent correspondence with friends. The letters reveal Newman's character and personality: he was witty and good-humored, frank, and precise. The letters are full of details. He mentions, for example, his habit of going to bed when the clock struck ten. At other times, he apologized for the scrap of paper he used, or for scribbling because his hand was tired from writing. He made humorous comments such as the following one to Maria Giberne: "I fear you have thought either your letter lost, or my memory—though both have been safe with me—and I have hoped every day for some leisure time to write."[24] It had taken Newman a little over a month to reply. He usually replied to correspondents within a day after receiving their letters.

During 1837, Newman corresponded often with William Wilberforce, Bowden, and Keble. Pusey, Rogers, Woodgate, Manning, and Jemima received a good share

---

24 *LD*, Vol. VI, JHN to Maria R. Giberne (May 3, 1837), 63-65; 63.

of letters. During this year and the following, Newman wrote his friend Thomas Dyke Acland, who was an M.P. for West Somerset, a number of letters with advice for his work in Parliament. Along with his wit and good humor, Newman's letters reveal his sensitivity to a friend's sorrow. Newman consoled Bowden upon his mother's death, and he showed the same finesse with Henry Edward Manning upon the death of his wife, Caroline, younger sister to Samuel Wilberforce's wife.[25] Newman reminded Manning that the happiness which is higher than any other consists in the awareness of God's closeness to man in his suffering. Newman comforted him with the reassurance that the loss of a loved one produces a calm detachment from the world.[26] Newman's effectiveness came from his own experience of the loss of family members.

Henry Edward Manning, a graduate from Balliol College and a Fellow at Merton College, became rector of a parish after leaving Oxford in 1833, and later Archdeacon of Chichester. Beginning in 1837, Manning had taken up Tractarian opinions and consulted Newman about parliamentary debates concerning the Ecclesiastical Commission, a body established to determine the distribution of the revenues of the Church of England.

Another correspondent, Lord James H. Lifford, wrote to Newman complaining about Newman's criticism of Evangelicals in "Self-Contemplation," one of the *Parochial Sermons*. In that sermon Newman had faulted the self-confidence and spiritual pride resulting from the contemplation

---

25 *LD,* Vol. VI, JHN to H. E. Manning (July 23, 1837), 102-3.
26 *Ibid.,* 102.

of self rather than of God. Newman suggested that Evangelicals "[D]estroy all positive doctrine, all ordinances, all good works; they foster pride, invite hypocrisy, discourage the weak, and deceive most fatally, while they profess to be the antidotes to self-deception."[27]

Newman replied to Lifford that he was not referring to individuals but to a system. Newman criticized the practice of the "direct contemplation of our feelings as *the* means, *the* evidence of justification."[28] He referred to "The Dairyman's Daughter," the third tale in *Annals of the Poor*, which has a deathbed scene in which a clergyman questions a dying person. This novel, which had wide distribution, made a "certain conscious state of feeling evidence of Justification."[29] Newman contrasted this scene with the deathbed examination of the sick prescribed in the Visitation of the Sick. In this service the dying person is asked to profess the articles of faith, examine his past deeds, repent of sins and receive absolution by a priest. This venerable and more ancient system considers the objects and fruits of faith as the direct and necessary evidence of Justification, not the inward, more subjective state of feelings.[30]

Newman indicted Evangelical literature in general, and specifically the widely published authors Hannah More, Thomas Erskine, and Jacob Abbot. These authors, he argued, jettisoned formal Catholic doctrines for the sake of including spiritually minded people in their society. He asked Lifford to look at *Tract 73*, "On the Introduction of

---

27 "Self-Contemplation," in *PPS,* Vol. II, 173.
28 *Ibid.,* 130.
29 *Ibid.,* 131.
30 *Ibid.,* 132.

Rationalistic Principles into Religion."[31] Finally he noted that the Hampden affair would awaken people to the danger of Socinianism among Evangelical party members. (Socinians denied the distinction of Persons in the Trinity and also the Incarnation.) The theme of the correspondence to Lifford: Newman's wariness of basing judgment on inconstant and subjective emotional feeling, was further developed in his writing on Baptism and Confirmation.

In a June letter to Jemima, Newman was particularly clear in his exposition of the dangers of the Protestants' and Evangelical Anglicans' reliance on feeling over doctrine and sacraments. Jemima had requested a doctrinal explanation on Confirmation. In the reply, Newman used as an example the long exhortations by Protestants at a "baptismal service," and compared this to Anglicans who focused on the "objects" or actions, as the laying on of hands in the ordination of priests or consecration of bishops. A similar action is found in the Confirmation service where the bishop imposes his hands on the one to be confirmed: "The *action* speaks."[32] It is a special blessing, he explained, tantamount to a prayer and does not require a long exhortation.

In this same letter, Newman patiently instructed Jemima in the doctrine of the Ancient Church: the Holy Spirit, who is the animating principle and Lord of the Church, communicates Himself in the sacraments: first in Baptism, which brings about forgiveness; then in Justification and the beginning of other gifts; and finally in Confirmation,

---

31 *LD,* Vol. VI, JHN to Lord Lifford (September 12, 1837), 128-33; 133.

32 *LD,* Vol. VI, JHN to Mrs. John Mozley (June 4, 1837), 78-81; 79.

which is the fullness of the sanctifying gifts given as a seed at Baptism. For the early Church, Confirmation was a part of the baptismal rite. Newman, however, did not consider Confirmation a separate sacrament; furthermore, he understood it to be a nonessential part of the baptismal rite. At that time, the Church of Rome administered Confirmation at the age of seven, which, Newman wrote, would be a good practice for Anglicans to follow since the specific grace of Confirmation is to perfect the Christian.

Newman acknowledged his lack of experience in the rite of Penance (Confession) since Anglicans marginalized this rite. Even so, on Saturday, March 17, 1838, Newman heard his first confession. He was vested with a surplice and seated against the rails at the altar at the north end of St. Mary's. Newman's first experience as a Confessor was in response to a young person who had come to Newman on the fifteenth and asked if he would hear his confession. The young man was preparing to receive the Holy Eucharist. Newman confided to the young man his feeling of awkwardness and told him of the sense of responsibility he felt in hearing someone's confession, but he agreed to hear the confession of his sins and grant him absolution.

The rite of Penance and the administration of absolution was not the only sacrament which raised questions in Newman's mind. He had questions about Baptism and the other sacraments. Besides the nature of the sacrament of Baptism, Newman had to contend with the form of administering this sacrament. For Catholics, a Baptism is valid when the one who baptizes invokes the name of each Person of the Trinity, while the person to be baptized has water poured on the head or is submerged in water three times.

An irregularity in the form used (the words and actions) is cause for an invalid Baptism. When asked about the validity of Baptism by clergymen who were Dissenters, Newman told Jemima that he advised "re-baptism" with the conditional form.[33] This was the case with Mrs. Pusey. On the eve of Easter 1838, he baptized a few persons; among them was Mrs. Pusey, whom he baptized conditionally. She had been baptized by a Dissenting clergyman and had doubts with regard to the validity of her Baptism. In light of her doubts, she had stopped receiving Communion for some months. Newman obtained the bishop's permission to give her conditional Baptism.

The consultations made by friends and joint work provided the occasion for a deepening in friendship. Two former pupils with whom Newman spent much time during the year 1837 were John Frederic Christie and Henry Arthur Woodgate. Christie, who had entered Oriel in 1824 and was elected Fellow in 1829, was actively involved in the Movement after becoming friends with Newman. Woodgate had been present with Isaac Williams at the dinner in 1828, when Mary Newman was taken ill. Newman later became godfather to Woodgate's eldest daughter, and Woodgate dedicated his 1838 Bampton Lectures to Newman. Woodgate and Rickards were the two friends about whom Newman wrote in the *Apologia,* who knew him best, but who in 1864 were no longer his friends. Later, how-

---

33 *LD,* Vol. VI, JHN to Mrs. John Mozley (October 6, 1837), 148-50; 149. Catholics believe that Baptism imparts a spiritual seal on the soul, so it is only given once to a person. When there is doubt about someone having been baptized, the priest baptizes using the words, "If you are not baptized, N., I baptize you in the name . . ."

ever, Newman and Woodgate saw each other frequently at Edgbaston and Rednal. In 1872, Newman dedicated *Discussions and Arguments* to Woodgate.[34]

Cultivating friendship was important to Newman. He made it a priority to visit his friends when time allowed. His time became more flexible after his mother's death in 1836. That year Newman visited Thomas Keble's parish at Bisley, J. F. Christie's parish at Badgeworth, and then spent two weeks at Thomas Mozley's parish in Cholderton. Robert Jeffries Spranger, a Fellow at Exeter College and Lecturer in Hebrew, served Newman as curate at Littlemore during this absence and on other occasions.

Some of Newman's letters are beautiful examples of prose. One, a letter to his friend Rogers, deals with the illness of Rogers's sister. Newman spoke to Rogers of how God calls to Himself those who are ready and that it is a privilege to be taken by Him: "Surely God would not separate from us such, except it were both for them and for us, and that those who are taken away are such as are most acceptable to Him seems proved by what we see . . ."[35] Newman commented on the relation of the petition in the Lord's Prayer, "Thy Kingdom come," and the privilege that it is to leave this world. Emily Rogers died in September of that year. It is in these letters that we glimpse Newman's deep spirituality and great humanity.

Newman's letters were also prompted by various pressing issues. For example, a new amendment to the Marriage Act of 1836, which provided that a superintendent's

---

34 *LD,* Vol. VI, Index of Persons and Places, 417.
35 *LD,* Vol. VI, JHN to Frederic Rogers (June 1, 1837), 75-76.

registrar certificate should be used instead of the publication of banns prescribed by the rubrics, caused a letter
from Newman to Perceval. Newman wrote that since the
rubrics had not been altered he would continue to use the
banns. Newman worried that the clause in the Act would
be the first of many innovations to follow. He confided in
Pusey that he was not advocating resistance, but that he
was disposed to decline to perform marriages on the license
of a registrar, shying away from this novelty. These letters show Newman's respect for the Church's practices and
norms and concern for their application.

Other letters record details of Newman's daily life. For
example, in September, on the first anniversary of the dedication of the chapel at Littlemore, an anonymous woman gave
a splendid chalice for St. Mary's altar. Bloxam's brother
gave candlesticks and an offertory bowl. John R. Bloxam,
whom Newman met in 1837, became Newman's curate at
Littlemore without remuneration. Besides these gifts from
his brother, Bloxam contributed stained glass windows for
the church. Other gifts recorded include a collection of £18
that was made for building a schoolhouse; the following
year on June 27, the first stone was laid. Some people from
Oxford asked for an evening service, and it was held.

In other letters to friends, he wrote about the spread of
Church Principles, a term describing the Movement. By
way of proof, he mentioned the good sales of the *Tracts*
and told an anecdote of a youth at a wine merchant who
had bought one of Pusey's *Tracts* and was later heard
"defending the cause very skillfully."[36] Clergymen in Chel-

---

36 *LD,* Vol. VI, JHN to Robert I. Wilberforce (October 6, 1837), 150-
51; 150.

tenham and Brighton were preaching Church Principles and the Bishop of Lincoln had praised the *Tracts.*

In September, Rev. George Townsend, Prebendary of Durham, began a series of accusations of alleged alterations of the liturgy introduced by Newman. Townsend found criticism with the use of a cross on the surplice, extra bowing, and the use of a table near the altar on which to place the bread and the wine. Pusey wrote to Bishop Bagot, refuting these accusations. Newman had attempted to revive some older liturgical practices such as using a lectern with an eagle instead of a simple reading desk and kneeling toward the east for prayer during services, facing *ad orientem,* the same way as the congregation. Newman knew this was an ancient Christian tradition, recommended by the Anglican Anthony Sparrow in his "Rationale of the Common Prayer." Newman would turn to the congregation in the parts addressed to them. Pusey told the bishop that Newman interpreted the rubrics with the primitive usage in the Church and with the practice of rites at some of the cathedrals. By October, Townsend admitted being misled by exaggerations; he retracted all that he had said and wrote an apology to Newman, who acknowledged the apology.

Older liturgical practices and Roman Catholic sacramental theology had a lasting effect on Newman, whereas his effort to construct a *Via Media* only gave him a transitory peace of mind. He could not find in the reality of ecclesiastical life of the Anglican Church what he was trying to formulate in theory. Preparation for the Lectures on Justification allowed him the opportunity to find in the Council of Trent's decrees an exposition of doctrine that accorded with the truths of Scripture and the Church Fathers. He argued that the Anglican Articles of Faith and *Homilies* were in keeping with the latter. Although he was attempting to show deficiencies in Roman Catholicism and to solidify Anglo-Catholic theology, he had embarked on a spiritual and ascetical path that was leading him slowly toward Roman Catholicism. Newman prayed with the Roman Breviary, practiced some fasting, and began to have a weekly Communion Service.

CHAPTER 24

UNDERSTANDING THE HOLY EUCHARIST

THROUGHOUT his years at Oriel College, Newman used the adjective "catholic"—for example, "catholic system" or "catholic ethos"—without referring to the Roman Catholic Church. He was an Anglican and believed that the Anglicans held the doctrine of the Church Fathers and first Christian centuries; he believed they were "Catholic" without giving allegiance to Rome. In 1838, however, by understanding further the difficulties in Anglican doctrine regarding the Holy Eucharist and prayers for the deceased, he realized how much Anglican theology had suffered with the Protestant Reformation. Newman began to think that Anglican theology lacked an internal presumption of truth. Instead of being a living body that grows and expands, it was like a group of contradictory doctrines heaped one on top of another.[1]

Whereas in 1837, Newman had continued his reflection on the sacrament of Baptism and the other rites considered sacraments by the Roman Catholic Church, in the year 1838 he advanced in his understanding of the Catholic doctrine on the sacrament of the Holy Eucharist. These developments took place as he looked for an editor for the

---

1 Morales, *Newman (1801-1890)*, 96-97.

British Critic. He eventually accepted the appointment himself at the beginning of 1838.

The *British Critic*, founded in 1793, was a conservative monthly which was eventually acquired by a group of High Churchmen in 1825, who turned the periodical into a quarterly. From the outset of the Oxford Movement, Newman chose to work within established publications instead of beginning a new journal. He thought the *British Critic* was one that would suit the Movement and arranged for like-minded men to write articles for the *British Critic* without pay. Soon, however, he became annoyed with the unorthodox views of the editor and felt he must stop writing for the *British Critic*.

In November 1837, the editor resigned and the search for a replacement began. The same month Newman wrote his friend, Edward Churton, rector of a church in Durham: "Men do nothing for *nothing*—what these men want, is an organ."[2] Newman knew that the men who wrote for the *British Critic* did not wish to be paid; instead, they sought a paper with a coherent internal ethos, a "Catholic temper." He hoped to convince Churton, who was a year older than he and sympathetic to the Oxford Movement, to become editor. Churton declined editorship, as did Manning, whom Newman asked next. Samuel Maitland, a historian from Cambridge University and librarian to London's Archbishop, took up the editorship on a trial basis, but resigned after only one issue. In January of 1838, Newman, against his will, was named editor; he did not wish the journal to fall into the hands of others.

---

2 *LD*, Vol. VI, JHN to Edward Churton (Nov. 21, 1837), 169-70; 169.

Without delay, Newman overhauled the journal. He asked Churton and others, such as Robert Francis Wilson and Manning, to contribute regularly for the sum of 7 guineas a sheet starting in July, concurrent with his editorship. He asked Henry Wilberforce to write four times a year, warning him the pay would be very bad. He regretted that Maitland had stepped down and commented: "But no wonder—he was setting out on a voyage of adventure with a rum crew and thought twice before he cut the cable."

The subject of the reviews and articles varied a lot. Newman asked Henry Wilberforce to write either on the Scottish Establishment or the Church extension system. Robert Isaac Wilberforce wrote one on the life of John Jay, Chief Justice of the United States. Of course, Newman would also write for the journal. He had trouble with the first issue of the *British Critic* under his editorship because some writers failed to send in their articles. Some of his closest friends got him out of the bind by writing articles. Bowden, Keble, Charles Le Bas, Rogers, Sewell, J. Mozley, Charles Thornton, and Newman himself were the authors of the articles for the first issue.

The January 1838 issue of the *British Critic* published an article by Rogers on "Froude's *Remains.*" Newman wrote to Wilson, praising the article and remarking on Pusey's astonishment at Froude, whom he had once considered merely a "good-natured, sharp schoolboy"; Pusey now exclaimed, "We have a giant."[3] William Froude wrote that his father was pleased with the book, and Sir Francis Palmer, a medieval historian and convert from Judaism,

---

3 *LD,* Vol. VI, JHN to R. F. Wilson (February 4, 1838), 196-97; 196.

wrote a favorable review of *The Remains* for the July issue
of *Gentleman's Magazine.*

Palmer wrote to Newman that he would have been glad
if some passages had been omitted, but people would recognize Froude's candor toward friends. Edward Churton
complained at first about passages and pages but later
acknowledged that people were misguided and needed
guides such as Froude. Newman told Manning that, as
expected, Froude's friends were getting into hot water in
some places about *The Remains,* but "if we can but turn it
into steam, and direct it aright, it may accelerate our motion
toward desirable objects."

For Newman and Keble, however, it had been very
important to publish Froude's papers. They contained not
only the Tractarian *ethos,* but they were also a sort of biography of Froude, which could have an important influence
on others. Froude had exerted a powerful influence on
Newman's religious path. Newman described it: "a stage
in the history of my own mind."[4]

At the end of March 1838, Newman's *Lectures on Justification,* which he had delivered the previous year, were
published. Newman remarked to Pusey that the Medieval
Schoolmen hardly touched the subject of Justification, and
since the Reformation much had been written on it. Earlier in January, a somewhat embarrassed Richard Bagot,
Bishop of Oxford, accepted Newman's kind dedication of
the *Lectures on Justification.* Newman confided to Henry
Wilberforce that it was this book that (until then) had cost
him the most in time and trouble. Unfortunately, the book

---

4 Morales, *Newman (1801-1890),* 93.

received a harsh review from Charles Web LeBas, a High Churchman and Cambridge alumnus, who was a frequent contributor to the *British Critic*. He asserted that the book was not only taxing to read but at times mystical.

While Newman did not criticize the bishops in his articles and sermons, he was aware of the harm caused by bad bishops and of the necessity for good appointments to vacant Sees. In 1837, in light of the disturbing state of deficient and unorthodox bishops, Newman confided to Maria Giberne that good Christians must hope in God without fearing the government or bishops. He even went as far as to say that "when a bishop is heretical, man, woman or child has license to oppose him."[5] However, out of respect for the office of bishop, Newman always obeyed; he reminded Maria that things were much worse off in the time of St. Athanasius. When the Arian Heresy was widespread, its erroneous ideas had fooled hundreds of bishops.

When Edward Denison, an Oriel Man, was given a political appointment in 1837 as the Bishop of Salisbury by the Whig Prime Minister, Lord William Melbourne, Newman commented that for the following ten to twenty years they must expect appointments like him, "very respectable men of no principles in a strict sense of the word."[6] Nonetheless, the following year he wrote to Miss Holdsworth that although it was lamentable when bishops were chosen by the State, their ordination was valid because they were consecrated by existing bishops who exercised the power of their office.

---

5 *LD,* Vol. VI, JHN to Miss M. R. Giberne (Dec. 3, 1837), 173-74; 174.
6 *LD,* Vol. VI, JHN to H. A. Woodgate (March 17, 1837), 44-45; 44.

There were, however, a few good bishops. One orthodox and courageous bishop was the Bishop of Exeter,
Henry Phillpotts. During a debate in the House of Lords
on a Church Discipline Bill, Phillpotts said that no one
would keep him from excommunicating a clergyman
who disobeyed. Phillpotts insisted that even if a bill were
passed to punish him, he would never act as to be unwor-
thy before Heaven. In a charge delivered to his clergy in
1836, the bishop had exhorted them to be faithful and regular in the use of all services in the *Prayer Book* and to
assert without fear the true authority of their ministerial
office.[7]

During this time when Newman was concerned both
with the doctrine of Justification and the appointment of
orthodox bishops, he continued to reflect on the subject
of the Holy Eucharist. In a letter dated February 1838, he
explained his understanding of the Eucharistic sacrifice
to Miss Holdsworth. Besides referring her to *Tract 81*, he
told her that the word "sacrifice" appears at least twice in
the Book of Prayers. He lamented that the Protestant inno-
vators did not use the word "altar," but, he explained, it
would only stand to reason that where there is a priest and
a sacrifice, there must be an "altar."[8] He wrote that the
Holy Eucharist "is not only a sacramental representation,
and also a real and proper sacrifice of bread and wine, but
a sacramental Presence of Christ Crucified—the shadow,
as it were, of the Cross on Calvary being continued to the

---

7 "Charge delivered to the Clergy of the Diocese of Exeter", Phillipots
(London 1836) cited in *LD,* Vol. VI, footnote, 13.

8 *LD,* Vol. VI, JHN to Miss Holdsworth (Feb. 6, 1838), 197-99; 198.

end of the world . . ."[9] He referred her to John Johnson's "Unbloody Sacrifice and Altar," and mentioned an essay on Eucharistic Sacrifice by Froude that would later appear in the third volume of *The Remains*.

This fundamental idea of the Holy Eucharist as a sacrament and as a sacrifice continued in the forefront of Newman's mind when, in March of 1838, he edited and wrote the preface to Christopher Sutton's "Godly Meditations upon the Most Holy Sacrament of the Lord's Supper." Also, in the following month, he married a couple who had asked to receive the Eucharist after the sacrament of Matrimony. In July, he replied to a comment made by his friend, Hugh James Rose, who, possibly upon reading Froude's *Remains*, argued for doctrinal reserve in speaking about the Holy Eucharist. Newman acknowledged the value in the first century custom of using reserve in speaking with non-Christians, but he asserted that ordinary men needed to hear about the Apostolic origins of parts of Eucharistic Service.

In the same letter to Rose, Newman also noted that when questions arose regarding the Eucharist, such as innovations, or omissions in the liturgy, the subject must be addressed. He expressed praise for the Roman Catholic use of the terms "sacrifice" and "memory" within the Mass and, at the same time, lamented the Roman Catholic refusal of the "Cup to the Laity."[10] The denial of the cup or chalice

---

9 *Ibid.,* 198.

10 *LD,* Vol. VI, JHN to Hugh James Rose (July 8, 1838), 262-63; 263. At that period of time, Roman Catholic laity were not allowed to receive the chalice with the Precious Blood of Christ. Catholic doctrine teaches that in receiving Christ under one form or species, one receives the whole Christ, Body and Blood.

with the consecrated wine to the laity became common in the thirteenth century. This was at first due to fear of profanation by spilling the Blood of Christ. At the same time, the usage was considered a way of teaching people that the whole Christ is present in each of the elements.

On May 13, the fourth Sunday of Easter, Newman preached a sermon titled "The Eucharistic Presence." In the sermon, he explained the meaning of Christ's words at the multiplication of the loaves as Christ's promise of the sacrament of the Holy Eucharist. According to Newman those words foreshadow Christ's words at the Last Supper when he instituted the Holy Eucharist. At this point Newman held an attenuated version of the Catholic doctrine of Transubstantiation, the teaching that with the words of Consecration, the bread and wine become the true Body and Blood of Christ, not a symbol, or a promise. He explained the Anglican position thus:

> The Church has never thought little of the gift; so far from it, we know that one very large portion of Christendom holds more than we hold. That belief, which goes beyond ours, shows how great the gift is really. I allude to the doctrine of what is called Transubstantiation, which we do not admit; or that the bread and wine cease to be, and that Christ's sacred Body and Blood are directly seen, touched, and handled, under the *appearances* of Bread and Wine.[11]

Only a week later, Godfrey Faussett, Lady Margaret Professor of Divinity, preached a sermon at St. Mary's titled *The Revival of Popery* in which he made scouring remarks on Froude's unguarded expressions and visionary sentiments in *The Remains*. He criticized Rome as the

---

11 "The Eucharistic Presence," in *PPS*, Vol. VI, 141.

Antichrist and the Tractarians for leading others toward popery. Faussett published his sermon, and Newman was able to publish a rebuttal almost immediately.

In his reply, Newman made a sharp defense against Faussett's accusations. He affirmed that Froude's opinions did not contradict the fundamental doctrines of Anglican Communion; he pointed out that Anglican theologians had held similar beliefs to those espoused by Froude. He quoted, for instance, various passages from the writings of Bramhall, Archbishop of Armagh, who in the seventeenth century stated that Anglicans did not deny that the Sacrament is the Body of Christ, but rather they disagreed on the manner of the Transubstantiation.[12] Newman noted that Froude had sharply criticized the Council of Trent for making some doctrines a condition for communion with the Catholic Church. At the same time, Newman argued that Anglicans who denounced those who did not accept Protestant errors, did for the Anglican Church what Trent had done for the Roman Church; they excluded some of its members from its communion.[13]

Froude thought that the condemnations of the decrees from the Tridentine Council were an insuperable obstacle in the union of Anglicans with the Roman See. Newman then put the question to Faussett:

"I will but ask by which of the Articles, by what part of the Prayer Book, is a member of our Church bound to acknowledge the Reformers, or to profess himself a

---

12 *Via Media*, II, A Letter Addressed to the Rev. the Margaret Professor of Divinity on Mr. R. Hurrell Froude's Statements Concerning the Holy Eucharist, n. 9, 211.

13 *Ibid.*, n. 6, 207.

Protestant? Nowhere. To force him then to do so, when he fain would not, is narrowing our terms of communion; it is in fact committing the same error which we urge against the Roman Catholics."[14]

Newman rebutted another accusation made by Faussett: that the Church of Rome was the Antichrist. Newman countered with the observation that if this were so, then the Anglican Church, whose origins dated to Pope Gregory the Great, was also a son of the Antichrist. He noted that by the same token, the same attack on the Church of Rome was now used by Dissenters on the Anglican Church. He wrote:

> If Rome has "committed fornication with the kings of the earth," then what must be said of the Church of England with her temporal power, her Bishops in the House of Lords, her dignified clergy, her prerogatives, her pluralities, her buying and selling of preferments, her patronage, her corruptions, and her abuses? If Rome's teaching be a deadly heresy, what is the Anglican Church, which "destroys more souls than it saves?"[15]

Newman was ashamed by the beliefs he had professed five years earlier and the language that he had used at that time. Then on a visit to Rome, Newman had alternated between condemning either the Church of Rome or Pagan Rome. At this point, there was no doubt in his mind about the meaning of chapters 17 and 18 of the Apocalypse:

"Take the chapters literally, and sure it is, Rome *is* spoken of; but then she must have literal merchants, ships, and sailors; therefore it is not Papal Rome but Pagan. Take them figuratively; and then, sure it is, merchants and

---

14 *Ibid.,* n. 11, 206-17.
15 *VM,* II, n. 13, 219-20.

merchandize, *may* mean indulgences and traffickers in them; but then the word Rome perhaps is figurative also, as well as her merchandize. Nay, I should almost say, it must be; for the city is called not only Rome but Babylon; and if Babylon is a figurative title, why should not Rome be?"[16]

> In his rebuttal of Faussett, Newman indicated Froude's condemnation of the seemingly idolatrous worship of saints among Roman Catholics and concurred with it, but admitted that it would be difficult to ascertain how much of this was truly the practice. He also expressed the idea that feelings of reverence for the crucifix should be understood as being similar to the feelings for the portrait of a loved one.[17]

The main part, however, of Newman's open letter to Faussett was on the Holy Eucharist. Here Newman reaffirmed his professed doctrine on the Eucharist: that the Real Presence of Christ with His body, blood, soul, and divinity is present in the consecrated species of Bread and Wine. Newman clarified this by explaining the position of the Anglican Divines, who believed that Christ is really present, not in an imaginary way, in the consecrated bread and wine, yet not present in a local space. The Divines objected that if Christ were present locally in Heaven, He could not be locally present at the same time in the consecrated bread. They believed that Christ was present in some unknown way but did not speak of the manner of His presence. As an Anglican, Newman asserted Christ's Body to be really present in the Holy Eucharist, but not locally. He

---

16 *VM,* II, n. 14, 221.
17 *Ibid.,* n. 10, 215

suggested that there may be a spiritual sense by which one perceives His presence, since Our Lord's risen body was not subject to the laws of space.[18]

Newman thought that the Roman Catholic theologian St. Robert Bellarmine spoke of Christ being present locally in two places at the same time. However, in a footnote he quoted Bellarmine, who actually spoke of Christ being present substantially, that is, on account of the substance rather than locally.[19] Bellarmine followed St. Thomas Aquinas, who had held that "the body of Christ is in this sacrament by way of substance, and not by way of quantity."[20] The entire Christ is in the Sacrament, but without extension. In the Eucharist the accident of quantity, by which a substance ordinarily occupies a place, is miraculously separate from the substance of Christ so that He is not localized in the dimensions of the bread and wine.[21] Newman's point of contention with Faussett was, however, not the precise theological question about the manner of Christ's Real Presence, but the general doctrine of Transubstantiation that Faussett mistakenly declared to be

18 *VM*, II, n. 22, 236-37.

19 *VM*, II, footnote n. 5.

20 Thomas Aquinas, *Summa Theologica* III, Q. 76, Art. 1, Ad. 3 (New York: Benzinger Brothers, Inc., 1947), Vol. 2, 2455.

21 Both as an Anglican and later as a Catholic, Newman rejected a "physicalist" explanation of the Real Presence. His understanding of Christ's spiritual presence would be commensurate with Aquinas's understanding of the substantial presence ("by way of substance"). Cardinal Ratzinger explained the extremes that this view avoids. See Ratzinger, Joseph, "The Presence of the Lord" in *God Is Near Us,* Ignatius Press, San Francisco, 2003, 74–93, in particular 84–85.

dangerous and contrary to Anglican theology.[22]

Newman reproved the Lady Margaret Professor of Divinity for taking a Lutheran view of the Holy Eucharist. Luther believed that Christ was present in the bread only in a spiritual manner, but not that the bread became the Body of Christ. According to Luther the Body and Blood of Christ coexist with the bread and wine (consubstantial presence). In his letter to the Lady Margaret Professor, Newman asserted that Anglican theology did in fact accept a doctrine of Transubstantiation, albeit it is different from that held by Roman Catholics. According to Newman, Anglicans believe that the consecrated elements are an efficacious sign of Christ's spiritual presence, yet they are more than a sign; "in some unknown way the soul becomes possessed at once of Christ according to its nature."[23] Because of Newman's belief in Christ's Real Presence in the Eucharist, he took great care of Eucharistic worship and the beauty surrounding it. Many people gave Newman gifts that helped him dignify the liturgical worship, both at St. Mary's and at the Church in Littlemore. In 1838, someone gave him an organ for Littlemore Chapel, and Bowden gave him stained glass. Newman commented that this was the law of faith and its reward: Ask much and you gain much. He also cared for the smaller details, such as the acquisition of proper altar cloths and a paten for distribution of Holy Communion. At this point in time, despite the writings of the Church Fathers and the Anglican *Homilies* that refer to Matrimony and the other sacraments, Newman

---

22 *VM II*, n. 10, 216.
23 *VM II*, n. 23, 239.

still restricted the number of sacraments to Baptism and the Holy Eucharist.

During 1838, Newman corresponded with Samuel Francis Wood and Henry Arthur Woodgate. Samuel Francis Wood, educated at Eton and later at Oriel under Newman, became an ardent Tractarian and a good friend of Newman. Wood lived in London, where he studied law. Wood suggested publishing extracts from John Johnson's *The Unbloody Sacrifice* to show the differences between Anglican and Roman Catholic doctrine on the Eucharist. The extracts were later included in Pusey's *Tract 81*. This *Tract* gathered the testimony of Anglican Divines against the Roman Catholic doctrine of Transubstantiation.

In 1838, Newman sent Woodgate a small sacrament case in which to carry the Sacrament to a sick person. Newman wished to thank him for kindness toward Mrs. Newman in the past. Woodgate, who frequently corresponded with Newman, sought him out for suggestions for his Bampton Lectures on the Authoritative Teaching of the Church. Woodgate dedicated these lectures, published in 1839, to him. Newman was in regular contact with other Tractarians: Isaac Williams, Robert Williams, and Richard William Church. Isaac Williams was busy in 1838; that year he published a book of poetry titled *The Cathedral*. The previous year he had written three *Tracts*. Robert Williams, Newman's former pupil, who attended Oriel in 1829, became a Conservative M.P. for Dorchester. Another Tractarian was Richard W. Church, who later wrote *The History of the Oxford Movement*. In April 1838, Church was elected Fellow at Oriel and Newman told his sister Jemima that he considered it to be a big gain for the college: "he is in every respect a desirable man, as far as one can judge—and of true and understanding Apostolical ἦθος (ethos)."[24]

Toward the end of the year Newman and the Tractarians were joined by a new group of men, consisting of Frederick W. Faber, William G. Ward, Frederick Oakeley, Dalgairns, and Thomas E. Morris. These Anglo-Catholic men, who were for the most part Newman's friends and students, were heading in a straight path toward union with Rome. They had learned from Newman and were drawing conclusions on their own, by questioning whether or not the Anglican Church was a true church and part of the one Catholic Church established by Jesus Christ. Newman provided unity between this new group, which was moving toward Rome, and the group composed of those like Keble and Pusey who wished to purify the Anglican Church by recovering Catholic truths, without moving toward Rome.[25]

Throughout the year visitors who were not Tractarians also came to see Newman at Oxford. These visitors ranged from strangers, such as clergymen from the United States, to friends, such as Manning, who sought his advice. Newman encouraged Manning, Archdeacon in the See of Chichester at that time, to be the principal of a theological college that was proposed for his diocese. Naturally the Tractarians also looked to Newman for guidance. Thomas Acland, M.P., who was at the center of a group of Tractarians in London, asked Newman for advice regarding plans for a national school system. Acland wished to know what role

---

24 *LD,* Vol. VI, JHN to Mrs. John Mozley (June 5, 1838), 253-54; 254.

25 Morales, *Newman (1801-1890),* 97.

the Church could play and how best to protect the Church's interest in education. Newman urged him to form a body of members of Parliament with his friends to oppose radical measures on the subject of education or other matters.

Others wrote Newman to criticize his views. Some of these were people he did not know and others were friends or acquaintances. Woods and Richard Church told Newman their disagreements openly. Newman respected their opinions even though they sometimes hurt his sensitivity. He was quite annoyed, however, when people spoke of him behind his back, as was the case with Samuel Wilberforce.

A controversial subject was prayer for the deceased. The Tractarians rediscovered this early Church practice through the study of Church History and the Church Fathers. Since the first century, Christians have prayed for eternal rest of loved ones and friends. Early Christian communities celebrated Masses asking God for the eternal happiness of the deceased. These Masses were celebrated in the catacombs, the early underground Christian burial sites, as well as in open cemeteries. Christians chose to bury their dead close to the tombs of Christians who had died holy deaths, especially martyrs.

Protestant Reformers of the Church in England interrupted the custom of praying for the souls of the deceased. The practice, however, did not become extinct; Newman noted that the Bishop of Bath and Wells prayed for the soul of Princess Charlotte Augusta in a sermon the week after her interment. Since the death of his sister Mary, Newman began to realize the necessity and naturalness of praying for the deceased. When Manning's wife died, Newman prayed for her deceased soul, albeit with some hesitation since it broke with Anglican customs.

Newman argued with George S. Faber on the orthodoxy of praying for the deceased. Newman told Faber that the whole of the faith can be found in Scripture, but ordinances, or concrete norms, such as prayer for the deceased, need not be shown in Scripture; they could be sanctioned by Catholic Tradition just as the Lord's Day had been changed from Saturday to Sunday. According to Newman, Catholic Tradition deemed this type of prayer "pleasing to God and in some unknown way useful to the dead." He wrote: "Why may I not believe a thing not in the Bible, if I do not force the belief on others?"[26] Newman considered this practice to be one left to private judgment, not an article of faith. He told George Faber that there are many rites and ceremonies, such as using the Cross in Baptism, that are not scriptural. When Faber pointed out that no author before Tertullian ever mentioned the practice, Newman retorted that testimony for the authenticity of some New Testament books was also scant and even less than that of prayers for the dead. If Faber believed in the canon of the New Testament he should believe in prayers for the dead.

From the exchange of letters with Faber it is clear that Newman now conceded a greater role to Apostolic Tradition than during his 1834 to 1835 controversy with Abbé Jager. Newman's sermons, letters, and books demonstrate a detailed knowledge of Sacred History and of the arguments and answers given to difficult biblical passages.

---

26 *LD,* Vol. VI, JHN to George Stanley Faber (April 11, 1838), 230-31; 231.

As the years went by, however, Newman realized that the content of the Creed cannot be proven by Scripture alone; it calls for the interpretation of the Apostles and their immediate successors.

That very month of May in which Newman wrote to Faber about Scripture proofs, Newman began a series of twelve lectures, "Lectures on the Scripture Proof of the Doctrines of the Church," in the Adam de Brome Chapel of St. Mary's. In the first lecture, Newman refuted the common objection that the necessary proof for doctrine contained in the Creed is that the stated doctrine must be explicitly found more than once in Scripture. Newman concluded this lecture stating:

> that it does not follow that a doctrine or rite is not divine, because it is not directly stated in Scripture; that there are some wise and unknown reasons for doctrines being, as we find them, not clearly stated there. To be sure, I might take the other alternative, and run the full length of skepticism, and openly deny that any doctrine or duty, whatever it is, is divine, which is not stated in Scripture beyond all contradiction and objection. [27]

Eight of the lectures were published that same year as *Tract 85*.

Besides the lectures, Newman worked on various projects. He devised setting up a house for writers ("young monks") who would help him and Pusey edit the translations of the Church Fathers. Mrs. Pusey, Robert Williams, and William Bowden each gave money for this project, and in October, Newman rented a house for this purpose

---

27 "Difficulties in the Scripture Proof of the Creeds" in *DA*, 125.

in Oxford on Aldate Street, opposite Christ Church. It was hard to find men for the house who would later aspire to Fellowships because by their association with Newman they would become marked men. The house was not the success that Newman expected, but three of the residents, Pattison, Christie, and Mozley succeeded in obtaining Fellowships.

A bigger project was one for the formation of clergy. In August of the same year, Newman supported a plan by Pusey to establish a college for clergy at Manchester. It was based on an earlier idea by Froude to impart religious education to the working classes of the manufacturing cities such as Manchester and Birmingham. Like Froude, Newman thought the celibate clergymen would make a greater impression on people. The potential patrons for the college in Manchester fell through, but despite the failure in starting a college, Pusey's generosity and efforts led to the construction of the Church of Our Saviour in Leeds.

More than by these failures Newman was saddened by the charge made by Richard Bagot, Bishop of Oxford, on August 14, 1838. Although the bishop praised the *Tracts* for recalling "forgotten truths," he faulted them for "ambiguity of expression" and the placing of others at risk of falling into superstition.[28] Newman considered discontinuing them and sought Keble's advice. Newman wrote Archdeacon Clerke asking him if he knew to which *Tracts* the bishop objected, so that he could remove them at once. Clerke suggested that Newman meet with the bishop.

---

28 *LD,* Vol. VI, Extract of Bishop of Oxford's Charge (August 14, 1838), 285-86.

Newman told Bowden that he felt the bishop had given them a slap. Nothing had been found in the *Tracts* that could be accused of Romanism; on the contrary, the *Tracts* were found to be sincere and to express the desirable recommendation of keeping fasts and festivals. Less positively, they had been found to have "expressions which might be injurious to particular minds."[29] Even though the bishop spoke of the importance of observing the rubrics, he had cast a general suspicion over all the volumes. Newman considered that these remarks by the bishop might simply be a check; yet for Newman, even the slightest disapproving word from his bishop (*ex cathedra*) was heavy.[30] Taking a different view than Keble, Bowden replied that withdrawing the *Tracts* would be like a recantation of all his principles; no one would believe that the withdrawal was done in deference to Episcopal authority. He urged Newman not to act unless he had a very clear directive from the bishop.[31]

When the charge was published, it had a footnote in which the bishop declared there was no censure on the *Tracts*; he stated that he believed the authors would always submit to his authority. Newman, however, felt dejected; he confided to Pusey that he felt like "a nobody" writing. He was neither bishop nor professor. The *Tracts* did not have the approbation of the bishop. Although the bishop was polite, he was not a friend. Newman understandably felt himself under a cloud of suspicion.

---

29 *LD*, Vol. VI, JHN to J. W. Bowden (August 17, 1838), 291-92; 291.

30 *Ibid.*, 291.

31 *LD,* Vol. VI, Extract of J. W. Bowden to JHN (August 1838), 292.

As in the previous year, Newman continued to reside at Oriel and to take part in the university life, even though he did not have any pupils at his college. He kept abreast of the appointments of college heads and university professors. He was satisfied by another type of appointment, the choice of Harrison, one of the Tractarians and a lecturer in Hebrew, to replace Ogilvie as chaplain to the Archbishop of Canterbury. While chaplain to the Archbishop, however, Harrison distanced himself from the Tractarian ideals.

At Littlemore, there was new activity: the construction of a school building, which Newman was happy to see completed even though he remarked that it was not a handsome building. For the chapel he commissioned a memorial of his mother from Richard Westamacott. It was to be a simple memorial with a female figure exchanging a measuring line or a plan with an angel.

During the long summer vacation of 1838, Newman remained at Oxford attending to his pastoral duties except for a one-week stay in London for repeated visits to the dentist. To J. F. Christie, one of his friends, he complained in jest of being alone: "I am solus here . . . *Do come up for the day.*"[32] Aside from his friends, he liked to be alone with his books; only five days later he wrote to James Mozley: "I am quite solus—you cannot think what a relief it is."[33] Although many of those days he dined alone in the Common Room, he did have occasional visitors, including Maria Giberne and her sister. Newman was also quite busy preparing

---

32 *LD,* Vol. VI, JHN to J. F. Christie (August 5, 1838), 278-79; 279.

33 *LD,* Vol. VI, JHN to J. B. Mozley (August 10, 1838), 281-82; 282.

lectures, making plans for printing the other volumes of *The Remains* and answering correspondence.

As usual, Newman maintained frequent correspondence with friends and family; sometimes his family members visited, and he tried to return the visits. In September Harriet and Thomas Mozley visited him, and in October, he visited his sister Jemima and her family in Derby. It had been two years since he had been at Derby. During this period his brother-in-law James B. Mozley married one of the daughters of James A. Ogle, a physician, ten years older than Newman, who had been his private Tutor at Trinity. Ogle became Regius Professor in 1851, and remained Newman's friend all his life.

The work on the *Library of the Church Fathers* advanced slowly but surely; the fourth and fifth volumes appeared in 1839. Except for the time of his visit to his sister Jemima at Derby, Newman continued to preach at St. Mary's, and in his diary, he recorded the title of the sermon that he preached each Sunday. He prepared for publication his four volumes of sermons, which appeared in November of 1838 with a dedication to his friend Hugh Rose. Evoking the meeting that began the Movement, Newman wrote of Rose: "When hearts were failing bade us stir up the gift that was in us and betake ourselves to our true mother."[34]

At Oxford, Newman's life was not tranquil. Because he stood for a strong religious ideal, he was inevitably drawn into controversies. From the start of 1838, Rev. Charles Golightly made plans to build a Memorial to the English Reformers—Thomas Cranmer, Nicholas Ridley, and Hugh

---

34 John Henry Newman, *PPS*, Vol. IV, Dedication (Nov. 19, 1838).

Latimer. They had been tried and executed for heresy by Queen Mary. The memorial was devised as a countermovement against the criticism of the Reformers in Froude's *Remains*. It became a test of anti-Roman sentiments, and Newman and other authors of the *Tracts* were urged to subscribe to it. Golightly had been Newman's curate at Littlemore, but when Golightly preached against Pusey's views on Baptism, Newman had dismissed him. Soon afterward, Golightly became an enemy of the Tractarians and sought every opportunity to attack them.

Bishop Bagot supported the project and urged Pusey to do likewise. Pusey was willing to commemorate certain aspects of the Reformation but not the Reformers. For this reason and because the plan was an attack on Newman, he declined to subscribe to it. Keble and Newman also declined. Despite their minor opposition, the Martyr's Memorial was erected in 1841. It was an imposing Gothic stone cross on St. Giles Street close to Broad Street.

On top of external criticism of the Tractarians, there were also internal struggles among the Tractarians that rose to a crisis. The men disagreed on plans for the proper translation and publication of the Roman Breviary and also with the editorship of the *Tracts*. At the beginning of 1838, Robert Williams and Samuel Wood began their own project of translating the Roman Breviary, which they wished to publish privately for subscribers only. Newman encouraged them, but they faced opposition from other Tractarians, who feared they would be labeled Romanists because of the translation. George Prevost, a supporter of the Oxford Movement and a pupil of Keble, asked Newman to suppress the publication of the Breviary and offered to pay the expenses incurred by the editors.

Earlier in the year, Newman had published a volume of a translation of Breviary hymns, *Hymni Ecclesiae, excerpti e Breviario Parisiensi,* with an English Preface. In this preface he wrote:

> [T]houghtful minds naturally revert to the discarded collections of the ante-reform era, discarded because of associations with which they were then viewed, and of the interpolations by which they were disfigured; but which, when purified from these, are far more profitable to the Christian than the light and wanton effusions which are their present substitute among us.[35]

It was a praise for the doctrinal depth and literary beauty of prayers put aside by reformers.

Keble advised omitting certain legends about saints and hymns, such as *Ave Maris Stella,* from the proposed translation of the Breviary. Newman prepared to make the necessary omissions, but Wood and Williams decided to suspend the project. They thought it would produce substantial alteration of the Breviary. After their decision to suspend the publication of the Breviary, Newman published a second volume of Latin hymns, *Hymni Ecclesiae, excerpti e Breviariis Romano, Sarisburiensi, Eboracensi et aliunde.*

This debate over whether or not to publish the Breviary signaled a growing division among the Tractarians. Although immediate problems had been averted, tension between them was growing. Newman was disappointed by

---

35 John Henry Newman, *Hymni Ecclesiae, excerpti e Brevario Parisiensi,* Preface, xiii.

the lack of trust and respect of some of his friends. Newman felt the loss of confidence of the group. After the reaction to *The Remains* and the tiff over the proposed publication of the Breviary, Newman felt attacked from all sides by friends and foes. He wrote Bowden, "It is just like walking on treacherous ice—one cannot say a thing but one offends someone or other."[36] Keble advised Newman to expect contradictions in his position as a leader. He also reminded Newman of his character: "[F]or you know, my dear N. you are a very sensitive person."[37]

Undergirding all these problems was one of greater weight. Newman and the translators of the Breviary wished to restore the Catholicism that had been destroyed by the reformers. He spoke of the Lutheranizing influence of the reformers on the *Book of Common Prayer*. For Keble, and also Pusey, the Reformation was a true reform—one that sought a more primitive and pure Catholicism.[38] Newman had agreed to the cessation of the publication of the Breviary because he realized there were no principles short of private judgment for adapting the Breviary for Anglican usage. The whole affair saddened Newman.

Like Newman, some of Tractarians were more inclined to the Roman Catholic Church. They believed in the Real Presence and tried to understand the doctrine of Transubstantiation. They prayed for the deceased, a practice they found in Christian Antiquity and Tradition. In a letter to Professor Faussett, Newman gave unwitting evidence to

---

36 *LD,* Vol. VI, JHN to J. W. Bowden (November 21, 1838), 343-44; 344.

37 *Ibid.,* 348.

38 Trevor, *Newman, Pillar of the Cloud,* 220-21.

the fact that he was becoming Roman Catholic. In it, Newman urged greater fidelity to the faith of their ancestors and commitment to holiness.

> This is the way to withstand and repel Roman Catholics; not by cries of alarm, and rumours of plots, and dispute, and denunciation, but by living up to the Creeds, the services, the ordinances, the usages of our own Church without fear of consequences, without fear of being called Papists; to let matters take their course freely, and to trust to God's good Providence for the issue.[39]

Newman had a very high respect for the Episcopal office and showed a refined reverence and obedience to the Bishop of Oxford. Not long after the bishop's charge, Bishop Bagot opposed Newman's editorship of the *British Critic* and the publication of *Tract 90*. In both matters, Newman obeyed his superior, but before then, in 1839, Newman had begun to face the first major problems in the Anglican Church.

---

39 *Via Media*, Volume II, 256 (n. 35).

CHAPTER 25

1839: FIRST ANGLICAN DIFFICULTIES

THROUGHOUT the year 1839, Newman's attention was consumed in great measure by his editorship of the *British Critic* and translations into English of works by the Church Fathers. The death of friends, the illness of others, various difficulties, and also many writing projects occupied his time and efforts. Perhaps the most significant development in Newman's life, however, came about as a result of his study on the early Church Fathers: both in the middle and at the end of the year, he was faced with the first real intellectual difficulties in adhering to the Anglican Church.

In January, Newman published an article in the *British Critic* on the theology of the first Church Father, St. Ignatius of Antioch. In the article, he argued in favor of the authenticity of St. Ignatius's Epistles. One of the arguments adduced in favor of their genuineness was that the epistles are missing the doctrine of the Trinity and baptismal regeneration that was enunciated centuries later. Newman pointed out that Ignatius transmits in his epistles the truths taught by Jesus' Apostles to the second generation of Christians. These truths were a religion, or Catholic system with a "definitive, complete and dogmatic form."[1] This system included most of the doctrines that comprise Catholic teaching today. With this article Newman was beginning to articulate the theory of dogmatic development that he would present in *The Development of Christian Doctrine* in 1845. Newman's arguments for the authenticity of Ignatius's Epistles and their record of Apostolic beliefs in the early years of the Church led him to conclude: "Give us, then, but St. Ignatius, and we want nothing more to prove the substantial truth of the Catholic system; the proof of the genuineness and authenticity of the Bible is not stronger; he who rejects the one, ought in consistency to reject the other."[2] Newman reasoned that the New Testament should be interpreted in accordance with the Church system described by Ignatius only a few decades after the death of the Apostles. This ancient Church system, in other words, contained the fundamental teachings of the Catholic Church of his day.

While Newman was thinking about the dogmatic foundations of Catholicism, he felt obliged to defend the Anglican faith, which he believed to be Catholic. In an article, *The State of Religious Parties,* for the April issue of the *British Critic,* he explained how the Oxford Movement upheld doctrines that were part of the Anglican tradition. He excused the excesses of some of its members as the legitimate exercise of private judgment. Furthermore, he

---

1 John Henry Newman, *Essays Critical and Historical I*, 258, available at: http://www.newmanreader.org/works/essays/volume1/index.html. After this it will be cited *Ess I.*

2 *Ibid.,* 261.

urged the clergy and individuals to refrain from suppressing Catholic impulses, because the Anglican Church was
acutely suffering from the absence of concrete and precise
doctrinal, liturgical, and disciplinary boundaries, as were
other Christian bodies that had separated themselves from
the See of Rome.

Also in January, Newman learned of the unexpected
death in Florence, Italy, of Hugh James Rose, who had
first asked Newman to write on the Church Councils and
had later helped to begin the Oxford Movement. Newman
wrote Mrs. Rose: "I will only say that in [sic] sorrowing
particularly for one who was always a kind, condescending
friend to me. In fact it was he who brought me into notice;
he was the first to introduce me to write on theological subjects, and then to praise me when I had written."[3]

Newman, desiring to revise his book on Arianism, wrote
to Williams: "I am this long vacation returning to my *own*
line of reading—the early controversies of the Church,
which I have suspended since 1835; not suspended of my
own wish, but it was pressing that subjects should be treated
more connected with what was going on in the Church."[4]
He hoped that the study of the Incarnation in the Church
Fathers would allow him to finish an edition of Dionysius
and a translation of Theodoret, a theologian from Antioch
who was born at the end of the fourth century. During the
course of translating the Church Fathers and in the reading necessary for editing others' translations, Newman

---

3 *LD,* Vol. VII, JHN to Mrs. Rose (January 29, 1839), 21.
4 *LD,* Vol. VII, JHN to Isaac Williams (July 18, 1839), 110-111; 110.

experienced his first major difficulties in adherence to the Anglican Church.

In June, when Newman began studying the fifth-century Monophysite heresy condemned by the Council of Chalcedon in 451, he began losing confidence in Anglicanism. The Monophysites believed that Christ has only one nature: a divine nature. The writings and authority of Pope Leo the Great led to a definition of faith at the Council of Chalcedon, affirming that Christ has a divine and a human nature, which are perfectly united. Newman was struck by the moral authority of the Pope that decided the outcome of the controversy. Newman would later write, "I saw my face in the mirror, and I was a Monophysite."[5] Newman told a friend that he was alarmed by discovering that Protestants and Anglicans were heretics like the Monophysites and that he too was a heretic. Until the fifth century, the criterion for choosing the authentic Church established by Christ was Antiquity, but now that foundation was challenged. The test for a true Church was its communion with the other churches and its communion with the See of Rome.

Just when Newman was concluding his study of the Monophysite heresy, the history of the fifth-century Donatist schism in the African Church convinced him that the judgments of the Roman See were definitive in deciding matters of the whole Church. In August, Nicholas Wiseman published an article, "Tracts for the Times: Anglican Claim of Apostolical Succession," in the *Dublin Review*. In the article, Wiseman argued that the Anglican Church was schismatic and thus could not claim Apostolic Succession.

---

5 *Apo.*, 114.

He based his argument on those adduced by St. Augustine, St. Optatus, and St. Jerome against the Donatists, but he applied them to the Anglican Church and the Tractarians' defense of the Branch Theory.

In mid-September on a walk to Littlemore, Robert Williams pointed out to Newman some key words in the article taken from St. Augustine that had escaped Newman's observation: "*Securus iudicat orbis terrarum*." The full sentence asserted: "Wherefore the entire world judges *with security* that they are not good who separate themselves from the entire world, in whatever part of the entire world."[6] Newman thought that these words went beyond the Donatists and applied to the controversy with the Monophysites. "They decided ecclesiastical questions on a simpler rule than that of Antiquity; nay, St. Augustine was one of the prime oracles of Antiquity; here then Antiquity was deciding against itself."[7]

These words and Wiseman's entire article were a strong blow not only to the Monophysites, but to Anglicanism and to the Tractarians who defended the Branch Theory of the Church. Newman wrote to Rogers: "Since I wrote to you, I have had the first real hit from Romanism which has happened to me. R. W., who has been passing through, directed my attention to Dr. Wiseman's article in the new

---

6 St. Augustine, *Cont. Epist. Parmen. Lib. iii, cap 3.* Quote by Wiseman, Nicholas, "The Anglican Claim of Apostolical Succession" in the *Dublin Review,* 1839, quoted from *Publications of the Catholic Truth Society,* Vol. XXIV, 1895, 23.

7 *Apo.,* 117.

Dublin. I confess it has given me a stomach-ache."[8] At the end of his article, Wiseman explained that some High Church Donatists had come up with the untenable idea that the Donatists were a part of the Church in communion with Rome. The arguments of the Church Fathers against such ideas were conclusive. Years later, Newman wrote that St. Augustine's words interpreted and summed up the long and varied course of ecclesiastical history. He acknowledged that with these arguments "the theory of the *Via Media* was absolutely pulverized."[9]

As Newman struggled with this new position, he believed that God would lead him. At about that time, he wrote a sermon on Divine Calls in which he praised being obedient to heavenly visions. Nevertheless, he "determined to be guided, not by imagination, but by reason."[10] Historical facts had a logical force that he could not ignore. He believed that the principle of dogma and Apostolic Succession, along with the sacramental system, were better safeguarded by Rome than by the Anglican Church. He felt that the argument for Anglican claims only lay in charges against Rome, but since 1833, he no longer considered the Church of Rome to be the Antichrist. He remarked: "I had no positive Anglican theory. I was very nearly a pure Protestant. Lutherans had a sort of theology, so had Calvinists; I had none."[11]

That Newman was heading toward Rome was evident. Earlier in the year, Newman had advised Manning on how

---

8 *LD,* Vol. VII, JHN to Frederic Rogers (September 22, 1839), 154-55; 154.

9 *Apo.,* 117.

10 *Apo.,* 119.

11 *Apo.,* 120.

to dissuade an Anglican who was thinking of becoming Roman Catholic. When Newman gave his advice, he surprisingly expressed the thought that it was only a question of time before some people would leave the Anglican Church due to its Protestant principles. Newman thought that men needed more of the external elements of worship which are part of the Roman Catholic Church; he blamed the Anglican bishops for their negligence in respecting this need and the Church's Tradition. He wrote to Manning:

> I think that, whenever the time comes that secessions to Rome take place, for which we must not be unprepared, we must boldly say to the Protestant section of our Church—"*You* are the cause of this. You must *concede*—you must conciliate —you must meet the age. You must make the Church more efficient—more suitable to the needs of the heart, more equal to the external pressures. Give us more services— more vestments and decorations in our worship—give us monasteries—give us the 'signs of an Apostle'—the pledge that the Spouse of Christ is among us. Till then you will have continual defections to Rome.[12]

To Manning's correspondent, Newman urged patience and reminded her of the duty to remain where God calls and to help one's fellow Christians "steeped and stifled in Protestantism" rather than "indulging" one's own feelings in the Communion of Rome.[13] He offered the same advice to others and soon applied it to himself.

While sincerely trying to remain an Anglican, Newman was embarrassed by two younger clergymen: Morris and

---

12 *LD,* Vol. VII, JHN to H. E. Manning (September 1, 1839), 133-34; 133.

13 *Ibid.*

Bloxam (who was his curate at Littlemore). One Sunday Morris preached on fasting to the congregation gathered at St. Mary's on St. Michael's Day. The following Sunday he preached to the congregation on the Roman doctrine regarding the Mass and condemning those who would not believe this doctrine. The Vice-Chancellor who had been present on both Sundays was very offended: Morris was admonished and reported to the bishop.

Bloxam, on the other hand, had been seen at the Roman Catholic chapel of the Earl of Shrewsbury at Alton Towers during the offering of the Mass. Bloxam defended himself, stating that he was praying in the chapel when he was surprised by Mass. Newman thought that it had been very imprudent of his curate but told the bishop that Bloxam was "a most active and valuable curate."[14] Bloxam, saddened by people's accusations, decided to leave the curacy at Littlemore. This, and the suffering of other friends, caused Newman pain.

Early in the year, Bowden was diagnosed with tuberculosis affecting his lungs. Newman was told that there was little likelihood of Bowden's recovery, and he wrote other friends asking for prayers for Bowden. He also wrote to Bowden inquiring about his health. After a small improvement, Bowden replied with the following expression of friendship: "At length, through God's mercy, I am enabled again to take up the pen myself, and it were strange if the first use which I made of this recovered faculty were not

---

14 *LD*, Vol. VII, JHN to Richard Bagot, Bishop of Oxford (December 9, 1839), 189.

to employ it in addressing you, the kindest, truest, of my friends.[15]

Edward Pusey also received consolation from Newman. Pusey's wife, who had been sick since 1837, died on Trinity Sunday in May of 1839. Newman preached for the first time "Peace in Believing," based on the text of Christ imparting the Holy Spirit to the Apostles the day after his Resurrection. As if speaking about Mrs. Pusey, he said:

> After the fever of life; after wearinesses and sicknesses; fightings and despondings; languor and fretfulness; struggling and failing, struggling and succeeding; after all the changes and chances of this troubled unhealthy state, at length comes death, at length the White Throne of God, at length the Beatific Vision. After restlessness comes rest, peace, joy;—our eternal portion, if we be worthy . . .[16]

Pusey and his wife had carried out many works of charity, including contributing funds for building churches. For a long time after the death of Mrs. Pusey, he was the only one that Pusey would see. He and Newman would go for daily walks. Pusey wrote to Newman that he had been like an angel sent to him by God, and he prayed "that He may make you what, as you say, there are so few of, a great saint."[17] Pusey signed another letter to his friend "ever yr very affect. and grateful friend E B Pusey."[18] Pusey's

---

15 *LD,* Vol. VII, J. W. Bowden to JHN (June 3, 1839), 96.

16 *PPS,* Vol. VI, "Peace in Believing," 369-70.

17 *LD,* VII, E. B. Pusey to JHN (July 16, 1839), 83.

18 *LD,* Vol. VII, E. B. Pusey to JHN (September 1, 1839), 142-43; 142.

suffering continued; next was the crippling illness of his son, and only five years later the premature death of Lucy, one of his daughters. Already an exemplary father, the widower now dedicated himself entirely to the care of his children and only gradually took up again his scholarly work.

The attention that Newman paid to his friends was all the more meritorious given the amount of work he had. The editorship of the *British Critic* consumed much of his time and energy, and Newman relied heavily on his brother-in-law Thomas Mozley and his friend Henry Wilberforce for articles for the *British Critic*. One month, two writers disappointed Newman, who was obliged to produce four sheets himself, extempore. On this and other occasions he complained of aching of his hands, due to excessive writing.

One of Newman's contributions to the *British Critic* was a pointed review of Henry Caswall's "America and the American Church" (1838), a narrative of the establishment of the Anglican Church in America. Caswall had optimistically remarked that the American Church was conducted on a "popular principle" because the American people were accustomed to republican procedures.[19] Without proper theological training and ordination to the clerical state, the laity stood on equal footing with the clergy in the church synods and committees.

Newman argued that although the American bishops believed in Apostolic Succession, they did not carry out a proper development of this truth: the bishops did not exercise the spiritual and ecclesiastical authority that derives

---

19 Henry Caswall, *America and the American Church* (London: John and Charles Mozley, 1851), 293.

from the Apostolic origin of their office. Newman put his finger on one of the main sources for this problem, namely, the democracy of religion. "The Americans boast that their Church is not, like ours, enslaved to the civil power; true, not to the civil power by name and in form, but to the laity, and in a democracy what is that but the civil power in another shape?"[20]

Although the *British Critic* was a voice for doctrinal views, it had a wide selection of articles, including some on church architecture. Earlier in the year the Oxford Society for Promoting the Study of Gothic Architecture was constituted at Oxford; its members included Bloxam, Isaac Williams, J. B. Mozley, C. Marriott, and W. Palmer. The society planned to collect architectural prints, drawings, and models, and house them in a museum. The members of the Oxford Movement were not only writing about the beauty of religious architecture, they were building or remodeling churches and contributing to the building of churches by others. In September, at the anniversary of the consecration of St. Mary's Littlemore, Newman made a collection that he sent to his friend, Simeon L. Pope, who was then building a new church. At about this time as well, Newman had three windows with seven figures installed at St. Mary's Littlemore.

On the publishing front, the *Tracts* continued to sell very well; the previous year approximately 60,000 *Tracts* had been sold. John Inglis, Bishop of Nova Scotia, sent Newman a letter praising the *Tracts*. Newman thought of the good effect this could have in the neighboring dioceses of

---

20 "The Anglo-American Church," in *Ess. I*, 356.

America, in particular, that of Vermont.[21] In January, Volume IV of the *Parochial and Plain Sermons* had been published in an edition of 1000 copies, and half a year later, a second edition was being prepared. One of the sermons in that volume was "The State of Grace," which Newman wrote with his Aunt Elizabeth in mind. Newman's sermons were often naturally motivated by events in the life of family and friends, as well as his own. This one, an insightful sermon on fasting, was a case in point. Newman wrote that fasting brings Christians into the realm of the supernatural, but that fasting could also open them to temptations from the Evil One. During Lent of 1839, Newman had been fasting much, often until 5 pm. Even with his increased prayer and his practice of fasting, his sentiments toward Roman Catholics only slowly improved.

On a trip to Europe, Rogers, his friend and former pupil, had met and spoken with a French priest. The priest had tried to convince Rogers of the errors of Anglicanism. Newman was amused by the account and admitted to Rogers that it is of little surprise that Roman Catholics did not have feelings of friendship toward Anglicans. Until the Catholic Relief Act of 1791, Catholic priests who celebrated Mass committed a felony. By contrast with some Roman Catholics' sentiments toward England, Newman's sentiments for Rome grew. Having just read Manzoni's *Promesi Sposi* he was captivated by the figure of the Capuchin, who had converted from his previous life to one of works of charity.

---

21 *LD,* Vol. VII, JHN to Isaac Williams (August 20, 1839), 123-24; 123.

Newman voiced a romantic dream that if matters got worse in the Church of England he would become a "Brother of Charity in London."[22]

All of these sentiments, however, would not impede Newman from reacting angrily to the allegiance by Catholics to Irish politicians. In January of the following year, Fr. George Spencer, a Roman Catholic priest, visited Oxford, asking Newman and others to join him in prayer for the unity of Christians. Newman declined dining with him in public. Manning and Pusey wrote Newman that Anglicans already prayed in their daily service for those in the "Catholic Church," whereas Roman Catholics prayed only once a year (on Good Friday) for the Anglicans, together with other heretics. To this Newman retorted that many Anglicans did not actually pray for Roman Catholics and instead reviled them. He added that if Roman Catholics practiced duplicity, they needed Anglicans' prayers all the more.

Only a month later, however, Newman wrote Fr. Spencer a letter with an angry tone in which he criticized an alleged alliance between the Roman Catholic Church and O'Connell as well as the Liberal Party in England.[23] Newman chastised Spencer: "[Y]our acts are contrary to your words; you invite us to union of hearts, at the same time you are doing all you can, not to restore, not to reform, not to re-unite, but to destroy our Church. You go further than your principles require. You are leagued with our enemies."[24] He also decried the lack of

---

22 *Ibid.*

23 See *LD,* Vol. VII, JHN to George Spencer (February 9, 1840), 233-35; 234.

24 *Ibid,* 233-35; 233.

recognition of the English Church in the speeches and letters of foreign ecclesiastics.[25]

Newman, who was normally a witty writer, filling letters
with humorous incidents as well as clever remarks, could
be, on the one hand, overly sensitive, and on the other,
caustic in his remarks. Although Newman's fault could be
partly justified by the almost desperate situation in which
he felt the Anglican Church to be, his response to Fr. Spencer's initiative was also due to Newman's sharp and sometimes inconsiderate reactions.

During this important year of Newman's first Anglican
difficulties, Newman's life at Oxford was anything but
secluded. His sermons and scholarly work and publishing
were done in the midst of demanding pastoral work.[26] He
had daily Morning Service at St. Mary's and weekly Communion Service. He walked back and forth to Littlemore for
marriages, baptisms, and burials. Newman visited the sick
and dying; for instance, on July 9 he noted that H. Loder,
a youth of his parish, had died. Newman prepared children
for Confirmation and held examinations for them at the
Adam de Brome Chapel. He was also a Rural Dean, which
meant he was the head of a deanery or geographic grouping
of clergymen, but had to resign due to lack of time.

In addition to his close ties with Bowden, Pusey, and Rogers, and work with Keble, William Wilberforce, Thomas
Mozley, and Christie, 1839 was the year Newman's friendship with James Hope grew, as noted by an increase in
correspondence between the two. These and other friends

---

25 *Ibid.*, 234.
26 Trevor, *Newman, Pillar of the Cloud,* 222.

manifested their admiration for Newman. When Woodgate published his Bampton Lectures, he dedicated them to his friend: "In token of a long and intimate friendship, / and as a tribute of respect / to the highest intellectual endowments, consecrated, throughout a life of consistent purity and holiness, to the cause of Christ's Church . . ."[27]

That year began another lifelong friendship for Newman. Edward Bellasis, a distinguished parliamentary lawyer and friend of Hope, had read the *Tracts* and Newman's sermons. In 1838, he went to Oxford to hear Newman preach and in 1839 went to Oriel to meet Newman. He would later become a Roman Catholic and remain a devoted friend of Newman, who would dedicate his book *Grammar of Assent* to him. Two of Bellasis's sons would later join the Birmingham Oratory with Newman.

As the year 1839 came to an end, Newman confided to a friend his interior disposition to seek and follow religious truth wherever it might lead him, referring to the Roman Catholic Church:

> I really believe I say truly that, did I see cause to suspect that the Roman Church was in the right, I would try not to be unfaithful to the light given me. And if at any future time, I have any view opened to me, I will try not to turn from it, but will pursue it, wherever it may lead. I am not aware of having any hindrance, whether from fear of clamour, or regard of consistency, or even love of friends, which could keep me from joining the Church of Rome, were I persuaded I ought to do so.[28]

---

27 *LD,* Vol. VII, Dedication of Bampton Lectures by H. A. Woodgate, 77.

28 *LD,* Vol. VII, JHN to Robert Williams (November 10, 1839), 180-81; 180.

In midyear he had been struck by the role of authority by the Roman See in deciding fifth-century heresies. He applied this to the position of the Anglican Church and felt for the first time a major blow to his Anglican membership. Newman, however, thought the Oxford Movement could still revive the Catholicism inherent in the Anglican Church. In November of 1839, he sent Keble a draft of an article: "Catholicity of the English Church," later published in the January edition of the *British Critic* of 1840. It was a feeble and failed attempt to defend the Anglican claims of Apostolic Succession.

CHAPTER 26

NEWMAN'S DOUBTS ABOUT HIS POSITION IN THE ENGLISH CHURCH

1840 was another very busy year for Newman, given his responsibility as editor of the *British Critic*, though it was his last year in this position, but especially it was a year of soul-searching and transition. In his conversations and correspondence, he sought to dissuade friends against converting from the Anglican Church to the Roman Church. All the while, he was wrestling within himself over the authority of the Roman Catholic Church, the obligation to remain in the Anglican Church, and his duty as an Anglican clergyman to refrain from giving people arguments that could dispose them in favor of Rome.

The previous year Newman had written to Rogers that: "[I]f at any future time, I have any view opened to me, I will try not to turn from it, but will pursue it, wherever it may lead."[1] In 1840, he was still unpersuaded that he must go over to Rome. One of the major points that Newman continued to debate in his mind was the justification for papal authority.

In the first few months of the year, Newman exchanged letters with Pusey and Keble, trying to establish what prayer and what day of the week could be used to pray for the intention of Christian unity. Although he had initially

---

1 *LD,* Vol. VII, JHN to Robert Williams (November 10, 1839), 180-81; 180.

disliked Fr. George Spencer's introducing this custom, he
now agreed on Friday, the day suggested by Pusey. Newman, already in the habit of daily prayer at set times, now
wished to pray more and also to fast. With these questions
in mind, he decided to spend Lent in Littlemore.

In late February, Newman announced his intention of
moving to Littlemore. He planned to live the season of
Lent with increased religious observance. At Littlemore, he
abstained from many items of food and fasted until 6 p.m.
on Wednesdays and Fridays. During Holy Week, his fasting was even more severe. Newman did this even though
it caused him fatigue and headaches, as fasting often does.
Newman sought the tranquility of a village, but there were
other reasons for his move to Littlemore: Bloxam, his
curate, was leaving to attend to his dying father, and the
school was in disarray, due to lack of discipline and attention by the headmistress, who had a drinking problem.

Newman wrote Jemima for practical advice on the care
of girls; he also asked what to do with the headmistress.
In April, he told Jemima that he had given up the idea of
dismissing the headmistress, but he had set himself the task
of teaching hygiene and manners to the girls:

> I have effected a great reform (for the time) in the girls'
> hands and faces—lectured with unblushing effrontery on the
> necessity of their *keeping their work clean*, and set them to
> knit stockings with all their might. Also I am going to give
> them some neat white pinafores for Church use, and am going
> to contrive to make them make them.[2]

---

2 *LD,* Vol. VII, JHN to Mrs. John Mozley (April 1, 1840), 284-85;
285.

Newman asked friends for books on education and recommendations for the school. He began to teach the schoolchildren to sing and accompanied them with the violin. They improved, and he was able to write to Bloxam, "We learned three tunes last week—and I am ambitious of teaching them Gregorian Chant this week."[3] Newman also began to teach the Catechism to the children.

Despite the problems at Littlemore, Newman was grateful to Bloxam. He wrote to him, warmly thanking him for his services at Littlemore, "You have inspired a general reverence for religion and love of the Church, and I see it in more ways that I can name."[4] After the death of his father, Bloxam returned at times and continued to assist Newman at Littlemore.

While there, Newman conceived the idea of establishing a monastery or house of prayer at Littlemore to which he might move definitively. This house could be a place to train men for the big cities. The plan might enable him to continue as Vicar of St. Mary's, taking the Sunday afternoon duty there, while living at Littlemore.[5] Newman wondered what Oriel College would say about this arrangement and whether he would become a nonresident Fellow. Pusey encouraged Newman with his plans but advised him to retain the pulpit at St. Mary's: "for your preaching there has certainly been made an instrument of great good."[6]

---

3 *LD,* Vol. VII, JHN to J. R. Bloxam (March 29, 1840), 282.

4 *LD,* Vol. VII, JHN to J. R. Bloxam (March 15, 1840), 261-62; 261.

5 *LD,* Vol. VII, Memorandum, Reasons for Living at Littlemore (March 17, 1840), 263.

6 *LD,* Vol. VII, E. B. Pusey to JHN (March 17, 1840), 266.

Pusey also suggested that he divide his time in the terms between Oxford and Littlemore.

Newman lost no time in looking for land to buy, and with Bloxam's help he began negotiations for nine or ten acres of land close to the church. In May, he was able to purchase the land for £800 borrowed from his friend Charles Marriot. He told Harriet his plans: "Our intention is, if we are prospered, here to build a retreat; and though while Fellows of Colleges, we are bound to Oxford, yet here we propose ultimately to pitch ourselves, so far as we can form plans in so changeable a world."[7] That same day he wrote to Tom, his brother-in-law, asking for advice for building on the property. He wished to begin building with a plan that would allow for later additions. The plans should include a library, an oratory or chapel, and cells; each cell would consist of three rooms: a sitting room, a bedroom and bathroom.

As with other projects, once Newman decided on a course of action, he thrust himself into the project, heart and mind. Reviewing plans for building, he suggested to Mozley that the cells be arranged around a cloister as at Magdalen College. Newman went over many artistic and financial considerations. For instance, he asked Mozley if they could avoid chimneys and fireplaces and replace them with hot water pipes. He also made plans for planting two acres with larch, firs, and elms, and in October and November, the college gardener planted several hundred trees on the property at Littlemore.

In 1840, Newman stayed at Littlemore only during Lent, but this stay had opened a new spiritual and pastoral

---

7 *LD,* Vol. VII, JHN to Mrs. Thomas Mozley (May 20, 1840), 328.

panorama for him. For the first time in twelve years, except for the Mediterranean trip, he had been away for an extended period from St. Mary's Church and Oriel College. While considering God's will, he had worked closely with educating children, fasted, prayed, and given free rein to his romantic imagination. In June, he wrote to his friend Henry Arthur Woodgate:

> We have bought a field of 10 acres at Littlemore close to the Church—there I intend to erect a coenobitium, and to end my days. And when parsons are turned out of their livings, and rail roads have superseded turnpikes, and you and yours are mounted on horses with one or two poneys for the luggage, I will give you bread and beer at the House of the Blessed Mary of Littlemore.[8]

At about this time, Walter Hook, an Anglican clergyman who was starting a community of nuns, wrote asking Newman for a prioress. Maria Giberne also inquired if Newman would be starting a monastery for nuns. Men such as Newman, Hook, and Pusey realized that monastic communities for women and for men would strengthen the life of the Anglican Church through their practices of piety and penance. Newman also thought that this monasticism would serve to dissuade possible converts to Roman Catholicism.[9]

Early in the year, Newman admitted to Bowden that Dr. Wiseman's article in the *Dublin Review* had unsettled some Tractarians and upset him personally because of its claims. According to Wiseman, if St. Augustine or St. Basil took a

---

8 *LD,* Vol. VII, JHN to H. A. Woodgate (June 11, 1840), 343-45; 343-44.

9 *LD,* Vol. VII, JHN to J. W. Bowden (February 21, 1840), 240-42, 240-41.

look at Christendom in the nineteenth century, they would say that Rome was the Catholic Church and that Anglican England was heretical. Newman wrote in order to counter the article, even though he thought there was a great deal in favor of its claim.

In the same letter, Newman mentioned that Pusey wished to set up a community of nuns, the Sisters of Mercy; he commented that this type of institution would be "the only means of saving some of our best members turning Roman Catholics, and yet I despair of such societies being *made* externally. They must be the expansion of an inward principle."[10] As on other occasions in the previous year, Newman was concerned with secessions to Rome; he would continue to dissuade friends as well as correspondents who wrote asking for his advice. However, as he had written Bowden, he did not see how the Established Church could maintain its members without the "inward principle" of dogma and apostolicity.

During 1840, Newman exchanged letters with two persons whom he tried to dissuade from conversion to Rome: Robert Williams and William Cowper Maclaurin. Newman knew Williams well and thought that his desire to become Roman Catholic was motivated by spiritual doubts and reliance on private judgment. Newman counseled him to pray and to be patient in wishing to resolve his doubts.

In a draft of an unsent letter to Williams, Newman argued that Williams had been born into the Anglican Church, and if it were in error, then he had been born into a state of error, and was not to blame. On the other hand, Williams

---

10 *Ibid.,* 241.

should admit the possibility of Rome being in error, and if this were the case, then he was "choosing and changing into error."[11] In acting in this way he would be acting on his own private judgment against the judgment of friends who were sincerely religious. A few days later, upon the suggestion of Wood, their common friend, Newman sent Williams a shorter and less passionate letter asking him to follow his judgment and remain in the Anglican Church.

William Maclaurin was a Scot who had become an Anglican clergyman. He eventually considered the Anglican Church schismatic—that is, outside of the legitimate communion with the Church of Rome. He wrote Newman that he remained Anglican with the hope that the Oxford Divines would propose a communion of the Anglican and Roman churches. Maclaurin preferred to seek unity with the See of Rome together with others, rather than individually. A few weeks later, he wrote to Newman, offering what was almost a reply to Newman's objection to Williams about private judgment in determining the true Church. Maclaurin said that "to go over with a body would be a very different step from doing it singly."[12]

Even so, Newman countered that Maclaurin was acting on his private judgment and very likely in a perplexed state of mind. He argued that for a person to feel the duty to change his present state, God would usually give "over-

---

11 *LD,* Vol. VII, JHN to Robert Williams (July 11, 1840), 354-55, 354.

12 *LD,* Vol. VII, W.C.A. Maclaurin to JHN ((July 18, 1840), 357.

powering evidence."[13] Newman wrote to Maclaurin that it would be better for him to remain in error than to change into error.

Lastly Newman added that the Anglican Church's foundation and internal consistency were being severely tested at Oxford; he did not think that God would leave the men there to remain in error. Newman advised his interlocutor to watch the steps of the body of deeply religious, gifted, and committed men at Oxford and to see where God was leading them. *"They are Church to you*—If Rome be true, they are her Messengers guiding you to her. If England be true, they again are hers."[14] This was a prophetic statement, since many men, including Maclaurin, would be led to communion with Rome by the example of the Tractarians at Oxford.

When Maclaurin replied, he argued that he had not been brought up an Anglican, and that it was through arguments that he had changed from being a Dissenting Independent to adopting the Reformed Episcopacy. Now his question was whether he should not go further and embrace Roman Catholicism, since the arguments in favor of papal succession were stronger than those for Apostolic Succession claimed by Catholics and Anglicans alike.

In his response, Newman admitted that if Maclaurin had arrived to the Anglican Church by private judgment, it would also be just to advance to Rome in the same manner. He counseled Maclaurin to be patient and to refrain from acting in a state of perplexity:

---

13 *LD,* Vol. VII, JHN to W.C.A. Maclaurin (July 26, 1840), 368-70; 368.

14 *Ibid.,* 370.

If I might venture to suggest, I would say that, were I in your present most painful state of mind, I think I should give over the *direct inquiry* for several years and give myself to fasting and prayer and practical duties. At the end of this time I trust that God would enlighten my judgment—at all events I should be in a better state of mind to judge how my duty lay.[15]

Newman was beginning to entertain doubts about Anglicanism, and he was doing exactly what he advised Maclaurin to do: fasting more, praying for Christian unity, and patiently waiting. In 1840, there were still Roman doctrines and practices that Newman could not accept. The principal doctrine with which he wrestled was the one concerning the office of the Pope.

NEWMAN'S POSITION IN THE ANGLICAN CHURCH

Newman realized that the office of the Bishop of Rome was important historically. However, when he preached a sermon titled "The Unity of the Church," he acknowledged the Apostolic origin of Baptism, but not of the papacy. Although an ingrained prejudice against the papacy remained firm in his subconscious, he was no longer equating the Antichrist with the Bishop, or the See of Rome. In 1840, Newman reviewed "Discourses on the Prophecies Relating to Antichrist in the Writings of Daniel and St. Paul," by James H. Todd, published that same year. Todd argued that despite corruptions in the Catholic Church, it

---

15 *Ibid.,* 404.

was wrong to name Catholics apostates and their bishops Antichrists. Newman agreed with Todd, and like him, asserted that Roman Catholics hold the essential truths of the faith.

Todd had adduced many arguments to show the errors of those who interpret the Prophet Daniel or St. Paul as indications that Rome or the Pope is the Antichrist. He had also traced the origin of the accusation of the Pope as the Antichrist to heretical groups, namely the Albigensians and the Spiritual Franciscans in the twelfth century. Calling Rome the Antichrist was an attempt to counter its doctrines by discrediting it. Newman agreed with Todd and argued that a mark of the true Church was its accusation of being the Antichrist by those who disagreed with certain doctrines. Newman went on at length to question the credibility of Bishop Thomas Newton, who in a book on prophecies had charged the greater part of Christianity with falling into a satanical error. Newman compared Newton, a worldly and mediocre bishop, with St. John Chrysostom, a holy and very generous bishop, who died persecuted for the faith, and asked, "Is this the man to sit in judgment on Chrysostom? is he the man to be trusted rather than Chrysostom?"[16]

In the review, Newman also described the holy lives of the sixteenth-century Bishop of Milan, St. Charles Borromeo, and the seventeenth-century Bishop of Annecy, St. Francis de Sales. Both of these men had lived exceptional

---

16 John Henry Newman, *Essays Critical and Historical*, *II*, "The Protestant Idea of Antichrist," 139, available at: http://www.newmanreader. org/works/essays/volume2/index.html. After this it will be cited *Ess. II.*

lives and had loved the Pope. Newman argued, "How can someone love the Antichrist and live in such a manner as these men?" After this, Newman put his finger on the crux of the matter:

> The only question then is this, "Has Christ, or has He not, appointed a body representative of Him on earth during His absence?" If He has, the Pope is not Antichrist;—if He has not, every bishop in England, Bishop Newton, Bishop Warburton, Bishop Hurd, is Antichrist; every priest is Antichrist, Mr. McNeile, Dr. Jortin, and Dr. Faussett inclusive.[17]

Newman also put forth various other arguments in favor of the Catholic Church; one was a historical one and the other a biblical one. The first one was a description of the Church's unequaled service to society. She has fulfilled her high mission. Newman offered examples from the lives of three bishops who were also saints: Ambrose, Basil, and Athanasius. The biblical argument was that wealth is not a mark of the Antichrist. What is evil and associated with the Antichrist is idolatry and attachment to material goods.

Writing to his close friend, Rogers, who was traveling in Europe, Newman admitted that the separation of the English Church was wrong, yet he would still not accept the authority of the Roman See: "It is quite consistent to say that I think Rome the *centre* of unity, and yet not to say that she is infallible, when she is by herself."[18] Looking back years later, however, Newman noted that upon reading quotes from St. Augustine regarding the catholicity of

---

17 *Ibid.,* 173.

18 *LD,* Vol. VII, JHN to Frederic Rogers (November 25, 1840), 448-52; 448.

the Church, he had seen the writing upon the wall, namely God's hand:

> It was clear that I had a good deal to learn on the question of the Churches, and that perhaps some new light was coming upon me. He who has seen a ghost, cannot be as if he had never seen it. The heavens had opened and closed again. The thought for a moment had been, "the Church of Rome will be found right after all" and then it had vanished. My old convictions remained as before.[19]

For Newman, the Catholic Church had three branches: the Anglican, the Roman, and the Orthodox. For a moment in 1839, he had seen that the center of the Church lay in Rome, but it would not be until 1841 that his confidence in Anglicanism was altogether shaken. Newman continued to tone down his way of speaking of Rome and to ask others to do the same. He had been doing this since the summer of the previous year.

Newman thought that the Anglican Church had Apostolic Succession, a sacramental system and the Primitive Creed, but he realized that in the Anglican system, the dogma and the ritual were much less strict than in the Roman system. He realized that for a long time he had accepted the statements of Anglican Divines without weighing them for himself. Now he concluded that while the Lutherans and Calvinists had a sort of theology, the Anglicans had none distinctively theirs.

Newman felt "very nearly a pure Protestant,"[20] but in addition to Baptism, he recognized the Holy Eucharist as a sacrament and used the word "Sacrament" to refer

---

19 *Apo.*, 118.
20 *Apo.*, 120.

to the Communion Service on Sundays. He continued to believe that Christ's Presence was a Real Presence and of a spiritual type rather than a "local" or physical presence. He acknowledged the sacrificial nature of the Mass and the Holy Eucharist, but misrepresented Catholic belief about the manner of Christ's Presence in the Holy Eucharist, which would lead to a friendly exchange in the following year with Fr. Charles Russell, an Irish priest.

In 1840, Mary Holmes, a young woman who was a musician and a writer and who had begun a religious life, introduced herself to Newman and began to correspond with him. In reply to a question about absolution, the sacramental forgiveness of sins, Newman explained that the Anglican Church accepted, as the Roman Catholic Church does, that absolution restores the soul to God's favor. Then he added without explanation that unlike the Roman Catholic Church, the Anglican Church "does not pronounce itself on the punishment incurred by sin."[21]

Newman had heard confession only once at Oxford, and it had been with some trepidation. Confession of sins and sacramental absolution had fallen out of use in the Anglican Church. Newman wrote Maria Giberne, his other frequent female correspondent, "I feel sure that we should be all in a much better state, were it practiced—but I see very great obstacles to reviving it. I think it should always be *sacramental*—performed in Church and face to face."[22] He commented that one of the obstacles to the practice of

---

21 *LD,* Vol. VII, JHN to Miss Holmes (July 19, 1840), 360-62; 360.

22 *LD,* Vol. VII, JHN to Miss M. R. Giberne (December 22, 1840), 465-67; 466.

confession was the lack of belief as a Church in this sacrament and concluded, "But I am sure that we are not a real
genuine Church, a Church all glorious within, till we return
to this primitive and Scriptural practice."[23]

Confession was not the only Catholic sacrament not considered so in the Anglican Church; Matrimony was, and
still is, considered a sacred rite in the Anglican Church,
yet it was not treated as a sacrament like Baptism. Newman held Matrimony in high esteem as a means, or path,
of Christian sanctification that had a specific rite and a holy
place in the Church. However, he did not speak of it in
terms of a sacrament.

Since his initial reaction to the marriage plans of Henry
William Wilberforce and other friends, Newman's acceptance of marriage for Oxford clergymen had changed. He
was more accepting of it and did not discourage Frederick
William Faber from a future marriage. Newman told Faber
that celibacy could be considered "as a penance for past
sin," but he added, "I consider it also a more holy state"[24]—
one that could not be strongly urged upon another. Newman advised Faber to wait for God's grace to show him the
path that he was to follow.

Newman was at a crossroads between the Church of England and the Church of Rome; this made him unsure of his
role as Vicar of St. Mary's, an Anglican Church. He thought
of resigning from St. Mary's because he feared that he was
misleading undergraduates toward Rome, but when he consulted Pusey about resigning from St. Mary's, the reply was

---

23 *Ibid.,* 466.
24 *LD,* Vol. VII, JHN to F. W. Faber (October 24,1840) 421-22; 422.

that he would cause more harm by leaving. At this time, Newman read at St. Mary's his sermon "Divine Calls." In it, he spoke of seeking to please God alone and of the shallowness of seeking human praise. He urged his parishioners: "Let us beg and pray Him day by day to reveal Himself to our souls more fully, to quicken our senses, to give us sight and learning, and touch of the world to come . . ."[25]

NEWMAN AT OXFORD

Despite Newman's doubts about his role at St. Mary's and at Oriel College, he was actively involved in the intellectual and religious life of the University. In 1840, he preached a few University Sermons upon the request of Heads of Houses.

In addition to his pastoral duties and Sunday sermons at St. Mary's Church, he met every month for theological meetings with his friends and took his turn presenting theological papers at these meetings. During this year he was involved with a few controversies, which were, however, less disturbing than those of earlier years. Newman summarized these to his sister Jemima: "I am in a lot of controversies—from Ward of T [Trinity] who was set on me for the article in the B.C. and from Mr. Hornby for the attacks on Knox in Froude's third volume. Also the egregious Goly has written 100 pages, but this requires no answer."[26]

George Robert Ward, a contemporary of Newman at Trinity College, published the statutes of Magdalen

---

25 *PPS*, Vol. VIII, "Divine Calls," 32.
26 *LD*, Vol. VII, JHN to Mrs. John Mozley (May 28, 1840), 334.

College and had a plan to publish the statutes of other colleges. Newman's friend James Hope wrote an article for the *British Critic* in which he criticized Ward. Newman asked Hope not to be severe with Ward, who had kind words to say about Newman, but the final article annoyed Ward.

As mentioned in his letter to Jemima, another controversy was with James Hornby, who voiced an objection to Newman on Hurrell Froude's *Remains*. Froude had denied that Knox held the doctrine of Apostolic Succession to which Hornby disagreed and for which he asked for an explanatory note in the *British Critic*. After the exchange of a few letters between Hornby and Newman, the latter declined to acquiesce to Hornby's demands.[27]

The third controversy was almost a one-sided attack upon Pusey and the Tractarians. Newman shrugged this one off as unimportant. It involved Golightly, who wrote the Bishop of Oxford a very long letter criticizing Pusey's "Letter to the Bishop" occasioned by the Oxford Memorial to the Reformers. Golightly, the leader for the memorial, actually sent the pamphlet to Newman, who replied with a simple thank-you note. To some friends, Newman referred to Golightly with humorous disdain, calling him "Golius." All these controversies were the inevitable consequence of Newman's publishing projects, especially as editor of the *British Critic*.

---

27 *LD,* Vol. VII, JHN to James J. Hornby (May 8, 1840), 320.

Editorship of the British Critic

This was the third year that Newman edited the *British Critic,* and again it was very demanding work. As editor, he suggested topics of articles and sources to his writers, corrected their submissions, and wrote articles. To Hope he explained: "If you can enter into a *reviewer's* [an editor's] feelings, you might divine that he *first,* on receiving an article, looks through it *negatively,* to see there is nothing which offends him . . ."[28] He was careful not to offend friends and bishops out of respect and prudence, not out of fear. He likewise sought the right timing to publish any critical review. For instance, when H. H. Milman published *History of Christianity,* Newman delayed publishing his review of it.

Even though Newman worked long hours as editor, he counted on the help of his friends, especially Tom Mozley, Henry Wilberforce, and John William Bowden. All of the writers were anonymous, yet they invested a great amount of time and energy in writing the articles. Soon after Newman took up the editorship, the sales increased steadily. Newman's position as editor obliged him to fill up the pages with spirited essays from his own pen, but one day toward the end of the year, he decided to give up the editorship. The decision may have been part of his desire to have more time to pray and to think about his position in the Church. He informed the publishers of his plans, and suggested that Mozley become the new editor. The publishers replied, thanking Newman for his excellent work and showing interest in Mozley as Newman's successor.

---

28 *LD,* Vol. VII, JHN to J. R. Hope (March 18, 1840), 268.

THE MOZLEYS AND OTHER FRIENDS

Tom Mozley was not only Newman's brother-in-law, he was also a close collaborator and friend to Newman. Often, Newman asked him to send articles sooner or to make corrections quickly for the sake of filling in the gaps in the review. Newman was grateful to him and opened one letter to him: "My dear Tom, You are what the Americans call a 'prime chap'; I only hope that I have not put you to great inconvenience."[29]

This year, James Mozley presented himself to a Fellowship at Magdalen College, and he was elected. Newman was delighted with the news of his former pupil and now brother-in-law. Newman wrote about the good news to his friends. He told Pusey, "Mozley passed a very good examination, and that told decidedly. It was a very near run thing."[30] A few of his opponents had not been present to vote. Newman was also very happy because the three residents at the house of writers at St. Aldate's Street: Pattison, Christie, and Mozley, had all been elected Fellows.

By midyear, Bowden returned to London from a long stay in Malta. When Newman went to London for the dentist, or other meetings, he paid Bowden at least two short visits. Bowden's health had improved, again he was able to write articles for the *British Critic,* and he managed to finish his book on Pope Gregory VII. Before publishing his book, Bowden asked Newman to allow him to dedicate it to him, but Newman declined, explaining that this was his principle to avoid the appearance of mutual praise

---

29 *LD,* Vol. VII, JHN to Thomas Mozley (September 6, 1840), 388.
30 *LD,* Vol. VII, JHN to E. B. Pusey (July 28, 1840), 371-72; 372.

among Tractarians.[31] He had declined a previous dedication by Pusey. Newman was touched by his friend's wish and wrote to him: "The loss of your Dedication is one of the most trying things I have had for some time. But Rogers to whom I mentioned it agreed with me. And then I had declined Pusey; how could I undo *this*?"[32]

Rogers was, in addition to Pusey and Keble, close to Newman. Although Rogers only wrote one article for the *British Critic*, he often ate meals with Newman at Oxford and also often went up to Littlemore with Newman. From April to December, William Copeland filled in as curate at Littlemore. Then, in December, Newman asked Arthur Haddan, a Trinity graduate and a newly ordained clergyman, to be his curate at Littlemore.

Friends often asked Newman for advice on books to read, or on books in which to find the answer to various questions. The advice that he gave to Miss Holmes, the young governess under his spiritual guidance, reveals the Church historians that Newman liked and his favorite books on the religious services of the Church. He recommended a Church history by E. Churton and another by Palmer. The book he found most useful for the services was *A Rationale upon the Book of Common Prayer of the Church of England,* by Anthony Sparrow; Newman had written the preface to the second edition.

In his letters, we also find the spiritual advice that Newman gave to his friends. He encouraged them to strive for

31 *LD,* Vol. VII, JHN to J. W. Bowden (October 13, 1840), 405-06; 405.

32 *LD,* Vol. VII, JHN to J. W. Bowden (November 6, 1840), 430-31; 430.

Christian holiness without leaving their present occupations and social surroundings. When Miss Holmes asked him about a newly converted Christian who wished to write books, Newman gave the following advice: "Let her turn her activity and energy upon herself; let her consider how much must be done by every one of us to enter life; how much is open to every one to do both to the glory of God and toward personal improvement; how high and wonderful a thing Christian Sanctity is; and what capabilities the regenerate soul has for improvement."[33] Next Newman advised her to study classical books of spirituality, namely, *The Imitation of Christ* by Kempis, *Pensées* by Pascal, and the devotional books of Bishop Taylor, Bishop Cosin, and Bishop Andrew. Newman continued with advice that he had been putting into practice for many years:

> Should she not give herself to the contemplation of obedience and holiness, and the reading of the lives of the Saints; and set herself deliberately to the business of self-government, of changing herself where she most requires it, of gaining perfect resignation to God's will, of unlearning worldly opinions, motives and principles, and of living as if in the sight of things invisible,—and that without impatience at apparent failure or apparent slow advance?[34]

More frequent than advice of an ascetical nature, Newman's letters contain comments and advice on church architecture and ecclesiastical matters of the day. Both subjects were of concern for the Oxford Movement.

---

33 *LD,* Vol. VII, JHN to Miss Holmes (May 29, 1840), 335-36.
34 *Ibid.*

CHURCH CONSTRUCTION

In 1818, Parliament passed the *Church Building Act* to provide money for building more churches and to settle problems, such as property rights and the division of tithes, derived from the creation of new parishes. Pusey and Newman pledged their support to the Bethnal Green churches, a project by the Bishop of London to build ten churches in the impoverished East End of London.

Some articles for the *British Critic* were on the subject of church architecture. Tom Mozley wrote one in 1839, and another in 1840, titled "New Churches." The Tractarians gave a lot of significance to church architecture because they realized that exterior beauty in sacred art is an expression of the holiness and beauty of God. The iconoclasm of the Protestant Reformation had gone hand in hand with a decreasing value given to doctrine, for the sake of greater inclusiveness of Dissenting bodies, and a focus on moral and social concerns. The doctrinal and spiritual renewal of the Church of England called also for a renewal in architecture and other sacred art. An important figure in this renewal was Augustus Welby Pugin, an English architect responsible for the revival of Gothic architecture in England. He became Catholic in 1834, and together with another convert and very wealthy patron, John Talbot, sixteenth Earl of Shrewsbury, built many beautiful Gothic churches in Staffordshire.

Various Tractarians and their friends were building or rebuilding churches with these ideals in mind. Newman wrote to Maria Giberne, "Iffley Church is going to be set to rights—and Sandford Church has had a tower built and inside reformed in a very Catholic way."[35] The Sandford Church was St. Andrew's Church at Sandford-on-Thames. Besides the addition of a tower, the arch of the chancel was rebuilt and new windows were added. At Ampfield in Keble's parish, a church dedicated to St. Mark was being built; Newman attended the consecration in April of 1841. In 1840, Newman had attended the consecrations of two other churches and congratulated others for their architectural labors.

Newman advised and encouraged Tom Mozley in his plans for a parish church at Cholderton. Mozley's church was small and in need of renovation. He drew up some architectural plans for it, but found resistance from the Provost at Oriel. Newman managed to obtain the college's approval, but told his brother-in-law not to send the Provost the elaborate plans nor mention Newman's financial support. Newman told Harriet, "You see I fear the Provost is *bent* on your not having a handsome Church—If Tom kicks, the said P. will write to the Bishop—*so let Tom quietly go to building,* now that he has got leave, saying nothing to nobody. The Provost cannot pull down. The P. does things so slowly, he will never guess what is going on till it is done."[36] Thus, in a stealthy manner, Mozley was able to begin construction of a beautiful church in keeping with his Tractarian ideals.

Newman also cared for the details within his church at Littlemore. In 1840, he added two more stained glass

---

35 *LD,* Vol. VII, JHN to Miss M. R. Giberne (July 17, 1840), 360.

36 *LD,* Vol. VII, JHN to Mrs. Thomas Mozley (November 23, 1840), 247.

windows to the church and made plans to add a small memorial to his friend, Hurrell Froude. The most significant addition was, however, an ornamental one made by his sister Jemima. He had asked her to make an altar cloth and had given her some instructions. She produced a very beautiful altar cloth, which exceeded all expectations and thrilled the women of the parish. Newman told his sister the reaction of the women and of Bloxam:

> It looks beautiful, and B is quite in ecstasies about it. As to Mrs. Barnes she dreamed of it of a night [sic] at first from astonishment at its elaborateness—and Eliza B. and several others, who are work women, look at it with amazement. Rogers, taking another view of it, is equally full of admiration. Indeed we are all so happy that one is afraid of being too happy.[37]

Even more urgent than proper care for the beauty of church architecture and liturgical rites was doctrinal clarity and faithfulness to the Creed and other apostolic traditions. The Church's bishops, who were entrusted with the mission to safeguard these truths, were failing in their responsibility.

ECCLESIASTICAL AUTHORITY

Newman had always acted with great respect and obedience for his bishop and the bishops in general, but he had also begun to lose his confidence in them. He was saddened by their general weakness in defending doctrines, as

---

37 *LD,* Vol. VII, JHN to Mrs. John Mozley (April 18, 1840), 312.

well as their apathy in responding to initiatives such as the prayer for the union of Christians.

When in 1840 Philip Shuttleworth was appointed Bishop of Chichester, Newman wrote to his friend Benjamin Harrison, chaplain to the Archbishop of Canterbury, expressing his fear that the consecration of this bishop would push some toward the Church of Rome. Newman also confided to Maria Giberne, "The new Bishop, Dr. Shuttleworth, will, I suppose, level some Episcopal Charges at us, but I don't suppose he will do much harm, which is the utmost one has a right to expect, sad to say, from appointments in these evil days."[38] Given the reigning religious liberalism, Newman noted with surprise two good appointments to lesser diocesan posts. Shuttleworth appointed Manning as Archdeacon of Chichester, and Hope was appointed Chancellor of the Diocese of Salisbury.

Newman believed that the bishops were responsible for maintaining communion in the Church, but he began to realize that many were unable to do so and others were afraid. Earlier in the year, Hope had mentioned to Newman that it would be fitting for the Chancellor of Oxford University to be a bishop, for there were precedents. Newman pointed out the risk of having a bishop appointed for life, because the choice of a bad one would favor Dissenters and unorthodox men such as Arnold and Hampden. Newman and the other Tractarians suffered from the failure of the bishops to uphold orthodox doctrine. By way of contrast, Newman portrayed in his writings the lives of holy

---

38 *LD,* Vol. VII, JHN to Miss M. R. Giberne (September 6, 1840), 387-88; 388.

bishops who had been champions of the faith during the early centuries of the Church. Newman's own sermons spoke of the same Church tradition of prayer, penance, and sacramental life.

CHURCH OF THE FATHERS AND PAROCHIAL SERMONS

In 1840, Newman continued to collect and organize his essays and sermons for publication. At the start of the year, he published *Church of the Fathers,* a collection of letters published in the *British Magazine* between 1833 and 1837. He continued to preach regularly at the University Church of St. Mary's and at St. Mary's in Littlemore. When traveling outside of Oxford, he was asked by friends to preach. On one occasion, while preaching at All Saints on Margaret Street where his friend Frederick Oakeley was the rector, a dangerous and at the same time humorous incident took place. He wrote to Harriet describing the event: "While I was sitting in my surplice at the altar in Margaret Chapel on Sunday, during the first lesson a large cat fell from the ceiling, down close to my feet, narrowly missing my head."[39] His friend, Mrs. Bowden, compared the story to her recollection of seeing a large cat at St. Mary Maggiore in Rome and with good humor remarked how closely the Chapel on Margaret Street resembled a Roman Catholic Church.[40]

The same year Newman arranged sermons that he preached in connection with the liturgical year, preparing

---

39 *LD,* Vol. VII, JHN to Mrs. Thomas Mozley (July 8, 1840), 352-53.
40 *Ibid.*

them for publication as Volume V of his *Parochial and Plain Sermons.* These were published in November in a larger printing than the previous volume. Most of the new sermons that Newman preached in 1840 would be part of the following volume of the *Parochial and Plain Sermons.* Some of the subjects were basic spiritual topics on which Newman insisted, such as sincerity in religious practice, repentance from sin, and resistance to worldliness. He also preached sermons written in previous years; one of these was on the practice of fasting. Although Newman was fasting regularly, a practice which he found difficult, he advised those who asked him about fasting to make instead small acts of self-denial. He wrote to Miss Holmes, "I would not abstain from food in a way to attract attention— but there are ways of denying oneself, where no one would suspect it."[41]

In another sermon, *The World Our Enemy,* Newman pointed out the mistake of thinking of a vague presence of evil in the world. Sinfulness, he explained, is due to man's corruption of the world and to man's disordered attraction to the good things of the world. Men live by sight instead of by faith; they wish the hundredfold promised in the Gospel without sacrifice and without looking toward the full reward in Heaven. The answer to temptations, wrote Newman, does not lie in fleeing from the world. With regard to a woman who frequented the Court, he wrote: "I do not think advisable you should break off your usual visits to the Court—particularly as your stay is limited. Nothing in the course of engagements in which

---

41 *LD,* Vol. VII, JHN to Miss Holmes (June 10, 1840), 341-42; 342.

you find yourself, is actually objectionable, and therefore you should continue in them."[42] Newman wished to stress that virtues could be lived in all settings.

Newman realized that the way to holiness is a prayerful life with the practice of self-examination and self-control. He explained further, "Though temptations present themselves to you in society, you would soon find temptations in solitude, were you to indulge your love of it. We cannot escape from *ourselves,* wherever we are—and *we* are the sinners, not the places in which we find ourselves."Other sermons were on circumstantial subjects such as the anniversary of the dedication of a temple or the unity of the Church. A few of the sermons would be published under two different collections, *University Sermons* and *Sermons on Subjects of the Day.*

Despite some shared religious beliefs, Newman's beliefs and practices had diverged from those of his family. Still, he tried to maintain the family ties, and in the midst of his consuming pastoral work he kept up correspondence with his siblings and occasionally saw them, except for Charles.

NEWMAN'S FAMILY

John Henry and Jemima corresponded often, and among his siblings, she was the one in whom John Henry confided most. In 1840, a new train line that went as far as Derby opened up, and Newman visited Jemima and John Mozley

---

42 *LD,* Vol. VII, JHN to Miss Holmes (July 19, 1840), 360-62; 361.

twice. John Rickards Mozley, Jemima's second son, was born in May. Years later, John Rickards would become a close correspondent with his uncle.

In October, John Henry and Frank met once at Cheltenham on John's way to visit Jemima in Derby. They had been estranged for a few years, following a letter by John Henry to Frank's wife, which had caused Frank jealousy. More importantly, both brothers could not agree on religious matters. Before their brief meeting, they exchanged some long letters explaining some of their religious beliefs. Frank told his brother that he would preach in any church when asked to do so, and that he considered the Baptist or Independent meeting "*as true* a church as yours, and yours as much a sect as those."[43]

There are no letters of correspondence with Charles that year, but occasionally John Henry had news about this brother from Frank. After one of these he told Jemima, "I have just heard from F.—C. [Charles Newman] is going on in his old way—writing him abusive letters. He seems to have written a whole *book* about him, which may dribble thro' the penny post. He is Honorary Secretary of the Bristol Statistical Society!"[44]

John Henry and Harriet corresponded a few times, and they were on good terms. She had written *The Fairy Bower, or History of a Month, A Tale for Young People,* a novel about their family that John Henry was reading. It was published the following year.

---

43 *LD,* Vol. VII, F. W. Newman to JHN (April 15, 1840), 307-09; 308.

44 *LD,* Vol. VII, JHN to Mrs. John Mozley (November 30, 1840), 453-54; 454.

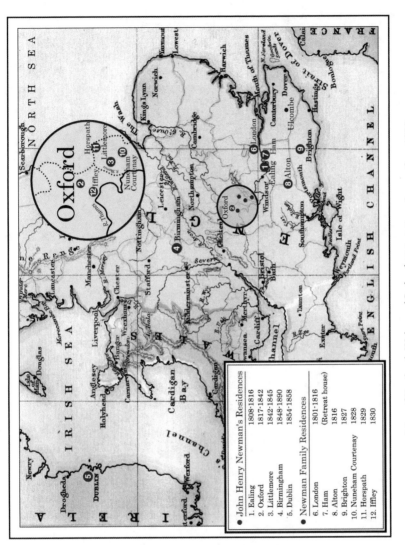

Map of England, Wales and Ireland (Adaptation of a map from 1876)
The Cross Lines divide the map into squares of 100 English miles.

● John Henry Newman's Residences
1. Ealing   1808-1816
2. Oxford   1817-1842
3. Littlemore   1842-1845
4. Birmingham   1848-1890
5. Dublin   1854-1858

● Newman Family Residences
6. London   1801-1816
7. Ham   (Retreat house)
8. Alton   1816
9. Brighton   1827
10. Nuneham Courtenay 1828
11. Horspath   1829
12. Iffley   1830

Family Group sketch by Maria Giberne (ca. 1830) (*Left to right*: Francis, Mrs. Newman, Harriet, John Henry, Jemima).

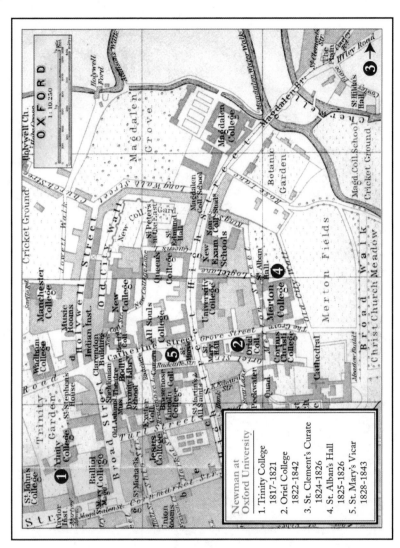

Partial Map of Oxford, 1901 (Adaptation from Wagner & Debes, Leipsic)

Newman at
Oxford University

1. Trinity College
   1817–1821
2. Oriel College
   1822–1842
3. St. Clement's Curate
   1824–1826
4. St. Alban's Hall
   1825–1826
5. St. Mary's Vicar
   1828–1843

Trinity College (Newman lived there from 1817 to 1821).

Trinity College Chapel.

Oriel Quad (Newman was a Fellow of Oriel College from 1822–1845).

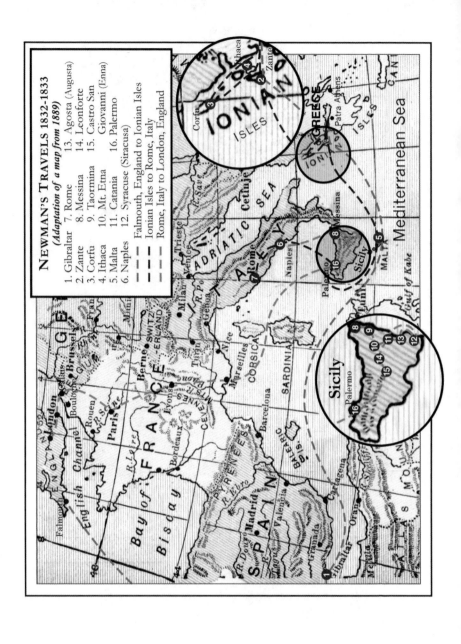

Newman's Travels 1832-1833
(Adaptation of a map from 1889)

1. Gibraltar
2. Zante
3. Corfu
4. Ithaca
5. Malta
6. Naples
7. Rome
8. Messina
9. Taormina
10. Mt. Etna
11. Catania
12. Syracuse (Siracusa)
13. Agosta (Augusta)
14. Leonforte
15. Castro San Giovanni (Enna)
16. Palermo

- - - Falmouth, England to Ionian Isles
—— Ionian Isles to Rome, Italy
- - - Rome, Italy to London, England

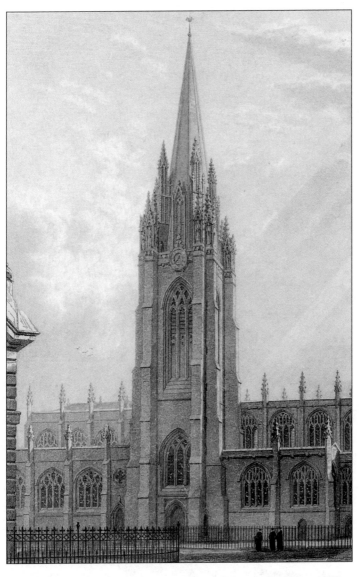

St. Mary, the Virgin, Oxford (Newman was the Vicar from 1828 to 1843).

The pulpit of St. Mary the Virgin. (Many students and Tutors went to hear Newman's Sunday sermons).

A restoration of Newman's "College" at Littlemore (Newman adapted some barns into living quarters and moved there in 1842).

Fr. Newman, ca. 1866.

St. Mary and St. Nicholas, Littlemore. (Newman ran a school at Littlemore and the children attended services at St. Mary's).

Living Room at Littlemore today (There, on the night of Oct. 8, 1845, Newman began his confession to Fr. Dominic Barbieri).

Newman's desk at Littlemore (On this desk he wrote *Development of Christian Doctrine*).

Photo of Cardinal Newman by Barraud (1885) (Pope Leo XIII made Newman a cardinal in 1879).

Newman's writing desk, Birmingham Oratory (This was in Newman's room where he lived and wrote from 1851–1890).

Cardinal Newman Library, Birmingham Oratory, Edgbaston (Newman moved there in 1851 and brought with him many of the books today in the library).

Cardinal's Private Chapel, Birmingham Oratory (Newman had portraits of his friends for whom he prayed at Mass).

Newman's Tomb at Rednal, outside of Birmingham (In 2010 his remains were exhumed and taken to the Birmingham Oratory Church).

As the year came to a close, Newman wished to remain Anglican and to fight the religious liberalism that vied for the soul of the Anglican Church and its bishops. Earlier, when discussing with Pusey the possibility of resigning from St. Mary's, he explained his state of mind in three points: the English Church was being tested, and although it had the risk of bursting, it might bear "infused Catholic truth;" all English Divines had created sympathy toward Rome, and; the real foe at the door was Liberalism and Rationalism; to leave St. Mary's would be to give the pulpit to the enemy.[45] For these reasons throughout 1840, Newman sincerely dissuaded friends and acquaintances from moving closer to Roman Catholicism, advising them to be patient and to pray for God's grace. While doing this, however, Newman himself felt more unsure about the claims of the Anglican Church and his own position in this church. With the publication of Volume V of the *Parochial and Plain Sermons* and his resignation as editor of the *British Critic,* Newman cleared his desk for some important change, as yet unknown to him. It would be an attempt to reconcile the *Thirty-Nine Articles* to true Catholic principles. In December of 1840, he began a draft of what would be the famous *Tract 90*, the last of the Oxford *Tracts.*

---

45 *Ibid.,* 450.

CHAPTER 27

THE CRISIS OVER *TRACT 90*

THE year 1841 would mark a major turning point in Newman's religious development. The main event of the year was his publication of *Tract 90* and the reaction that it unleashed in Oxford, among the English bishops and throughout England. The crisis over *Tract 90* would lead Newman to stand firm in his defense of Catholic principles and to question the authority of Anglican bishops. Toward the end of 1841 another crisis, over the establishment of an Anglican–Lutheran See in Jerusalem, led Newman to begin to doubt that the English Church was a branch of the true Catholic Church.

The *Thirty-Nine Articles*, drafted in 1571, and approved by the bishops, were an attempt to define the doctrine of the Anglican Church. Together with a set of prescribed *Homilies* and the *Book of Common Prayer* they formed a body of the teaching and liturgy of the Anglican Church. The three elements were a compromise between Roman Catholic and Protestant doctrinal beliefs and liturgical practices. English clergymen and students studying at Oxford University were obliged to subscribe to the *Articles*.

In 1840, Newman noted that his friend Robert Williams and others thought that the Articles opposed Catholic truths taught by the Roman Catholic Council of Trent. Newman set out to show that this was not the case; the

Articles opposed only abuses by the Church of Rome. He completed the tract in late January 1841, and as soon as it was published in February, its content provoked a protest at Oxford.

In *Tract 90*, Newman examined fourteen of the Articles. In a notice to the tract he wrote, "THIS Tract was written under the conviction that the Anglican Thirty-Nine Articles of Religion, of which it treated, were, when taken in their letter, so loosely worded, so incomplete in statement, and so ambiguous in their meaning, as to need an authoritative interpretation . . ."[1] Newman asserted that only the Catholic Church and what it had taught always and everywhere could supply that interpretation. Article XXXV mandated the reading in church of Homilies from the *Book of Homilies,* which explained Anglican doctrine.

Regarding Articles VI and XX on Holy Scripture and the Authority of the Church, Newman asserted that "not a word is said, on the one hand, in favour of there being no *external* rule or method to fix the interpretation of Scripture by, or, as it is commonly expressed, of Scripture *being the sole rule of faith*; nor on the other, of the *private judgment of the individual* being the ultimate standard of interpretation."[2] In support of this he quoted from Anglican theologians that the Holy Scriptures form together with the Creed a rule of Faith instead of two different rules of Faith.

Newman argued that the *Articles* stated only broad principles. Concerning *Article VI* on Justification by faith, for example, Newman pointed out that the words do not

---

1 *Tract 90,* notice, 261.
2 *Tract 90,* 276.

deny Baptism's role in Justification. Furthermore, the *Articles* left open points of controversy, such as the manner of Christ's Spiritual Presence in the Holy Eucharist. The authors of the *Articles* did not define the manner of Christ's Presence, except to affirm that He is present in a heavenly and spiritual manner. Christ's presence is not a local presence because the Body of Christ is in Heaven. Article XXVIII held that Transubstantiation (the change of bread and wine into the Body and Blood of Christ) is a doctrine contrary to Scripture. By this the framers of the *Articles* rejected the belief held by some Roman Catholics that following the words of Consecration Christ is present under the form of an ordinary human body. Newman explained:

> What is here opposed as "Transubstantiation," is the shocking doctrine that the body of CHRIST, as the Article goes on to express it, is not given, taken, and eaten, after an heavenly and spiritual manner, but is carnally pressed with the teeth; that It is a body or substance of a certain extension and bulk in space, and a certain figure and due disposition of parts, whereas we hold that the only substance such, is the bread which we see.[3]

Later, as a Roman Catholic, Newman maintained much of what he had written in the *Tract*, except for his understanding of Transubstantiation and the section on Article XXXI which rejects the Mass as a sacrifice and the practice of private offering of the Mass by a priest without a congregation. Article XXXI condemned the doctrine that Christ is offered in the Mass for the remission of sins of both the

---

3 Tract 90, 315, ed. 1883.

living and the dead. This was the position held by Anglican theologians and the Tractarians.

Newman explained that, when writing *Tract 90*, he had agreed with the doctrine of seventeenth-century Anglican Divines that Christ is not offered in the Mass. He noted how Pusey had explained in *Tract 81* that the early Christians offered their gifts to God and that God in turn gave Himself to them, but Christ Himself was not offered. For the Tractarians the sacrifice consisted in the offering or oblation of bread and wine to God and the communication by God to men of the Lord's Personal Presence. However, "there was no real offering up of Christ, because there was no Transubstantiation. He was really present, but as our spiritual food, and as the Lamb that had been offered once, but not as then being offered; not as the Lamb of the Mass."[4]

At this time, Newman preached a sermon, "The Spiritual Presence of Christ in the Church," in which he looked at different Gospel passages that indicated the Risen Christ's Presence among His disciples. Newman attempted to show that, in a way that cannot be humanly explained, the Body of Christ that was in Heaven was simultaneously present to His disciples. St. Luke narrated Christ's visible presence to the Disciples of Emmaus, and how it became an invisible or spiritual presence: "He vanished from sight that He might be present in a sacrament; and in order to connect His visible presence with His presence invisible . . . ."[5] After the Ascension, Christ appeared to Saul in a

---

4 *Tract 90,* 353, ed. 1883.

5 *PPS,* (Ignatius Edition) Vol. VI, "The Spiritual Presence of Christ in the Church," 1262-1271; 1269.

visible yet mysterious manner on the way to Damascus. By means of this analysis of New Testament passages, Newman aimed to underscore Christ's Spiritual Presence in the Holy Eucharist.

In *Tract 90,* however, Newman misrepresented Roman Catholic doctrine about the manner of Christ's Presence in the Holy Eucharist. Charles Russell, an Irish Catholic priest ten years Newman's junior, was sad to hear that Newman accepted the Protestant misrepresentation of this doctrine. Where Richard Wiseman had failed, Russell, who was a humble and clever priest, managed to get through to Newman. Russell wrote a letter to Newman on Holy Thursday expressing an ardent love for Christ in the Eucharist. Russell told Newman that Roman Catholics believe Christ is present in His glorified body in the Eucharist, not in the manner of ordinary human flesh. Newman thanked him and later acknowledged in the *Apologia Pro Vita Sua* Russell's contribution to his conversion to Roman Catholicism. A few years after writing *Tract 90,* Newman began to believe that in the Transubstantiation, the bread and wine become the Body and Blood of Christ offered for mankind.

One of the main contentions of *Tract 90* was that the *Articles* were intended to denounce abuses by a system called Romanism, or popery, in contrast to authentic Catholic doctrine present in the teachings of the ancient Church. Prominent among such abuses were the sale of indulgences and Masses, the multiplication and adoration of relics, the Roman doctrine on Purgatory, and the excessive tribute, tantamount to idolatry, given to saints. With regard to Purgatory, Newman indicated that one of the *Articles* and the *Homily Concerning Prayer* opposed the Roman belief of

Purgatory as a temporal punishment, or a substitute for Hell and a way of obtaining pardon for those who had died in sin.[6]

Very soon after the *Tract* was published, Golightly, once Newman's curate, initiated and organized opposition against it. He asked Philip Wynter, the university Vice-Chancellor, and the bishops to censure it. The Heads of Houses met to deliberate on the *Tract*, but since they had not read it they postponed deliberation to another date. Pusey wrote to Philip Wynter in defense of Newman, and asked that Newman receive the same toleration granted to those rejecting baptismal regeneration.[7] Newman wrote a public letter addressed to R. Jelf, once a Fellow with him at Oriel, in which he explained unclear parts of *Tract 90*, and he asked Hawkins to have the Heads delay their second meeting for less than a day, giving him time to publish his explanatory letter.

Hawkins asked the Heads to wait for Newman's letter, but they did not. On March 15, the Heads called Newman's interpretation of the *Articles* an evasion rather an explanation of the *Thirty-Nine Articles*.[8] The same day Newman wrote to Bowden, "If you knew all, or when you know, you will see that I asserted a great principle, and I ought to suffer for it—that the Articles are to be interpreted, not according to the meaning of the writers, but (as far as the wording will admit) according to the sense of the Catholic Church."[9]

---

6 *Tract 90,* 298.

7 *LD,* Vol. VIII, E. B. Pusey to Philip Wynter (March 12, 1841), 73-74.

8 *LD,* Vol. VIII, Censure on *Tract 90,* 77.

9 *LD,* Vol. VIII, JHN to J. W. Bowden (March 15, 1841), 77.

Newman thought that the compilers of the *Articles* had intended the words they used to bear several senses in order to keep Catholics in the English Church.[10] Newman thought that in judging *Tract 90,* the Heads had usurped authority that was reserved for the Bishop of Oxford.

Keble, who had read proofs of the *Tract*, and Pusey supported Newman. The three conferred on how best to proceed since the authorship of the *Tract* was anonymous. Newman thought that the protest was a storm that would soon pass and he wished not to make any noise. Harriet wrote her brother a beautiful letter of support: "The tug of war must come some day; let it be now, *if you are* prepared. And that I hope is the case." She assured him of the good wishes and prayers of all.[11] Arthur Perceval, offering to support Newman, commented that the *Tract* would raise "a cry of war to the knife." He asserted, "Yet I think it one of the most important papers that had been put out, and calculated, under God's Blessing, to do much good."[12] William Palmer of Worcester College also wrote Newman, praising *Tract 90* as the most valuable one in the series.

Newman's *Letter to R. W. Jelf, Canon of Christ Church, in Explanation of No. 90, in the Series called Tracts for the Times* appeared in the *Morning Post.* Newman defended his *Tract*, which condemned what he called the "authoritative teaching of the Church of Rome" as manifest in public devotional practices. Referring to the Roman Church he

---

10 *LD,* Vol. VIII, footnote, 76.

11 *LD,* Vol. VIII, Mrs. T. Mozley to JHN (March 14, 1841), 67.

12 *LD,* Vol. VIII, A. P. Perceval to JHN (March 10, 1841), 68.

wrote: "I think it goes very far indeed to substitute another Gospel for the true one. Instead of setting before the soul the Holy Trinity, and Heaven and Hell; it does seem to me, as a popular system, to preach the Blessed Virgin and the Saints, and Purgatory."[13] As he had done in the *Tract,* Newman explained that the *Articles* had been drawn up before the Council of Trent; therefore, its censures were against Roman abuses rather than decrees of this council.[14] In fact, he asserted that Trent had protested against many of the errors that the *Articles* and *Homilies* condemn.[15] Newman noted that invocation of saints is not idolatry, but tends toward it. He explained that adoration of images and relics is unwarranted and unscriptural, and produces practical idolatry.

Newman defended the use he made of the term "ambiguous formularies" in the *Tract* by arguing that there are open questions in the Anglican Church, a point that was nothing new.[16] The most important and sacred doctrines of the Anglican religion are contained in the Creed, and the *Articles* do not define these doctrines; they existed before the *Articles*. Newman maintained that the Anglican Church allows a great diversity in doctrine except for what is taught in the Creed. In support of this assertion, he quoted Anglican Divines.[17] Bull and Stillingfleet spoke of the *Articles* as

---

13 *LD,* Vol. VIII, JHN to R. W. Jelf, Canon of Christ Church, in Explanation of No. 90, in the Series called Tracts for the Times (March 13, 1841), 79.

14 *Ibid,* 78-88; 80.

15 *Ibid.,* 84.

16 *Ibid.* 78-88; 80.

17 *Ibid.,* 85.

help for the preservation of peace and tranquility, whereas the Creed contains the articles of Faith. Newman saw in various English Divines "much greater freedom in the private opinion of individuals" subscribing to the *Articles* than the freedom that he had taken.[18]

In letters to his friends, Newman explained that he had written *Tract 90* to keep men from going over to Rome. Frederick Oakeley, writing to Pusey about *Tract 90*, confirmed the success of Newman's intent:

> There are persons about me, among the most valuable members of the Church whom I know, and I could mention elsewhere, who have long felt considerable perplexity about certain passages in the 39 Articles and who certainly would not, except upon supposition of a Catholic interpretation of the *Articles* conscientiously subscribe them.[19]

On March 17, Bishop Bagot sent Newman a note through Pusey asking that for the peace of the Church, there should be no more mention of the *Articles* in the *Tracts for the Times*. The Archbishop of Canterbury suggested to Bagot that the publication of the *Tracts* be discontinued forever.[20] Newman complied with both petitions and he continued to wait, hoping for the storm to pass. He informed Pusey that some bishops wanted him to suppress *Tract 90*, which he could not in conscience do. "And they use me against myself. They cannot deliver charges of a sudden, but they

---

18 *Ibid.,* 87.

19 *LD,* Vol. VIII, Frederick Oakeley to E. B. Pusey (March 15, 1841), 95.

20 *Pusey,* Vol. II, Liddon, 190.

use me to convey to the world a prompt and popular condemnation of my own principles."[21] Although Newman was ready to suppress the *Tract* if the bishop ordered him to do so, he planned to resign his living at St. Mary's at the same time.

The crisis point finally arrived. Under the influence of the Archbishop of Canterbury, the Bishop of Oxford asked Pusey to communicate to Newman that *Tract 90* should be suppressed and not republished and that Newman should tell the world that this was at the request of the bishop. Pusey advised Newman that the bishops would not censure *Tract 90*, and Newman considered it a tacit compromise between the bishops and himself that if he remained silent, they would not censure the *Tract.* More and more Newman did not wish to suppress *Tract 90*, but he informed the bishop that he would comply with his order to cease the *Tracts* entirely. Newman wrote Maria Giberne, "If the view were silenced, I could not remain in the Church, nor could many others—and therefore since it is *not* silenced, I shall take care to show that it is not."[22]

Newman wrote Bishop Bagot defending himself and his views. Revealing his personal disposition, he wrote that he sought holiness in private life and in the life of the Church. He thought that without this "sanctity of heart and conduct," political reunion was meaningless. "If we be holy, all will go well with us."[23] He asserted that sanctity is the

---

21 *LD,* Vol. VIII, JHN to E. B. Pusey (March 24, 1841), 115-17; 115.

22 *LD,* Vol. VIII, JHN to Miss M. R. Giberne (October 17, 1841), 298-99; 298.

23 *LD,* VIII, JHN to Richard Bagot, Bishop of Oxford (March 29, 1841), 129-44, 142.

great "Note" of the Church that he discerned in the Established Church of Scotland, but not in the Roman Church in Ireland.[24] Newman claimed that he respected those within the Anglican Church with whom he differed in opinions. He urged people to love one another and to love what is good in the other, for "Argumentative efforts are most useful for this end under this sacred feeling . . ."[25]

Newman closed the long and poignant letter to Bishop Bagot, conveying sorrow for having caused him anxiety and professing that he had acted before God for the good of the Church and always with reverent submission to his bishop. Despite Newman's moving letter and convincing arguments, Bishop Bagot was unable to sufficiently enter into Newman's concern and arguments, and the year after the publication of *Tract 90* he joined other bishops in censuring the *Tract.*

Newman's friends, such as Isaac Williams, were greatly pleased with Newman's letter to the bishop. John F. Christie thought the letter was admirable; it was a practical commentary to all the *Tracts* worth more than five more volumes, as well as an example of the respect given to the Episcopacy.[26] At the same time, Keble and Pusey prepared publications concerning the views put forth in *Tract 90.* At Newman's petition Keble did not publish his pamphlet. Pusey instead did publish a 217-page commentary on the *Tract.*

---

24 *Ibid.,* 143.

25 *Ibid.*

26 *LD,* Vol. VIII, J. F. Christie to JHN (April 10, 1841), 171.

While Newman was forced to defend the Catholic principles of the Anglican Church and to show that the *Articles* could be read in a Catholic sense, his knowledge about Catholics and his own contact with them increased.

DEALINGS WITH ROMAN CATHOLICS AND THOUGHTS OF UNION WITH ROME

During 1841, Newman and his circle of friends had more contact with Roman Catholics. Frederic Rogers and James R. Hope visited Rome, and while there, they had many conversations with Catholic clergymen, including a clever Irish Jesuit who debated with them and kept them laughing for two hours and a half.[27] Rogers and Hope also visited Milan, where they met with Alessandro Manzoni, the Italian novelist. Hope spoke with Jesuits and went into the mountains to visit monasteries.[28] He likened the Benedictines to the Fellows of the Oxford Colleges but with more simplicity of life and discipline. He met an old and shrewd Trappist monk who one night gave him a book on the Blessed Virgin Mary by St. Alphonse Liguori and exacted a promise that if Hope ever became a Roman Catholic, he must write the monastery to tell of his conversion.

Newman himself met with Fr. Spencer, who visited Oxford to promote prayer for Christian unity. Newman also corresponded during 1841 with various Catholic priests and laymen. Although he had not initiated the contacts, he cor-

---

27 *LD,* VIII, Frederick Rogers to JHN (December 9, 1840), 7-10, 12.
28 *LD,* VIII, F. Rogers to JHN (no date, 1840), 29.

responded with Fr. Charles Russell and Ambrose Phillipps. In June, Fr. Russell visited Newman at Oxford. Russell was polite and friendly, and did not speak with Newman about religious questions. He only gave him some Catholic books.

Newman was concerned that visits to St. Mary's College Oscott, a Roman Catholic seminary, would cause scandal to Anglicans and lead some to go over to Rome. He advised Ward not to visit Oscott, but to no avail.[29] Later in the year Francis D. Wackerbath, a clergyman from Lichfield, also visited Oscott. Wackerbath was impressed by the learning and holiness of men that he met there and by the beauty of the liturgy. Despite the effort of dissuasion by Newman and others, Wackerbath joined the Roman Catholic Church shortly afterward.

In February 1841, Bloxam began a lengthy correspondence with Ambrose L. Phillipps, the heir of a wealthy family, who at the age of fifteen had become Roman Catholic.[30] Phillipps had the vision of a Catholic England; he wished the reunification of the Anglican and Roman Catholic churches and hoped that Newman and other Oxford men would help in this project. Referring to his correspondence with Phillipps, Newman told Bloxam that there was more holiness in the Church of England.[31] Roman Catholics would convert England if they went barefooted and preached the Gospel like St. Francis Xavier. Little did

---

29 *LD,* Vol. III, W. G. Ward to E. B. Pusey (December 6, 1841), 364-366; 366.

30 Trevor, *Newman, Pillar of the Cloud,* 251.

31 *LD,* Vol. VIII, JHN to J. R. Bloxam (February 23, 1841), 41-43, 42.

Newman know that a small Italian priest, Fr. Dominic Barbieri of the Passionist Order, had then recently landed in
England and had begun to do just that: preach barefooted
in the manufacturing towns.[32] Newman yearned for the
likes of other Bernards and other Borromeos. Newman told
Bloxam that only if the Anglican Church rushed into heresy and the Roman Church cleansed herself would it be a
duty to leave the church; otherwise, it would be a sin.[33]

Newman did not think that a direct union between
the Anglican Church and Rome would take place in his
lifetime, but he advised a union of hearts and a focus on
improving their own bodies respectively. He expressed
the opinion that Tractarians had done a lot to improve the
"English Communion." Mr. Phillipps was a good example
of the Roman Catholics, but they should do much more.
Newman urged that Roman Catholics live charity better,
influence the tone of their publications, give up "uncatho-
lic" things, such as using churches for music recitals, and
preach sanctity and moral reformation.[34] He argued that
reunification was only the prerogative of those in authority,
namely the bishops, and that the time was not yet ripe for it.

In the same letter, Newman expressed his common-
place prejudice of Rome as "hollow, insincere, political, ambitious and unscrupulous."[35] Again he asserted
that Rome did not have the mark of sanctity. The Roman
Catholic Church had many societies and publications,

---

32 Trevor, *Newman, Pillar of the Cloud,* 252-253.

33 *LD,* Vol. VIII, JHN to J. R. Bloxam (February 23, 1841), 41-43,
42-43.

34 *Ibid.,* 43.

35 *LD,* Vol. VIII, JHN to J. R. Bloxam (March 2, 1841), 48-50, 49.

but little of inward religion. Newman especially faulted Irish Roman Catholics for siding politically with English Dissenting bodies. Phillipps also lamented this, but asked Newman that the High Church Party in England break up its political connection with the Orangemen of Ireland.[36] For his part, Nicholas Wiseman wrote to Newman telling him that although O'Connell had sincere religious feelings, he was misguided in foreign and domestic politics. Wiseman reminded Newman that he (Wiseman) had protested strongly against Catholics acting in league with Dissenters to advance the cause of religion through political agitation.[37]

Newman unjustly claimed that Rome had able controversialists but few men with the spiritual depth and real charity of writers like St. Francis de Sales (a bishop), and Pascal, both of whom were Roman Catholics. Newman argued that Pusey, unlike most Catholics, had the spirit of these men.[38] He urged Bloxam to tell Phillipps that sending foreign Divines to Oxford would only work against Phillipps's goals.[39] Later on, Newman insisted that Phillipps was going too fast and that proselytism to Rome would only do harm to the cause of union.[40] Surprisingly, in September, Newman met with two priests that Phillipps sent to visit Bloxam and see Oxford.[41]

---

36 *Ibid.,* 50.
37 *LD,* Vol. VIII, R. Wiseman to JHN (May, 1841), 195.
38 *LD,* Vol. VIII, JHN to J. R. Bloxam (March 2, 1841), 48-50; 50.
39 *LD,* Vol. VIII, JHN to J. R. Bloxam (March 3,1841), 51.
40 *LD,* Vol. VIII, JHN to J. R. Bloxam (June 27, 1841), 210-11.
41 *Ibid.* 279.

After *Tract 90* Newman and Phillipps began to correspond directly with one another. Phillipps told Newman
that he prayed to God that Newman would not be remembered as an "eminent *Protestant Divine,*" but as the Father
of the English Church in its Catholic Restoration.[42] Newman acknowledged that the unity of the Catholic Church
was near to his heart. "I do not see any prospect of it within
our time, and I despair of its being effected without great
sacrifices on all hands. Were the Roman Church in Ireland
different from what it is, one immense stumbling block
would be removed."[43]

When Newman objected that for three hundred years
there had been hopes of healing this "great schism" but
it had not been achieved, Phillipps replied that even after
many years they must continue to pray and labor for a healing of the schism. Fr. George Spencer wrote Newman again
expressing his hopes for restoration of unity in the Church.
This time Newman replied with a different tone than he had
done before. Newman acknowledged that Roman Catholics
were acting in a more Christian manner toward Anglicans.
He wrote Spencer, "Let me express the great satisfaction
I have felt at seeing the kind spirit, which many persons
of your communion have displayed during the past year
toward the English Church."[44]

In September, Newman admitted to Phillipps that in
addition to the main obstacle to union, a political one,
there were two important obstacles to unity: the Roman

---

42 *LD,* Vol. VIII, JHN to Ambrose L. Phillipps (April 7, 1841), 165.
43 *Ibid.*
44 *LD,* Vol. VIII, JHN to George Spencer (August 19, 1841), 251.

Catholic doctrine of Transubstantiation and devotion to Mary. He maintained that this Eucharistic doctrine and Marian piety were not found in early Christianity. Newman later retracted his position on the antiquity of devotion to Mary. Surprisingly, only a day after this exchange with Phillipps, Newman corresponded with Acland on the prayers for union. Also at about this time, Newman preached a sermon, "Weapons of the Saints," which referred to the humility expressed in Mary's *Magnificat*. And in a letter to Henry Wilberforce, he confided to his friend that he had been repeating the words, "All generations shall call me blessed," which opens this Marian canticle.[45] Newman did not object to following the example of the Mother of Christ, but did object to excesses in external devotion and preaching about her.

Newman wrote a letter to Nicholas Wiseman to explain his position, but he never sent it. He insisted that Catholics should improve their tone, remove abuses and conciliate Anglicans in words and deeds. "Such conduct on both sides must tend eventually to unity, *in God's time,* though, it may be, not in our day."[46] Newman continued to argue for corporate reunion and opposed individual conversions. A few weeks later, on October 13, he wrote another letter to Wiseman, which also was never sent. For the first time in correspondence, Newman spelled out four specific points that he suggested Roman Catholics do in their efforts to achieve unity with Anglicans. They must 1) aid the Conservative

---

45 *LD,* Vol. VIII, JHN to Henry William Wilberforce (October 27, 1841), 310.

46 *LD,* Vol. VIII, JHN to Nicholas Wiseman (October 14, 1841), 297-98; 298. The letter was not sent.

party, 2) admit what is wrong and defective in their own body, 3) win the hearts of their enemies by acts of mercy, and 4) instead of directing their attention to members of the Church of England, direct their attention first to the religiously ignorant in the cities and to the Dissenting bodies.[47] With this in mind, Newman believed that progress must be made prudently and that unity would be achieved by a Church body, not by individuals.

FEAR OF INDIVIDUAL CONVERSIONS

Throughout all of 1841, Newman was very concerned that Anglicans, and in particular Tractarians, would become Roman Catholics. His advice to those considering converting to Roman Catholicism was the same: patience and prayer as well as trust in Divine Providence. For Newman, conversion to Roman Catholicism was an act of private judgment in religious matters. He told his friends that in matters of religion no one should act on private judgment and wrote an essay for the *British Critic* on this very subject. He argued that the Anglican Church had, despite its isolation from other Christianity at large, notes of true Catholicism.

Newman made it clear to his bishop and to others that his intention with *Tract 90* had been to keep people within the Anglican Church. He had had in mind people who would go over to Rome if forced to renounce a Catholic interpretation of the *Thirty-Nine Articles*. His friends' letter expressing that they found comfort in this interpretation of the *Articles* confirmed Newman's concern.

---

47 *Ibid.*

Newman felt great responsibility not to mislead men who looked up to him, and he felt the constant scrutiny of the public eye. Some junior men at Oxford said, "I will go if N. goes" or "Would you go over if K and N did?"[48] Some friends asked him questions about future events, which Newman did not wish to think about yet. At the start of 1841 he wrote his friend Henry Wilberforce, who was contemplating conversion to Roman Catholicism, "*How long* do you want before you turn R. C.? will two years do? Let me know this important point."[49] Toward the end of 1841, following the condemnation of *Tract 90* and other significant events, Newman then told various friends, including Henry Wilberforce, that he did not discard the possibility of one day going over to Rome, but not suddenly.[50] Even then Newman was concerned with countering the rumor that he and others were seceding to Rome.[51]

Miss Holmes wrote Newman about her desire to become Roman Catholic. Newman tried to dissuade her by telling her that one should not act on first inspirations. She should instead think and pray about God's will, "To any friend who asked me what to do, I should prescribe three years, during which his thoughts and prayers should be directed

---

48 *LD*, Vol. VIII, JHN to Henry Wilberforce (November 8, 1841), 320-322; 322.

49 *LD*, Vol. VIII, JHN to Henry William Wilberforce (March 1, 1841), 45-46; 46.

50 *LD*, Vol. VIII, JHN to Henry Wilberforce (November 8, 1841), 320-22; 321.

51 *LD*, Vol. VIII, JHN to Mrs. J. Mozley (November 16, 1841), 334-35; 334.

this one way, to learn God's will."[52] This is what Newman did in his own case.

Miss Holmes was especially drawn by the Roman Catholic teaching on Transubstantiation. Newman did not accept this doctrine but believed that the Eucharist is the Real Presence of Christ. He told Miss Holmes that "The Presence of Christ is still with us" in the Most Holy Sacrament.[53] Days earlier, on November 28, he had preached for the first time the "Invisible Presence of Christ" in which he argued that Christ's Presence was experienced through the service, sermons, the Most Holy Sacrament, the religious seasons and other personal communications.[54] When Christ said that the Kingdom of God is within you, He was teaching that God acts inwardly, "touching the secret heart." In the unsettled situation of the Church, Christ's interior presence in the Christian is a source of consolation: "Since then, in this our age, He has in judgment obscured the visible and public notes of His Kingdom among us, what a mercy is it to us that He has not deprived us of such as are personal and private!"[55]

Newman told Miss Holmes that when individuals leave a religion they are acting upon private judgment. He advised her to wait and see if the English Church got better or worse, and then to move with others, but not alone. In the "Invisible Presence of Christ" Newman echoed this sentiment: "When, then, we are overwhelmed, as we

---

52 *LD,* Vol. VIII, JHN to Miss Holmes (August 8, 1841), 238-39.

53 *LD,* Vol. VIII, JHN to Miss Holmes (December 6, 1841), 366-67; 366.

54 "Invisible Presence of Christ," in *OS,* 308-23.

55 *Ibid.,* 318.

well may be, at the confusion of all things around us, as Psalmists and Prophets have been before us, let us turn to the thought of that gift which Psalmists and Prophets had not as we may have, and which is personal and incommunicable and unspeakable, but known to religious men."[56]

Newman told Miss Holmes that the Church of England was a true branch of the Church and that she should be content to be placed by God in it. He said of himself: "In her I have been baptized, and the question is, why am I to change? Rather is it not God's will that I should labour in it, with the hope of amending what is wanting in it?"[57] In November Newman insisted once more that Miss Holmes wait because she was risking schism, even if the Church of Rome were right.

To another friend, Samuel Wood, who worried that Newman was about to become Roman Catholic, Newman wrote, "I trust I have been favored with a much more definitive view of the (promised) inward evidence of the Presence of Christ with us in the Sacraments, now that the outward notes of it are being removed."[58] Wood was unsettled about becoming Roman Catholic and Newman advised him to do some penance. Wood replied that he "would leave all external changes to wiser heads" than his and that until Newman and Robert Williams left the Church he would mind his own business.[59] As far as penance goes, he told

---

56 S.D., "Invisible Presence of Christ", n. 21, 319.

57 LD, Vol. VIII, JHN to Miss Holmes (August 15, 1841), 247-49; 248.

58 LD, Vol. VIII, JHN to S. F. Wood (December 13, 1841), 374-75; 375.

59 LD, Vol. VIII, S. F. Wood to JHN (December 28, 1841), 375.

Newman that he had gained good advice from St. Francis de Sales, which was presumably the value of small acts of self-denial. Wood sent Newman a copy of De Sales's *Treatise on the Love of God.*

Despite Newman's efforts, some Anglican clergymen became Roman Catholics. This was the case with Mr. Francis Wackerbath, a clergyman from the Lichfield Cathedral. Richard Waldo Sibthorp was another clergyman who became Roman Catholic after visiting Oscott. When Sibthorp was about to set out for Oscott, Newman had warned him not to go there, but he went anyway.[60]

Newman wrote to another friend, Richard Westamacott, "I have not thought whatever of going over to Rome, or letting others—but I have a great wish to make our Church more Catholic in its tone, and to introduce into it the good points of Rome—and if the consequence is a more friendly feeling between the Churches, it may tend to the improvement of Rome itself."[61] He admitted that both Churches have their excellences and that both are injured by enmity, but commented that if some individuals went over to Rome it would only do harm.

Newman continued to think that corporate reunion was not possible then, and he argued against individual conversions. He wrote Phillipps: "I must ask your leave to repeat on this occasion most distinctly that I cannot be a party to any agitation, but mean to remain quiet in my own place,

---

60 *LD,* Vol. XXIX, JHN to John Fowler (April 12, 1881), 363.

61 *LD,* Vol. VIII, JHN to Richard Westmacott (April 8, 1841), 166-67, 167.

and to do all I can to make others take the same course."[62] Despite his intentions it was impossible for Newman to stay still because the matters at hand were too important. He was soon at the center of a heated university contest over the election of a new Professor of Poetry; the contest had a strong religious element.

POETRY PROFESSORSHIP

John Keble, who had been Professor of Poetry, was expected to retire after the maximum of two five-year terms. He wished Isaac Williams, a talented Latinist, to succeed him to the Chair of Poetry. Unexpectedly, James Garbett, a less qualified Evangelical clergyman from Brasenose College, said that he would run against Williams. A heated controversy arose at Oxford over the contest. Williams was identified with the Tractarians and their Church Principles. Williams could withdraw from the contest, but retreat would seem equivalent to defeat of Church Principles. Newman, consumed with the idea of this contest, considered the opposition to Williams as one more affront in a series of disavowals by the University and feared that Williams's defeat would embolden Convocation to "drive the Tractarians out of the university."[63] Newman complained to his friends that for eight years he and his friends had not only not been encouraged; they had been silenced by the bishops. *The Record* and its ultra-Evangelical sponsors wrote against Williams. *The Standard* also agitated against the Tractarians.

The academic contest between Williams and Garbett

---

62 *LD,* Vol. VIII, JHN to Ambrose L. Phillipps (June 28 1841), 213-14.
63 *Ibid.,* 339.

became a heated one; it was a party battle reminiscent of earlier ones. In 1837 and 1839, the Tractarians had opposed on religious grounds the nomination of F. D. Maurice to the chair of Political Economy and of H. H. Vaughan to a Logic Praelectorship. For the sake of peace at the University and in the Church, William Gladstone had the university draw up a petition inviting both candidates to withdraw their candidacy and asked Bishop Bagot to intervene. In the end, the President of Trinity College compared pledged votes. Garbett had 921 against 623 for Williams. Given this calculation of the outcome, Williams withdrew his candidacy on January 20, 1842, and shortly afterward James Garbett took the Oxford Chair of Poetry.

Williams's loss was emblematic of the powerful opposition by Oxford men to the Catholic principles in the English Church. Newman had fought for Williams's election precisely for fear that his loss would further embolden those who opposed the Tractarian ideals. Newman kept his allegiance to the Anglican Church, but during 1841, he encountered other serious objections to its external notes as part of the Catholic Church.

THREE DECISIVE BLOWS CONCERNING THE ANGLICAN CHURCH

The initial reaction of the university authorities to *Tract 90* was a heavy blow to Newman, but from July to November of 1841, Newman experienced three other blows that shook his convictions regarding the Anglican Church.[64] As a result of these, he began to doubt seriously that

---

64 *Apo.*, 139-46.

the Anglican Church was a true branch of the Catholic Church and turned his attention more to Rome. During this year he became more familiar with the mentality and devotion of Roman Catholics through his dealing with Roman Catholic priests and through the books that Fr. Russell had given him, in particular the *Sermons* of St. Alphonse Liguori.

The first blow came with Newman's study of the Arian Heresy. In 1841, while studying once more St. Athanasius and the Arian Heresy, Newman was gripped again by the thought he first had in 1839. He realized that the Arians were equivalent to the Protestants; the semi-Arians were like the Anglicans, and Rome held the position she had always had. "The truth lay, not with the *Via Media*, but with what was called 'the extreme party.'"[65]

The second blow was the censure of *Tract 90* by many of the bishops. At the start of the year only a few bishops had voiced their disapproval, but by the end of the year seven had denounced it in their triennial charges, and even more did so in the following year.[66] Newman had kept silent about *Tract 90* under a tacit "understanding" with Bishop Bagot that the *Tract* would not be censured or removed. Newman felt betrayed and dejected;[67] while he tried to defend the Catholic principles of the Anglican Church, the bishops disowned them. He thought that the bishops were making the Church Protestant. The different Charges repudiated practices of ancient Christianity in favor of the

---

65 *Apo.,* 139. Morales, *Newman, (1801–1890),* 111.

66 By 1844, twenty-four bishops had censured *Tract 90.* Trevor, *Newman, Pillar of the Cloud,* 257.

67 *Apo.,* 139.

Reformers of the Church of England. They accused Newman of party spirit and fanaticism and claimed that his Catholic interpretation of the *Articles* was mere sophistry.[68]

Some of these bishops were intolerant of those who held orthodox beliefs and punished them. One such case was the refusal of the bishop of Winchester, C. R. Sumner, to ordain Peter Young, a deacon who was Keble's curate at Hursley. The bishop was upset by Young's denial of the Presence of Christ in the Eucharist as merely figurative. Keble felt that it was a "deliberate beginning of serious vexation on the part of authority."[69] *The Record* described the rejection of Young as a defense against encroaching Puseyism, the name given to the position of Pusey's disciples, and boasted two other victories for the Protestant cause: Jenkyns had removed W. G. Ward from his Tutorship and Dr. Hawkins had likewise removed R. W. Church.

In September, C. R. Sumner came out with a Charge in which he protested against the Oxford Tract writers on six grounds. One was their denial of the doctrine of Justification by faith alone, and another was *Tract 90*'s method of interpreting the *Articles*. Keble was worried that his bishop wished him to resign from his living.[70] Regarding his curate, James R. Hope advised Keble to ask Bishop

---

68 "1841-1842, Bishops Charging," in Trevor, *Newman, Pillar of the Cloud,* 249-62, 258-59.

69 *Ibid.,* 227.

70 *LD,* Vol. VIII, John Keble to JHN (September 30, 1841), 286.

Sumner to have Young's case studied by a diocesan commission and sent to the Court of Arches (of the Province
of Canterbury) for a definitive judgment.[71] In the end,
Keble decided to send a Protest to the Archbishop. With
respect to his own standing in the diocese, Keble asked
Bishop Sumner if he had permission to remain in the
diocese.

After the blows derived from the study of the Arian Heresy, and the censure of *Tract 90*, came the third and perhaps strongest blow to Newman. It was the plan concocted
in 1841 by the government and William Howley, the Archbishop of Canterbury, to establish an Anglican bishop
in Jerusalem with jurisdiction over a body of Anglicans,
Lutherans, and other Christians. It was a political move to
increase English political presence in Jerusalem. For Newman, the plan entailed complete disregard for the spiritual
and doctrinal nature of the Church.

The king of Germany, Frederick William IV, wished to
carry out a reorganization of the Evangelical communion
in Germany by establishing ten metropolitan bishops. The
king was inspired by ideas from Hooker's *Ecclesiastical
Polity* and Baron Christian J. Bunsen, a Protestant clergyman. Bunsen was a German married to an English woman
and an admirer of the English Church and the ideas of Dr.
Thomas Arnold. Archbishop Howley, Bishop Blomfield,
and Lord Anthony Ashley, a social reformer and Oxford
graduate, together with the Evangelicals, favored the
scheme advanced by Bunsen.

---

71 *LD*, Vol. VIII, JHN to John Keble (December 26, 1841), 389-90;
389.

Bishop Blomfield asked William Gladstone to be a trustee of the funds for this project and of plans for the new diocese. At first Gladstone went along with the idea, but soon realized it was fraught with ecclesiastical and theological difficulties. Gladstone sought Hope's advice who, in turn, wrote to Newman for advice on both the ecclesial implications of such a union and the theological grounds for it. Newman's reply was summed up in a letter to Jemima: "It is a formal recognition of the Protestants by communicating with them as a Church without reconciliation on their part."[72] If this new diocese were accepted, it would undercut the Branch Theory and therefore the Anglican claim to catholicity.

Gladstone realized that Howley and Blomfield did not wish to consult the body of the bishops, and that their project approximated the English Church to Protestant communions. The plan did not distinguish between Orthodox and heretical Churches of the East. With this realization, Gladstone wrote a long letter to Bishop Blomfield in which he declined the trusteeship.[73]

Newman thought that the scheme was a totally misguided one. In a letter that he unsuccessfully attempted to publish in *The Times,* he argued that the Church should not advance political ends, nor should episcopacy be forced on German Protestants who did not hold orthodox Catholic principles. "Surely it is an evil great enough to find Bishop

---

72 *LD,* Vol. VIII, JHN to Mrs. J. Mozley (November 21, 1841), 338-41; 340.

73 *Ibid.,* W. E. Gladstone to the Bishop of London (Nov. 30, 1841), 249-54.

heretics, without going on to make heretics Bishops."[74] Newman told Bowden that if this took place, "I shall not be able to keep a single man from Rome."[75]

Newman explained that, except for travelers, some officials, and a few Jewish converts, there were no Anglicans in Jerusalem. He pointed out the absurdity of having Anglicans and Lutherans under the same bishop without regard to doctrinal disparity. Lastly, there was even talk of Turkish Druses and Monophysites uniting under an English bishop. Newman said that this would be the last straw that breaks the horse's back.[76] Dr. Michael Solomon Alexander, a Polish Jew and convert to Christianity, who had taken Anglican Orders and taught Hebrew at King's College, London, was chosen to be Bishop of Jerusalem. In October, he was consecrated bishop by Archbishop Howley. Newman commented that the Archbishop "is doing all he can do to unchurch us."[77]

Newman wrote a formal protest, which he sent to Bishop Bagot. Newman told Hope that Protestants required agreement in doctrine rather than bishops. Anglicans required Confirmation before receiving Holy Communion. The Protestants would have neither and yet wished to be

---

74 *LD,* Vol. VIII, JHN to the Editor of the *Times* (November 1, 1841), 314-16; 316.

75 *LD,* Vol. VIII, JHN to J. W. Bowden (October 10, 1841), 288-89; 289.

76 *LD,* Vol. VIII, JHN to J. W. Bowden (October 12, 1841), 294-96; 295.

77 *LD,* Vol. VIII, JHN to Mrs. T. Mozley and Mrs. J. Mozley (October 12, 1841), 296-97; 297.

admitted into ecclesiastical communion.[78] Newman asked rhetorically, "are we to set up bishops over Methodist, Baptists and Unitarians?"[79] He told Woodgate, "I repeat, if we are now to recognize the Protestants as Catholic brethren (a question which was *open* till this Jerusalem matter) the ground is cut from under me. I shall have taught people that there is a Church,—*somewhere*—and the Archbishop will teach them it is not to be found at home."[80]

Newman finally broke his silence and spoke about the Church's state from the pulpit of St. Mary's. On four consecutive Sundays, starting November 28th, Newman preached his Samaritan Sermons on the Notes of the Church. He used Scripture to interpret the situation of the English Church, comparing it to Samaria, the northern kingdom of Israel when it was separated from Judah. In that biblical situation, the Prophet Elijah, who lived in the northern kingdom, had not told the people to go to worship in Jerusalem. The sermons were later published in the volume of *Sermons on Subjects of the Day*.[81] In the sermons, Newman offered arguments to keep people within the English Church, but his faith in the Anglican Church had been shattered.[82] Newman spoke of the Invisible Presence of God in the Church. "Since then, in this our age, He has in judgment obscured the visible and public notes of

78 *LD,* Vol. VIII, J. R. Hope to JHN (November 30, 1841), 346.

79 *Ibid.,* 347.

80 *LD,* Vol. VIII, JHN to H. A. Woodgate (November 12, 1841), 326-27; 327.

81 *SD,* sermons nn. 21, 22, 23, and 24.

82 *Apo.,* 143.

His Kingdom among us, what a mercy is it to us that He has not deprived us of such as are personal and private!" [83]

Newman's arguments were no longer in defense of the Anglican Church, but an invitation to trust in God's Providence and to remain where one had been placed by God. An important reason for remaining in the Anglican Church was Christ's Invisible Presence within it. "And we will cling to the Church in which we are, not for its own sake, but because we humbly trust that Christ is in it; and while He is in it, we will abide in it. He shall leave before we do."[84]

A private experience may have led Newman to speak thus about God's sacramental presence in the Church.[85] He had hinted to his friends, Samuel Wood and Miss Holmes, of having been favored with an inward evidence of the Presence of Christ in the sacraments. Wilfrid Ward soon told people that Newman had "seen Our Lord" in the sacrament of the Holy Eucharist. Newman naturally tried to put an end to the rumors, but his strong yet restrained feelings in "The Invisible Presence of Christ" suggest that he may have actually had such a unique experience of God's love. In this sermon he said:

> [I]f you have come to Service, and been favoured with the peace or the illumination you needed; or if you can recollect times when you visited holy places, and certainly gained there a manifestation such as the world could not give; or if sermons have come to you with power, and have been blessed to your spiritual good; or if your soul has been, as it were, transfigured within you, when you came to the Most Holy Sacrament . . . O!

---

83 *SD*, n. 21, "Invisible Presence of Christ," 318.

84 *Ibid.*, 322-23.

85 Trevor, *Newman, Pillar of the Cloud*, 261-62.

pause ere you doubt that we have a Divine Presence among us still, and have not to seek it.[86]

Newman drew strength from the Holy Eucharist and prayer in general, but as he later wrote in his *Apologia*, "From the end of 1841, I was on my deathbed, as regards my membership with the Anglican Church, though at the time I became aware of it only by degrees."[87] The absurd project of the government and the Archbishop of Canterbury to establish a joint Anglican–Lutheran Episcopal See in Jerusalem had brought Newman "to the beginning of the end"; but he later considered this "one of the greatest mercies" bestowed on him by God.[88] Newman realized that he could no longer sustain that the Anglican Church was one of the three branches of the Church.

Newman still felt Anglican, but for him, Anglican meant Catholic. Although he defended himself, he was shunned by many Anglicans, including the bishops in authority. There was little room for Catholic principles in the Established English Church of the mid-nineteenth century. There was no longer room for Newman and some of his Tractarian friends in the Anglican Communion. Understandably, Newman was upset that many people asked him what he would do in the future. He simply wished to do what was right, acting day by day without anticipating the future.

---

86 *SD,* n. 21, "Invisible Presence of Christ," 321-22.

87 *Apo.,* 147.

88 *Apo.,* 146.

CHAPTER 28

DEBATE ON HOW TO
MAKE MEN MORAL

D URING the crisis of *Tract 90,* Newman wished to remain quiet, hoping that the storm would blow over. For such a prolific writer, his silence could only be but a relative one. He was silent to the public at large about *Tract 90,* but otherwise he wrote a considerable amount during 1841. His primary focus was the translation of treatises by St. Athanasius, but he wrote seven articles for *The Times,* several articles for the *British Critic,* and prepared another volume of sermons for publication.

In January, at the opening of a new library and reading room at Tamworth, Sir Robert Peel delivered an address on education, which soon drew a lot of attention. Peel was a Member of Parliament for this town in Staffordshire, Northeast of Birmingham. Peel argued that natural sciences would improve the lot of farmers and industrial workers and would lead to an elevation of moral character. He stipulated that the library would not have books with controversial religious views, and although its board would include two clergymen, no discussions on religious differences would be permitted.

John Walter II, son of the owner of *The Times,* and his father convinced Newman to reply. The result was seven letters published during the month of February in

The Times under the name "CATHOLICUS." The letters anticipated parts of Newman's *Idea of a University* written twenty years later. The letters were a sharp criticism of Lord Henry Brougham's educational and religious philosophy. Brougham, a major proponent of the Reform Bill, had been one of the leaders promoting the so-called Diffusion of Useful Knowledge and the establishment of the University of London in 1827. One of his main ideas, typical of the enlightened deist, was the exclusion of religion from higher education.

Newman criticized Peel, who despite his sincere adherence to the Anglican Church, followed Brougham's notions that learning in physical sciences makes persons moral individuals:

> [T]hat the mind is changed by a discovery, or saved by a diversion, and can thus be amused into immortality,—that grief, anger, cowardice, self-conceit, pride, or passion, can be subdued by an examination of shells or grasses, or inhaling of gases, or chipping of rocks, or calculating the longitude, is the veriest of pretences which sophist or mountebank ever professed to a gaping auditory. If virtue be a mastery over the mind, if its end be action, if its perfection be inward order, harmony, and peace, we must seek it in graver and holier places than in Libraries and Reading-rooms.[1]

Newman focused on the deist's underlying idea that religion is superfluous and that man is either in no need of salvation or that he is saved by the awe produced by nature

---

1 John Henry Newman, *Discussion and Arguments,* "Tamworth Reading Room," Letter II, 268; available at: http://www.newmanreader.org/works/arguments/tamworth/section2.html.

and the knowledge of its order and complexity. Newman ridiculed the assertion made by Peel of the power of scientific knowledge to someone on a deathbed. In contrast to Brougham's deistic ideas, Newman asserted that only grace could heal and cleanse man of his moral diseases. Vice cannot be removed by human methods. He wrote that "Christianity, and nothing short of it, must be made the element and principle of all education."[2] Newman was far from dismissing the benefits of poetry, metaphysics, history, physics, or mathematics. He was pointing to the experience that Christianity, not literature or philosophy, converts men.

In the fourth letter to the *The Times,* Newman addressed Brougham's view of study of the New Testament as opinion, and Peel's notion of doctrine as "controversial divinity." Unlike Brougham, Peel thought that science leads to religion, albeit through a long and unsafe road that most cannot travel. Wishing to avoid controversy, however, he ended up putting religion aside. Newman took offense at Peel's caricature of doctrine and his belief that secular knowledge is the principle of social unity. For Peel, religion and political parties were synonymous; religious controversy was divisive and should be put aside for the sake of the State. According to Newman, Peel, inspired by Brougham, rejected faith as the fulcrum of society, and substituted it for secular knowledge. The old bond that united men was faith; the new one is knowledge. Faith was the source of division. Displaying great mastery in his

---

2 John Henry Newman, *Discussion and Arguments,* DA Letter III, 274, available at: http://www.newmanreader.org/works/arguments/index.html.

command of satire, Newman described Brougham's new pantheon of saints whose members were characterized for their "pursuit of knowledge," including the likes of Julian the Apostate and Cromwell.

In another letter, Newman insinuated the proper relationship between faith and reason. Religion suggests to science the conclusions that science reaches after its own study. "Science gives us the grounds or premises from which religious truths are to be inferred; but it does not set about inferring, much less does it reach the inference—that is not its province."[3] It is up to Christianity to take facts, give them meaning and draw conclusions from them, but people live and die upon a dogma; no one will die a martyr for a conclusion.[4] Newman asserted that for the majority of people, logical syllogisms are not the way to know God, and that "Life is not long enough for a religion of inferences: we shall never have done beginning if we determine to begin with proof."[5]

Newman refuted the idea that secular knowledge is the moral foundation for people's lives. "Life is for action. If we insist on proofs for everything, we shall never come to action: to act you must assume, and that assumption is faith."[6] Faith comes to us in many ways, including Revelation, the influence of others, the effect of events and history. With his capacity for irony Newman wrote: "But if we commence with scientific knowledge and argumentative proof, or lay any great stress upon it as the basis of personal

---

3 *DA*, Letter VI, 292-93.
4 *Ibid.*, 293.
5 *Ibid.*, 295.
6 *Ibid.*, 295.

Christianity, or attempt to make man moral and religious by Libraries and Museums, let us in consistency take chemists for our cooks, and mineralogists for our masons."[7]

In his last letter to the *The Times,* in reply to Peel's *Address at the Tamworth Reading Room,* Newman repeated the idea that physical science does not lead necessarily to religious thoughts or practice. It only does so in the person who is already religious. The reason that science cannot make men religious is that it does not seek the final causes as philosophy does.[8] The created world can be read as a work or as a machine. If it is considered a creation, then it is studied with awe; if it is considered a machine, then it is studied with mere curiosity.[9] But this awe in itself is no substitute for religion. In fact, for Peel, awe makes man feel the "the moral dignity of his exalted nature" as if man were fine without religion.[10]

Brougham had gone further, expressing that knowledge of the marvelous works of the Great Architect of Nature was reason for gratification of man's natural strength and the powers of his mind. Newman commented that this self-worship of man was deplorable. He agreed that nature is more wonderful than any manmade object, such as a watch, "but wonder is not religion, or we should be worshipping our railroads. What the physical creation presents to us in itself is a piece of machinery, and when men speak of a Divine Intelligence as its Author, this god of theirs is not

---

7 *Ibid.,* 295-96.
8 *DA,* Letter VII, 299.
9 *Ibid.,* 300.
10 *Ibid.,* 301.

the Living and True, unless the spring is the god of a watch, or steam the creator of the engine."[11]

At Trinity College Newman became interested in mathematics and the physical sciences like astronomy. He realized though that in the empirical sciences one deals with tangible realities, and that these can actually lead to a desire to explain all of reality from material principles. He wrote: "To those who are conscious of matter, but not conscious of mind, it seems more rational to refer all things to one origin, such as they know, than to assume the existence of a second origin such as they know not. It is Religion, then, which suggests to Science its true conclusions; the facts come from Knowledge, but the principles come of Faith."[12]

Far from discarding the physical sciences he wished to establish that faith points the way to science, and that the reverse is not always true. He would expound on this relationship between science and theology in *The Idea of a University.*

Although an attempt was made to keep the authorship of the Letters secret, Newman worried that his attack on Peel would jeopardize Pusey's chance of becoming bishop. The keenness of his accusations and the severe tone of the Letters are somewhat surprising. They conjure the image of a ferocious lion springing upon his prey, but the tone was characteristic of Newman when he thought something serious was at stake. More than an attack on Peel's belief about the place of religion and theology in education, the Letters

---

11 *DA,* Letter VII, 302.
12 *Ibid.,* 300.

were an attack on deistic principles concerning not only useful knowledge acquired through physical science, but also the underlying premises of the power of knowledge to procure man's moral excellence without religion.

NEW EDITORSHIP FOR THE BRITISH CRITIC

In April, Newman gave advice to Thomas, the new editor: "Do begin and write some articles yourself at once—there's a good fellow, and get a stock. Your present articles are MAGNIFICENT."[13] He warned him to be careful in personal comments on people: "You will get horsewhipped if you do so often."[14] In the transition period, he spent a lot of time teaching the new editor his work and suggesting topics for articles as well as writers. Newman helped Thomas prepare his first issue as editor, which came out in July, and also wrote for the July issue an article titled "Private Judgment."

The new editor got off to a bad start with an article on Godfrey Faussett titled "The Oxford Margaret Professor." Faussett had come out with a pamphlet against *Tract 90* and the Tractarians. Newman thought it was a good idea to write about Faussett, whom he called "a fat dog who comes out to bark once to two years [sic]," and told Thomas: "I think you can be strong and yet be *bland* and temperate."[15] Newman, however, did not see the article before it came out and later regretted its un-Christian tone. A few days

---

13 *LD,* Vol. VIII, JHN to Thomas Mozley (April 1, 1841), 150-51; 151.
14 *Ibid.*
15 *LD,* Vol. VIII, JHN to T. Mozley (June 12, 1841), 204.

later he composed a prayer asking God's forgiveness for any judgmental and critical spirit toward Faussett.[16]

Mozley's first issue raised complaints from readers, and Keble asked Newman to do something about Mozley, but Newman stuck by him. Pusey raised a larger issue with Newman: would the *British Critic* represent all or some in the Movement? He was quite upset at Oakeley's article on the English Reformers in which he had accused the Reformers of being at first a political movement lacking in doctrine.[17] Pusey thought the journal should express all views or say nothing about the Reformers. Newman replied that he had tried to make the journal literary and scientific instead of theological but had failed.[18]

In September of 1841, the Archbishop of Canterbury summoned Pusey to Lambeth Palace, asking him to keep Newman from controversy in the *British Critic*. A few months later in December, Newman voiced the idea of stopping the *British Critic*. He asked Mozley for his opinion and told him, "I think our course is *to be quiet* . . . The strength of our opponents is in there being something to *attack*. It is truly Protestant. If we are silent, they are a rope of sand."[19] After the second issue of the *British Critic* under Mozley, attacks upon the Tractarians had increased. Newman only wrote one more article for the *British Critic*. The end of Newman's editorship of the *British Critic* was the

---

16 *AW,* 216-17.

17 *LD,* Vol. VIII, E.B. Pusey to JHN (July 27, 1841), 232-34; 233.

18 *LD,* Vol. VIII, JHN to E. B. Pusey (July 30, 1841), 234-35; 234.

19 *LD,* Vol. VIII, JHN to Thomas Mozley (December 13, 1841), 373-74; 373.

close of another rich chapter in Newman's life and writing. In 1842 he moved definitively to Littlemore with the hope of living in a more peaceful setting and dedicating more time to prayer.

LITTLEMORE AND ATHANASIUS

Newman had already spent Lent in 1841 at Littlemore. In July he again stayed at Littlemore. He rented a second-story bedroom and a study on the ground floor from a Miss Sarah Burford. Here Newman worked with intensity on a translation of Athanasius for the *Library of the Church Fathers*. For a few weeks during the winter of that year, he even worked ten to twelve hours per day on the translation.[20] He had the help of Christie, and consulted Dr. Routh on certain passages.[21] In July, Newman bought some stables and a barn that formed the shape of an L adjacent to the property that he had bought in May of the previous year. Newman made plans to turn the stables into one room "cottages" that would serve as cells for him and other men who might join him later on. In February 1842, Newman moved to Littlemore for the season of Lent. In addition to dedicating more time to prayer, he supervised the construction of bookcases and turned the barn into a library. When the bookcases were ready, Newman transferred his library to Littlemore. The previous year Newman had spent £858 acquiring books. He wrote to his sister Jemima that these

---

20 *LD,* Vol. VIII, JHN to H. A. Woodgate (November 12, 1841), 326-27; 327.

21 *LD,* Vol. VIII, JHN to M. J. Routh (November 15, 1841), 333-34.

books were an investment.[22] Dalgairns said that Newman's library was enviable and that men without a Fellowship could come and read under Newman. At this time Newman had a new resident curate at St. Mary's in Oxford, David Lewis from Jesus College. Copeland continued as Newman's curate at Littlemore.

Onlookers considered the "monastic life" as a sign of his future conversion to Rome. Richard Jelf, a Tutor at Oriel, was alarmed by Newman's monastic plans, and when the bishop of Oxford heard similar rumors he wrote to Newman asking for an explanation.[23] Newman replied that he was not starting a monastery. He had withdrawn from all public discussions of Church matters and wished to devote himself to theological studies, the concerns of his parish, and practical works. He sought a place for a "life of greater religious regularity"[24] and to have some guests spend time with him. He did not intend to establish a monastery; the house would not have a chapel or refectory. Newspapers misrepresented Newman's intentions, and Newman told the bishop that he was hurt that sacred matters of his conscience were made public talk.[25]

The leader of the Oxford Movement sought peace and quiet to pray and to study. As the attacks on *Tract 90* continued, he needed to be out of Oxford. In some sense

---

22 *LD,* Vol. VIII, JHN to Mrs. John Mozley (February 12, 1841), 34, and footnote n. 4.

23 *LD,* Vol. VIII, Richard Bagot, Bishop of Oxford to JHN (April 12, 1842), 504.

24 *LD,* Vol. VIII, JHN to Richard Bagot, Bishop of Oxford (April 14, 1842), 504-07; 505.

25 *Ibid.*

Newman was pushed out of Oxford; he had been silenced and almost "exiled" by his bishop and other bishops. Surely Newman felt inspired by St. Athanasius, Bishop of Alexandria, who in the fourth century had been exiled from his See by the emperor for preaching the truth. Newman considered Athanasius a great champion of the Catholic faith.

Newman never intended a formal monastery, but writing to intimate friends he called the home at Littlemore their μονε, or monastery. When his friend H. A. Woodgate hinted that Newman could be named bishop, Newman made the humorous retort:

> You forget that I am an incipient Monk, in my noviciate at the least. I am preparing a Monastery at Littlemore and shall shortly retire from the world—so if the great prospects are destined for me you speak of, I shall be the first Bishop from the Cloister for the last three hundred years—and while I am about it, think (since Sir R.W. said that everyone had his price) that I will not come out of it except for the Papacy.[26]

At Littlemore during July 1841, Newman reflected on the state of the English Church. In the article "Private Judgments," he advocated that when a person looks at two religious bodies that profess to be Catholic and are bearing good fruits, a person should remain in the one in which Providence has placed him, instead of risking making an unwarranted mistake. Newman now believed the English Church suffered the note of schism, but he argued that the Roman Church suffered the practical error of idolatry

---

26 *LD,* Vol. VIII, JHN to H. A. Woodgate (September 22, 1841), 276-78; 277-78. R.W. was Robert Walpole, the British Statesman (1667-1745).

by superstitious veneration of Mary and the saints. He concluded a long discussion of instances of "private judgment" in the Bible as follows:

> It is then a Note of the Christian Church, as decisive as any, that she is not idolatrous; and any semblance of idolatrous worship in the Church of Rome as plainly dissuades a man of Catholic feelings from her communion, as the taint of a Protestant or schismatical spirit in our communion may tempt him to depart from us. This is the Via Media which we would maintain; and thus without judging Rome on the one hand, or acquiescing in our own state on the other, we may use what we see, as a providential intimation to us, not to quit what is bad for what may be worse, but to learn resignation to what we inherit, nor seek to escape into a happier state by suicide.[27]

It was in this same month, however, that Newman was visited a second time by the "ghost of antiquity." Some years before, he had seen how in the fourth century, the voice of Rome had decided Trinitarian controversies with the Arians. Now studying Athanasius's writings on the Arians he realized that the modern day Anglicans resembled the semi-Arians of the 5th century, while the Church of Rome was the center of orthodoxy. Newman was left in a state of perplexity regarding the Anglican Church's claim to catholicity. His doubts only grew as attacks on *Tract 90* increased and the plans to establish the joint Anglican–Lutheran Jerusalem Bishopric were drawn up.

Newman decided to divide the publication of *Select Treatises of St. Athanasius in Controversy with the Arians* into two volumes. The first volume appeared in 1842 and

---

27 "Private Judgment" in *Ess. II,* 370. First published in *British Critic,* July 1841.

the second one in 1844. The translation was a literal one because Newman knew that a non-literal translation would fan fears about the Catholic principles of the Tractarians. At the end of his life Newman undertook a freer translation of some of Athanasius's works, which would remain faithful to the bishop's teaching. It would be the last book that Newman published in his life. The study of St. Athanasius had been both Newman's first and last "passion."[28]

During this "exile" at Littlemore, Newman said the translation of Athanasius had led him to understand the state of schism of the Anglican Church. Even so, Newman endeavored to find reasons to remain in the Anglican Church and to speak of the duty to do so. The result of these thoughts on the subject was expressed in his article "Private Judgment" in the *British Critic* and the four sermons on the Notes of the Church.

The year 1841 following the publication of *Tract 90* had been a painful one. Newman had acquiesced to his bishop's desire that the *Tracts* be stopped, and at the middle of the year had relinquished the editorship of the *British Critic*. It was a painful time for him because many bishops fired their charges against him and the Tractarians, and out of obedience to his bishop he was unable to respond. The bishops had not done the same to the extreme Evangelicals, who ignored the *Articles* concerning Baptism and Justification, or to the Liberals such as Arnold and Hampden, who held a rationalist interpretation of Scripture and theology.[29]

---

28 *LD,* Vol. XXVII, JHN to Edward B. Pusey (April 20, 1874), 56-7; Ian Ker, 714.

29 Trevor, *Newman, Pillar of the Cloud,* 258.

CHAPTER 29

STORM AND CALM
AFTER *TRACT 90*

THE crisis precipitated by the publication of *Tract 90* in January of 1841 never subsided as Newman had expected or wished. In 1842, the reaction became a storm which pushed him further into semi-retirement at Littlemore. The storm became continuous: Many of the Anglican bishops preached charges in their triennial diocesan visits in which they strongly condemned, not only *Tract 90,* but the entire Tractarian Movement, questioning the High Church Principles that the Movement was trying to restore. The charges were relentless, like rain storms one after another. Many bishops voiced great indignation against the Tractarians' criticism of Protestant principles and the sixteenth-century Protestant Reformers.

The charge by R. Mant, Bishop of Down, Connor, and Dromore, began with civility by the acknowledgment of the good intentions of the authors of the *Tracts for the Times.* Soon it turned to criticize the Tractarian adoption of the Roman notion of Tradition.[1] Mant, who pitted Scripture against Tradition, criticized the Tractarians for

---

1 *LD,* Vol. IX, R. Mant, "A Charge Intended For Delivery at the Visitation of the Clergy of Down and Connor, by their Bishop, June 1842," 613-21, 614-15.

reviving prayers for the dead, which he thought had no scriptural foundation.

Bishop Mant asserted that the *Articles* should be understood in their literal grammatical sense. He argued that the points on which latitude of interpretation was sought were the very points on which the national church was at variance. The bishop objected twice to Newman's description in *Tract 90* of the Church teaching "with the stammering lips of ambiguous formularies."[2] Mant also objected to the Tractarians' praise of the Roman liturgy, and in particular its Breviary.[3] Newman and his friends, on the contrary, were keenly aware of the liturgical ignorance and lack of authority in the Anglican Church.

The charge that struck Newman most deeply came from his own bishop, Richard Bagot, who delivered his verdict in May 1842, at Newman's church, St. Mary's, with Newman in attendance. Bagot noted that the Tractarians "had been exposed to a storm of abuse as violent as it has been unceasing—to calumnies and misrepresentations of the most wanton and cruel description . . ."[4] He praised the Tractarians for their Christian moderation and forbearance under such insults. Next, Bagot proceeded to condemn the doctrines promulgated by the Tractarians as erroneous and heretical.

---

2 *Ibid.,* 618-19.

3 *Ibid.,* 620-21.

4 *LD,* Vol. VIII, Richard Bagot, A Charge delivered to the Clergy of the Diocese of Oxford by Richard Bagot, D.D., Bishop of Oxford, and Chancellor of the Most Noble Order of the Garter; at his Fourth Visitation, May 1842; Appendix 2; 605-12; 606.

Bagot remarked that the *Articles* had been drawn with a view of including rather than excluding men of various opinions and that Calvinists had stretched the interpretation of the *Articles* more than *Tract 90*. He thought, however, that by the subtle interpretation put forth by *Tract 90* "the Articles may be made to mean anything or nothing."[5] Newman was naturally very hurt by these words. Although Bagot admitted that there should be license in interpreting the *Articles,* he found fault with the careless language of the younger members of the Movement.[6] Bagot expressed his concern that students without clear minds who opposed Puritanism or Calvinism would easily go to the opposite extreme of Romanism.[7] In making his case, Bagot accused the Roman Catholic Church of being subtle, deceptive, schismatic, and even anti-Christian. Ingeniously Bagot called for a renewal of sacramental practice, fasting, and adherence to the *Book of Common Prayer* while criticizing those who were bringing it about. He spoke of a gradual renewal brought about by an "expansive principle" which was in fact no other than the Catholic principles revived by the Movement.[8]

Newman told his friend Keble: "You will be glad to hear that the Bishop's charge delivered yesterday was very favourable to us, rather to our cause—for some of us suffered."[9] Indeed, Newman suffered, but he hardly showed it in his writing. He was in part stunned by his own

---

5 *Ibid.,* 608.

6 *Ibid.,* 609.

7 *Ibid.,* 610.

8 *Ibid.,* 611.

9 *LD,* Vol. VIII, JHN to John Keble (May 24, 1842), 14-15; 14.

bishop's remarks, but expected the bishop would modify the published text. A few months later, when the bishop published the charge, Newman commented: "*Ours* put a note to his charge which took off whatever was severe in his text."[10]

Although Newman was able to restrain ill feelings, he thought the bishops had things backwards. It was not the Tractarians who were acquiescing to heresy, but the bishops. Newman felt that the educated laity, in particular barristers, had to stem the tide of doctrinal error.[11] During 1842, he had frequent correspondence with Edward Badeley, Edward Bellasis, and James R. Hope, lawyer friends in London about the events of the time. Bellasis suggested that a hundred barristers sign a declaration in support of *Tract 90*. Newman liked the idea, but in the end it did not materialize.

During all these attacks, Newman's patient forbearance was conveyed in his numerous letters. It is surprising, for he expressed no anger, neither did he make disparaging remarks. Newman even went as far as to counsel calm obedience to Tom Mozley, after Mozley's bishop had criticized the *British Critic* for espousing Catholic principles. Even in the case of his own bishop's criticism, Newman's reaction was self-controlled and charitable, though his sentiments were bruised.

UNIVERSITY EVENTS

On May 24, the very next day after Bishop Bagot's Visitation and Charge, the Heads of Houses passed a motion

---

10 *LD,* Vol. VIII, JHN to Thomas Mozley (September 17, 1842), 97-98; 97.

11 *LD,* Vol. VIII, JHN to Charles Crawley (January 2, 1842), 404.

to repeal the censure against Renn Hampden. This censure was due partly to Newman, who, in 1836, had actively campaigned against Hampden for his Latitudinarian approach to doctrine. This time Newman decided not to take an active part in forming a committee at Oxford against Hampden, but encouraged friends to do so. On the appointed day, a large number of non-resident Fellows came up to Oxford for the vote. The proposal to rescind the censure was defeated by 334 *Non-placets* to 219 *Placets*. The Heads of Houses had no doubt been emboldened by Bishop Bagot's strictures. However, despite the Episcopal Charges against the Tractarians, a sufficient number of Oxford graduates opposed Hampden's theological opinions.

Notwithstanding this vote against Hampden, endorsed by a few bishops, five years later in 1847, the Whig Prime Minister, Lord John Russell, nominated Hampden to be Bishop of Hereford. Hampden was consecrated bishop for that See in the following year. The same type of political influence that had obtained Hampden's appointment as Regius Professor of Theology at Oxford in 1836 now obtained for him an Episcopal See.

Although Hampden had been defeated twice, opposition against the Tractarians was increasing at Oxford. Edward Hawkins, Provost of Oriel and friend of Hampden, did not like R. W. Church's friendship with Newman and his support of *Tract 90*. In 1841, following the publication of the *Tract,* Church offered to resign his Tutorship at Oriel. After some hesitation, Hawkins accepted the resignation and was left with only one Tutor at Oriel since two others had resigned to marry.

Other Tractarians felt the side effects of the struggle against Hampden. Shortly after the Hampden vote, the Bishop of Oxford refused to accept Albany James Christie as a candidate for Deacon's Orders. Christie lacked the necessary testimonial letters. Hawkins refused the College Testimonials on account of Christie's association with the Tractarian Movement. Christie eventually became a physician and entered the Roman Catholic Church. In 1842, the same year of Church's resignation, Isaac Williams, Tutor at Trinity College, who had lost the contest for the Poetry Professorship, married and left the university.

The criticism of the *British Critic* continued, and in September 1842, Edward Denison, Bishop of Salisbury, took the journal to task for its favorable opinion of Roman Catholicism and its exaggeration of the ills of the principles of the Protestant Reformation. Newman was upset that the bishop singled out one publication, leaving radical Evangelical papers untouched.[12] He asked Mozley to write the bishop. Since Mozley, who lived in Denison's jurisdiction, thought this might make matters worse, Newman insisted that they should follow St. Ignatius of Antioch's rule: "Do nothing without the Bishop." He urged Mozley to write his bishop. Instead Mozley wrote an article titled "Episcopal Charges of the Past Year" which appeared in the January issue of the *British Critic* for 1843.

Bishop Denison was not the only one annoyed by the articles of the *British Critic*. Another was Pusey, who had a different idea of the Protestant Reformers and was upset

---

12 *LD,* Vol. IX, JHN to Thomas Mozley (September 14, 1842), 89-90; 89.

with Newman's review of *The Remains and Publications of the Late Rev. John Davison*, a Fellow and Tutor at Oriel College in 1810. In *The Remains,* Davison, an admirer of Bishop Jewel as the great exponent of the English Reformation, claimed that during the Dark Ages the secluded virtue of monks had been exalted as the perfection of Christian spirit. Newman ably refuted this alleged injustice; he argued that the monks were those who best lived both the spirit and the letter of the law in the Gospels. For Newman, monks were the set of men nearest to Christian perfection.[13] But monks did even more—they shut themselves to pray and do penance for the sake of the world and to intercede for God on its behalf. Newman knew this not only from his reading, but from personal experience. The subject matter of this defense could not have been any closer to his heart since he was living like a monk in Littlemore.

LITTLEMORE

Newman had read St. Athanasius's *Life of St. Anthony* and written about it in a series of articles titled "Church of the Fathers" which appeared in 1833, in the *British Critic*. St. Anthony, who had lived in the third century, led an ascetic life of frequent prayer and penance, devotion to Christ and love of neighbor.[14] St. Anthony's penance consisted primarily in fasting in imitation of Jesus Christ in the desert.[15]

---

13 *Ibid.,* 218.

14 John Henry Newman, *Historical Sketches,* Vol. II, The Church of the Fathers, *"Anthony in Conflict,"* 101.

15 *Ibid.,* 111.

Since 1839, while at Littlemore, Newman had observed a rigorous Lent fast, and he recorded the details in notes titled "Personal and most private."[16] On Wednesdays and Fridays he abstained from food until 5 p.m. During Holy Week the rigorous Lent fasting which he had begun in 1839 increased. In a diary entry he wrote, "I have this Lent abstained from fish, fowl, all meat but bacon at dinner; from butter, vegetables of all sorts, fruit, pastry, sugar, tea, wine, and beer and toast. I have never dined out. I have not worn gloves."[17] Newman lived on bacon, eggs, milk, barley-water, and water. He missed tea and he felt weak in his limbs, but he was able to read and write as usual.[18] On Sundays, he did not abstain or fast.

In 1841 and 1842, Newman kept similar abstinence and fasting during Lent and in addition abstained from milk. Instead of milk he drank tea, a stimulant which he had missed in the former two Lents.[19] However, by the end of Lent 1842, he felt weak and began to have milk and bread, which made him feel stronger again. He also added butter to the bread and on some occasions had wine, but he felt exhausted and in consequence sometimes did not pray the Breviary. On a few occasions, he had to take Sulfate Quinine pills as an analgesic for pain in his face. During Lent, Newman also did not read the newspaper. He tried sleeping on the floor, but it was too cold for him to get to sleep, so he desisted.[20]

---

16 John Henry Newman, *AW*, 215-22.
17 *Ibid.*, 217.
18 *Ibid.*, 218.
19 *Ibid.*, 219.
20 *Ibid.*, 221.

At Littlemore, Newman established a schedule for daily prayer of the Breviary and house rules.[21] The day began at five with Matins, followed by Lauds and Prime. At eleven, he and his companions went to the Church for Morning Prayer and again at three for Evensong. The simple main meal was supper at six. There was silence before two and after eight to facilitate prayer and study. The day ended with Vespers at seven and Compline at nine. Compline was prayed in Latin unless someone was present who did not understand, in which case it was prayed in English. Each person had various jobs and cared for his own room, while a servant took care of the fires, set up for breakfast, and cleaned.

For all the fasting and prayer, Littlemore was not a dull place. Sometimes after dinner Newman played sonatas on the violin in the library. Soon he had the stable company of some men with good humor and laughter. The first to move in was John Dobrée Dalgairns, a young graduate of twenty-three who had lost a Fellowship to Jesus College by one vote because of his Catholic ideas. Dalgairns wished to be ordained a deacon, in part to relieve the disappointment of his parents.[22] Newman helped support him because his father gave him a very small and insufficient allowance.[23]

After Dalgairns, the next to move in was William Lock-

---

21 *LD*, Vol. IX, Memorandum: Order of the Day at Littlemore, 81.

22 *LD*, Vol. IX, JHN to J. L. Richards (October 10, 1842), 122-23; 122.

23 Trevor, *Newman, The Pillar of the Cloud*, 273.

hart, a twenty-two-year-old connected with Sir Walter Scott. Lockhart's family sent William to Newman to keep him from going over to the Roman Catholic Church. Before allowing him to move in, Newman made Lockhart sign an agreement that for three years he would put aside the question of becoming Roman Catholic.[24] By August of 1842, five men were living with Newman at Littlemore. And in December, they were joined by Frederick Bowles, a nervous young man whose brother had been at Oriel and died at a young age. Bowles was ordained a deacon on December 18, and the following day, he became Newman's curate at Littlemore.

The men who went to Littlemore were all much younger than Newman. This led to gossip at Oxford that Newman surrounded himself with "inferior men" and "junior admirers" over whom he could have complete sway. The reality is that they were bright men and good students who had given up academic advancement to be with Newman. Some sought him out for advice and others were referred to him by friends or family members. Lockhart later recorded that Newman refused to be treated as a superior and wanted to be called simply Newman.[25] This was too much for his companions, who instead addressed him omitting his name.

Other young men came and went from Newman's place. One such visitor gave rise to a humorous incident. This visitor walked to Littlemore with great enthusiasm and

---

24 *LD,* Vol. IX, JHN to E. B. Pusey (August 20, 1842), 67-68.
25 Trevor, *Newman, The Pillar of the Cloud,* 273.

stayed two nights, but the Spartan arrangement frightened him. Newman wrote: "I could not conceive what ailed him—for he looked at me as if I had been a ghost or wizard—spoke in his most solemn voice—would not laugh—was sick all night and did not get a wink of sleep—and next day looked thin and yellow."[26] Upon his returning to Oxford, he was at once restored to "his beaming looks and lovely spirits."

Almost as humorous was the spying carried out by a pugnacious Evangelical, Mr. McGhee, which occurred at the festive dedication of the church at Littlemore. On this occasion, Newman arranged for a procession with children and clergymen singing Psalm 24.[27] Between sixty and seventy persons received Holy Communion. The spy, who during the service cried out that it was "popish," wrote a letter, published by *The Record,* complaining of the procession with children and bells, and of Newman kneeling before a wooden cross.[28] The spy was corrected in a letter to the *Plymouth Herald* indicating that the children had worn smocks, the "wooden cross" was a "stone cross" and the procession was about twenty paces, from the schoolhouse to the church.[29]

The accusations caused Bishop Bagot to inquire from Newman about the activities at Littlemore. Newman was

---

26 *LD,* Vol. IX, JHN to Charles Marriot (September 6, 1842), 83.

27 *LD,* Vol. IX, JHN to Miss M. R. Giberne (September 25, 1842), 112-13.

28 *LD,* Vol. IX, *Clericus* to the Editor of the *Record* (September, 29, 1842), 113-15.

29 *LD,* Vol. IX, JHN to the Editor of the *Plymouth Herald* (December 3, 1842).

able to allay the bishop's fears and convince him that at Littlemore, he sought greater prayer, quiet, and study in private. During Advent of 1842, Newman and his companions lived an even stricter lifestyle, waking up at three for Matins and then going to bed until six in the morning. After breakfast at eight, they fasted until five in the evening. While living at Littlemore, Newman continued to assist others in many ways. He looked for employment for the son of a college servant, he sought a nursery maid for Jemima, and taught Latin to a boy in the village. Newman continued his letter writing, including to Anglicans thinking of becoming Roman Catholics.

ADVICE TO POTENTIAL CONVERTS

One of his correspondents was Miss Holmes, who had first written to him in 1840. Newman had managed to keep her from becoming Roman Catholic. Even though Miss Holmes asked for his advice, she was headstrong and rarely followed it.[30] Instead she involved Newman in helping her to find employment and in publishing a book on church architecture. In 1842, Miss Holmes begged to be allowed to meet Newman on her way through Oxford to a new job as a governess. When they met in Oxford, she expected to find a venerable sage and rudely expressed her childish disappointment. Newman wrote to her a few days later to excuse himself and added: "As for myself, you are not the first person who has been disappointed in me. Romantic people always will be. I am, in all ways of going on, a very ordinary

---

30 Trevor, Newman, *the Pillar of the Cloud,* 277-78.

person."[31] With his good humor, Newman reported to his sister Harriet that the young lady "was almost disgusted to find me so young. She said she had thought my hair was grey—so you see I must like Pythagoras shut myself up in a cave and never be seen by anyone."[32]

For some years, Newman continued to help Miss Holmes, a difficult young woman who was very impatient with her imperfections. He wrote her: "Our very work here is to overcome ourselves—and to be sensible of our hourly infirmities, to feel them keenly, is but the necessary step to overcoming them."[33] And he advised her to spend time in daily prayer: "giving half an hour every morning to the steady contemplation of some one sacred subject."[34] He also suggested that she picture Christ standing over her.

During 1842, some Anglicans who were not from Newman's circle became Roman Catholics. Newman was informed about them and some of them contacted him. One of the converts was Isabella Young, a wealthy twenty-six-year-old woman whom Pusey had been advising to remain Anglican. Upon his request Newman also wrote to her. She was a perplexed and emotionally unstable woman. Acting against Pusey's advice she was received into the Roman Catholic Church by Dr. Wiseman, and soon entered the novitiate of a religious order.[35] As much as this gave pain

---

31 *LD,* Vol. IX, JHN to Miss Holmes (November 20, 1842), 153.

32 *LD,* Vol. IX, JHN to Mrs. T. Mozley (November 16, 1842), 149-50; 149.

33 *LD,* Vol. IX, JHN to Miss Holmes (December 27,1842), 184-85.

34 *Ibid.*

35 *LD,* Vol. IX, E. B. Pusey to JHN (October 28, 1842), 135-36.

to Pusey, it could not compare with William E. Gladstone's pain at the news of the conversion to Rome of his sister Helen. Dr. Wiseman had also been involved in the reception of this young woman.[36]

Another convert to Roman Catholicism was Bernard Smith, a Fellow of Magdalen College, Oxford. In 1839, Smith had been appointed rector of a church in the diocese of Lincoln. In the course of beautifying his church, J. R. Bloxam introduced him to the church architect August W. Pugin, who in turn introduced him to St. Mary's College Oscott and to Bishop Wiseman. On a visit to a dying person with a Catholic priest, Smith was greatly moved by the effect of the Last Sacraments on the dying person.[37] Not long after that, in December of 1842, Smith attended a retreat preached by Wiseman and asked to be received into the Catholic Church.

Earlier John Kaye, the Bishop of Lincoln, had complained to Smith for introducing objectionable liturgical practices that had existed in earlier times, such as having candlesticks and a cross on the altar, turning toward the altar in prayers, and crossing himself in the service. Newman had written a letter to Smith attempting to keep him from joining the Roman Church. Smith, however, saw other difficulties in the Anglican Church besides liturgical abuse. When writing to a friend about Smith's decision Newman explained: "one idea got possession of him that

36 *LD,* Vol. IX, JHN to E. B. Pusey (July 24, 1842), 48 and footnote n. 2.

37 Wilfrid Ward, *The Life and Times of Cardinal Wiseman,* London 1897, Vol. I, 409-12.

the English Church, as being out of communion with the whole Catholic world, Greek and Roman, was in schism, and therefore unsafe to live and die in, according to the judgment of antiquity . . ."[38]

Although Newman tried to dissuade Anglicans such as Isabella Young and Bernard Smith from going over to Rome, his own contacts with Roman Catholics gradually increased, as did their prayers for the conversion of Newman and his friends.

In November 1842, Fr. Charles W. Russell wrote to Newman from St. Patrick's College, in Maynooth, Ireland, thanking Newman for the gift of Volume V of his *Parochial Sermons*. Russell asked Newman if he in turn would accept a volume of sermons by St. Alphonse Liguori. Russell closed the letter by telling Newman that he never went to the "Holy Altar" without praying that Newman would be brought into the "external membership of the one true fold."[39] Newman, who was at the time preaching the Samaritan Sermons, replied to Russell: "There is a divine life among us, clearly manifested, in spite of all our disorders, which is as great a note of the Church, as any can be. Why should we seek Our Lord's presence elsewhere, when He vouchsafes it to us where we are? What *call* have we to change our communion?"[40] Still Newman was thankful to Russell and invited him to visit if he should be passing by

---

38 *LD*, Vol. IX, JHN to J. W. Bowden (December 29, 1842), 188-89.

39 *LD*, Vol. IX, Charles William Russell to JHN (October 31, 1842), 154-55; 155.

40 *LD*, Vol. IX, JHN to Charles William Russell (November 22, 1842), 155-56; 156.

Oxford. In August of the following year, Russell was able to visit Newman at Oxford.

Despite these sermons and his correspondence with Russell, Newman wrote a retraction to his extreme anti-Catholic statements made in the 1830s. Newman felt he had to publish this retraction to relieve his conscience. In a letter to the editor of the *Oxford Conservative Journal* he explained that he had been following the language of Anglican Divines, but he also admitted that with his language he had hoped to find approval among those whom he respected and to repel the charge of Romanism.[41] For some years prior to the retraction, Newman had ceased to make inflammatory remarks about the Roman Catholic Church and commented in letters that to make these comments was uncharitable. He intended this retraction to be published at Christmas, hoping that during this season of conciliation, his statement would be less startling to Anglicans. Newman considered the possibility of publishing the retraction in a newspaper in the United States instead of England, but in the end it was published in the January 1843 issue of the *Oxford Conservative Journal*.

Meanwhile, many Roman Catholics continued to pray for Newman's conversion. One Roman Catholic priest who was fervently praying was Fr. Dominic Barbieri, a priest of the Passionist Order. Barbieri had read an article that Dalgairns had published the previous year in *L'Univers*, a French newspaper, on the obstacles to reunion between the Anglican and the Roman Catholic churches. Barbieri wrote

---

41 *LD,* Vol. IX, JHN to the Editor of the Oxford Conservative Journal (December 12, 1842), 167-72; 171.

a letter of introduction to Dalgairns in which he expressed his love for England.[42] Although he appealed more to the heart rather than to reason, Barbieri pointed out that contrary to *Tract 90,* some of the *Thirty-Nine Articles* could not be reconciled with Catholic teaching and the decrees of Trent.

Dalgairns replied to Barbieri that although the English Church was sick, it was still a living member of the Church with signs of life, such as succession, sanctity, orthodoxy, and persecution. With this exchange, a frequent and affectionate correspondence ensued between these two men, one which was shared with the community at Littlemore. Dominic Barbieri perceived that his vocation was the conversion of Englishmen and bringing the English Church back to the common fold. Newman appreciated Fr. Dominic's ardent love and saw in it the action of Providence.[43]

In 1842, Barbieri wished to visit Littlemore, but Dalgairns wrote with regret that it would not be advisable.[44] Instead of the proposed visit, Barbieri sent a copy of the Passionist Rule to the men at Littlemore, who read it with interest. Eventually, with Newman's approval, Dalgairns invited Barbieri to visit Littlemore; his first visit would take place on June 24, 1844.

In October 1842, Ambrose Phillipps visited Oxford to meet Newman and to introduce him to Fr. Luigi Gentili, who admired Newman's preface to a translation of Fleury's *Ecclesiastical History.* Born in Italy the same year as

42 Alfred Wilson, *Blessed Dominic Barbieri, Supernaturalized Briton,* Sands & Co Ltd., London, 1967, 289-90.

43 *Ibid.,* 295.

44 *Ibid.,* 294.

Newman, Gentili was a lawyer, a brilliant linguist, and a gifted musician. He had been suitor to an English Catholic heiress, but when her family refused his suit, the course of his life changed. Instead he joined the Institute of Charity, founded by philosopher priest Antonio Rosmini. Gentili came to England to work among Catholics in industrial towns. Phillipps thought that Fr. Gentili was the person who could convert Newman. Phillipps reported that both he and Gentili had been enchanted by Newman, "whose amiable manners are only equaled by his gigantic learning and talents."[45]

Although Newman had tried to keep Anglicans from becoming Roman Catholic, often he had not succeeded. His correspondence and friendship with Catholics had also increased. This and his public retraction of anti-Catholic statements made in the 1830s were an indication of his changing views of the Catholic Church. The sharp criticism leveled by numerous Episcopal Charges against Newman and the Tractarians, especially by his own bishop, had been painful, yet his semi-monastic life at Littlemore enabled him to have peace and react with charity.

Newman no longer defended the Anglican Church as a *Via Media* between Protestant churches and the Roman Catholic Church, or as a branch of the Catholic Church. He urged his fellow Anglicans, however, to remain in the Anglican Church because he believed that they should remain where God had placed them and that despite its many weaknesses, God still was present in the Anglican

---

45 *Purcell,* Vol. I, 257-58. JHN to Lord Shrewsbury from Ambrose Lisle Phillipps, cited in *LD,* Vol. IX, 129.

Church. Newman did not know what would follow for him or for his friends and for the English Church. He only knew that he had to pray and fast, and this he did. He was seeking God in prayer and as a result had greater strength and a certain inner peace in the midst of the uncertainty.

In the meantime, the unity of the Oxford Movement had begun to fracture with Oakeley and Ward, who, representing the younger generation, had certain control over Tom Mozley and the *British Critic*. Newman sided with Oakeley and Ward's views of the English Reformers and the logical conclusions reached by his friends, but he was not ready to make the statements that they made or to do so in the manner in which they did.

CHAPTER 30

NEWMAN'S RESIGNATION FROM ST. MARY'S UNIVERSITY CHURCH

A FTER more than two years of voluntary withdrawal to Littlemore, Newman's situation in the Anglican Church failed to improve. Although Newman dedicated a great deal of time to a new writing project, he inevitably felt more and more out of communion with the Anglican Church. He debated whether he could retain his post as Vicar of St. Mary's; he had considered resigning from St. Mary's for over two years. He had consulted with Keble, who had urged him to remain. In January, he wrote to a friend: "I have such a dreadful impression of our corruptions and heresies and unrealities, viewing us a body, that holiness of individuals, and the good that is doing in external and on its surface, are insufficient to overcome this deep despondency . . ."[1] Newman believed that the English Church "had been so radically Protestantized."[2]

Newman's growing dissatisfaction with the English Church contributed to his retraction of anti-Catholic statements. The retraction appeared at the end of January in the *Oxford Conservative Journal* under the headline "Oxford and Rome." Other local papers and the *English Churchman* reprinted the retraction. The *Churchman* agreed with

---

1 *LD,* Vol. IX, JHN to C.H.J. Anderson (Jan. 21, 1843), 210-211; 210.
2 *Ibid.,* 211.

Newman in censuring his own hard words and insults against Catholics, and called for "well-weighed and temperate statements of 'Anglican doctrine,' and a recurrence to Anglican practices and discipline in all their details."[3] Soon afterward the Roman Catholic *Dublin Review* also reprinted Newman's words.

Oddly, the retraction was anonymous, but people immediately recognized it as Newman's. The wealthy Catholic, Ambrose Phillipps, wrote Newman, congratulating him for what he termed God's goodness shown in this act of humility on the part of Newman.[4] With the letter he sent a copy of a "Prayer for England" composed some years earlier by Fr. Dominic Barbieri. However, Golightly and others were quick to criticize Newman. He was censured by the bishops and ostracized in the Anglican Church. He felt unsettled and more and more a Roman at heart. This made him feel guilty, for people still thought him to be an Anglican. He told his friend William Henry Wilberforce, "Yet what can I do? how is it possible to give men the right impression of what I would say, when every word is sure to be misunderstood, every admission to be exaggerated, every avowal to be but a hint of what is unsaid?"[5] Newman no longer had confidence in his Anglican beliefs and was worried by the thought of unsettling others, who still had confidence in him. He told William, "It is so very difficult to steer between being hypocritical, and revolutionary."[6]

---

3 "Severe Language against Rome," *English Churchmen, LD,* Vol. IX, 217.

4 *LD,* Vol. IX, Ambrose Lisle Phillipps to JHN (Feb. 10, 1834), 327-28.

5 *LD,* Vol. IX, JHN to Henry Wilberforce (Feb. 3, 1843), 223-24; 223.

6 *Ibid.,* 224.

Pusey assured Newman that he was loved and respected by many.[7] Newman thanked his friend for the kind words, but confessed that for some years he had lacked confidence in himself and consequently wished for others to have less in him.[8] Pusey tried to calm Newman's worries that he might be misleading people. He wrote Newman: "Any how, young men ought to trust you, and cannot help it; it is plainly part of God's appointments; He draws people around you, in the first instance against your will, in a way they are drawn around no other; and since such is His will, it will be yours to accept it."[9] He acknowledged that for Newman this entailed suffering, but that he should accept the cross that God wished him to carry.

Newman's state of mind was one of uncertainty, and not surprisingly he acted with prudence and advised others to do the same. In a candid letter to Miss Holmes, he admitted his own condition and counseled her not to visit the Roman Catholic, Dr. Wiseman: "Do consider that you are about to be submitted to temptation; that is, the temptation of acting, not on *judgment* but on *feeling*. Your feelings are in favor of Rome, so are mine—your judgment is against joining it—so is mine. Yet I would not trust myself among R[oman] Catholics without recollecting how apt feeling is to get the better of judgment—and I warn you of the same."[10]

7 *LD,* Vol. IX, E. B. Pusey to JHN (Feb. 4, 1843), 227.

8 *LD,* Vol. IX, E. B. Pusey to JHN (Feb. 4, 1843), 227-28; 227.

9 *LD,* Vol. IX, E. B. Pusey to JHN (Feb. 6, 1843), 228.

10 *LD,* Vol. IX, JHN to Miss Holmes (Feb. 8, 1843), 231.

Thoughts of Resignation from St. Mary's

Aware of his feelings and conscious of his responsibility as a pastor at St. Mary's, Newman once again thought of resignation. He had first considered this in 1840, and had spoken to Keble about it. Now he did so again. Newman told Keble that the undergraduates attended his services and sermons against the wishes of their Tutors. Newman realized that the influence that he exerted was in the direction of the Church of Rome. At one time he had tried to balance this by making strong statements against Rome, but now he could no longer do that. What worried Newman most was that almost all the English bishops had censured *Tract 90*, and in conscience he could only hold his position at St. Mary's based on his commentary on the *Thirty-Nine Articles* in which he asserted their compatibility with Roman doctrines.[11] With the almost unanimous rejection of his *Tract* by the bishops, he thought he had nothing to fall back upon. Newman wished to retain his pastoral work at Littlemore by separating Littlemore from St. Mary's. Hawkins, the Provost of Oriel, had declined this petition in 1840. Newman would not be allowed to keep Littlemore.[12] Charles Eden, a Tutor six years Newman's junior, was ready to take St. Mary's and Littlemore.

In May, Newman told Keble that as a beneficed clergyman he wished to quietly withdraw instead of being asked to take the Oath of Supremacy, and in conscience having to refuse.[13] Newman considered that he could no longer teach

---

11 *Ibid.*, 280.

12 *LD,* Vol. IX, JHN to John Keble (May 4, 1834), 327-28.

13 *LD,* Vol. IX, JHN to John Keble (May 18, 1843), 346-50; 348.

at St. Mary's without misleading younger men who had faith in him. While entertaining these thoughts, Newman worked hard at finding writers for a series titled *The Lives of English Saints*. Newman had conceived this project as a way of directing the attention of persons who were in danger of leaving the Church of England to go from doctrine to history, and from speculation to fact. He wished for them to find "interest in English soil and to keep them from seeking sympathy in Rome and her views."[14] It was also Newman's way of staying away from controversial subjects and arousing suspicion and criticism. He instructed contributors to stay away from doctrinal subjects. He wanted to give the public an account of the holy lives of native saints, in many cases somewhat obscure, and he hoped that this scheme would actually support the ideas of *Tract 90* by presenting the beliefs and practices of Ante-Reformation times.

PUSEY CENSURED

Newman was not the only Tractarian attacked by the Liberals at Oxford. Newman's enemies turned on Pusey on the occasion of a sermon on the Real Presence of Christ in the Eucharist, which he delivered on the Fourth Sunday of Easter at the Oxford Cathedral, May 14, 1843. Dr. Faussett, Lady Margaret Professor of Divinity, lodged a formal complaint with the Vice-Chancellor, Dr. Wynter. Pusey was accused of holding the Roman Catholic doctrine of Transubstantiation. Wynter convened six doctors, including Hawkins, Provost of Oriel, and Faussett himself,

---

14 *Ibid.*, 349.

and summarily censured Pusey, and suspended him as university preacher for two years. A bewildered Pusey sought Newman's advice. In his characteristic manner, Newman worked behind the scenes and consulted with his friends, Badeley, James Scott, and Roundel Palmer, all experts in ecclesiastical law. After various consultations, it was decided not to pursue a legal suit against the Vice-Chancellor.

People quickly compared Pusey's censure to that of the Regius Professor of Divinity, Renn Dickson Hampden, but it was altogether a different case. Hampden's opinions were in 1836 specifically detailed in extracts from his writings, and he, unlike Pusey, knew the specific accusations lodged against him.[15] The action by the university authorities was an abuse of power and justice, but despite appeals, the Vice-Chancellor and his "Star Chamber" remained adamant that they were complying with university statutes.

The censure of Pusey, a respected Hebrew scholar, as well as an exceptional family man and generous almsgiver, was part of a much larger attack on anything that hinted at Catholic principles and practices traditionally accepted by the Anglican Church. The previous year, Keble's curate had not been admitted to Orders for holding traditional views. Within the same week as Pusey's sermon, another clergyman, Thomas Edward Morris, preaching also at Christ Church Cathedral, was accused to the Chancellor for referring to William Laud as "the martyred Archbishop, who let

---

15 *LD*, Vol. IX, JHN to the Reverend Wynter from Francis Atkinson Faber (June 5, 1843), 372-73.

us trust, still intercedes for the Church."[16] Richard Church, wrote years later about the atmosphere at this time, saying a "climate of jealousy, mistrust, miserable tittle-tattle, sometimes of the most slanderous and sometimes of the most ridiculous kind, was set going all over Oxford." The Heads of Colleges and their Tutors were at odds; candidates for Fellowships were closely examined on their opinions, as were candidates for Holy Orders. They were cross-examined over the infallibility of General councils, Purgatory, the worship of images, the *Ora pro nobis*, and the intercession of saints.

Pusey published his sermon and protested to the Vice-Chancellor for his unjust treatment, yet humbly endured the censure. In July, a striking juxtaposition occurred. While Pusey was censured for holding orthodox Anglican teaching on the Real Presence of Christ in the Holy Eucharist, an American who had once been a Unitarian minister was awarded an honorary degree by Oxford. The students were outraged by this and were so vocal interrupting the University Commemoration that the University gathering was dissolved before the awards ceremony. That same month Faussett was unanimously reelected as Lady Margaret Professor of Divinity.

Although *The Lives of the English Saints* and Pusey's censure took up much of Newman's attention, Newman spent much energy and time, as in the immediately preceding years, trying to dissuade Anglican friends from becoming Roman Catholic.

---

16 *LD*, Vol. IX, Quote from Sermon by Rev. Thomas Edward Morris, XXIX.

ADVICE TO PROSPECTIVE CONVERTS

One of these friends was Charles B. Bridges, a graduate from Oriel who had been living at Littlemore since October of the previous year. Edward Hawkins, the Provost of Oriel, wrote Newman to tell him that Bridges was in danger of joining the communion of Rome. Hawkins asked Newman to counsel him. In correspondence with the Provost it became clear that Newman only knew in general about Bridges's unsettled religious ideas. Newman had accepted him at Littlemore, hoping that Bridges would resolve his difficulties, but Newman did not ask Bridges any particulars, because he refrained from asking people for their religious beliefs. He did not ask people for their beliefs unless they wished to speak about them.

The case with Miss Holmes was quite different. She told Newman about her changing emotional state of mind and asked him many questions. As was expected, Newman counseled self-control. He wrote to her, "All your powers of mind and capacities of usefulness will go for nothing, till you use them. They will war against each other, like a country in insurrection. You are in one frame of mind one day, another the next. You depend on what people say of you."[17] He counseled her to seek peace in prayer, and recommended that she read *The Spiritual Combat,* a book on the spiritual life by Laurence Scupoli, a Catholic priest. Earlier, Newman had also suggested that she read *The Imitation of Christ* by Thomas à Kempis and not put aside the reading of Sacred Scripture.[18] Besides seeking advice from

---

17 *LD,* Vol. IX, JHN to Miss Holmes (April 29, 1843), 319-20; 319.

18 *LD,* Vol. IX, JHN to Miss Holmes (March 8, 1843), 272-75; 275.

Newman, she sought advice from Oakeley. In doing so, she wore Newman's patience thin. He wrote to her, "You cannot tell half to Mr. O. and half to me—tell him all, or me all. If you tell me all, I can advise you, if you tell him, he can advise you."[19]

Still Newman continued to advise Miss Holmes. She wanted to become Roman Catholic, and to enter a convent as a nun. Newman, who knew her better than she knew herself, did not think she was fit for conventual life. And even more, he told her that she was not ready to become Roman Catholic, running the risk of leaving that communion after a short while. That same year, Richard Sibthorp, a Fellow from Magdalen College, who had become Roman Catholic in 1841, had reverted to the Anglican Communion. Thus, Newman advised Miss Holmes, "I cannot conceive a more painful situation, [than] that for a person to find himself joined, committed irreversibly, to the Church of Rome— and then to find he wanted something more or less, which he could not get."[20]

Ambrose St. John was a young clergyman and Fellow at Christ Church College, Oxford, whom Henry Wilberforce introduced to Newman in June of 1843. Ambrose agreed to write the life of St. Simon Stock for the series of *Lives*. In July, while assisting the vicar of a country parish, Ambrose wrote to Newman confiding in him worries about taking the oath for the *Thirty-Nine Articles*. In particular, Ambrose believed that he could not profess what the *Articles* state about Transubstantiation and Invocation

---

19 *LD,* Vol. IX, JHN to Miss Holmes (May 14, 1843), 340.

20 *LD,* Vol. IX, JHN to Miss Holmes (August 16, 1843), 461.

of Saints. Ambrose thought that the notion of Transubstantiation in the Catechism of the Council of Trent was correct, and that when the Anglican Church condemned the word "Transubstantiation" it meant something quite different from what the Church of Rome meant. He also believed that it was the will of God for men to ask the saints for their prayers, and especially the Virgin Mary.[21]

In a reply letter, Newman sympathized with Ambrose and offered him a place to stay at Littlemore. Newman, however, wished Ambrose to have a place to pray and think for himself rather than give him answers to his doubts. He told the young man, "It is no good my attempting to offer advice, when perhaps I might raise difficulties instead of removing them. It seems to me quite a case in which you should, as far as may be, make up your mind for yourself."[22] Acting this way was not false humility on Newman's part; on the one hand, he was unsure of himself, but more importantly he felt a sacred obligation to teach the Anglican faith without leading others to Rome.

In August, Ambrose moved in with the community at Littlemore. Dalgairns and Bridges were living with Newman. Frederick Bowles, who since December of the previous year was Newman's curate at Littlemore, was temporarily kept away from Littlemore by his mother, whose daughter Emily had been received that year into the Roman Catholic Church. A few years later both Frederick and his mother also became Roman Catholic.

---

21 *LD*, Vol. IX, Ambrose St. John to JHN (July 13, 1843), 427-28; 427.
22 *LD*, Vol. IX, JHN to Ambrose St. John (July 16, 1843), 429.

Another case was that of Charles Seager, a married man and a scholar at Worcester College, who was Pusey's assistant in Hebrew. At the start of 1842, Pusey asked Newman to help keep Seager from falling into Roman errors, but Newman's attempts were in vain. Seager's conversion was a source of pain and embarrassment for Pusey, and his enemies seized the occasion to belittle him. Concerns with possible converts had become a common part of daily life for Newman, but he managed to carry on with his work on the *Lives*, and normal life at Littlemore. During this time he considered when would be the best moment to resign.

RESIGNATION FROM ST. MARY'S

Newman's resignation, however, was precipitated by unexpected events. On August 25, William Lockhart wrote to Newman to inform him that he was about to begin a retreat under Fr. Gentili after which he would most likely become Roman Catholic. He asked Newman and those at Littlemore to pray for him to know God's will. At the end of the retreat, Lockhart became a Roman Catholic, and Newman reported this to Bishop Bagot. Lockhart's mother corresponded with Newman, and she thanked him for all he had done to try to keep her son an Anglican. A few years later, however, Mrs. Lockhart, like Mrs. Bowles, became Roman Catholic.

Newman wrote to his sister Jemima, "As to Lockhart's matter, I own that, were there no other reason, it would be sufficient to have made me resign (if left to myself). It is a very great scandal under the circumstances—and I could not hold up my head again as Vicar of St Mary's."[23] Newman felt he could no longer keep his position as Vicar of St. Mary's, and in September he submitted his letter of resignation to the bishop. He wished to remain in "lay communion," that is, a layman in the Church of England.

Newman had contemplated this step for over two years, and in March of 1843, he had written once more a long letter to Keble laying out the reasons that were prompting him to resign from St. Mary's. Keble replied that he thought the time had come for Newman to retire from St. Mary's, but "I am not sure that I should say this, if it involved your retiring from the exercise of the Ministry." He agreed with Newman that by managing to keep Littlemore he would be able to give advice to people's consciences and avoid the appearance that he was recklessly throwing away what Providence had given to him. Newman, however, was not allowed to keep St. Mary's at Littlemore.

On Sunday, September 25, 1843, Newman presided at his last service at Littlemore, and delivered his farewell sermon, "The Parting of Friends." In this homily Newman spoke of God's plans and blessings. King David was not allowed by God to build a temple, but he had rejoiced in God's presence. Although Newman had built a temple, with a certain sadness he compared himself to David: "We too, at this season, year by year, have been allowed in our measure, according to our work and our faith, to rejoice in God's presence, for this sacred building which He has given us to

---

23 *LD,* Vol. IX, JHN to Mrs. John Mozley (September 5, 1843), 504-5; 504.

worship Him in."[24] With gratefulness but heavy heart, after seven years, a symbol of perfection, Newman spoke of his exodus as that of the Israelites from Egypt.[25] Alluding to the Anglican Church, he lamented that his Mother had abandoned the one who would have died for her.[26]

Newman closed the sermon with a touching description of his solicitude for those who had been under his care, and he asked for their prayers, "remember such a one in time to come, though you hear him not, and pray for him, that in all things he may know God's will, and at all times he may be ready to fulfill it."[27] After the sermon Newman received communion, and then stopped officiating the service. Pusey continued, although overcome with emotions. Many years later Newman's friend, Edward Bellasis, wrote:

> [T]he sermon I can never forget, the faltering voice, the long pauses, the perceptible and hardly successful efforts at restraining himself, together with the deep interest of the subject, were almost overpowering; Newman's voice was low, but distinct and clear, and his subject was a half-veiled complaint and remonstrance at the treatment which drove him away.[28]

Bellasis concluded his reminiscence: "And thus the services of the greatest man of our times, the acutest and most laborious, and most energetic of the sons of the English Church is lost to us, he retires into lay communion."[29]

---

24 *LD*, Vol. IX, "The Parting of Friends," Appendix 7, 733-40; 735.

25 *Ibid.*

26 *Ibid.*, 739.

27 *Ibid.*, 740.

28 Edward Bellasis, *Memorials of Mr. Serjeant Bellasis. 1800-1873*, London, Burns and Oates, Ltd, 1893, 53.

29 *Ibid*, 54.

While drafting his resignation letter, Newman heard the unexpected news that his brother-in-law, Tom Mozley, was going to resign from the *British Critic* and was about to become Roman Catholic. Newman was alarmed. Tom had been in Normandy, accompanying Harriet, who was recuperating from fatigue brought about by insomnia. There, Tom had become friends with two good Catholic priests (brothers) and their sister, and Tom had embraced the desire of becoming Roman Catholic. As he received the news, Newman wrote to Tom and asked him not to act in haste. Newman told him, "If you ask me, I must plainly tell you that you are under excitement, and in no fit state to act for yourself."[30]

Matters were worsened because Harriet thought Newman was an accomplice to her husband's sudden plans. Newman was particularly concerned with the abruptness of Tom's decision made without adequate warning to his wife, considering the harm this would cause. In the end, on September 4, he traveled to Cholderton, just north of Salisbury, where Tom lived, and persuaded him to wait for at least two years before taking his proposed step and advised him to finish the restoration of his parish church. Tom desisted from his plans to become Roman Catholic, but he resigned from the editorship of the *British Critic*. Tom's last article, titled "Six Doctors," appeared in the July 1834 issue of the *British Critic*, the last issue under the hands of the Tractarians.

---

30 *LD,* Vol. IX, JHN to Thomas Mozley (September 21, 1843), 530-31; 530.

The article was a severe criticism of Pusey's secret trial and unjust censure.

The reactions to Newman's resignation were to be expected. His friends were sympathetic while his enemies were happy to see him go. Bishop Bagot did not try to stop Newman or lament his loss. He only asked him to submit a notarized letter of resignation. Newman had not given the bishop his reasons for resigning, but there was almost no need to do so. For any keen observer, it was evident that the hierarchy of the Anglican Church was responsible in great measure for Newman's step. Newman told his sister Harriet: "I do so despair of the Church of England, I am so evidently cast off by her, and, on the other hand I am so drawn to the Church of Rome, that I think it *safer*, as a matter of honesty, not to keep my living."[31] By contrast to his treatment by the Anglican bishops, the Episcopal Bishops of New York, New Jersey, Maryland, and North Carolina expressed their satisfaction at a proposed American edition of Newman's *Parochial Sermons*.[32]

During this sad and trying time for Newman, Jemima was an affectionate support to her brother. In addition to Keble and Pusey, others such as Manning were also kind to Newman. During 1843, Manning corresponded often with Newman, and upon hearing of Newman's resignation, Manning expressed his sorrow to him. In subsequent correspondence, Manning asked Newman to consider that it would take more than a few years to change the opinions

31 *LD,* Vol. IX, JHN to Mrs. Thomas Mozley (September 29, 1843), 537-38; 537.

32 *LD,* Vol. IX, "To the Editor of the Oxford Herald" (March 25, 1843), 292-94.

and prejudices of a whole life in the English Church, and he praised him for all that he had done for the Church. Then with reference to the Church of England, Manning asked rhetorically: "For years, who has been more loved and revered?"[33] Finally Manning, who shared Newman's letters with Gladstone, urged Newman to be more patient.

Newman replied to his friend's kind note, recounting in a chronological manner the events which had led him to resign.[34] He told Manning that he had not acted out of irritation or impatience, but because he thought the Church of Rome to be the Catholic Church, and the Anglican Church no longer in communion with the Catholic Church. Newman held that he could no longer honestly teach in the Anglican Church.

It is hard to imagine the effect and significance of Newman's resignation. He was no longer acting as a clergyman in the Church of England. For the first time since his appointment as curate at St. Clement's in 1824, he did not have a Sunday Service, nor did he preach any more. He no longer had the care of parishioners and visits to the sick. This change was the first step in Newman's formal separation from the Anglican Church. Newman needed some rest, and in October he went away to London. On two Sundays he attended the services at St. Margaret Chapel where Oakeley was the vicar; Newman appreciated the beautiful Gregorian Chant sung in the services. From there, he went to Derby to visit John and Jemima Mozley. Besides

---

33 *LD,* Vol. IX, H. E. Manning to JHN (October 23, 1843), 584-85; 584.
34 *LD,* Vol. IX, JHN to H. E. Manning (October 25, 1843), 585-86.

speaking with his brother-in-law and sister, he spent time playing with his sister's children and playing the violin.

Newman was beginning a new and final stage in his life as Anglican. He was figuratively reduced to lay communion in the Anglican Church. After the short visit to family and friends, he continued his extended retreat at Littlemore. Although his position and condition were quite different from what it had been as Vicar of St. Mary's, Newman had mentally prepared for this inevitable step. There, in the quiet of Littlemore, he followed a demanding plan of spiritual exercises; he continued his study and writing. Visits and correspondence with friends also kept him occupied.

For some time, Newman's energies remained focused on the publication of *The Lives of English Saints*. Dalgairns, who was living with Newman at Littlemore, wrote the life of St. Stephen Harding, the first one of the series to be published. It was followed by *The Family of St. Richard the Saxon* by Thomas Meyrick, an undergraduate at Corpus Christi College, and *St. Augustine* by Frederick Oakeley. Frederick W. Faber was then writing on St. Wilfrid, a seventh-century Archbishop of York. Many others wrote for the series, but both Dalgairns and Faber contributed the most.

Dalgairns acted almost like a son to Newman, and while away visiting his mother, he wrote to Newman, lamenting the extension of his family vacation, and being absent from Littlemore. He humorously remarked that being thrown back upon childhood acquaintances for six weeks, he was not much of a monk any longer.[35] Newman addressed him in

---

35 *LD,* Vol. IX, J. D. Dalgairns to JHN (October 19, 1843), 580-81; 581.

letters with the affectionate Latin superlative "carissime."[36] Ambrose, Lockhart, and other young men also looked up to Newman with love and admiration.

Despite the intimate following that Newman had, the Tractarian Movement had changed because its leaders had changed, and a few had come to an early death. In April 1843, Samuel Francis Wood died at the relatively young age of thirty-four. Newman noted that Froude and Wood, two of their Littlemore brothers, had died within seven years. Keble and Pusey were loyal friends and faithful Anglicans, but they did not have Newman's leadership capacity or desire to go further than they already had in their conclusions about the Anglican Church. And now Palmer was criticizing that legacy of the *British Critic* and disowning the Tractarians. With the latter in mind, Newman told Maria Giberne that "the Tractarian party *is* in process of being broken up."[37] There was more to the breakup; the Oxford Movement had evolved, and was no longer so much a force of reform in the Anglican Church as a statement on the doctrinal and juridical nature of the English Church. The natural consequence was that some of the newer generation wished to become Roman Catholic. Newman's heart was now with Rome, but he urged friends, including Tom Mozley, not to take this step without more prayer.

---

36 *LD,* Vol. IX, JHN to J. D. Dalgairns (April 26, 1843, October 14, 1843), 313-14; 565-67.

37 *LD,* Vol. IX, JHN to Miss M. R. Giberne (October, 27, 1843), 589-90; 589.

In May, Newman had confided to Keble, his friend and spiritual guide, "I am very far more sure that England is in schism, than that the Roman additions to the Primitive Creed may not be developments, arising out of a keen and vivid realizing of the Divine *Depositum* of faith."[38] Protestants held that the Roman Catholic Church had corrupted the Gospel teaching by its additions. Over a number of years Newman had come to realize that in doctrinal matters this was not the case. He could now affirm that the Anglican Church was in schism with the true Church founded on the Apostles. He jotted down notes for study concerning his theses on development. Newman thought that the Roman Catholic Church had correctly developed doctrines that it had received from Christ's Apostles. The entries continued until May 1844, and they indicate how he matured the ideas for his book, *An Essay on the Development of Christian Doctrine,* completed in October 1845. In March 1843, he wrote: "*Supposing* the Catholic Religion to be true, qu. [sic] whether some great judgment is not *likely* to have come upon us English for our dreadful suppression of it through three centuries by national *acts*—If so, are not the misconceptions we form of it, only to be expected conformably with the state of the case?"[39] The next day an entry was on the Roman invocation of saints. He asked how one could believe that God is the God of St. Paul without believing that the saints live and are present to us.[40]

Earlier, in February of 1843, Newman published fourteen University Sermons under the title *Sermons, chiefly*

---

38 *LD,* Vol. IX, JHN to John Keble (May 4, 1843), 327-29; 328.

39 *LD,* Vol. IX, Diary entry (March 18, 1843), 283.

40 *LD,* Vol. IX, Diary entry (March 19, 1843), 286.

on the *Theory of Religious Beliefs, preached before the University of Oxford,* commonly known as his *Oxford University Sermons.* The volume contained sermons from the period of 1826 to 1843, which dealt with the relationship between faith and reason. As the years advanced, Newman was more precise in his definitions and analysis. For example, he described three improper senses of the word reason: explicit reason, evidential reason, and secular reason. By the latter, he referred to the error of applying secular maxims to religion and disregarding the first principles proper to religion. Newman argued that faith is an assent of the mind that is based on antecedent reasons, and starts with religious principles. He wrote, "Faith is an exercise of presumptive reasoning, or of reason proceeding on antecedent grounds."[41] In another sermon, "Implicit and Explicit Reason," Newman argued against the notion that accuracy in stating doctrines is indispensable for correct reasoning. Specifically he dismissed the idea that to believe a revelation one has to have good evidence.

Newman explained that reason can be implicit, as in mental reasoning, and explicit, as in arguing a point. "The process of reasoning is complete in itself and independent. The analysis is but an account of it; it does not make the conclusion correct; it does not make the inference rational."[42] He indicated that the process of reasoning is mysterious and that it is complete and independent of analysis or argument. Newman continued, "Faith, then, though

---

41 "Love, the Safeguard of Faith against Superstition" in *US,* 231.

42 "Implicit and Explicit Reason" in *US,* 259, available at: http://www. newmanreader.org.

in all cases a reasonable process, is not necessarily founded on investigation, argument, or proof; these processes being but the explicit form which the reasoning takes in the case of particular minds."[43]

Newman asked what safeguards faith from credulity and superstition? And he replied that it was not reason, because faith is not founded on logical reasoning:

> And thus I would answer the question how it may be secured from excess, without the necessity of employing what is popularly called Reason for its protection,—I mean processes of investigation, discrimination, discussion, argument, and inference. It is itself an intellectual act, and it takes its character from the moral state of the agent. It is perfected, not by intellectual cultivation, but by obedience.[44]

Newman would develop the arguments of these sermons in his *Essay in Aid of a Grammar of Assent*, published in 1870. In a third edition to the volume of *Oxford University Sermons*, Newman added the important sermon, "The Theory of Developments in Religious Doctrine," which was preached in February shortly after the volume was published.

In November of 1843, Newman published another series of sermons, titled *Sermons on Subjects of the Day*; these had been preached over a number of years, and had some bearing on particular occasions. As customary, Newman did so after having consulted Keble. The latter included his "Four Sermons" on the notes of the true Church and on

43 *Ibid.*, 262.
44 *Ibid.*, 249-50.

the English Church, which he had preached in 1842. With regard to these sermons Newman wrote to Keble, "The feeling comes on men [sic] 'Light has been given to *me*—*I* have had the suggestion, which others have not, that our Church wants the notes of a true Church."[45] He worried, "If I were to die, I should be in a state which others are not in."[46] Nonetheless, in the sermons Newman had urged patience and staying where one had been placed by God.

One of the sermons in the volume was "The Apostolical Christian," delivered in February of 1843. In this sermon, Newman quoted many texts from Scripture to support the thesis that the first Christians were men and women detached from the world with their minds and hearts in Heaven, which could only be achieved through habitual prayer, as was evidenced in the early Christians. Next he explained how some Christians were called to a stricter life, yet they were often scorned by fellow Christians. Newman concluded,

> But, if the truth must be spoken, what are the humble monk, and the holy nun, and other regulars, as they are called, but Christians after the very pattern given us in Scripture? What have they done but this—perpetuate in the world the Christianity of the Bible? Did our Saviour come on earth suddenly, as He will one day visit it, in whom would He see the features of the Christians whom He and His Apostles left behind them, but in them?[47]

---

45 *LD,* Vol. IX, JHN to John Keble (September 6, 1843), 509-10; 509.
46 *Ibid.*
47 "The Apostolical Christian," *SD*, 290-91.

Newman urged his fellowmen to study what a Bible Christian was, to pray about it, and wished for each one to apply it to his own life, depending on his own particular calling. In reading this sermon it is clear that Newman discerned that he was called to a stricter rule of life, and he had embraced it with his small group of friends at Littlemore. Like those following Christ, he felt mocked at times and his private life scrutinized by the curiosity of others. In the end, no longer supported by his own bishop and censured by most of the bishops, Newman did not feel authorized to teach in the Church of England. The volume of *Sermons on Subjects of the Day* closed with "The Parting of Friends," Newman's sad and personal farewell address to his congregation and friends.

With Newman's resignation from St. Mary's in 1843, the Oxford Movement lost its primary leader. The Movement, which sought the doctrinal, spiritual, and liturgical reform of the Anglican Church, could not count on Newman because he was finally convinced that this Church was no longer part of the Catholic Church; it was a body that had separated itself from the Church. Concerning the Anglican Church, Newman confided in a letter to his friend, H. A. Woodgate, "we are all coming to pieces."[48] He explained that the Anglican Church could barely keep men such as Tom Mozley and Frederick Faber within its fold. Newman ended the letter with a premonition, "The fact is our system is rotten and won't hold together."[49]

---

[48] *LD,* Vol. IX, JHN to H. A. Woodgate (October 2, 1843), 548-49; 549.

[49] *Ibid.*

These candid words written to a longtime friend expressed Newman's sad conclusions.

CHAPTER 31

REACHING CERTITUDE OF CONVERSION TO ROMAN CATHOLICISM

A FTER the major step in September 1843, the remaining months of the year and the following year were difficult ones in which Newman tried to settle his mind about the theological status of the Anglican Church and his obligation to remain in the Anglican Church. He had a growing conviction about the truth of his conclusions, but had some doubt about whether he might be under some error or delusion.

That Advent, Newman and some of his companions at Littlemore made a five-day silent retreat. Each day had three exercises or points for meditation on the traditional subjects of the end of man, the Fall, Sin, Death, and Judgment, and the Incarnation. During the exercises Newman was sleepy and had trouble concentrating due to his severe fast.

Referring to this retreat, Newman wrote, "I tried to give up to Him, if for His greater glory, my fellowship, my Library, the respect of friends, my health, my talent, my reason—but added 'Lord, be merciful.'"[1] He examined his conscience and wrote, "I thought of my three sins, & prayed to be able to get rid of them, indulgence of the appetite, self conceited thoughts, & wanderings in prayer."[2] He

---

1 *LD,* Vol. X, Notes from Littlemore, Advent Retreat, 1843, 64-8; 65.
2 *Ibid.,* 65.

also admitted to impatience, impetuosity, rudeness, and inaccuracy in speech.[3] Newman was trying very hard to discern the path before him.

As 1843 wore on, the contentious matters swirling about Newman and his writings did not calm down, not even after Newman's resignation from St. Mary's. And even the supposedly neutral content of *The Lives of the English Saints* and its tone became a controversial matter. The *Lives,* which he had hoped would divert attention from doctrinal differences, actually made matters worse and brought various questions to the fore.

LIVES OF THE ENGLISH SAINTS

Francis Rivington, publisher for the *Lives*, worried that the volumes would contain teaching offensive to the Anglican Church and a tone favorable to the Church of Rome. Newman sought out the opinion of James R. Hope and W. E. Gladstone concerning Dalgairns's *Life of Stephen Harding*. When Hope criticized the tone, Newman rejoined that it was very difficult to give mere facts without commenting on them, and that it was impossible to avoid three elements in Church History: miracles, monks, and popes. He wrote: "If any sympathetic feeling is expressed on behalf of persons and events of Church History, it is a feeling in favor of miracles, or monkery, or popery, one or all."[4] Newman explained to Hope that he had reluctantly taken the editorship because none of the original promoters

---

3 *Ibid.,* 67.
4 *LD,* Vol. X, JHN to James R. Hope (Nov. 6, 1843), 12-14; 12.

of the project had done so. Since then young men, who expected monetary compensation, had written, and others were writing other *Lives*. However, Newman ended his letter with the most important argument in favor of publishing the *Lives*, "If the plan is abandoned, this significant question will be, nay is already, asked 'What then, cannot the Anglican Church bear the Lives of her Saints?'? [sic]"[5] Newman was correctly inferring that the Church of England had disowned its rich Catholic past. After perusing the *Lives*, Rivington politely informed Newman that, as a Church of England bookseller, he would not be able to publish this work, which he thought would lead people to join the Roman Communion.[6]

After further correspondence with Hope, Newman decided to abandon the post of editor for the *Lives* because of the misgivings of Pusey and Gladstone, and the possibility that the bishops would censure the series. The publication of *St. Stephen Harding*, the first of the *Lives*, was met with both praise and criticism from the readers. Newman thought that Gladstone should realize that the apprehension and resistance against the project only verified and substantiated Newman's conviction that the catholicity of the English Church was untenable.[7]

Newman spent a great deal of time corresponding with publishers regarding expenses, copyright, book cover, book wrapping, prefaces, and so forth. The architect Augustus W. Pugin made the cover design for the first volume,

---

5 *Ibid.,* 14.

6 *LD,* Vol. X, Francis Rivington to JHN (Nov. 10, 1843), 22-23; 22.

7 *LD,* Vol. X, JHN to James Robert Hope (March 14, 1844), 164-65; 164.

St. Stephen Harding, and for at least ten other *Lives*. James Toovey, a London publisher, advertised and distributed the *Lives*, the first one printed by Rivington and the next ones printed by Mozley. In February, *The Family of St. Richard the Saxon*, the second of the *Lives,* was printed. Newman asked that his initials be dropped from the preface of the *Lives* to follow.[8] By June, the fifth volume of the series was published. The series and Newman's influence soon reached across the ocean to the United States, as a letter from a New York clergyman shows.[9] Another correspondent, Sir Francis Palgrave, a medieval historian and Deputy Keeper of the Queen's Records, wrote to Newman, making a suggestion that the *Lives* point out how Medieval Christianity was supported by Sacred Scripture. In his thank-you note, Newman explained his decision to quit the series, remarking that he felt the need to disconnect from the direction of this work because it would be a mark for the bishops to rally against.

For a good part of 1844, Newman continued to be significantly involved in the publication of the *Lives*. In the lives of the Medieval English saints, Newman saw continuity and development with regard to doctrine and practice. In his correspondence with friends, he began to explain this development, and in the process, he began to trace the development of his own religious views, a very important step forward.

---

8 *LD,* Vol. X, JHN to James Toovey (June 4, 1844), 256-57; 256.

9 *LD,* Vol. X, JHN to John Henry Newman from J. W. Williams (November 4, 1844), 385-86; 386.

DEVELOPMENT OF NEWMAN'S
RELIGIOUS BELIEFS

In December of 1843, Mrs. William Froude wrote to Newman, asking him about his beliefs concerning the Roman Catholic Church. For years she had read Newman's writings and had been convinced by them that when the Anglican Church seceded from Rome, it had not lost its Apostolic Succession. Newman acknowledged that some of his opinions had changed since his *Lectures on the Prophetical Office of the Church, Viewed Relatively to Romanism and Popular Protestantism*, but that the central ideas of that work, such as the primary role of Scripture, had remained in place.[10] The purpose of his book, he explained to Mrs. Froude, had been to try to defend the system under which he had been brought up, even though a great part of the book was Anti-Protestant.[11] He wrote to her:

> Time alone can turn a view into a conviction—It is most unsatisfactory to be acting on a syllogism, or a solitary, naked, external, logical process. But surely it is possible in process of time to have a proposition so wrought into the mind, both ethically and by numberless fine conspiring and ever-recurring considerations as to become part of our mind, to be inseparable from us, and to command our obedience. And then the greater the sacrifice, the more cogent the testimony shall we have to its authority, for to overcome impediments is a token of power.[12]

With these words, Newman was describing his change in

---

10 *LD,* Vol. X, JHN to Mrs. William Froude (Dec. 9, 1843), 51-54; 52.
11 *Ibid.,* 51-52.
12 *Ibid.,* 53

religious views as the convergence of many simultaneous considerations acting on his mind.

Although he was corresponding on these matters with Mrs. Froude, his correspondence with Keble and Pusey decreased for some months. Finally, in January, Keble broke the silence and wrote to Newman, pointing out reasons for Newman to remain in the Anglican Church.[13] One of the arguments Keble used was that many people, who looked to Newman as a guide, would be confused and perplexed were he to leave them. Another argument was that only an unequivocal act of heresy should lead Keble or Pusey to leave the Anglican Church.

Newman replied to his friend with certain embarrassment for his silence, thanking him and opening his state of mind to him. He confided in Keble, "I am in no distress of mind at present—that is, whatever is truth, and whatever is not, I do not feel called to do any thing but to go on where I am, and this must be peace and quietness—and whatever is before us, in this one may rejoice, and not take thought for tomorrow."[14] He continued explaining that he had a growing conviction about the mistaken situation of the English Church, and that his reading in Church History led him toward Rome.

He felt a sense of duty remaining where he was, yet he realized that at some point, those under the Mosaic Law had been led from their beliefs to the Gospel truths. He admitted that there comes a time when convictions overrule the

---

13 *LD*, Vol. X, John Keble to JHN (Jan. 22, 1844), 100-101; 100.
14 *LD*, Vol. X, JHN to John Keble (Jan. 23, 1844), 101-103; 101.

duty to remain in one's place, and although many people were unsettled, this "Unsettling may be a blessing . . ."[15] In his own defense, Newman commented on St. Paul, who must have unsettled many good and conscientious Jews. But even so, Newman confided: he did not wish to trust his own judgment and move on his own. He reasoned, "[I]f I am right, Pusey, Manning etc may be brought forward; but if Pusey, Manning etc are right, I may be brought back—that nothing, if it be possible separate us."[16] Still, Newman conveyed his fear of dying in the English Church. He commented that if he were faced with that prospect of imminent death, he would probably convert to Roman Catholicism.

Keble and Pusey resumed their correspondence with Newman. Their letters were a mix of affection and pain due to Newman's serious doubts and some hope that he would not leave the Anglican Church. Newman felt that these friends could no longer understand him. At the same time he continued correspondence with the Froudes concerning the claim that he was unsettling people. He explained that he was seeking real objective truth, and that when someone was brought up in "a system *short* of truth," change was necessary to read the truth.[17] In one letter, he outlined for his friends the stages of his change of opinion toward Rome. In 1839, Newman was struck by the role Pope Leo had played in fighting the Monophysite heresy at the fifth-century Council of Chalcedon. Between the Catholic and the extreme Monophysite party there was a large middle

---

15 *Ibid.,* 103.

16 *Ibid.*

17 *LD,* Vol. X, JHN to Mrs. William Froude (April 4, 1844), 189-92; 189.

party, or *Via Media,* supported by the emperor. Newman found a parallel with the Reformation, where the Anglican Church was on the anti-Catholic side.[18]

Upon coming to this realization, Newman found a key to interpreting other important passages of history.[19] In particular, he understood more clearly the role played by Pope Julius in the fourth century in defense of St. Athanasius's resistance to the Arians, who denied Christ's Divinity. Pope Julius appealed, as Pope Leo did later, to his own Episcopal authority, claiming to fill the See of St. Peter. Whereas the Arian heretics appealed to Scripture grounded on a liberal interpretation, St. Athanasius appealed to an ecclesial interpretation of Scripture. The Arians also objected to novel philosophical terms such as "consubstantial," adopted for the Creed by the Council of Nicaea. The emperor and other civil authorities supported the heretics. In the mode of Scripture interpretation, and the civil government's usurpation of doctrinal authority, Newman saw a parallel with the doctrinal and ecclesial abuses of the Anglican Church. In yet another letter, Newman told the Froudes about a third event in Christian history, the Donatist controversy, which had opened his eyes to the English Schism.[20] As with the Monophysite and Arian heresies, Newman saw in the Donatist heresy a close parallel with Anglican heresy and schism.

These historical parallels, recounted to the Froudes, had given Newman doubts about the Anglican Church, but he

---

18 *LD,* Vol. X, JHN to Mrs. William Froude (April 5, 1844), 195-98; 196-97.

19 *Ibid.,* 197-98.

20 *LD,* Vol. X, JHN to Mrs. William Froude (April 9, 1844), 200-204; 200-201.

held that it was right to resist doubts and to put aside objections to the religious system of which one was a part. He concluded that if God wished, He could give light to a person's mind: "If it is His will to lead us from them, if the doubt comes from Him, He will repeat the suggestion . . . He will make our way clear to us. Fancies, excitements, feelings go and never return—truth comes again and is importunate."[21]

Throughout May and June, Newman continued his correspondence with the Froudes. He discussed the belief, professed in the Creed, that the Catholic Church is one. Next he asked the logical question: How can the Church be one, if Roman Catholics in England are considered heretics and schismatics? Newman agreed with a lawyer who had written to him, "how preposterous that a man across the Channel believes in Purgatory, Mass, the Pope's supremacy etc must all of a sudden, if he comes to England, change his creed and worship, and become a member of a local community which denies all that he has hitherto received?"[22] Then he proceeded to write about the Pope and his power over all the Church. He explained how in early Church Tradition there was a sense that each individual bishop presides over the entire Church, while at the same time the bishops preside together over the whole Church. Individual bishops have immediate jurisdiction for a diocese. "Their power is restrained. The Pope instead is not restrained"; he exercises his power over the entire Church. Newman

---

21 *Ibid.*, 201.

22 *LD,* Vol. X, JHN to Mrs. William Froude (May 19, 1844), 237-44); 239.

presented testimonies in support of this belief from the first three centuries of Christianity: from St. Clement of Rome, St. Ignatius of Antioch, St. Irenaeus, Tertullian, Pope Victor, Pope Stephen, and Pope Dionysius, which proved that in these centuries the authority of the popes was decisive on debated matters of doctrine and discipline.[23]

In June, Newman again wrote to the Froudes and began to espouse his principle of development of doctrine. He referred to the development of papal power over the first few Christian centuries as an example of doctrinal development. As an Anglican, Newman believed that there had been developments of Scripture with regard to the doctrine of the Holy Trinity and the Incarnation, but now he believed that development was not limited to the early centuries.[24] He also had come to realize, as he affirmed in his last *University Sermon* dedicated to this subject, that developments are not limited to explanations of the sense of the Creed, but to other doctrines arising from the Creed.[25] In another letter in July, Newman elaborated further on his theory of development, which made possible his reconciliation with modern aspects of Roman Catholicism.[26] He argued that the Church had the promise of divine assistance to develop special doctrines.

After this flurry of letter writing, in 1844, Newman apologized to Mrs. Froude and John Keble for dwelling so much on his thoughts in the letters. All the while, though, Newman worried about his friends and their suffering. He

---

23 *Ibid.,* 242-43.

24 *Ibid.,* 264-65.

25 *Ibid.,* 266.

26 *LD,* Vol. X, JHN to Mrs. William Froude (July 14, 1844), 297-98.

prayed for them, wrote to them, and went to visit them in time of grave illness. This year he was especially close to the suffering of the Pusey and the Bowden families.

DEATH OF FRIENDS

Newman's loyalty to friends was especially evident in his care for them during their illnesses or in the death of their loved ones. For example, in early April 1844, Pusey informed Newman of the imminent death of his daughter Lucy. Lucy sent Newman a message, "Give him my respectful love, and thank him for his kindness to me."[27] Like her deceased mother, Lucy had treasured Newman's affection and sermons. Newman comforted Pusey, writing him that his daughter Lucy had been prepared by her father to be an heir of Heaven—Pusey was presenting her to God as a "holy blameless sacrifice." He continued, "Dear Lucy has been made His in Baptism, she had been made His in suffering, and now she asks to be made His by love."[28] On April 22, 1844, after a long illness of the lungs, young Lucy died. Newman wrote of her, "She was a saint."[29] He supported Pusey throughout, even helping him with the epitaph and funeral arrangements.

Lucy was not the only one who met death in 1844; for, unfortunately, John W. Bowden's consumption was

---

27 *LD,* Vol. X, Edward Bouverie Pusey to JHN (April 9, 1844), 206.

28 *LD,* Vol. X, JHN to E. B. Pusey (April 10, 1844), 206-07.

29 *LD,* Vol. X, JHN to Matthew Holbeche Bloxam (April 23, 1844), 217-18; 218.

worsening. In June, a fever from a lung abscess prompted a visit from Newman, who went to London to see him. Newman was edified by the peacefulness of Bowden and his wife, both fully aware of Bowden's critical condition. Newman felt that the separation brought by death was a way by which God would prepare him for an even more painful separation: he felt cut off from Oxford. "I do fancy I am getting changed. I go into Oxford, and find myself out of place. Every thing seems to say to me, this is not your home."[30] Losing Bowden, his first association with Oxford, he felt severed from all that was dear in Oxford.

Indeed, September 11, 1844, was the last time that Newman saw his dear friend. On that day Newman gave him Holy Communion, and returned to Oxford. On the fourteenth, Newman wrote a letter to Keble telling him about Bowden's piety and resignation and how verses from Keble's *Christian Year* had been on Bowden's lips during the last few days of life. Newman recalled that, on his first day at Oxford, Bowden had met him, and since that day 27 years earlier, they had been intimate friends. John William Bowden died at his home in London on September 15. His widow, Elizabeth Bowden, asked Newman to read a service for them, and if possible, give them the Holy Eucharist.[31] Newman went straightaway to London and remained with Bowden's family until the funeral on the twenty-third.

The death of Bowden, deeply felt by Newman, marked a significant moment in Newman's spiritual journey. Just as Newman no longer felt at home at Oriel College or Oxford,

---

30 *LD,* Vol. X, JHN to Mrs. John Mozley (August 13), 312-13; 312.
31 *LD,* Vol. X, Elizabeth Bowden to JHN (September 15, 1844), 340.

Bowden's death was a severing of Newman's ties with his Anglican past. Newman had not had the strength to sadden Bowden with his thoughts of becoming Roman Catholic. Writing to Keble, Newman confessed, "And now for several years past, loving him with all my heart, I have shrunk from him feeling that I had opinions that I dared not tell him, and that I must be constrained or almost hypocritical if I was with him."[32] But Bowden's death did not end Newman's ties with Bowden's family, which continued throughout his life.

Others were blessed by Newman's attentions that year. During the summer of 1843, his friend Oakeley, who was editing the series of the *Lives*, fell gravely ill. Newman prayed for his recovery and visited him in London. By September, Oakeley had improved. At the end of the year, he visited Robert Williams, a lawyer friend, who also lived in London and was scheduled to have surgery. Newman traveled to London expressly to keep him company the day of surgery and returned to Oxford after spending time with his friend. Newman's attention to the sick sometimes included prolonged care. Beginning in January 1844, Newman brought Holy Communion to Miss Elizabeth Lenthall, an Oxford resident, until her death in July 1845.

Although Newman shared the pain brought about by the death of his friends and their loved ones, his sorrow in 1844 was just as great for their spiritual suffering and confusion over his position in the Anglican Church.

---

32 *LD,* Vol. X, JHN to John Keble (September 14, 1844), 335-37; 337.

PREPARING FRIENDS FOR HIS
FUTURE CONVERSION

Friends and acquaintances prayed for Newman, and some wrote to tell him that they were doing so. They were aware in different measure of his movement closer to the Roman Catholic Church, and most sincerely wished that he would not take the step of renouncing the Anglican Church. Pusey's response to Newman's position shows that, by and large, Newman's friends simply wished the best for him. Pusey, replying to a birthday letter from Newman, confessed that news of Newman's divided heart had shattered him. Pusey wrote that he felt left on shore with the tide sweeping by, but he soon regained his peace, for Pusey had a strong faith in the Anglican Church's teaching, although he did not deny that God gave others more light, expecting them to act upon it.[33]

Even with these brave words, in reality Pusey could not reconcile himself with the loss of Newman to the Anglican Church. He wrote: "In a word, write or speak or act as I may, I do not believe that it ever can be; it goes against my whole nature to believe it. I cannot think that we should be so utterly deserted as that it should be permitted."[34] Newman told his friend not to shut his eyes to the painful reality.[35] Newman had already for five years had the conviction that the Anglican Church was not part of the Catholic

---

33 *LD,* Vol. X, Edward Bouverie Pusey to JHN (August 21, 1844), 316.

34 *LD,* Vol. X, E. B. Pusey to JHN, footnote 324, quoted from *Pusey,* II, by Liddon, 406.

35 *LD,* Vol. X, JHN to E. B. Pusey (August 28), 324-25.

Church. Newman desired to attenuate the shock and unsettlement of his friends and those who trusted in him. With this end in mind, Newman asked Henry Wilberforce and Mrs. Froude to tell others of his doubts dating back to 1839, so that all would be prepared. He did not want his friends to know, however, how close he was to his final decision.[36] He wanted his friends to have time to prepare for a step that he might take in the future.

It was not only his friends' reactions that worried Newman—especially those who for a long time had looked up to him to prepare for his move, but also his family's reactions. So, even though in May he had told Jemima that he was not about to make any move, he admitted to her that over the years his feelings toward Rome had grown stronger.[37] Then in June, he confided in her not to be surprised if he gave up his Fellowship.[38] He added that he felt cheerful while trying to serve God without worldly ambitions. Yet it is obvious that he felt the pain of his friends, as witnessed by his correspondence at the time. Newman confided to Edward Badeley that over the previous years he had at times felt as if he were asleep and dreaming, and wondered whether his feelings were the result of excitement or some delusion. To Badeley, he compared the Anglican Church to a dying or dead system. He said that after living in the Anglican Church, "We cannot, we will not, believe what the real state of the case is. We cannot be persuaded to open our eyes. Every ominous fact admits of an explanation,

---

36 *LD,* Vol. X, JHN to Henry Wilberforce (June 8, 1844), 263; JHN to Mrs. William Froude (May 28, 1844), 251.

37 *LD,* Vol. X, JHN to Mrs. John Mozley (May 21, 1844), 247.

38 *LD,* Vol. X, JHN to Mrs. John Mozley (June 3, 1844), 255-56; 255.

and in it we take refuge. Consider the shock with which a child, parent, or wife hears of the inevitable blow. It is like a dream."[39]

Newman expressed unbelief about his actions, but he was not in a daze; he was considering his next step, which he confided to close friends like Elizabeth Bowden. In October 1844, he told her about his plans to retire from Oxford.[40] This caused her sorrow because of her love for the University. Newman regretted that he had caused her pain.[41] She, however, replied that she had been defending him in conversations and preferred to know his thoughts. She told him that her pain was for having caused him pain.[42] Newman considered voluntarily resigning his Fellowship at Oriel, but thought that Provost Hawkins might instead oblige him to resign.[43] With these confidences Newman revealed to friends his sentiments and future plans.

At the end of the year, the situation for Newman became more distressing, especially after Charles P. Golightly publicized a false letter from Newman to Isaac Williams, stating that Newman was joining the Roman Catholic Church.[44] The letter appeared on November 4 in the London

39 *LD,* Vol. X, JHN to Edward Badeley (September 9, 1844), 331-32; 332.

40 *LD,* Vol. X, JHN to Elizabeth Bowden (October 15, 1844), 365-67; 366-67.

41 *LD,* Vol. X, JHN to Elizabeth Bowden (October 21, 1844), 370-71.

42 *LD,* Vol. X, Elizabeth Bowden to JHN (October 23, 1844), 372.

43 *LD,* Vol. X, JHN to Henry Edward Manning (November 24, 1844), 433.

44 *LD,* Vol. X, Charles Portales Golightly to William Simcox Bricknell (November 1, 1844), 384.

Standard, Herald, and *Morning Chronicle.* It was no surprise that the following day *The Churchman's Newspaper* ridiculed Newman, Ward, Charles Penny, and others
who had embraced the "heresy and schism" of the "Popish
sect." Williams wrote to the Editor of *The Times* asserting
that the claim was false.[45] Newman also wrote to Keble
and others disclaiming the truth of the rumor. To Maria
Giberne he wrote, "Two things, however, seem plain:
first that everyone is prepared for such an event, next that
every one expects it of me. Few indeed who do not think
it suitable, fewer still who do not think it likely."[46] A few
days after the newspaper debacle, Newman asked the
publisher of *The Lives of the English Saints* to place an
announcement in the paper, *The English Churchman*, stating that Newman's role as editor had ended with the second
volume.[47]

Despite the falsehood of this and other rumors, and
Newman's strong reaction, the desired effect was obtained:
people began to prepare for the inevitable. Golightly predicted that thirty Masters of Arts of the University and
a total of one hundred members of the Anglican Church
would become Roman Catholics by the end of the year.[48]
On the other hand, others who admired Newman wrote

---

45 *LD,* Vol. X, Isaac Williams to the Editor of the Times (November 7,
1844), 390.

46 *LD,* Vol. X, JHN to Miss Maria Rosina Giberne (November 7, 1844),
390.

47 *LD,* Vol. X, JHN to James Toovey (November 9, 1844), 395-96; 395.

48 *LD,* Vol. X, Charles Portales Golightly to William Simcox Bricknell
(November 1, 1844), 384.

him respectful letters asking him to pause from the step he
wished to take.[49] A clergyman pleaded, "Ah! Newman do
stop with us—What shall we do without you!"[50]

Another kind letter came from his friend, Edward
Coleridge, a clergyman and Master at Eton College, who
made an earnest appeal for him not to leave the Church of
England unless he was absolutely obliged by conscience.[51]
Coleridge argued that Newman's secession would have an
effect on numerous people who relied implicitly on Newman's steps and would actually follow him acting against
their own consciences. Newman replied, "The pain that I
feel at the distress I am causing others, at the great unsettlement of mind I am causing, and the ties I am rending, is
keener than I can say."[52] Then Newman made a remarkable
statement: that the only motive upon which he acted was a
sense of duty, "imperative to my salvation."[53] Newman's
intellectual reasoning had become a moral conviction. He
felt obliged in conscience to act in obedience to a higher
law for the sake of his salvation.

Newman explained to his friend Manning that he had
no plans for moving for a long time, but that the unexpected rumor served a good purpose: to prepare people.

---

49 *LD,* Vol. X, William Smith Dear to JHN (November 4, 1844), 385;
William Robert Browell to JHN (November 11, 1844), 397-98; William
Elliott to JHN (November 7, 1844), 392.

50 *LD,* Vol. X, William Robert Browell to JHN (November 11, 1844),
397-98; 398.

51 *LD,* Vol. X, footnote, 399.

52 *LD,* Vol. X, JHN to Edward Coleridge (November 12, 1844), 398-
99; 398.

53 *Ibid.,* 399.

He reiterated his reasoning: "And, as far as I know myself, my one paramount reason for contemplating a change is my deep unvarying conviction that our Church is in schism and that my salvation depends on my joining the Church of Rome."[54] His motivation was undiluted by other reasons to which skeptics might point, for he did not have many Catholic friends or a desire for change. He had no enthusiasm to bolster him, nor heroic feelings for which to make the sacrifice, yet his conviction remained firm.[55] Manning showed the remarkable letter to Gladstone, who lamented that it would be the greatest crisis that the Church had known since the Reformation. Gladstone, future Prime Minister of Great Britain, asserted that Newman's loss would be the apostasy of one of the most intelligent men of his age who had headed the most important movement in the Church for at least two centuries.[56]

Not only did Newman have no external motives drawing him toward Catholicism, but he opined to both Keble and Coleridge that he had spent very little time with any Catholics.[57] So it was not for tangible benefits that he sought Roman Catholicism; his primary concern was indeed his own salvation. He told Keble: "I don't think I *could* die in our communion—Then the question comes upon me, is not death the test? shall one bear to live, where die one

---

54 *LD,* Vol. X, JHN to Henry Edward Manning (November 16, 1844), 412-13; 412.

55 *Ibid.*

56 R. Shannon, *Gladstone, 1809-1865,* Vol. 1, London 1982, 143-44.

57 *LD,* Vol. X, JHN to John Keble (November 21, 1844), 424-27; 426; JHN to Edward Coleridge (November 16, 1844), 416-17; 416.

cannot?"[58] In the same letter Newman challenged his friend, "What I have asked myself is 'Are you not perhaps *ashamed* to hold a system which is so inconsistent, so untenable?' "

Friends, not knowing exactly how to respond, tried to reassure Newman of how much he had done for Oriel, Oxford, and the Church, and how much they personally owed to him. One of these was John Frederick Christie, a former pupil,[59] and another was William E. Gladstone. Weighing in on all this drama, Jemima told her brother that the report of his conversion had caused both her and their Aunt Elizabeth pain, but she (Jemima) had felt unable to write Newman. She was sorry that her silence had caused Newman pain. Like their aunt, she prayed for Newman to do whatever was right.[60] Newman reminded Jemima of his aversion to change.[61] At his age he did not wish to change, but he was ready to accept it if it was God's will for him. In the meantime, he tried to convince himself that he was not under the power of any delusion; he was buying time to see if this was the case.

At the same time, Newman was hurt by the accusation that he was dishonest. Some people, including journalists, were calling him a liar. Coleridge desired a strong defense,

---

58 *LD*, Vol. X, JHN to John Keble (November 21, 1844), 427.

59 *LD*, Vol. X, John Frederic Christie to JHN (November 17, 1844), 419-20; JHN to William Ewart Gladstone (November 18, 1844), 420-421.

60 *LD*, Vol. X, Mrs. John Mozley to JHN (November 20, 1844), 424.

61 *LD*, Vol. X, JHN to Mrs. John Mozley (November 24, 1844), 433-35; 435.

perhaps some type of public declaration of esteem for Newman. Characteristically, Newman thought it would be better to accept the cross. He confided in Keble that any such
declaration would make him more proud, and would, in the
end, only increase the unsettlement of those who sympathized with him.[62]

In the midst of a year filled with anxieties like this one
and various significant losses, Newman continued to offer
spiritual advice to various persons. One of these was Mary
Holmes.

SPIRITUAL ADVICE TO MARY HOLMES

Mary Holmes, who had continued her frequent correspondence with Newman, found herself being urged to
remain in the Anglican Church by Newman. Miss Holmes
was hurt by the dry tone of some of his letters, especially
since she had him on a pedestal. Newman warned that she
was treating him as a sort of idol.[63] To this Miss Holmes
replied: "You are very patient, dear Mr. Newman, and I
am very unreasonable. It is absurd for me to expect all
I did from you."[64] She informed him that in six months,
on October 15, the eve of her own birthday and also the
feast of St. Teresa of Avila, she would be received into
the Roman Catholic Church. She had already spoken
with Bishop Wiseman, who urged immediate action, but

---

62 *LD*, Vol. X, JHN to John Keble (November 21, 1844), 424-27.

63 *LD*, Vol. X, JHN to Miss Mary Holmes (March 14, 1844), 165-66;
165.

64 *LD*, Vol. X, Miss Mary Holmes to JHN (March 16, 1844), 167.

following Newman's advice, she decided to wait for six months. Holmes made the decision to be received into the Roman Catholic Church during Benediction at Vespers in a Catholic Church. She wrote Newman, "I had laboured in vain to 'believe,' to feel Christ's Presence, in the Protestant sacrament; but at Benediction when the Host was lifted up, all came spontaneously—tears burst forth, tears of joy at feeling my Saviour really near me. It was so unexpected; I had no idea I should feel conscious of the Real Presence in that way."[65]

Newman then had to tell her that he would no longer be able to provide her spiritual direction since she was not on a six-month trial; she had already determined to become Roman Catholic. Newman also apologized for any earlier harshness or inconsiderate behavior toward her. He made a surprising display of affection, writing, "In losing you, I lose what I can seldom expect to meet with—an affectionate heart."[66]

Mary Holmes, who revered Newman and was attached to him, did not have a romantic infatuation, but a real desire for Christ and the truth. Despite Holmes's sentimentality, she posed some real challenges to Newman's idea of invocation of saints and the role of feelings in spiritual life. She claimed that Newman urged people to stay in the Anglican Church based on feelings, even though convictions are a safer guide to truth. She boldly wrote, "There is no warrant in Scripture or the Fathers for staying one hour separated

---

65 *LD,* Vol. X, Miss Mary Holmes to JHN (April 20, 1844), 216.
66 *LD,* Vol. X, JHN to Miss Mary Holmes (April 22, 1844), 217.

from the Church, when once you have a conviction that the sect you have been brought up in is not the Church."[67] She went on, "I am afraid that you are in a state of doubt and perplexity yourself. You seem unwilling to forbid my invoking the Saints, and yet I feel you cannot sanction it."[68] Newman's response was to accuse her of being unsettled—that her feelings waxed and waned since she lacked firm convictions. For these reasons, he had dissuaded her from joining the Church of Rome. Accordingly, Newman advised Holmes to refrain from invoking the saints because it would be mixing two systems.[69] Newman explained to her that he thought it was correct to ask God's allowance for the Blessed Virgin Mary to pray for one's intentions, but he believed it wrong to pray directly to the Blessed Virgin Mary.

It was not only Miss Holmes who received this advice. So too did Frederick William Faber (often called simply William Faber), who was under Newman's spiritual direction for nearly a year. He also pleaded with Newman for permission to invoke Mary directly.[70] Faber greatly desired this, but Newman replied to Faber as he had to Holmes: one should not mix religions.[71] If one did so, one would be in danger of making private judgments in matters of religion,

---

67 *LD,* Vol. X, Miss Mary Holmes to JHN (June 13, 1844), 272-73; 273.

68 *Ibid.,* 273.

69 *LD,* Vol. X, JHN to Miss Mary Holmes (June 10, 1844), 267.

70 *LD,* Vol. X, Frederick William Faber to JHN (November 28, 1844), 438-39.

71 *LD,* Vol. X, JHN to Frederick William Faber (December 1, 1844), 442-44; 443.

which could lead to the sins of presumption and disobedience, particularly grievous for a clergyman. Faber appreciated Newman's advice. He resolved to halt his inquiry into another system of religion until God cleared the way.[72] In the meantime he promised he would strive to improve in virtue, directing his whole life to God. However, Faber confided to Newman a fear he had, which he didn't realize Newman shared: "the fear of being '*damned*', as out of the Church."[73]

Meanwhile, Holmes was trying to follow Newman's advice: to receive the Protestant sacrament, not to invoke the Saints, and to leave the Catholic household in which she lived. She had scruples, however, about receiving Holy Communion in the Anglican Church, and she subsequently became rather hysterical in her letters, for she believed Newman was displeased with her, and she feared his abandonment.[74] She begged him to take her back under his guidance until October and promised to do everything he said with regard to devotions, books, friends, and residence.[75]

Newman was extremely patient with Holmes, who continued to write to him about her daily state of emotions. In one of his replies Newman explained his notion of spiritual direction: "Real direction implies the relation of Confessor and penitent. It is grave and sacred—it is oral not in

---

72 *LD,* Vol. X, Frederick William Faber to JHN (December 12, 1844), 454-55.

73 *Ibid.,* 454.

74 *LD,* Vol. X, Miss Mary Holmes to JHN (June 20, 1844), 279-80.

75 *LD,* Vol. X, Miss Mary Holmes to JHN (June 22, 1844), 281-82; 282.

writing—it is ratified by the seal of absolution. How different what you call by the name!"[76] Newman, who apparently
had a very demanding idea of spiritual direction, insisted
that Holmes had never been under his obedience. He had
only given her advice, and acquiesced to give her advice
until October.[77]

Miss Holmes, following Newman's advice, eventually
moved to the countryside, away from her Roman Catholic
employers, but it was only a few months later that she was
received into the Roman Catholic Church. She wrote Newman about her experience in receiving the Sacraments, and
apologized to him for the worries she had caused him. In
her characteristically bold manner she asked Newman if he
was obedient to the one appointed by Christ as the Head
of the Church, and continued: "Who is Dr. Pusey, that you
should bow down to him? Is he not a fallible man? Could
St. Thomas of Canterbury, St. Anselm and Venerable Bede
rise from their graves, can you doubt an instant which side
they would take? Would they submit to Dr. Wiseman or to
the Bishop (so-called) of Oxford?"[78]

Newman carried out all this correspondence and guidance
from Littlemore, where he stayed all that year except for
the trips he made to visit Bowden. Occasionally he walked
into Oxford to call on Pusey or to meet with someone else,
but the rest of the time he worked at Littlemore, where,

---

76 *LD,* Vol. X, JHN to Miss Mary Holmes (June 23, 1844), 283-84;
283.

77 *LD,* Vol. X, JHN to Miss Mary Holmes (June 25, 1844), 286-87;
287.

78 *LD,* Vol. X, Miss Mary Holmes to JHN (November 30, 1844), 441-
42; 442.

besides his daily time for prayer, study, and answering correspondence, he attended to visitors.

LIFE AT LITTLEMORE

The growing library afforded Newman with the means to further his study without having to leave Littlemore. His library at Littlemore grew with volumes that friends or acquaintances sent him. Fr. Charles W. Russell sent Newman some Italian devotional books and another volume of St. Alphonsus Liguori's sermons. Fr. Gentili sent Newman a copy of J. Marchetti's *Critique de l'Histoire Ecclésiastique de Claude Fleury*. Newman spent the large sum of money, which Bowden had bequeathed to him, to buy many books. Newman consulted his friend Edward Badeley about buying various collections of history books and classics, and about booksellers.

As for performing the duties of a clergyman, he only gave assistance to friends who were ill or to their families, but no longer acted publicly in the role of clergyman. An exception to this was June 2, when Newman assisted Eden with Holy Communion at St. Mary's. However, when Eden, the new Vicar of St. Mary's, invited Newman to preach at the commemoration at Littlemore on September 25, 1843, Newman declined the invitation. Eden repeated the invitation in 1844. Newman, annoyed at Eden's patronizing attitude, thanked him for the invitation, but declined again, offering this explanation: "My preaching days in our Church are over."[79]

---

79 *LD,* Vol. X, JHN to Charles Page Eden (September 14, 1844), 333.

Since at Littlemore there were "no sacramental services," religious vows or ecclesiastical authority, Newman
strongly encouraged those who lived at Littlemore to seek
sacramental Confession.[80] Occasionally someone not living at Littlemore sought Newman for confession. One of
these was Thomas William Allies, who in April became
convinced that post-baptismal sin required sacramental
Confession, and went to see Newman for that purpose.
Allies, chaplain of the Bishop of London from 1840 to
1842, published a collection of sermons, which he dedicated to Newman with the words: "by one thankful for
his teaching and still more thankful for his example . .
."[81] Sacramental Confession had become a regular part of
Newman's spiritual life. Friends like Allies who admired
Newman had also discovered the spiritual benefits of
this sacrament.

During his time at Littlemore, Newman's health failed,
partly due to his voluntary privations from food and rest
and partly due to his inner conflict. He complained to Dr.
Babington, his doctor, that he had unsteadiness in his hands
and frequent drowsiness. Dr. Babington advised him to eat
better and to obtain sufficient rest. He warned Newman
that otherwise he would fall into the state of a helpless and
almost invalid person.[82] Newman complained to some of
"a literal pain in and about my heart,"[83] which most likely

---

80 *LD,* Vol. X, JHN to William Dodsworth (March 18, 1844), 170-71.

81 *Sermons on the Epistle to the Romans and others,* Thomas W. Allies,
1844, cited in *LD,* Vol. X, footnote, 73.

82 *LD.* Vol. X, George Gisborne Babington to JHN (September 26,
1844), 351.

83 *LD,* Vol. X, JHN to Mrs. John Mozley (November 24, 1844), 433-
35; 434.

was gastritis and esophageal reflux due to his emotional stress. Years later, Newman told his friend Robert I. Wilberforce that before becoming a Catholic, the separation from friends had weighed so heavily on him that it significantly deteriorated his health.[84] Tired, run down, and emotionally drained in December, Newman fell sick from influenza. Events at Oxford contributed to Newman's malaise, for the Vice-Chancellor and the Heads of Houses had growing animosity to anything that was not according to the Low Church and Evangelical views of the Anglican Church.

WILLIAM G. WARD'S "IDEAL OF A CHRISTIAN CHURCH"

In June, William G. Ward, a Fellow from Balliol College and a Tractarian, published a book that created a stir equal to that of *Tract 90*. In his work, *Ideal of a Christian Church,* Ward argued that a man could hold all that the Church of Rome teaches and remain under the *Articles* and formularies of the Anglican Church. Newman, who had nothing to do with its publication, did not agree with Ward's theory.[85] Newman believed that the *Articles* were not compatible with the whole circle of Roman doctrine.[86] In October, the Heads of House met to discuss what course of action to take

---

84 *LD,* Vol. XVI, JHN to Robert Isaac Wilberforce (September 1, 1854), 242.

85 *LD,* Vol. X, JHN to John Keble (December 16, 1844), 462-63; 462.

86 *LD,* Vol. X, JHN to John Keble (December 29, 1844), 474-76; 475.

against Ward and his book. Earlier in October, Ward had antagonized Benjamin P. Symons, the future Vice-Chancellor of Oxford. Ward had organized a party to oppose the nomination of Symons as the new Vice-Chancellor of Oxford, whose turn it was by order of rotation of colleges. Wynter, the outgoing Vice-Chancellor, endorsed Symons, one of the six doctors who had censured Pusey. Newman asked various persons beforehand to consider refraining from a fight since Symons's victory was almost assured. Sure enough, on October 8, Convocation met and Symons obtained a majority of 700 votes.

On the following day, an editorial in *The Times* asserted that the only possible reason for the unprecedented break in university custom was self-defense against academic censures and deprivations. It urged the new Vice-Chancellor to abstain from making his own religious views the standard for his academic duty and warned against the power of changing majorities.[87]

The editorial agreed with Newman, who told Elizabeth Bowden that he did not like opposing the Heads of Houses. He would only do so for questions of faith, and this made the last agitation (against Hampden) a painful one for him. Foreseeing his departure from Oxford, Newman felt this was the last time that he would vote in Convocation.[88]

Following Symons's victory, Dr. Jenkyns, Master of Balliol College, banned Ward from acting as chaplain and reading morning and evening prayers in the College chapel.

---

87 *LD,* Vol. X, Editorial in *The Times* (October 9, 1844), 360-61.

88 *LD,* Vol. X, JHN to Elizabeth Bowden (October 15, 1844), 365-67; 366.

On October 28, when Ward attempted to read the Epistle at
the Communion Service, Jenkyns went to the lectern at the
right side of the altar and read the Epistle out loud, making
deliberate emphasis and pauses on condemning words that
he applied to Ward.[89] The next insult to Ward occurred in
early 1845, when the Heads decided to put three propositions to vote in Convocation. The first two were to condemn Ward's book and to deprive him of his B.A. and
M.A. degrees. The third proposition was to establish a test
for all those who in the future were suspected of unsound
opinions. Whoever was tested must declare that he subscribed to the *Thirty-Nine Articles* in the sense in which
they were originally drawn up, and interpreted by the university at the present time. Newman quickly advised Pusey
to draw up a declaration against the third proposition, and
urged that he get one or two prominent men to refuse the
Test.[90] Pusey published a letter on the following day in *The
English Churchman* declaring that he could not take such
a test. He argued that such a test would undo the intention
with which the *Articles* were framed: to admit two parties
within the Anglican Church, the High and Low Church,
rather than exclude either with a stringent interpretation.[91]

Newman foresaw the injustice of such a test. The *Articles,*
he explained, must be accepted in a literal and grammatical
sense, which was open to various interpretations. In *Tract*

---

89 *LD,* Vol. X, quote from *William George Ward and the Oxford Movement* by Wilfrid Ward, 1889, 325.

90 *LD,* Vol. X, JHN to Edward Bouverie Pusey (December 16, 1844),
463-64; 463.

91 *LD,* Vol. X, E. B. Pusey to the Editor of *The English Churchman*
(December 17, 1844), 464-66; 465.

90, Newman argued that the *Articles* could be interpreted in a Catholic sense. Newman explained that the Anglican Church relied on two standards: the *Articles* and the *Book of Common Prayer* which served as the interpretative key for the *Articles.* The *Book of Common Prayer* and the *Homilies,* which formed part of it, contained much of the Anglican Church's Catholic liturgy and Tradition. Without these texts, the *Articles,* which were partly Lutheran and Calvinistic in origin, would usurp the Anglican Church's Catholic Creed and liturgy.[92]

Newman keenly realized the import of Ward's censure. He also thought a defeat of the proposed Test would be like a virtual repeal of the censure of *Tract 90.*[93] Newman was correct. Some of the opponents of the Tractarians wished Convocation to censure *Tract 90* by means of this Test. Newman asserted, "If the Test passes, the state of things will be as miserable as can be conceived—some men ejected, others straining their conscience—and suspicion, distrust, reserve, dissimulation everywhere. It would in fact be the reign of Inquisition. The Vice-Chancellor would be able, and would not scruple, to summon a Tutor before him for his Lectures on the Articles on the information of his Pupils! It would be the reign of Golightlyism."[94]

Newman believed that both the Liberal and High Church party would protest against, and defeat the Test. Despite his

---

92 *LD,* Vol. X, JHN to Elizabeth Bowden (December 27, 1844), 472-74; 473.

93 *LD,* Vol. X, JHN to Mrs. John Mozley (December 22, 1844), 467-69.

94 *LD,* Vol. X, JHN to Elizabeth Bowden (December 27, 1844), 272-74; 273-74.

hopes for the outcome of Convocation, the publication of Ward's book had manifested the doctrinal malaise of the Anglican Church.

CONVERSIONS

In June 1844, when Robert C. Burton, an Anglican clergyman, wrote to Newman in June about his imminent conversion, Newman replied, "The question is not whether the Church of Rome is right, but whether it is the duty of A. or B. to join it. It is not an abstract theorem, but a practical question. It is a far less evil to remain in error, in which we were born, than to change into error."[95]

Burton rejoined: "Am I to imply from this that the Church of Rome is right—is, in fact the true Church of Christ? And if so, can I be justified in remaining in the English Communion? am I not trifling with God's grace and tempting Him to deprive [myself] of it, when He has led to [sic] me to the light, and I nevertheless turn away from it?"[96]

Newman had advised Burton not to act on private judgment, but to wait for greater light from God and to act in a group with others who serve as "a guarantee and a verification of each other's judgment."[97] Newman was entering the last lap of his race as an Anglican. He was only waiting for more grace to take the step forward to Roman Catholicism. The question in many people's minds, not only family and friends, but countless persons in England was: "When would

---

95 *LD,* Vol. X, JHN to Robert Clerke Burton (June 23, 1844), 284-85.
96 *LD,* Vol. X, Robert Clerke Burton to JHN (June 29, 1844), 290.
97 *Ibid.,* 284.

Newman convert?" On June 24, the Italian Passionist priest, Fr. Dominic Barbieri, visited Littlemore at the invitation of John D. Dalgairns and met Newman for the first time. Newman was not yet thinking of making any moves.

Another convert was George Tickell, Oakeley's curate. In the fall of 1844, while traveling in Belgium, Tickell joined the Roman Catholic Church. When Oakeley learned about it in the newspapers, he was very upset. Charles Bridges, a resident at Littlemore, also converted. Bridges left Littlemore early in the morning of December 25, and joined the Roman Catholic Church the following year.[98] Prior to all this, Newman had tried to avert Bridges's move to Littlemore in order to avoid a compromising situation.

In November and December 1844, Newman worked hard to finish a second part of his translation of texts by St. Athanasius. By December, he was busy working on the essay on the development of Christian doctrine. He had jotted down many ideas and wished to organize them. He wished to answer the question about what he should do: whether or not to join the Roman Catholic Church.[99] He had decided that if, once he wrote the book, his conviction about the Catholic Church was not weaker, he would join it.

Over five years, Newman had grown in the conviction that the Roman Catholic Church is the only true Church. It was this belief in its infallibility and the authority granted by God to the Successor of Peter that led Newman toward Rome. Although external events served as catalysts, in the

---

98 *LD,* Vol. X, JHN to Charles Marriot (December 23, 1844), 469-70.
99 *LD,* Vol. X, Memorandum (December 1844), 459-60.

end, it was the conviction that the Church of Rome was the true Church established by Jesus Christ. With this in mind, he accepted all the other doctrines it held, such as the canon of the Sacred Scripture, and practices, such as prayer for the dead. He expressed this belief with a short phrase, "I must either believe all or none."[100]

During this time, he had experienced the loss of friends and name, as well as position. What worried him most was how his change of ideas could cause others to fall into skepticism, indifference, and even religious infidelity.[101] Newman, however, worried even more that he might be withholding others called by God from dying within the Roman Communion; and that some whom he kept from Roman Communion would end up in the Latitudinarian party of the Anglican Church. Although Newman had a strong conviction about the truth of the Roman Catholic Church, he still entertained the doubt that he might be under some delusion or temptation.[102]

---

100 *Ibid.,* 377.
101 *Ibid.,* 262.
102 *Ibid.,* 262.

CHAPTER 32

1845: LAST PREPARATIONS FOR CONVERSION

JOHN Henry Newman was well on his way to becoming Roman Catholic. Before taking the step of formal communion with the Roman Catholic Church, he wished to convince himself that he was not under some delusion, because he had once been persuaded into thinking of the Church of Rome as the Antichrist. The year 1845 was a year of final preparation for this momentous step. At the beginning of the year, he told Jemima, Keble, Maria Giberne, and others that he did not yet have plans for any immediate move.[1] Jemima expressed grief at the approaching separation of her brother from their common religion.[2] Charles Marriot found out about Newman's situation and wrote to him, telling him that he felt Newman's pain, yet wished to continue to be close to him, despite their differences.[3]

Newman continued living at Littlemore, which he dubbed *Domus Sanctae Mariae*, the House of Mary, but he was able to travel to visit friends with a little more ease since he had no pastoral, or college duties. In January, Newman offered encouragement to William Faber, who

---

1 *LD,* Vol. X, JHN to Maria Rosina Giberne (January 8, 1845), 484-85.

2 *LD,* Vol. X, Mrs. John Mozley to JHN (January 8, 1845), 485.

3 *LD,* Vol. X, Charles Marriot to JHN(January 13, 1845), 491.

had been criticized in the *British Magazine* for his life of St. Wilfrid. Then in February the big controversy from the preceding year unfolded.

FEBRUARY CONVOCATION TO CONDEMN WARD

Dr. Wynter, the Vice-Chancellor, persisted with the plan to bring to vote three propositions at the Oxford Convocation. The first proposition sought to condemn Ward for his book and the second one sought to revoke his academic titles. Wynter and the Hebdomadal board wished to pass a third proposition, obliging a new type of Subscription to the *Articles*. This would require Subscription based on the interpretation of the reigning University authorities, which were liberal. A great stir surrounded the weeks preceding the Convocation. Members of the University wrote pamphlets for and against the proceedings.[4] Ward's friends advised him that he would be able to appeal to the Queen as Visitor of the University. Sir John Dodson, Queen's Advocate, presented the opinion that depriving Ward of his degrees, or establishing a new Test, was illegal.[5] According to Dodson the university granted a degree by grant from the Crown, but it did not have power to take away a degree.

---

4 *LD*, Vol. X, Declaration, footnote, 492; "Reasons for voting against the proposed censure of certain propositions extracted from a Work lately published by Rev. W. G. Ward, M.A., Charles Marriot (January 18, 1845), 498-99; 498.

5 *LD*, Vol. X, Opinion of Sir John Dodson, Queen's Advocate, and Richard Bethell, Q.C. on the Legality of Ward's Proposed Degradation (January 17, 1845), 506-07.

He also argued that the law required a cleric who subscribed to the *Articles* to take them in a literal and grammatical sense, not in the sense in which he believed they
were originally framed, or later accepted by the university.[6]
The Provost of Oriel was furious at the opposition to a new
Test and wished to pass it at all cost, but the Heads decided
to drop the third proposition because the general opinion
indicated that it was unlikely to succeed.

When the Vice-Chancellor publicly announced to withdraw the third proposition, disgruntled members of the
University plotted to inflict a more severe blow to Newman and the Tractarians.[7] On January 25, 1845, the fifth
anniversary of the publication of *Tract 90*, one of the Heads
of Houses proposed that a vote be taken at the next Convocation for a formal censure of the principles contained in
Tract 90 and a solemn repudiation of its mode of interpreting the *Thirty-Nine Articles*.[8] Four hundred and seventy-
four votes, including those of Lord Ashley, and the Bishops
of Llandaff and Chichester, were collected and presented to
the Vice-Chancellor and Heads, who accepted the petition.
This was the same Test under a different dress. Frederic
Rogers, Newman's former pupil, and Edward Badeley both
wrote against the proposed censure of *Tract 90*. James R.
Hope objected in a legal opinion to the censure of *Tract 90*,
which would actually establish a practical test of opinion

---

6 *Ibid.,* 507.

7 Richard William Church, *The Oxford Movement: Twelve Years 1833-
1845,* London, 1900, 379-80.

8 *LD,* Vol. X, Formal Condemnation of the Tract Ninety by the University of Oxford (January 25, 1845), 511-12.

in the University; as proposed, the Test would be vague and extensive since it would involve matters of much controversy.[9]

Despite these protests, and without observing a required ten-day timetable, a proposition to censure *Tract 90* was added to the Convocation on February 13. Marriot, who was Fellow and Dean of Oriel, wrote a letter of complaint to the Vice-Chancellor.[10] Gladstone also wrote to the Provost of Oriel, pleading for the same practice of due deliberation used in the House of Commons.[11] He appealed to the study of all of Newman's works, not just his *Tract 90*, and urged that Newman's great service to the University and the Church be recognized.

James Bowling Mozley, Newman's brother-in-law and friend, wrote to inform Newman of the events. Newman replied that he was, in the words of the *English Churchman*, "a dead man."[12] He added, "Hebdomadal Boards can do me neither good nor harm."[13] In April, James Bowling Mozley wrote an article in the *Christian Remembrancer* that caused Newman to write to him: "I knew you love me, as I do you—I was not prepared for what you say—and now, as is the law of such things, I know it is just when I

---

9 *LD*, Vol. X, Legal Opinion of James Robert Hope on Censure of Tract 90 (February 8, 1845), 538-40.

10 *LD*, Vol. X, Charles Marriot to the Vice-Chancellor (February 5, 1845), 524-26.

11 *LD*, Vol. X, William Ewart Gladstone to the Provost of Oriel College (February 6, 1845), 526-27.

12 *LD*, Vol. X, JHN to James Bowling Mozley (February 5, 1845), 522.

13 *Ibid.*, 522.

am losing it. You speak as if writing a funeral oration, and so it is."[14] Newman confided in Mozley that he planned to resign his Fellowship, and suggested that Mozley share this news with anyone he thought appropriate.

Newman told Pusey that if a decree were passed condemning *Tract 90* it would constitute for Newman a long-awaited external circumstance to confirm his course.[15] He wrote to Mrs. Bowden and Isaac Williams that there must be some meaning in all this, implying a confirmation of his departure from the Church of England.[16] But Newman's friends wished to defend him. Manning wrote to tell Newman that although he had not planned to vote in the censure of Ward, he would go to Oxford to vote for Newman: "I owe to you more than to any one living."[17]

Jemima, who wrote frequently to Newman during 1845, was appalled at the cowardly persecution against her brother, a behavior that she considered "so unlike the English."[18] She knew that her brother was calm, but worried for his health, and felt the great injustice inflicted on him.[19] Newman thanked his sister for her affection and sympathy, and

---

14 *LD,* Vol. X, JHN to James Bowling Mozley (April 2, 1845), 612-13.

15 *LD,* Vol. X, JHN to Edward Bouverie Pusey (February 6, 1845), 528-29.

16 *LD,* Vol. X, JHN to Elizabeth Bowden (February 7, 1845), 531; JHN to Isaac Williams (February 7, 1845), 531-32; 531.

17 *LD,* Vol. X, Henry Edward Manning to JHN (February 6, 1845), 531.

18 *LD,* Vol. X, Mrs. John Mozley to JHN (February 7, 1845), 533.

19 *LD,* Vol. X, Mrs. John Mozley to JHN (February 9, 1845), 541.

through her thanked Anne Mozley, his sister-in-law. But
he explained that people's sympathy produced both satisfaction and pain. It caused pain due to the suffering that
it produced in others, and because an increase in people's
goodwill toward him would suggest ungratefulness on his
part if he were later to disappoint them.[20]

Although he was grateful for the signs of consideration
and friendship that he received, he was almost numb from
inward pain. He told Manning that he had very little interest in the results of the vote: "I have ills which Heads of
Houses can neither augment nor cure. Real inward pain
makes one insensible to such shadows."[21] To another friend
he wrote, "But now I have no pain about ecclesiastical
movements—I am too far gone for that."[22]

The two Proctors of the University had power to veto a
measure brought before Convocation. Richard W. Church,
Newman's friend and one of the Proctors that year, wrote
to Newman a few days before the vote to tell him that he
would veto the measure.[23] Newman indicated to Jemima
that this was likely to happen. He told her that a condemnation of *Tract 90* would turn people toward Rome, but that
this would not be a good motive for conversion: "Disgust
makes no good converts; change of opinion is, commonly

---

20 *LD,* Vol. X, JHN to Mrs. John Mozley (February 10, 1845), 542-43;
543.

21 *LD,* Vol. X, JHN to Henry Edward Manning (February 9, 1845),
540-41; 541.

22 *LD,* Vol. X, JHN to Charles Miller (February 11, 1845), 545-46;
546.

23 *LD,* Vol. X, Richard William Church to JHN (February 8, 1845),
535.

speaking, the work of a long time. People who are disgusted one way, may be disgusted the other."[24]

On February 13, a snow-covered winter day, Convocation met and voted 776 to 368 to censure Ward's book, and 568 to 511 to degrade Ward of his degrees.[25] Newman was not present to vote. After the votes against Ward, voting for the third proposition to censure *Tract 90* began, but as soon as it started, the two Proctors stood up and vetoed the measure. The Vice-Chancellor left the assembly amid the hissing of undergraduates. A declaration of thanksgiving with the signatures of 341 masters at Oxford was presented to the Proctors. The defeated proponents of the censure immediately called for another vote to take place in the following term, once new Proctors were appointed, but through Gladstone's mediation, Pusey obtained assurance from the Archbishop of Canterbury that there would be no further proceedings of the sort at Oxford.[26] The future Prime Minister of England and Archbishop Howley, the Head of the Church of England, had acted kindly, but it was too late.[27] Newman's course was already decided.

Although Newman's course seemed certain, he was grateful to Pusey for informing him of the Archbishop's words. Newman implored his friend to see things as they were: "I am as much gone over as if I *were already gone*. It is a matter of time only. I am waiting, if so be, that if I am

---

24 *LD,* Vol. X, JHN to Mrs. John Mozley (February 11, 1845), 546-47.

25 *LD,* Vol. X, footnote, 550.

26 *LD,* Vol. X, William Ewart Gladstone to Edward Bouverie Pusey (February 22, 1845), 570.

27 Henry Liddon, *Life of Edward Bouverie Pusey,* II, 436-38.

under a delusion, it may be revealed to me . . ."[28] Newman told Pusey that he looked to external events, such as the attempted censure of *Tract 90,* not as a cause for his actions but as confirmation.

Interest in *Tract 90* was widespread. The renewed controversy over *Tract 90* occasioned the revocation of Frederick Oakeley's ecclesiastical license. The case against Oakeley was initiated by a letter which he had written to the University Vice-Chancellor in Newman's defense. Oakeley was a High Church Anglican and Tractarian, rector of the well-known St. Margaret Street Chapel in London. His letter provoked the anger of Bishop Blomfield of London, who asked Oakeley to resign, but Oakeley resisted. Subsequently Blomfield pressed charges against Oakeley in the Court of Arches, a court of appeal under the jurisdiction of the Archbishop of Canterbury. Oakeley agonized on whether to defend himself with legal action because his decision would affect his friends, many of whom wished him to resist the bishop.[29] He relied on Newman's advice and the legal counsel from Newman's friends, Hope and Bellasis, who paid for his legal defense. Oakeley finally decided against an appeal to the Privy Council, the highest court of appeals short of the monarch.[30] Oakeley resigned

---

28 *LD,* Vol. X, JHN to Edward Bouverie Pusey (February 25, 1845), 573-74; 574.

29 *LD,* Vol. X, Frederick Oakeley to JHN (May 26, 1845), 673-74.

30 *LD,* Vol. X, F. Oakeley to JHN (April 14, 1845), 625.

his position at St. Margaret Street Chapel,[31] and contrary to Bellasis's advice did not pursue defense against the bishop's suit. In June, Oakeley did not appear in court for his trial, nor was he represented.[32] At the end of the month the ecclesiastical court found Oakeley guilty and revoked his ministerial license.[33]

Oakeley's case was only one of several cases of abusive authority being used to squelch opposition among the orthodox clergy: Pusey's censure, Newman's forced retirement, and Ward's degradation. But it was also part of a larger attack registered in other quarters against Tradition, namely the country parishes. This was the case with Henry William Wilberforce, who had been accused the previous year by his curate and some parishioners of altering the liturgy and teaching Roman doctrine. At Oxford, the University's Hebdomadal Board had become a party organ instead of an impartial university office. To carry out its plans it resorted to bringing nonresidents of Oxford, who lived in the country, to come to vote in Convocation.

Despite his proven intellectual talent and moral character, Newman was disrespected and mistreated by the university authorities. Newman only felt respected by one man with authority at Oxford, Martin J. Routh, President of Magdalen College. In 1845, as on many occasions since

---

31 *LD,* Vol. X, F. Oakeley to JHN (June 3, 1845), 689.

32 *LD,* Vol. X, Edward Bellasis to JHN (June 1, 1845), 687-89.

33 *LD,* Vol. X, footnote, 722; quote from the *British Magazine,* XXVIII, 1845 (Aug.), 177-83; 183.

1837, Routh asked Newman to be examiner for the John-son scholarship. This year Newman was obliged to decline. In his thank-you note, a grateful Newman told Routh, "You are the only person in station in Oxford who has shown me any countenance for a long course of years, and much as I know your kindness I did not expect it now."[34] This comment seemed an exaggeration, but it was in fact true. Most of those who admired Newman were undergraduates and his peers, many of whom were no longer residing at the University.

SPIRITUAL GUIDANCE OF FUTURE CONVERTS

Despite his serious misgivings about the Anglican Church, Newman was especially respectful of the duties proper to Anglican clergymen and his loyalties to the Anglican Church. In his condition as an Anglican clergyman, he was very careful of what advice he could give to Anglicans and non-Anglicans, and of the duties that he had toward his superiors. Because of this conduct Newman did not hesitate to suspend correspondence with any Anglican who joined a Roman Catholic college or stayed at a Roman Catholic institution.

The case of George Montgomery, an Irishman of English and Scottish descent, residing in Dublin, is illustrative. Montgomery, an Anglican who began a correspondence with Newman, became a Fellow of St. Columba's College,

---

34 *LD*, Vol. X, JHN to Martin Joseph Routh, President of Magdalen College (February 21, 1845), 568.

a Roman Catholic institution. When he informed Newman, the latter replied that he would no longer be able to correspond with him. Based on Newman's reply, Montgomery resigned from St. Columba's College and wrote to inform Newman. In addition, Montgomery posed to Newman a qualm of conscience that other future converts had voiced to Newman: could a person with serious misgivings about the Anglican Church partake in Anglican services and receive Holy Communion in the Anglican Church without committing a sin?[35] For those who thought that the Anglican Church was not the true Church, this dilemma of conscience was a pressing one. And they turned to Newman for advice.

In April, Montgomery visited Newman at Littlemore in a state of distress regarding the salvation of his soul if he were to remain an Anglican any longer.[36] Newman decided he should not speak with him about the subject, and instead asked Pusey to speak with him. Later Newman remarked that Pusey was too severe with Montgomery so that, half in jest, Newman told Dalgairns, "I venture to say that the said M. is the first person who has been driven out of the Church of England by the severity of her discipline."[37] In the end Montgomery became a Roman Catholic, and in 1849 was ordained a priest.

Earlier in the year Newman tried to dissuade another Anglican, Richard Stanton, from becoming Roman Cath-

---

35 *LD,* Vol. X, George Montgomery to JHN (March 10, 1845), 585-86; 586.

36 *LD,* Vol. X, JHN to Edward Bouverie Pusey (April 17, 1845), 628-29; 629.

37 *LD,* JHN to John Dobree Dalgairns (May 18, 1845), 662-63; 663.

olic. Stanton, who wished to spend some time at Littlemore, was an ordained deacon and Newman advised him to submit his mind and heart to the system in which he had been raised. Unable to do so, Stanton decided to resign his position as assistant at a parish, and in June, he joined the Littlemore community. Another future convert to Roman Catholicism was Thomas Francis Knox, who obtained a B.A. at Trinity College. In March, he wrote to Newman expressing a desire to receive for the first time sacramental absolution. Newman sent him to Pusey since he was not exercising any ministerial function in the Anglican Church.[38]

Often those who sought Newman's spiritual advice were his friends. Early in the year, Maria Giberne asked Newman about the propriety of attending Roman Catholic services. Newman replied that it would be a scandal unless she were a catechumen, that is, someone receiving formal instruction to become Roman Catholic. He also told her that invocations to the saints were not required by the Church of Rome.[39] More importantly, since the English Church did not sanction them, Newman did not like using them. This advice was the same that he had given Miss Holmes, who continued to seek Newman's spiritual counsel. Despite her pleadings, he insisted that he could not give her spiritual direction because she was a Roman Catholic.[40]

---

38 *LD,* Vol. X, JHN to Thomas Francis Know (March 10, 1845), 584-85.

39 *LD,* Vol. X, JHN to Miss Maria Rosina Giberne (January 26, 1845), 515.

40 *LD,* Vol. X, Draft of JHN to Miss Mary Holmes (February 4, 1845), 521-22.

Other friends asked Newman to act as an intermediary with their families. One of these was John Dalgairns, who lived with Newman at Littlemore. He asked Newman to write on his behalf to his father regarding his becoming Roman Catholic. Newman wrote to John Dalgairns, Senior that his son was not acting rashly since for three years his son had considered the decision to become Roman Catholic.[41] Newman added that after writing for *The Lives of the English Saints,* John had acquired a literary name. His writings not only prepared people for a future step, they gave him weight and authority. Dalgairns, Senior accepted that his son join the Roman Catholic Church and agreed with the idea for him to be ordained a priest in France.[42] Newman advised Dalgairns to keep open the option of ordination at Oscott. Dalgairns was impatient to begin his studies in France. Most of all, however, Dalgairns was impatient about taking the step to communion with Rome.

Converts Moving as a Group

Despite Newman's attempts at dissuading future converts, in 1844, and even more in 1845, Littlemore became a place where future converts to Roman Catholicism visited or wrote for advice. Without planning for it, what he had hoped and prayed for occurred: a joint movement toward Rome of many Anglicans. The Movement was not so much

---

41 *LD,* Vol. X, JHN to John Dalgairns Senior (February 18, 1845), 564-66.

42 *LD,* Vol. X, John Dobree Dalgairns to JHN (May 7, 1845), 650-51.

that of a group *per se* but of many taking the step to Rome, some before Newman and many after.

One of the first converts in 1845 was Thomas Meyrick, author of *The Family of St. Richard*. In late February, Meyrick, although troubled by intellectual pride, told Newman that he was afraid of delaying entrance into the Roman Catholic Church lest the grace of the Holy Spirit pass by him. He had held back because others did so, not because he doubted the truth of the voice of Rome. He finally resolved to separate himself from those to whom he looked up, and informed Newman of his plan to enter the Roman Church, which he did shortly thereafter.[43]

Albany J. Christie, John Frederic's brother and a Fellow at Oriel, heard that Oakeley had begun to think of joining the Roman Catholic Church. He learned from Oakeley that Newman wished for people to join as body rather than individually.[44] Christie wrote Newman that he had some temporal advantages by remaining a Fellow, but that he set his confidence on him. In March and later in May, Christie spent some days with Newman at Littlemore.

Converts like Holmes and Tickell tried to speed up Newman's conversion. In March, during Holy Week, George Tickell, who had converted in December 1844, wrote Newman, telling him that many people and communities prayed for him that he would receive the gift of faith in the "loving authority of the Church and of making profession of

43 *LD*, Vol. X, Thomas Meyrick to JHN (February 24, 1845), 571-72.

44 *LD*, Vol. X, Albany James Christie to JHN (March 17, 1845), 599-600.

her Faith."[45] He also wished to thank Newman for having been an instrument for bringing him into the Catholic Church. Later in May, Tickell dined twice with Newman at Littlemore. On the first day, with the enthusiasm of a recent convert, he tried for two minutes to convert Newman, but he did not go any further. Newman wrote to Dalgairns, "I have kept my gun loaded and cocked, intending to discharge upon him, if he made a second attempt, but he has kept his peace."[46] Afterward, Tickell tried to do the same with Pusey.

A week later, Tickell sent Newman a miraculous medal from France with the image of the Immaculate Conception. The Virgin Mary had appeared at a chapel in Rue du Bac in Paris in 1830, and use of her medal spread very quickly. On August 22, 1845, Newman wrote the word "medal" in his diary. This was the day that he began to wear the medal around his neck.[47] In 1867, following a controversy with Pusey over devotion to the Virgin Mary, Newman would tell Pusey that it was the twenty-second anniversary of the day "I saw my way clear to put a miraculous medal round my neck." The editors of Newman's *Letters and Diaries* consider it likely that with his letter Newman sent Pusey a medal with an explanatory leaflet. Otherwise the reference

---

45 *LD,* Vol. X, George Tickell to JHN (March 19, 1845), 607-8.

46 *LD,* Vol. X, JHN to John Dobree Dalgairns (May 9, 1845), 651-53; 652.

47 *LD,* Vol. X, G. Tickell to JHN (May 13, 1845), 658-59; 658; and explanatory note, *ibid.*

to the miraculous medal would not have meant something to Pusey.[48]

Ambrose St. John and John Dalgairns were part of a different category of future converts. They lived with Newman and were among his closest friends. In 1844, St. John was prepared to join the Roman Catholic Church, but his mother thought it would be a grave sin and opposed. In April, St. John paid a visit to his family and wrote Newman in distress due to his mother's attitude.[49] Newman greatly encouraged him, and sent him news about George Bridges, Tickell, and Montgomery; Bridges was just about to convert.

Newman teased Ambrose St. John about his long and out-of-fashion name; he addressed him with the affectionate Latin word *carissime* (dearest), as he also addressed Henry Wilberforce.[50] Writing to the latter he said, "Tell St. John I have just got his letters—and tell him that his letters are like violets, in my forlorn estate. How thankful I ought to be that if I lose some friends I gain others. His account of himself is cheering."[51] Both St. John and Dalgairns had gone to visit their respective families; Newman was alone at Littlemore.

During 1845, a concerned Newman followed the steps of Frederick Sellwood Bowles, who had resided for some time at Littlemore. Bowles had gone to the Isle of Wight,

---

48 *LD,* Vol. X, JHN to Edward B. Pusey (August 22, 1867), 658.

49 *LD,* Vol. X, Ambrose St. John to JHN (April 8, 1845), 620-21; 620.

50 *LD,* Vol. X, JHN to Ambrose St. John (April 26, 1845), 638-39; 638; JHN to Henry Wilberforce (April 27, 1845), 639-42; 639.

51 JHN to Henry Wilberforce (April 27, 1845), 639-42; 639.

where he was trying to study the basics of religion. He felt ignorant about religion and was determined to read a book by Thomas Scott, recommended by Newman. But Bowles needed to be under someone's care, so Newman asked Henry Wilberforce and Robert F. Wilson to take Bowles in at their rectories. Newman told them that Bowles needed to rest and study at his leisure.[52] By association with Mrs. Bowles and her son, Newman thought of Mrs. Lockhart and her son. Newman spoke to a friend about Lockhart, who had left Littlemore to become Roman Catholic and had entered the Institute of Charity, a religious community.[53] Lockhart's mother, who had been worried about her son's intentions of becoming Roman Catholic, was happy to see a year later that her son was calm, and very cheerful, as well as interested in the family. She began to show an inclination to the Church of Rome, and was eventually received the following year.[54]

After further correspondence between Newman and Bowles, Newman advised Bowles to be frank with his mother, and to sort out his religious beliefs before returning to Littlemore. Newman, who wrote to him with the affection of a father, did not wish to exert undue influence over him.[55] At first Mrs. Bowles thought Newman had not been transparent with her as far as his views went.

---

52 *LD,* Vol. X, JHN to Frederick Sellwood Bowles (April 11, 1845), 623.

53 *LD,* Vol. X, JHN to Mrs. William Froude (April 20, 1845), 634.

54 *LD,* Vol. X, JHN to Elizabeth Bowden (May 13, 1845), 657, and footnote.

55 *LD,* Vol. X, JHN to Frederick Sellwood Bowles (April 24, 1845, 635-36), 636.

Newman defended himself; he had tried to inform her through her son of his resignation from St. Mary's before it was made public.[56] Mrs. Bowles, whose daughter Emily had become Roman Catholic in 1843, was worried that her son too would become Roman Catholic, but she apologized to Newman for any unkind words conveyed in a letter to her son.[57] She trusted that Newman acted seeking the glory of God, and that God would lead her son to his eternal salvation.

Newman maintained the desire not to leave the Church of England based on his private judgment alone. This subject came up in correspondence with Edward B. Fortescue, a friend of Henry Wilberforce who visited Newman a few times in 1844–1845. Fortescue was quite unsettled about remaining Anglican, and he told St. John that he expected as many as 100 would follow Newman.[58] When Newman heard about this he commented that Fortescue's mindset and Oakeley's increasing direction toward Rome were a comfort to him inasmuch as they were a confirmation of his own desire to move to Rome with a large group of men.[59] Fortescue and his wife did become Roman Catholics, but many years later.

When advising prospective converts, Newman was careful to point out the need for them to give sufficient warning to family members and those under their care. This was the

---

56 *LD*, Vol. X, JHN to Mrs. Bowles (June 17, 1845), 706-07.

57 *LD*, Vol. X, Mrs. H. S. Bowles to JHN (July 1, 1845), 722.

58 *LD*, Vol. X, Ambrose St. John to JHN (April 29, 1845), 643.

59 *LD*, Vol. X, JHN to John Dobree Dalgairns (April 27, 1845), 643.

case with John Moore Capes, an Anglican clergyman who was on the verge of joining the Roman Catholic Church. He had written to Newman for advice. Newman replied to Capes that for six years he (Newman) had the growing conviction that the Church of England was in schism, but he had considered it his duty to set himself against his conviction. He had only shared his thoughts with Frederic Rogers and Henry Wilberforce.[60] In a follow-up letter, Newman pointed out that a clergyman should not surprise people with news of abandoning his church because this would be unfair to a congregation. A congregation had a right to know that its spiritual guide has a set of opinions which they implicitly trust.[61] Newman wrote to Capes, "I feel very strongly indeed on the point of clergymen stepping as it were from their pulpit into another communion."[62] Newman led by example; he had stepped down from St. Mary's in September 1843. But Capes could not wait. In June he was received into the Roman Catholic Church, and his wife followed him some time afterward.

Newman's advice to Capes was one of many proofs of the respect that he had for both his duties in the Anglican Church and also for Anglican congregations. At the same time, he was mindful of people's rights. Capes had spent a big part of his fortune building a church in Bridgewater. Newman thought that, out of justice, it should not be taken away and suggested that Pusey speak on Capes's behalf to the diocesan authorities. Newman considered it to be another thing if

---

60 *LD,* Vol. X, JHN to John Moore Capes (June 4, 1845), 690.

61 *LD,* Vol. X, JHN to John Moore Capes (June 8, 1845), 694.

62 *Ibid.*

Capes wished to give up the church on his own.[63] Newman later praised Capes's sacrifice in his *Lectures on the Present Position of Catholics in England*; Capes remained a layman, leaving behind his means of subsistence.[64]

Another convert to Roman Catholicism was Michael Watts-Russell, a clergyman who wrote to Newman in June. Watts expressed the same reasons for conversion as Newman: he thought the Roman Catholic Church was the true Church established by Christ and believed the Anglican Church to be in schism. Watts thought that the Anglican Church retained, by God's mercy, a valid sacrifice and consequently true sacraments, but that it had forfeited the daily sacrifice and the reservation of the Sacrament in churches. Watts believed in the authority and influence of the Roman See, but had no doubt regarding the validity of his Orders, so he had no plans to leave the Anglican Communion. However, upon hearing of Newman's imminent conversion, Watts felt bewildered:

[S]ince I have heard that you Sir, whom I can never look upon but as my Father, have been taught by God that it is time to go elsewhere, I feel oppressed with a sense of forlornness in being deserted, and my heart bounds to follow your steps . . .[65]

Watts did not wish to act rashly and asked Newman, whom he saw as an instrument for the reconciliation of

---

63 *LD*, Vol. X, JHN to John Moore Capes (August 13, 1845), 746-47.

64 John Henry Newman, *Lectures on the Present Position of Catholics in England*, Lecture VIII, "Ignorance Concerning Catholics the Protection of the Protestant View," 359-62; 359, available at: http://www.newman-reader.org/works/england/lecture8.html#capes.

65 *LD*, Vol. X, Michael Watts-Russell to JHN (June 19, 1845), 710-711.

the Anglican Church with Rome, for advice. At the end of August, Watts visited Newman in Littlemore. Watts and his family would be received into the Church of Rome in November 1845.

All the while the vexing Mary Holmes continued to write Newman, sometimes daily. Finally, his patience ran out, and he told her that he would not give her any further advice or correspond with her any more. Concerning their correspondence he told her: "After your recent letters, I have come to the resolution of breaking it off altogether. I have many reasons for this. It is enough to say to you that you have no claim whatever on me to continue it. I have already given up much time and thought to you, to the loss of others who have a real claim on me."[66] He wrote to her spiritual director, George Spencer, a priest at Oscott, to inform him of the situation.[67] Although Newman told Miss Holmes, "I have been patient *beyond* my duty," she continued to write to him.[68] This was one of the few times Newman expressed his annoyance in a personal letter. For the most part Newman responded patiently to the objections and questions posed by friends or acquaintances.

PARTING WITH FRIENDS AND FAMILY

By the beginning of 1845, Newman began to part with his friends. Even if differences in religious beliefs were not an obstacle for friendly intercourse, the absence of similar engagements and circles of friends would still create a

---

66 *LD,* Vol. X, JHN to Miss Mary Holmes (May 31, 1845), 681.
67 *LD,* Vol. X, JHN to George Spencer (May 31, 1845), 681.
68 *LD,* Vol. X, JHN to Miss Mary Holmes (May 31, 1845), 681.

separation. Nonetheless, the previous year Keble had written to Newman that their affection would always remain the same. On February 20, 1845, the eve of Newman's birthday, Keble sent Newman an affectionate and congratulatory letter. Keble wished to meet with Newman and recall memorable conversations they once had had with Hurrell Froude.[69] Sadly, Newman did not receive any other letters from Keble until October 3 and 11 of the same year. After Newman's conversion, he did not see Keble again until September 1865.

Pusey, however, continued to consult Newman about difficult cases of spiritual doubts that people brought to him. Concerning a woman who was dwelling too much on her sins, Newman told Pusey:

> Clearly it seems to me that she ought not just now to think of our Lord's Passion—Indeed I should have a fear, judging without knowing a person, that her mind was oppressed with over-meditation etc, and that active duties would be good for her. I think she probably is right in anticipating illness, if she does not change the course of her thoughts.[70]

Newman's advice was practical; he exercised moderation in guiding souls. He advised people to be patient and act cautiously. Since Pusey was sad, thinking of his future separation from Newman, in the same letter Newman continued to prepare his friend. With reference to neglecting God's calls, he told Pusey: "One must make no other person's impressions a guide to oneself. I put it as an

---

69 *LD,* Vol. X, John Keble to JHN (February 20, 1845), 567.

70 *LD,* Vol. X, JHN to Edward Bouverie Pusey (March 12, 1845), 586-87.

illustration. Nor am I speaking prominently about myself when I say, what I ought to say, yet shrink from saying, that I suppose Christmas cannot come again without a breakup—to what extent or to whom I do not know."[71]

A date for Newman's reception into the Roman Catholic Church was drawing near; Newman would be received before Christmas. In vain, Pusey gave his dear friend arguments to keep him in the Anglican Communion. He argued that a token of Christ's Presence with the English Church were signs of growing life within her and the experience of the grace of the sacraments by her members.[72] Newman agreed with his friend's assertion, but he maintained that the Anglican Church was outside the Catholic Communion. Also, Newman replied that the unsettlement he produced in people was his "one overpowering distress," which had made him physically ill the previous year; yet in proportion as his course became clearer, it was more bearable.[73] In response to Pusey's claim that Newman caused disunity among the families of converts, Newman retorted:

> The disunion of families indeed remains, and it is enough to turn one's head; but in proportion as one feels confident that a change is right, in the same proportion one wishes others to change too; and though it is any thing but my wish that they should change because I do, of course it cannot pain me that they should take my change as a sort of warning, or call to consider where the Truth lies.[74]

---

71 *Ibid.,* 587.

72 Henry Liddon, *Life of Edward Bouverie Pusey,* II, 448-49.

73 *LD,* Vol. X, JHN to Edward Bouverie Pusey (March 14, 1845), 591-94; 591.

74 *Ibid.*

Newman's desire to follow the truth in religion was his guiding principle, or passion, one which made his pain bearable and justified the pain which he caused others. Newman's *ethos* contrasted with that of his late friend, Blanco White, who died a pantheist. Newman was appalled and saddened by White's autobiography. Newman also criticized the superficial notion of truth conveyed in a biography on White: "[H]is biographer actually calls him in his last moments a *Confessor*—confessor to what? not to any opinion, any belief whatever—but to the *Search* after truth; ever wandering about and changing; and therefore great."[75] Newman continued, "For years I have had an increasing intellectual conviction that there is no medium between Pantheism and the Church of Rome."[76]

Both White and Newman had sought religious truth, but White had ended in skepticism. Newman's careful and persistent study led him instead to an objective truth that was greater than himself; it was Truth itself. This Truth was knowable both through reason and Revelation, and concerned not only the knowledge of God's existence and attributes but moral law and the divinity of the Church.

The day before Pusey's letter, Jemima had written John Henry a moving letter in which she told him that although he had sufficiently warned her, she felt great pain: "It is like hearing that some dear friend must die."[77] She begged him to reconsider, but asked him to forgive what on her part

---

75 *LD,* Vol. X, JHN to Henry Wilberforce (April 27, 1845), 639-42; 639.

76 *Ibid.,* 640.

77 *LD,* Vol. X, Mrs. John Mozley to JHN (March 13, 1845), 594.

might seem inconsiderate. Newman replied to his sister that he had wanted to wait seven years and would like to wait longer, but the years were passing by and he was getting old.[78] As far as his convictions went, he had reached the conclusion that by not moving he was offending God. He candidly told her that he loved ease and that he was making a large income from the sale of his sermons. He was ready to sacrifice it all only because of an imperative necessity. He again argued that with God's grace he had been living a stricter life and had improved in many respects; how then could he at the same time be so grossly blind in a matter of such importance?[79] He reasoned with his sister that at one time or another, anyone who is a heretic faces a trial, as he did, when he comes to realize his state. Jews who became Christians were cursed by their friends. Nestorians, Dona-tists, or Monophysites had to break all ties to return to the Christian Faith.

Newman prepared for the step he was to make, trusting that God heard the prayers many good people were making on his behalf. And he prayed every day for light: "Continu-ally do I pray that He would discover to me, if I am under a delusion—what can I do more? what hope have I but in Him? to whom should I go? who can do me good? who can speak a word of comfort but He? who is there but looks on me with a sorrowful face? but He can lift up the light of His countenance upon me."[80]

---

78 *LD,* Vol. X, JHN to Mrs. John Mozley (March 15, 1845), 595-98; 595.

79 *Ibid.,* 596.

80 *Ibid.,* 596-97.

Newman was depending almost solely on his trust in God. Except for his companions at Littlemore, few understood and accepted his disposition and trial. But Newman was not angry at his sister, and he entreated her, with other spiritual considerations, to trust in God's ways, which are beyond our human ways. He told Jemima that in October or November, at the latest, he would give up his Fellowship; since his earlier correspondence with Pusey, he had advanced the date by one month.

Newman and Jemima exchanged other letters clarifying their positions. Newman was perplexed that what was a rule for him was not a rule for others, "as if there were two truths"—which is not the case; but he told his sister that they must submit at that moment to a sort of mystery.[81] Jemima clarified that she was not judging her brother's actions. Besides these considerations, brother and sister considered what would be the least painful way to communicate the news to Aunt Elizabeth Newman.

Among the few Anglican friends who accepted Newman's convictions, besides Henry Wilberforce, were Maria Giberne and Mrs. Elizabeth Bowden. Mrs. Bowden did not argue with Newman. Instead she accepted his conscientious and thorough study of religious truth. She remained a close friend to him; their friendship was the continuation of Newman's friendship with John William Bowden, her husband. That year, on the date of the birthday of both her late husband and of Newman, she wrote to Newman, "I know that we must be in your thoughts this day, and I

---

81 *LD*, Vol. X, JHN to Mrs. John Mozley (March 22, 1845), 606-07; 606.

cannot help writing to you—not that I can say anything more than you know, but it is a pleasure to me—we always used to talk of you."[82]

Newman's correspondence with Mrs. Bowden increased. As he confided more in her, she understood his views about the Church of Rome better. She told him, "There is hardly any comfort in the prospect, but I trust I am right for the present in thinking I have to do nothing but wait."[83] She kept Newman informed about her family, and also asked him to help with the preface for a book entitled *Thoughts on the Work of the Six Days of Creation*, which her husband had been writing before his death. After Newman wrote the draft for the short preface about the life of his friend, Mrs. Bowden suggested that he make some minor changes and add something about the friendship of her husband with Newman: "I should be sorry to speak of his entering at Oxford without alluding to the beginning of your friend-ship—which was, as you well know he always thought it, the most important event in his life—would you mind say-ing something about it?"[84] Mrs. Bowden also asked New-man to place his initials to the preface.

The following month Mrs. Bowden told Newman that their mutual friend, Mrs. Charlotte Wood, widow of Sam-uel Francis Wood, a deceased lawyer and Tractarian, had made big strides toward Rome in little time. Mrs. Bowden

---

82 *LD,* Vol. X, Elizabeth Bowden to JHN (February 21, 1845), 569-70; 569.

83 *LD,* Vol. X, Elizabeth Bowden to JHN (March 31, 1845), 611-12; 611.

84 *LD,* Vol. X, Elizabeth Bowden to JHN (May 26, 1845), 671-72; 671.

added, "After all how can I think her wrong following you!"[85] Mrs. Wood eventually came into the Church, in 1845, following Newman's lead.

Newman told Maria Giberne that his convictions were as strong as they could be, although he could not tell if they were a call of reason or of conscience. He made a distinction between seeing something clearly and acting out of duty.[86] He also told her of his plan to give up the Oriel Fellowship in October and to publish a book between October and Christmas to explain his beliefs: "I wish people to know *why* I am acting as well as *what* I am doing . . ."[87] This would reduce people's surprise and strengthen those who wished to take the same step but needed reasons. He added by way of explanation, "And I think people have a claim on me, since I said one thing formerly, now frankly to say the other."[88]

During May, Maria Giberne made plans to speak personally with Newman, but due to other visits from Oakeley and the Bowdens, Newman was unable to see her. Newman was busy trying to write his final essay, but had many interruptions from visitors. Giberne grew quickly in the conviction that the Church of Rome was the true Church, and was unsure of receiving Holy Communion in the Anglican Church. Newman was surprised at the speed with which

---

85 *LD*, Vol. X, Elizabeth Bowden to JHN (June 26, 1845), 714-15; 715.

86 *LD*, X, JHN to Miss Maria Rosina Giberne (March 30, 1845), 609-10; 610.

87 *Ibid.*

88 *Ibid.*

she advanced toward joining the Church of Rome: "Your mind has come on so quickly, that I cannot trace its steps and do not quite know your position."[89] Newman told her that by an extraordinary grace Christ's Real Presence in the Holy Eucharist could be communicated to those in schism. At the same time, he advised that prior to a change it would be fitting to withdraw for some time from attending Holy Communion.[90]

A few weeks earlier Newman wrote to his friend, Richard William Church, who had vetoed the proposed censure of *Tract 90*. Newman thanked him for his kindness and courage at the February Convocation. Many years later, Newman dedicated the third uniform edition of *University Sermons* to Church, then Dean of St. Paul's Cathedral in London. He explained that he had not done this earlier because he felt that an association with any work of his at that point would have been a burden. Newman thanked Church for having given a welcome ear to his anxieties in February 1841 (after the publication of *Tract 90*), and wrote: "[M]uch less can I lose memory of your great act of friendship, as well as of justice and courage, in the February of 1845, your Proctor's year, when you, with another now departed, shielded me from the 'civium ardor prava jubentium,' ['frenzy of his fellow citizens.' Horace, *Odes*, Book III, line 2]" . . .[91]

---

89 *LD*, Vol. X, JHN to Miss Maria Rosina Giberne (May 25, 1845), 670.

90 *Ibid.*

91 John Henry Newman, *Oxford University Sermons,* 3rd Edition, Dedication, v-vi, available at: http://www.newmanreader.org/works/oxford/index.html#dedication.

Newman walked in a sort of spiritual darkness. He felt anxiety that he was acting based on some hidden sin or weakness that led him to wish to become Roman Catholic. In this spiritual state, he acknowledged the bittersweet praise of friends such as Rogers, James Mozley, and Blanco White. In his autobiography, White had praised Newman. Reflecting on White's praise, Newman humbly commented that White could not be speaking of "I, this old dry chip who am worthless, but of a past I. No one has spoken well of me."[92] The former was a confession of his inner thoughts, the latter was an overstatement, but he was referring to Whately, Hawkins, the Heads of Houses, Golightly, and a large number of men at Oxford. Newman confided to his friend Wilberforce that he felt in the dark. He quoted for him words from one of his own poems: "O! may we follow undismay'd / Where'er our God shall call!"[93] The words were reminiscent of his thoughts in the other poem, "Lead Kindly Light," composed in 1833 on the eve of the Oxford Movement's birth.

Later in the year, Newman told another friend, "In Mercy are the consequences of our actions concealed from us, that there may be room for faith, room for good deeds, room for boldness. We are all walking in the dark, and are led on in the dark."[94] Newman realized that it was not only he who could not see beyond the present moment. His friends and many of those who read his sermons were looking for their

---

92 *LD,* Vol. X, JHN to Henry Wilberforce (April 27, 1845), 639-42; 641.

93 *Ibid.,* 642. Words from the final stanza of "To F.W.N, A Birthday Offering" written on January 27, 1826, for Frank, his brother.

94 *LD,* Vol. X, JHN to Edward Coleridge (July 3, 1845), 723-24; 724.

way in the midst of the doctrinal confusion and spiritual mediocrity of the moment; they were looking for religious truths that they did not find in the Anglican Church.

The year 1845 would be Newman's final year as an Anglican. As he told his friend Pusey, he was not moving toward Rome because of external circumstances in the English Church, nor out of expectation of personal gain in the Roman Catholic Church. His reasons were arguments based on doctrinal principles and Church History.

Summarizing Newman's spiritual journey up to this point, one can say that various external events had served to confirm his view that the Church of England had separated from the Catholic Church and lacked its doctrinal integrity and the authority invested in St. Peter's successors. In 1841, the creation of a joint Anglican–Lutheran See in Jerusalem had demonstrated the doctrinal errors of the English Church. In 1845, the censure and degradation of William G. Ward at the February Oxford Convocation and the failed attempt to censure *Tract 90* had demonstrated the Protestant anti-dogmatic ideology of the university authorities. Bishop Blomfield's attack on Frederick Oakeley because of his orthodoxy had further confirmed Newman's view that the Church of England was not a branch of the true Church.

Newman began to prepare his family and friends for his inevitable separation from the Church of England and union with the Church of Rome. Many did not understand, but he patiently explained his reasons to them. During the year some friends and acquaintances also began to prepare to join the Church of Rome. Many of them sought Newman's advice. In the end, this joint movement, albeit the sum of individuals moving to the Church of Rome, was a confirmation of Newman's judgment. His move toward Rome would not be the result only of his "private judgment"; it would be the consensus of many men and women ultimately moved by God's Providence.

As much as Newman acted upon reasoned convictions, his planned move to the Church of Rome depended on a spiritual process which involved waiting on God. Newman felt "*solus cum solo*," alone with God. Newman felt that he was walking in the dark and awaiting some final confirmation by God that he was not deluding himself, as he had when as a young man he had accepted anti-Roman beliefs and sentiments. Newman prayed and suffered a great deal; except for some friends, he felt alone, and he felt responsible for many who had once placed their trust in him. But in the midst of his suffering, he was confident that God would show him the way.

CHAPTER 33

NEWMAN'S ESSAY ON DEVELOPMENT AND HIS FINAL CONVERSION

NEWMAN had resigned from St. Mary's in 1843, and during the second half of 1844, he ceased going to Oriel College. In 1845, he only went a few times and did not attend the Oriel election in March.[1] Newman was ready to resign his Fellowship at Oriel, but before doing so he wanted to finish the book that he had begun. In writing this book he wished to test his ideas against the measure of Church History and to articulate the reasons for his convictions. He later wrote: "As I advanced, my difficulties had so cleared away that I ceased to speak of 'the Roman Catholics,' and boldly called them Catholics."[2]

DEVELOPMENT OF CHRISTIAN DOCTRINE[3]

Although, when he finished his work on St. Athanasius in December 1844, he hoped to rest from writing, the idea of writing a new book weighed heavily upon him. He wrote to a friend:

---

1 *LD,* Vol. X, Diary entry and footnote (March 28, 1845), 608.

2 *Apo.,* 234.

3 John Henry Newman, *An Essay on the Development of Christian Doctrine,* 6th ed., University of Notre Dame Press, Notre Dame, 1989, from the Foreword by Ian Ker, xvii-xxvii.

And then I found all of a sudden this new work come before me, and I could not deny its claim on me. I have been thinking about some work or other since last March year [sic], and turning the subject in my mind at odd times—yet in spite of that, I have lost, if that is the word when it could not be helped, or rather consumed several months this Spring, in working upon it in ways which will not turn to any direct account.[4]

The previous year he had lost his good friend William Bowden and had suffered the anxiety of telling friends about his plan to become Roman Catholic. In the winter he had been ill with repeated bouts of influenza and had had many interruptions from the correspondence surrounding the February Convocation.[5]

By June 1845, Newman had worked for over four months on his new project and he had abundant material, but he needed to finish working out the principle of development—the subject upon which the book rested. He worked six to seven hours a day and finished three chapters out of a projected five. He rewrote every part but was still not satisfied with the results, or the progress. Newman did not want people to know that he was writing, but in June, an Oxford paper rumored that he was composing a manifesto before leaving the Anglican Church.[6]

---

4 *LD,* Vol. X, JHN to Mrs. William Froude (June 1, 1845), 686-87; 686.

5 *LD,* Vol. X, JHN to Mrs. William Froude (June 10, 1845), 695-97; 696.

6 *LD,* Vol. X, John Dobree Dalgairns to JHN (June 24, 1845), 713.

Newman had been jotting notes for his book in his diary during 1844, and even earlier. He also kept a little notebook with thoughts for his new book. The notion that Christian doctrine develops through the centuries was one dealt with by authors as early as the Scholastic period. Newman had referred to the notion of development in his early writings. He wrote in one of the *Tracts for the Times* that the "articles of faith" which secure the Church's purity from successive heresies and errors were all hidden in the Church's bosom from the start and brought into form according to the occasion.[7] In 1836, Newman answered the objection that the Church of Rome had departed from Primitive Christianity, for development of Gospel truths was also found in Anglicanism since the Anglican system itself is not found complete in the first Christian century.[8]

As a Tractarian, Newman claimed that the Anglican Church held the "note" of Apostolicity, or that it only taught the doctrines of the Church at the time of the Apostles. He held that the Roman Catholic Church held the "note" of catholicity or universality, which the Anglican did not. Newman, like others, initially thought that the Roman Catholics had added dogmas (such as Transubstantiation), practices (such as devotion to Mary and prayers to the saints), and the belief in Purgatory. Study of different fourth- to fifth-century heresies, however, led Newman to think that Rome, not Canterbury, had the "note" of Apostolicity, along with that of catholicity. Gradually, Newman began to consider that the doctrines and practices which

---

7 *Tracts N. 28, The Via Media,* Vol. 1, 40.
8 *Apo.,* 111.

he once believed were additions were actually authentic developments from Primitive Christianity.

Newman studied the notion of development and its implication for an understanding of Revelation more than any earlier persons had done before him. In one of his most original sermons from the *University Sermons,* Newman indicated that developments were not simply explanations of doctrines already formulated but new doctrines that arose from the original dogmas.[9]

During the year 1845, Newman refined the idea of development in doctrine and Church practices and tested the idea against the history of Christianity. In the first edition, published in December of the same year, he spoke of "tests" to examine whether a doctrine is a true development or a corruption of Primitive Christianity. He explained to Pusey that "One age corrects the expressions and statements of even the Saints of the foregoing." Unless the theory of development were accepted, general skepticism would follow. Since saints and theologians had contradicted each other, people might conclude that religious truth is arbitrary. At the same time, Newman reasoned that if development were correct, there would be no reason to stop with the English Church. He wrote: "I cannot hold precisely what the English holds and nothing more. I must go forward or backward—*else* I sink into a deep skepticism, a heartless acedia, into which too many in Oxford, I fear, are sinking."[10]

---

9 John Henry Newman, *An Essay on the Development of Christian Doctrine,* 6th ed, University of Notre Dame Press, Notre Dame, 1989, from the Foreword by Ian Ker, xix.

10 *LD,* Vol. X, JHN to Edward Bouverie Pusey (March 14, 1845), 591-94; 593.

Newman wrote to a friend: "I cannot make out why I am to believe just what the English Church allows me to believe and nothing more. The early ages of the Church seem to me to have taught either more or less—less if we ask for a very rigid proof of what they held, more if we are content with rough and general proofs—but in no case as we teach in England."[11]

He perceived that the teaching of the Church grows as a child grows to become a man. To live is to grow, to develop; "In a higher world it is otherwise, but here below to live is to change, and to be perfect is to have changed often."[12] Doctrines are ideas that are alive and have the power to influence people. These ideas are developed by communities of men and their leaders in a complex interplay with other people and their ideas. An idea "grows when it incorporates, and its identity is found, not in isolation, but in continuity and sovereignty. This it is that imparts to the history both of states and of religions, its special turbulent and polemical character. Such is the explanation of the wranglings, whether of schools or of parliaments."[13]

In his book, Newman pointed out that the philosopher Joseph De Maistre and theologian Johannes Mohler had written about the increase and expansion of the Christian Creed and ritual over 1800 years. He agreed with them that from the nature of the human mind, time is necessary for the full comprehension and perfection of great ideas; and

---

11 *LD,* Vol. X, JHN to Charles Crawley (July 14, 1845), 750.

12 John Henry Newman, *An Essay on the Development of Christian Doctrine,* 6th ed., University of Notre Dame Press, Notre Dame, 1989, 40. After this it will be cited *Dev.*

13 *Dev.,* 39.

that the highest and most wonderful truths, though communicated to the world once for all by inspired teachers, could not be comprehended all at once by the recipients, but, as being received and transmitted by minds not inspired and through media which were human, have required only the longer time and deeper thought for their full elucidation.[14]

Newman called this "the theory of Development of Doctrine," a theory to explain the "necessary and anxious problem" posed by the 300 years of the Protestant Reformation.

As a historian of Church doctrines Newman articulated what he perceived to be seven "tests" or "notes" to distinguish true development in the history of Christianity from corruption. These notes verify the unity and identity of an idea, or doctrine, through all the stages of its development. Newman explained:

> To guarantee its own substantial unity, it must be seen to be one in type, one in its systems of principles, one in its unitive power toward externals, one in its logical consecutiveness, one in the witness of its early phases to its later, one in the protection which its later extend to its earlier, and one it its vigour with continuance, that is, in its tenacity.[15]

The first "note" Newman studied, preservation of type or identity, was the view people had of Christianity in the first five centuries. He indicated how in each of these centuries, the Church was a religious community, claiming a divine commission and holding its surrounding bodies to be heretical. The Church was a well-organized and disciplined

---

14 *Dev.,* 30.
15 *Dev.,* 206.

body, spread throughout the world. It was considered a natural enemy to governments, an intolerant force, and a society that breaks laws and divides families. It was accused of being superstitious and responsible for foul crimes. It was likened to many sects. Throughout these five centuries, the Church maintained the same identity in the eyes of external observers.[16] The pagan writers Tacitus, Seutonius, and Pliny associated Christianity with the Oriental superstitions that were extending throughout the empire.[17] These heathen rites had some external similarity with Christianity. Later on Celsus and Porphyry confused Christianity with Gnosticism.[18]

These Roman philosophers and authors considered Christianity and many Oriental sects a threat to the cohesion of the Empire; they frowned on its ascetical discipline, initiation rites, concern for proselytism and what they mistakenly thought was a somber view of life and sins. Christianity was seen as "a religion which men hate as proselytizing, anti-social, revolutionary, as dividing families, separating chief friends, corrupting the maxims of government, making a mock at law, dissolving the empire, the enemy of human nature, and a 'conspirator against its rights and privileges . . .' "[19]

This was the identity of Christianity throughout its first centuries, which had continued into the nineteenth century. The Roman Catholic Church, which claims continuity with early Christianity, was characterized in modern times in the

---

16 *Dev.,* 208, 246.
17 *Dev.,* 211.
18 *Dev.,* 223.
19 *Dev.,* 247.

same way as it had been characterized in the first centuries. In the fourth century, when Christianity became the imperial religion, it kept its identity, but it was no longer compared with the Oriental sects; rather, it was compared to the Manichean religion and many Christian sects such as the Arians, Donatists, and Apollinarians. Externally, there were some similarities between the Church and these Christian sects, but the Church professed Apostolic Succession and obedience to the Bishop of Rome. The Church was known for a zealous adherence to its own creed and an intolerant view of what it considered error. Newman explained, "In one point alone the heresies seem universally to have agreed,—in hatred to the Church."[20] She was called a seducer, harlot, apostate, Antichrist and devil by heretics. Its opponents continually subdivided into many other sects while it remained one. "The Church is everywhere, but it is one; sects are everywhere, but they are many, independent and discordant."[21] A few heresies became widespread, yet they were only the same in name, for in no two places were they the same in their beliefs and practices, and unlike the Church Fathers none claimed the name "Catholic" for itself.

Newman illustrated the preservation of type or identity between the Catholic Church in modern times and the Church of the fifth and sixth centuries of Christianity. When Arianism spread among the Vandals in Africa, the Visigoths in France and Spain, the Ostrogoths in Italy, and the Suevi in Portugal, Arians robbed the Catholics of their

---

20 *Dev.,* 253.
21 *Dev.,* 251.

churches and the treasures of their shrines, yet they never claimed the title "Catholic," and they called Catholics by the name "Romans."[22] Newman saw the parallel between the Catholic Church of early Christianity and that of modern times. The English Church, like Arianism, was a heretical body in the state of schism under the patronage of the monarchy.

In the fifth and sixth centuries the test of catholicity did not suffice to refute heresy. The Arian and Nestorian heresies, based on the literal interpretation of Scripture, led to serious errors about the Divinity of Christ and Mary's role as Mother of God. When the Monophysite heresy arose the Imperial Court supported Eutyches, the originator of the error, and the emperor convoked a general council of the Church's bishops to decide the doctrinal question. After a violent council, which ended with the murder of the patriarch of Constantinople, the Monophysites had their way for a short time until Pope St. Leo, Bishop of Rome, set matters straight. St. Peter Chrysologus urged Eutyches, "submit yourself in everything of what has been written by the blessed Pope of Rome; for St. Peter, who lives and presides in his own See, gives the true faith to those who seek it."[23] Leo convoked the Council of Chalcedon which met on October 8, 451 and was attended by the largest number of bishops of any Council before. At Chalcedon, the doctrine of Christ's dual nature and the power of the Bishop of Rome, based on the succession from St. Peter, was reaffirmed by the bishops. Newman commented that despite

---

22 *Dev.,* 279.
23 *Dev.,* 307.

the errors of bishops within the Church, frequent heresies, the occupation of its churches and oppressions of its people, "there is but one Voice for whose decisions the people wait with trust, one Name and one See to which they look with hope, and that name Peter, and that See Rome . . ."[24]

Examining the record of history, Newman had proven to his satisfaction the identity of the modern Roman Catholic Church with Christianity of the first six centuries. The developments in those centuries, like the role of papal power, catholicity as a test of authentic Christianity, the practice of correcting heresies with excommunication (the exclusion from ecclesial communion), and reliance on Church Fathers for the interpretation of Scriptures, were still maintained in the nineteenth century. The same false accusations and the claim that the Church of Rome was the Antichrist, as well as persecution by governments, were also maintained by its opponents in the nineteenth century.

In his *Essay on Development,* Newman examined from a historical point of view a whole series of other subjects, such as Purgatory, the practice of sacramental Confession, Indulgences, Prayer for the Dead, Prayer to the Saints, Devotion to the Mother of God, and the Mass. He dedicated the majority, though, to establishing the identity of the modern Roman Church with the ancient one. In 1845, one of the principal thoughts on his mind was that the Church of England was heretical; it had fallen into schism as had so many other bodies in early Christianity. Newman wished to live and die in the Church founded by Christ upon the Apostles.

---

24 *Dev.,* 322.

The rest of Newman's essay dealt with other important elements, even though he did not elaborate on them as much. To explain the second note of true development, or continuity of principles, Newman enumerated nine principles that he derived from the Incarnation, the central truth of Christianity: dogma as definitive and necessary, the supremacy of faith, the principle of theology, the sacramental principle (God's revelation of Himself through the material and visible as in the Incarnation), the mystical sense of Scripture, the principle of grace whereby God makes us like Himself, asceticism, the evil of sin, and the sanctification of matter. Each of these principles had been vigorously maintained in the Church at all times.[25] Later Newman considered that the theory of development was itself another principle. This principle gave character to the whole course of Christian thought. "It was discernible from the first years of Catholic teaching up to the present day, and gave to the teaching a unity and individuality."[26] Newman explained that principles give rise to doctrines and illustrated how the principles of the early Church were the same as those of the later Church, so that even though there were variations in belief, the similarity was greater than the difference.[27]

On the other hand, Newman noted that heretics violated these principles. The Arians and Nestorians denied the allegorical rule of interpreting Scripture; the Gnostics substituted knowledge for faith, and most violated the

25 *Dev.*, 326.
26 *Apo.*, 198.
27 *Dev.*, 353.

dogmatic and sacramental principles.[28] Newman asserted that in modern times Protestantism likewise had reversed the principles of Catholic theology, such as the dogmatic principle, the mystical interpretation of Scripture, and the sacramental principle.

In the *Essay on Development,* Newman hardly referred to the Holy Mass, but in March, as he began to write the *Essay,* he told Pusey that Our Lord could grant His grace through the sacramental rites of the English Church.[29] Newman thought that even though a Church was schismatic, Christ made Himself present on its altars if it had Apostolic Succession and the true form of Consecration. Newman told Maria Giberne that prior to St. Augustine, who expounded a theory on sacraments administered to heretics, there had been a controversy over the validity of Baptism performed by heretical clergy.[30] St. Cyprian had argued that those baptisms were invalid. St. Stephen, Pope at the time of St. Cyprian, instead had taught that those baptisms were valid and should not be repeated if they were properly administered. The teaching of the Pope once again had prevailed.

St. Augustine had taught that for a sacrament to be valid the minister must be validly ordained and the matter and form of the sacraments must be correct. Each sacrament requires a given element (matter) and precise words (form). This teaching applied not only to Baptism, but also to the

---

28 *Dev.,* 354.

29 *LD,* Vol. X, JHN to Edward Bouverie Pusey (March 14, 1845), 591-94; 593.

30 *LD,* Vol. X, JHN to Miss Maria Rosina Giberne (June 1, 1845), 682-84.

other sacraments. With regard to the Mass, if a minister was rightly ordained, the Holy Eucharist contains the Real Presence of Christ. Schism produces an obstacle or obex for grace to flow to the recipient. In the case of infant Baptism, for instance, the obex of being part of a heretical body was removed when the children conformed to the Church, or when they received the sacrament of Confirmation. Newman believed that in the case of the Eucharist, the obex is solved by love. If someone is within a schismatic Church due to invincible ignorance and that person adores Christ, the grace of the Eucharist flows into that person's soul.[31]

As an Anglican, Newman grew in his appreciation and love for the Holy Eucharist. In 1837, he had begun to celebrate a weekly Communion Service. In 1838, Newman spoke about the sacrificial character of the Mass as verified in the ancient prayers of the liturgy. He reasoned that a priest and a sacrifice called for an altar, more than a table. But Newman soon came to appreciate the complete rite of the Mass and its beauty even more. In 1846, Newman wrote his novel, *Loss and Gain*, a fictional account based on his conversion. The novel had as one of its poignant scenes the first time the protagonist enters a Roman Catholic Church during the Sacrifice of the Mass. The convert in the novel conveyed his awe:

> I declare . . . to me nothing is so consoling, so piercing, so thrilling, so overcoming as the Mass, said as it is among us. I could attend Mass forever and not be tired. It is not a mere form of words—it is a great action, the greatest action that can be on earth. It is, not the invocation merely, but, if I dare use the word, the evocation of the Eternal. He becomes present

31 *Ibid.*, 683.

on the altar in flesh and blood, before whom angels bow and devils tremble. This is that awful event which is the scope, and is the interpretation, of every part of the solemnity.[32]

Newman was not the only one concerned about the validity of the Anglican sacraments. Miss Jane Parker, a friend of T. W. Allies who wished to become Roman Catholic, also asked Newman about the validity of the Eucharist in the Anglican Church. Though Newman thought that the Anglican Church was in schism, he believed that by an extraordinary mercy, the grace of the sacraments could be transmitted to the recipients of the holy elements. Newman also believed in the validity of sacramental Confession in the Anglican Church. In the spring of 1844, when Allies visited Newman for sacramental Confession, he left a record of the visit: "As I walked over I could not think how great was the privilege to be near and to have means of intercourse with the greatest man the English Church in her separated state has ever produced, and a *saint*."[33]

One of the last questions that Newman had trouble understanding before becoming Roman Catholic was the Church's belief and veneration of the Virgin Mary. A gradual development in Newman's devotion to the Virgin can be divided into four periods.[34] During a first period, until 1834, the central role of Mary in the mystery of the Incarnation led Newman to doctrinal veneration of the

---

32 John Henry Newman, *Loss and Gain,* 327, available at: http://www. newmanreader.org/works/gain/index.html After this it will be cited *LG.*

33 Mary H. Allies, *Thomas William Allies,* London 1907, 46-47.

34 John Henry Newman, *Mary, The Virgin Mary in the Life and Writings of John Henry Newman,* ed. Philip Boyce, Grand Rapids 2001, 27-32.

Virgin Mother. In a second period, until 1837, he accepted
the difference between intercession and invocation of Mary
and the saints. This was a distinction tacitly recognized by
the *Articles*; intercession was allowed, whereas invocation
was condemned. At first Newman thought that invocation
of the saints was not practiced in early Christianity. He
thought that it obscured the unique mediation of Christ and
that it could lead to idolatry. When he and his companions
at Littlemore prayed the Divine Office they refrained from
praying *ora pro nobis* (pray for us) and instead prayed *oret
pro nobis* (may she intercede for us), and they omitted the
ancient hymn *Salve Regina*. Out of obedience to the Anglican Church, Newman followed Anglican practice until his
reception into the Roman Church. In a third period, from
1837 to 1839, he condemned as unscriptural her external
veneration by modern Catholics, yet his own veneration for
her continued to grow. In a last period, from 1839 to 1845,
as Newman's understanding of true doctrinal development
and practices grew, he finally understood and accepted
modern Catholic veneration of the Virgin Mary.

Some of the last pages of the *Essay on Development* were
dedicated to the development of Christian belief and devotion to saints (to the Blessed Virgin Mary in particular). By
studying the ante-Nicene Fathers, St. Justin, St. Irenaeus,
and Tertullian, Newman came to realize that already in the
second and third centuries, the Fathers spoke of the Blessed
Virgin Mary as the New Eve, and gave her a singular type
of honor as the Mother of the New Adam.[35] As an illustration of the sixth note of true development, the conservative

---

35 *Dev.*, 416-18.

action of development on earlier doctrine, Newman asserted that devotion to the Mother of God provides protection and confirmation about the Divinity of her Son.[36]

Devotion to the Mother of God was no longer an obstacle for Newman. In the *Apologia* he later wrote:

> The idea of the Blessed Virgin was as it were magnified in the Church of Rome as time went on,—but so were all the Christian ideas; as that of the Blessed Eucharist. The whole scene of pale, faint, distant Apostolic Christianity is seen in Rome, as through a telescope or magnifier. The harmony of the whole, however, is of course what it was. It is unfair then to take one Roman idea, that of the Blessed Virgin, out of what may be called its context.[37]

By mid-1845 Newman no longer had any intellectual doubts about Roman Catholic doctrine, yet while he labored over the *Essay on Development,* his family and friends continued to give him unsolicited suggestions and advice against his intended step.

FAMILY AND FRIENDS

Newman's family, except for Jemima, was not able to understand his reasons for reception into the Catholic Church. Newman remained in contact with Jemima and, on a lesser scale, with Harriet. He had very little contact with Charles, who early in the year wrote from Germany asking for money after having been in a debtors' prison. Early in 1845, Charles wrote Frank from Bonn: "I believe almost

---

36 *Dev.,* 425-36.
37 *Apo.,* 196-97.

the whole family is in a false position from not finding proper society; only, I am more aware of this than others; and I am less mad, because I admit I am mad. My madness takes a different turn from yours and John's."[38] On the assumption that John Henry's income would decrease significantly upon becoming Roman Catholic, Frank offered to take wholly upon himself the care for their Aunt Elizabeth and for Charles. Frank also offered John Henry to come to visit, or stay at his home for as long he needed, or wished.[39] It was a generous offer although not without a tinge of condescension and a show of disregard for Roman Catholicism.

False reports and rumors about Newman continued throughout the year. His friend Albany J. Christie reported to him that some people were calling him (Newman) a skeptic. Newman wrote to Christie to refute the calumny and to explain that he had never felt the temptation to skepticism.[40] Newman anticipated that some, if not many, would take the step toward Rome with him, but he thought the Church of England would be seriously affected when the Protestant party succeeded in throwing out its antagonists, the Tractarians: "I suppose there will be a dreadful move toward liberalism."[41] According to Newman the Bishops of Exeter and London were enforcing stricter rubrics as

---

38 *LD,* Vol. X, Charles Robert Newman to JHN (May 7, 1845), 647.

39 *LD,* Vol. X, Francis William Newman to JHN(May 1, 1845), 644.

40 *LD,* Vol. X, JHN to Albany James Christie (April 8, 1845), 619.

41 *LD,* Vol. X, JHN to Simeon Lloyd Pope (March 20, 1845), 603-04; 604.

long as they could cast aside Catholic doctrines and principles. They allowed for the use of a surplice by the priest, but they did not acknowledge that an altar implies that the Mass is a sacrifice.[42]

Defending himself from false rumors did not diminish Newman's charity toward his friends and neighbors. Newman did more than theorize about theology and history; he genuinely lived by the spirit of the Gospel. The practice of charity characterized his relations with others. In 1845, his diary and correspondence indicate that he followed with charitable interest the lives of some youths whom he knew. Henry William Weltch, a nephew of Ambrose St. John, was a young lad whom Newman had tutored in Euclid and Greek at Littlemore since 1843. In January 1845, Newman arranged for the young man to study at St. Mark's College, the National Society's Training Institution for Schoolmasters.[43] Newman took a great deal of interest in the lad's progress in London, and Henry William was in turn grateful to Newman and kept him abreast of his progress.[44] Another youth who was the object of Newman's concern and affection was his godson, Octavius Ogle. When he became a young man, Newman wrote to him and sent him one of his books.[45] During 1845, Newman also followed with concern the health of Marianne, one of Bowden's daughters, then confined to bed for months due to an ailment of her hip.

---

42 *Ibid.,* 604.
43 *LD,* Vol. X, JHN to Derwent Coleridge (January 8, 1845), 486.
44 *LD,* Vol. X, Henry William Weltch to JHN (March 17, 1845), 599.
45 *LD,* Vol. X, JHN to Octavius Ogle (April 22, 1845), 624.

In his conversations and letters there was no bitterness toward his Anglican brothers or animosity toward the bishops. Although he was frank and privately criticized what he thought mistaken, Newman practiced charity in dealings with others, with the occasional intemperate response to an annoying correspondent as the exception. Newman's charity was evident in his understanding for those who had not, like him, received the spiritual and intellectual grace to believe the Church of Rome to be the true Church.

Not all, however, was false rumors regarding his conversion and other contradictions; Newman had good friends who valued him greatly and spared no expense to show their love for him. In the early nineteenth century, when only wealthy or important persons had their portraits made, Wilberforce, recognizing the importance of his good friend, commissioned two portraits of him. In May, Newman went to London and sat on three different days for a portrait by Sir W. Ross, a miniature painter. In July, he visited Mrs. Bowden and Mrs. Wood in London and sat for Sir Ross again. During the same visit to London he sat for a portrait by George Richmond, also commissioned by Henry Wilberforce.

On his return to Littlemore, Newman heard of the death of Miss Lenthall. For over a year Newman had paid weekly visits to Miss Lenthall, a parishioner of St. Mary's in Oxford, who was ill. Newman read prayers with her and took her Holy Communion. When she died on July 21, 1845, Newman told Pusey about the news: "I have just heard it—it has affected me much—she is my last link with St. Mary's."[46]

---

46 *LD,* Vol. X, JHN to Edward Bouverie Pusey (July 22, 1845), 736-37; 737.

MORE REACTIONS FROM FRIENDS
AND WELL-WISHERS

As the year 1845 advanced, Newman's friends began to accept the inevitable end of his spiritual journey, albeit with varying reactions. Pusey, who had tried to deny the reality of Newman's step, began to accept it and to put on a good face. Newman wrote a friend about Pusey, "[H]e is trying to smooth it over—as if it involved no great separation."[47] But for Pusey and Keble, who knew and loved Newman so well, the loss would be great. Both had prayed that their friend would not leave the Anglican Communion, but were finally accepting of what would happen in some months' time.

On June 17, Gladstone met with Judge Coleridge, Robert Wilberforce, and Manning to discuss Newman's intended step. They wished Newman to be received into the Catholic Church outside of England, and wrote to Pusey and Keble to convince Newman to do so.[48] Newman mused, "Can it be for any reason except to hide my thinking the English Church in Schism?"[49] Newman thought going abroad to be received would misrepresent him in such a solemn act. When he pressed for the reason, he found out that their plan was for him to leave England for good. Surprised,

---

47 *LD*, Vol. X, JHN to Elizabeth Bowden (June 25, 1845), 713-14; 714.

48 *The Gladstone Diaries, III, 1840-1847,* ed. M.R.D. Foot and H.C.G. Matthew, Oxford, 1974, 461.

49 *LD*, Vol. X, JHN to John Dobree Dalgairns (June 29, 1845), 720-21; 720.

he wrote, "I could hardly help saying how cool."[50] Newman told Mrs. Bowden about this and argued that if the
Church of England were not the lawful authority, why
should he go abroad?[51] He would no longer be accountable to the Anglican Church.

The efforts of those trying to dissuade Newman from
becoming Roman Catholic multiplied. He was often
amused by what people wrote to him in letters, but at
times, he expressed annoyance. One letter occasioned an
entertaining reaction on Newman's part. John William
Burgon, a graduate from Worcester College and win-
ner of the Newdigate prize for the best composition in
English verse, wrote Newman a very long letter exhort-
ing him to remain in the Anglican Communion. Newman
remarked, "Mr. Burgon has sent me a sermon, very well
meant. It should have been in verse. You know he has got
the Newdigate."[52] Burgon, who also went to Littlemore to
"preach" to Newman, told him that by becoming Roman
Catholic, he would undo all that he had done through his
writing.

One whose efforts met a less gracious, but humorous,
response was Tresham Dames Gregg, an Anglican clergy
man in Ireland, who tried to scare Newman with the degrad-
ing character of popery in Ireland. Gregg had sent Newman
a borrowed copy of a book by Joseph Meade, who regarded

---

50 *Ibid.,* 720.

51 *LD,* Vol. X, JHN to Elizabeth Bowden (June 25, 1845), 713-14;
714.

52 *LD,* Vol. X, JHN to John Dobree Dalgairns (June 29, 1845), 720-21;
721.

the Pope to be the Antichrist. Newman replied that since he had not asked for the book and had enough books to read himself, and since Meade wished the book back, he would lose no time in returning it.[53]

Newman had various strangers writing or calling on him to advise him against leaving the Anglican Church. One of these strangers who went to Littlemore even resorted to indecency, claiming that on account of madness in his family, Newman should not leave the Church of England.[54] Another stranger wrote Newman that people err by mistaking what their duty is, and exhorted him not to travel faster than God would ordain.[55] Newman sent a terse reply to the author of the letter telling him to treat others with reverence, and not to advise others without good knowledge of them.[56] The gentleman sent an apology to Newman, who then in turn replied kindly.[57]

Richard Westamacott, a classmate of Newman's from childhood days at the Ealing School, also tried to dissuade Newman from his plans. In this case, Newman thanked his friend and explained to him the reasons for his plans to join the Roman Catholic Church.[58] Westamacott replied, "We shall have to avoid one subject—but I cannot forget you

---

53 *LD*, Vol. X, JHN to Tresham Dames Gregg (July 17, 1845), 733.

54 *LD*, Vol. X, William Brudenell Barter to JHN (June 2, 1845), 6 88.

55 *LD*, Vol. X, Henry Anthony Jeffreys to JHN (June 5, 1845), 692.

56 *LD*, Vol. X, JHN to H. A. Jeffreys (June 8, 1845), 695.

57 *LD*, Vol. X, H. A. Jeffreys to JHN (June 9, 1845), 695; JHN to H. A. Jeffreys (June 12, 1845), 703-04.

58 *LD*, Vol. X, JHN to Richard Westamacott (July 11, 1845), 729-30.

are an old schoolfellow, and have been my good friend for many a long year—and so let us go on through life thinking kindly of, and wishing well to each other."[59]

NEWMAN'S LAST MONTHS AS AN ANGLICAN

After all those attempts to dissuade Newman, the Anglican clergyman made his last farewells. At the start of August, Newman thanked his sister, Jemima, for speaking with their Aunt Elizabeth about his impending step.[60] Newman had a close tie with his aunt and was sorry to cause her pain. Later in the month, he told Jemima that the appearance of his book would be a signal of "his going."[61] Writing the *Essay* was taking a toll on Newman, and upon the news of the death of Edward Elmes, a clergyman who had once been a master at the school in Ealing, Newman told his sister that he felt old. He confided that the book that he was writing was "a work of labour and pain" to him.[62] He had rewritten the last chapter a few times and was still dissatisfied with it. Newman closed the letter to Jemima with the wish: "May I never lose your esteem and approbation, as I think I never shall lose your love!"[63] He never lost her love, but once he became Roman Catholic their correspondence lost its intimacy; she

---

59 *LD,* Vol. X, Richard Westamacott to JHN (July 16, 1845), 732.

60 *LD,* Vol. X, JHN to Mrs. John Mozley (August 6, 1845), 743-44.

61 *LD,* Vol. X, JHN to Mrs. John Mozley (August 17, 1845), 748-49; 748.

62 *Ibid.,* 748.

63 *Ibid.,* 749.

shut out of her life everything connected with Newman's new life.[64]

Later in the month, he wrote Maria Giberne that the sign of his going over would be the resignation of the Fellowship at Oriel, probably in October, but he did not think he would finish the book by then.[65] In any case, he thought his change would be soon, whether before or after the publication of his book. He had tried to tell only his close friends about the book he had written and instructed the publisher not to let the printer know the name of the author until the release of the book. Newman sought some peace and quiet from intruders. Understandably, he shunned being the object of curiosity and idle public scrutiny in the newspapers.

In August, Frank wrote John Henry again, but this time to make the ridiculous suggestion that he form an Anglo-Episcopal Free Church with a succession of bishops derived from New York or Scotland. This church would later be a means to union with Rome.[66] John Henry replied that he thought the Roman Church to be the only true religion and the English Church to be in schism.[67] He was not going to Rome because he thought that particular religion more bearable, or because of some other personal fancy.

---

64 Trevor, *Newman, The Pillar of the Cloud*, 351.

65 *LD,* Vol. X, JHN to Miss Maria Rosina Giberne (August 24, 1845), 751-52; 752.

66 *LD,* Vol. X, Francis William Newman to JHN (August 6, 1845), 744-45.

67 *LD,* Vol. X, JHN to Francis William Newman (August 7, 1845), 745.

Newman added that except for involuntary ignorance, there is no salvation outside the Church of Rome.[68] Newman jotted down a comment on his brother's letter to him: "That I could be contemplating questions of Truth and Falsehood never entered into his imagination!"[69] For Newman the change of religion was a matter of religious truth of the utmost importance, not a strategy in religious affairs.

On August 9, Dr. Wiseman, Catholic Bishop for the Central District of England, visited Newman at Littlemore, but the subject of their conversation was never made public. Some months earlier, Wiseman had written to Newman, who had replied with greater warmth than he had any time earlier.[70] Newman explained that his "cold and formal" tone in previous correspondence had been due to the position he had as an Anglican clergyman. Newman had felt that to act otherwise was to betray a sacred obligation and obedience to his own bishop; however, Newman wished to apologize and express his esteem for Wiseman.

Wiseman had expected Newman to be received into the Church in February 1845, but when the month passed by, he had grown impatient. Some from old Catholic families maliciously suggested that Newman would not convert.[71] Wiseman did not wish to embarrass Newman by a personal visit, so he sent Bernard Smith to visit him at Littlemore. Newman invited Smith to dinner, and at the time for the

---

68 *Ibid.*

69 *LD,* Vol. X, Francis William Newman to JHN (August 6, 1845), 744-45, 745.

70 *LD,* Vol. X, JHN to Nicholas Wiseman (April 16, 1845), 626-27.

71 Wilfrid Ward, *The Life and Times of Cardinal Wiseman,* Vol. I, Longmans, Green, and Co., London, 1897, 424.

meal, Newman appeared dressed as a layman. Smith knew that this was Newman's avowal to him and to Wiseman of the impending move. Smith reported it to Wiseman, who failed to see the meaning of the sign.[72] Even so, Dr. Wiseman would soon have the long-awaited joy of Newman's reception into the Catholic Church. As a Roman Catholic, Newman would fall under Wiseman's jurisdiction.

In August, Newman met in Oxford with Lady Georgiana Fullerton, whose husband had been received into the Roman Church in 1843.[73] Lady Georgiana, who was a novelist, biographer, and poet, would follow her husband into the Church in March 1846. Also in August, Newman corresponded with a woman whose identity was kept anonymous, and who also sought his advice. Newman no longer abstained from giving advice in favor of the Roman Catholic Church. The anonymous woman had been presented with some historical arguments against the orthodoxy of Pope Honorius I.[74] Newman told his correspondent that she was not prepared to judge the historicity of the arguments. He explained, "No truth, no conclusion about what is true, is without its difficulties. You must give up faith, if you will not believe till all objections are first solved."[75] Instead of examining questions beyond her competence she should take the general view of Catholicism and Anglicanism

---

72 *Ibid.,* 428.

73 *LD,* Vol. X, Diary entry (August 16, 1845), 747.

74 This seventh-century pope advocated Monothelism, the doctrine that Christ has only one will, the divine will, a heresy, which was condemned after his death by the Third Council of Constantinople.

75 *LD,* Vol. X, JHN to An unknown Correspondent (August 1845), 750.

and consider which answers better to the idea of a Divine Messenger, and which has always spoken to the whole world with authority.

On August 24, Newman attended the Sunday Communion Service at the church in Littlemore, but did not receive the Sacrament. He was taking yet another step before his final move. The next day, Fr. Randal Lythgoe, the Provincial of the English Province of the Jesuit Fathers, stopped to visit Newman. The diary entry for that day reads: "Mr. Lythgoe called—I did not see him."[76] Even though he was about to make his move, he wished to do it as quietly as possible. He had met Wiseman, whom he had known for a long time, but it was not the same with Fr. Lythgoe, to whom Newman wrote to apologize that "his circumstances should have prevented" their meeting.[77]

At the start of September, William George Ward and his wife wrote to Newman, informing him that they would be received into the Roman Catholic Church at the Jesuit Chapel in Bolton Street, London. William G. Ward had been almost literally pushed out of the Anglican Church when he was censured by Oxford University and deprived of his degree. Despite this injustice, which also deprived him of an ecclesiastical license, his joining the Roman Catholic Church was labeled a secession from the Anglican Church. Mrs. Ward told Newman of the great peace and joy that both she and her husband had experienced that very day

76 *LD,* Vol. X, Diary entry (August 25, 1845), 752.

77 *LD,* Vol. X, JHN to Revd. Mr. Randal Lythgoe, S.J. (August 25, 1845), 752.

in joining the Catholic Church. She wished to thank Newman for the valuable help that he had given to her through
his writings and advice.[78] After teaching theology at St.
Edmund's College in Hertfordshire, he later became editor
of the *Dublin Review,* an influential Catholic journal.

In September, Simeon Lloyd Pope, one of Newman's
contemporaries at Oxford, wrote, asking Newman to dis-
avow the rumors that he had heard about his intentions.
Newman replied to his friend that no one had a right to
be surprised. Two years earlier, he had resigned from St.
Mary's (September 18, 1843), and almost a year earlier he
had made public his intentions through some friends. Newman repeated to Pope what he had written to Frank: "I am
convinced that (*to those who are enlightened see it*) the
Church of Rome is the only place of salvation. I do not
think I can remain outside of it, and yet remain in God's
favor."[79] Newman considered that he had spent seven years
in probation. During that time he had fulfilled his duty as an
Anglican clergyman to teach Anglican doctrines and support the Church of England. His love for the truth and his
conscience did not allow him to continue in the same situation any longer.

For Newman, reception into the Catholic Church had
become a matter of duty. He was impelled by his conscience to remain no longer an Anglican. Newman had
moved from reasoned arguments in favor of the Roman
Catholic Church to a serious sense of duty to act according

---

78 *LD,* Vol. X, Mrs. William George Ward to JHN (September 5, 1845),
757.

79 *LD,* Vol. X, JHN to Simeon Lloyd Pope (September 18, 1845), 762-
63; 763.

to his convictions. He believed that given his knowledge of Revelation and religious truths, he endangered his eternal salvation by not fully embracing these truths. He was, however, cognizant that this step was not an obligation for others without sufficient knowledge of the truth and the necessary divine grace.

Reception into the Catholic Church of a baptized person consisted, as it does today, in a profession of faith, sacramental Confession with absolution of sins, and the reception of two other sacraments: First Communion and Confirmation.[80] Reports of Anglicans from the upper social classes and clergy who were becoming Roman Catholics began to increase. *The Tablet*, a Catholic periodical, reported on September 20 that Mr. and Mrs. Ward were received into the Church.[81] Bishop Wiseman confirmed the Wards at St. Mary's College, Oscott. The news report mentioned former Anglican clergymen who were at Oscott: Spencer, Talbot, Bernard Smith, Montgomery, and Capes. The article asserted that Newman would soon convert and no longer wished that his intention should be kept secret.

Toward the end of September, events at Littlemore quickly unfolded; Newman's young companions were unable to restrain any longer their eagerness to be received into the Church. On the twentieth, John Dalgairns wrote to Fr. Dominic Barbieri, asking to be received into the Roman

---

80 After making a profession of faith, candidates to be received into the Roman Catholic Church recite some sentences in which they reject all the errors condemned by the Church and profess obedience to the local bishop and Roman Pontiff.

81 *LD,* Vol. X, Confirmations at Oscote [sic] The Recent Conversions (September 20, 1845). From the *Tablet Evening Edition,* 763.

Catholic Church. Fr. Dominic, who had prayed and offered many sacrifices to God for this intention, replied, praising God and inviting Dalgairns to Aston, a Passionist house just outside Birmingham. Fr. Dominic sent regards to Dalgairns's "holy companions" at Littlemore. An exultant Fr. Dominic continued:

> Dear Littlemore, I love thee! A little more still and we shall see happy results from Littlemore. When the learned and holy Superior of Littlemore will come, then I hope we shall see the beginning of a new era. Yes, we shall see again the happy days of Augustine, of Lanfranc, and Thomas. England will once more be the Isle of Saints, and the nurse of new Christian nations destined to carry the light of the Gospels coram gentibus et regibus et filiis Israel.[82]

In the second half of September, Newman sent the *Essay on the Development of Christian Doctrine* to Toovey and reviewed proofs. He asked Robert F. Wilson, Keble's curate, to tell Keble that he had sent his book to the press and would soon resign his Fellowship. Wilson, like so many others, asked Newman about the step he was to take and whether the Anglican Orders would be valid. Newman replied that his conviction about the truth of the Church had grown over the years. He would not bargain, or ask for concessions about Anglican Orders: "If I believe the One Church is infallible in doctrine, and to be obeyed in all things, how can I be asking a point in detail, such as whether she receives Anglican Orders? Far deeper feelings

---

82 Denis Gwynn, *Father Dominic Barbieri,* Desmond & Stapleton, Buffalo, 1948, 199-200.

ought to be urging me on, or I ought not to move at all."[83]

Within one week, there was a flurry of conversions to Roman Catholicism from the group at Littlemore. On September 27, Dalgairns traveled to Aston House to be received by Fr. Dominic on Michaelmas Day. Ambrose St. John gave up his scholarship at Christ Church College and left for Prior Park College, near Bath, where he would be received into the Church on October 2. Christie left for London, where he in turn would be received into the Church on October 18.

On October 2, Richard Stanton wrote Newman, asking him where he should go to be received into the Church. Stanton wished to avoid the notoriety of Oscott and thought of going to Stonyhurst College, a Jesuit school, or to Aston House.[84] Newman replied that he expected to be received into the Church by Fr. Dominic at Littlemore and welcomed Stanton to join him. Stanton was very grateful for Newman's invitation and decided to join him at Littlemore.

Finally, on October 3, Newman wrote to Provost Edward Hawkins, resigning from his Fellowship at Oriel. He wrote to Pusey, Elizabeth Bowden, Christie, Mrs. William Froude, Mr. Phillips, Jemima, and Henry Wilberforce to inform them what he had done. Mrs. Bowden replied, "[W]e must hope you will still be allowed to guide and benefit us who yet remain—it is impossible not to be sadly perplexed and every month adds to my perplexity—yet I cannot feel that I should be right in changing now, and so I

83 *LD*, Vol. X, JHN to Robert Francis Wilson (September 25, 1845), 766.

84 *LD*, Vol. X, Richard Stanton to JHN (October 2, 1845), 770-771.

hope and pray that the right way may in some way become more clear before us . . ."[85] She added, "I would not give up the right, if I may say so, to talk to you."[86] Mrs. Elizabeth Bowden would see her way to the Church of Rome in 1846.

On October 3, Keble began a letter to Newman that he was only able to finish on October 11, at midnight, since his wife was gravely ill. Besides thanking Newman for praying for his wife, Keble described Newman's departure as an expected thunderbolt. Keble felt grief for losing a guide and a helper, but he wrote to express his love to his friend:

> My dearest Newman you have been a kind and helpful friend to me in a way in which scarce any one else could have been and you are so mixed up in my mind with old and dear and sacred thoughts, that I cannot well bear to part with you: most unworthy as I know myself to be: and yet I cannot go along with you: I must cling to the belief that we are not really parted . . .[87]

AT LAST, FULL COMMUNION WITH THE CATHOLIC CHURCH

October 5 was a Sunday and Newman stayed indoors all day preparing for a general confession of his sins prior to his reception into the Church. He marked the diary entry with a cross. On the sixth, Newman completed the advertisement for his *Essay on the Development of Christian Doctrine*. The book remained unfinished, and would be published in this state before the end of the year.

---

85 *LD,* Vol. X, Mrs. Elizabeth Bowden to John Henry Bowden (October 7, 1845), 772.

86 *Ibid.*

87 *LD,* Vol. X, John Keble to John Henry Newman (October 3, 1845), 774-75.

William Faber wrote to Newman on the fifth, confiding his affection for Rome and his attraction to its doctrines. Faber had some doubts about the need to remain where God had placed him, as Pusey enjoined him to do, and he wished Newman's advice. A few weeks later, in November, Faber was received into the Church of Rome at Northampton by Bishop William Wareing, Vicar Apostolic of the Eastern District.

On the afternoon of the eighth, Dalgairns, who had returned to be with Newman at Littlemore, went out to meet Fr. Dominic at the Angel, the Oxford coach stop. Only then did Newman tell Dalgairns his precise intention to be received into the Church. The coach was delayed by the weather, and Fr. Dominic, who had been five hours on the top of the coach, was soaked.[88] They took a chaise to Littlemore, where they arrived at about eleven at night. While Fr. Dominic sat down by the fire to dry his clothes, Newman entered the room. Fr. Dominic later wrote to his superiors:

> The door opened—and what a spectacle it was for me to see at my feet John Henry Newman begging me to hear his confession and admit him into the bosom of the Catholic Church! And there by the fire he began his general confession with extraordinary humility and devotion.[89]

Newman began his confession that night and completed it on the following day, Thursday, October 9. That day, Fr. Dominic also heard the confessions of Richard Stanton and Frederick Bowles. Then at six in the evening, before

---

88 Trevor, *Newman, The Pillar of the Cloud*, 358-60.
89 Gwynn, *Father Dominic Barbieri*, 204.

an overjoyed priest who gave them a conditional Baptism, each made his profession of faith. On the following day, Fr. Dominic said Mass at Littlemore, using a writing desk as an altar, and he gave Communion to those present. Newman had written the *Essay on the Development of Christian Doctrine* on this very desk. John Henry Newman, the 44-year-old Oxford scholar and leader of the Oxford Movement, was at last a Roman Catholic, received into the Church without public spectacle in the quiet village of his former Anglican parish.

In the novel *Loss and Gain*, which was Newman's first work as a Roman Catholic, he described his own sentiments about reception into the Church of Rome:

> A VERY few words will conduct us to the end of our history. It was Sunday morning about seven o'clock, and Charles had been admitted into the communion of the Catholic Church about an hour since. He was still kneeling in the church of the Passionists before the Tabernacle, in the possession of a deep peace and serenity of mind, which he had not thought possible on earth. It was more like the stillness which almost sensibly affects the ears when a bell that has long been tolling stops, or when a vessel, after much tossing at sea, finds itself in harbour. It was such as to throw him back in memory on his earliest years, as if he were really beginning life again. But there was more than the happiness of childhood in his heart; he seemed to feel a rock under his feet; it was the soliditas Cathedræ Petri. He went on kneeling, as if he were already in Heaven, with the throne of God before him, and angels around, and as if to move were to lose his privilege.[90]

Before leaving Littlemore, Fr. Dominic walked to see the Woodmasons, one of the two families that had made

---

90 *LG,* 384.

Littlemore more genteel. Mathias Woodmason, his wife, and two daughters were received that day into the Church of Rome. Their son Charles was received at St. Mary's College, Oscott, in November.

The Italian Passionist had never before seen "any monastery so poor," and he gave Newman a rule of life with less austerities than he and his companions had been practicing.[91] Fr. Dominic wrote of Newman to his superiors: "In my judgment he is one of the most humble and lovable men I have met in my life."[92] At the same time, Newman wrote of him to Mrs. Bowden: "I wish all persons were as charitable as he. I believe he is a very holy man." Newman saw Fr. Dominic only a few times more before his death in 1849. Thirty years after Dominic's death, Newman testified for Dominic's process of canonization:

> Father Dominic was a marvelous missioner filled with zeal. He had a great part in my own conversion and in that of others. His very look had about it something holy. When his form came into sight, I was moved to the depths in the strangest way. The gaiety and affability of his manner in the midst of all his sanctity was itself a holy sermon.[93]

On Sunday, October 12, the five converts: Newman, St. John, Dalgairns, Stanton, and Bowles, walked to St. Clement's, the Catholic chapel at Oxford, to attend Mass. Newman had prepared his friends and readers, yet he had evaded the curiosity of the press. For Newman, reception into the Roman Catholic Church was not a victory,

---

91 Gwynn, *Father Dominic Barbieri,* 207.
92 *Ibid.,* 205.
93 *Ibid.,* 211.

but rather like a ship coming out of rough waters to port. It brought the peace that follows accomplishment of duty. Many people wrote Newman to congratulate him or to express their perplexity. Many criticized him, and others said that he would convert back to the Anglican Church. Some were happy to see him go. Keble and Pusey both wrote beautiful letters to their friend. Pope Gregory XVI sent his Apostolic Blessing, which served as a consolation during the loneliness that Newman soon experienced at Littlemore after the severing of many friendships.

Newman would not see some of his good friends for a very long time; many of his friendships were interrupted for years. Newman's friendships with Keble and Pusey also suffered. In 1865, Newman visited Keble at his home in Hursley and unexpectedly met Pusey there; they had not seen each other since 1846. The three had aged; initially Newman and Keble had not even recognized one another at the door. The three spent four hours together. At intervals, while Keble attended on his sick wife, Pusey and Newman spoke alone. Later when Pusey went to read the Evening Service in Church, Keble and Newman spent some time alone. Newman described the scene to a friend: "We walked a little way, and stood looking in silence at the church *and* churchyard, so beautiful and calm. Then he began to converse with more than his old tone of intimacy, as if we had never been parted, and soon I was obliged to go . . ."[94] After their reunion, Keble wrote Newman many notes. In one he quoted from *Macbeth*: "When shall we

---

94 *LD,* Vol. XXIV, JHN to Sir John Coleridge (September 17, 1868), 142-43.

three meet again? . . . When the hurlyburly's done. When the battle's lost and won."[95]

Newman's love for the truth had prevailed over many previous prejudices in religion, the modest comfort of his life, and the feeling of separation from his English culture and close friends. It was not only through assiduous study but also through prayer and the practice of mortification that Newman had reached moral certainty about religious truths.

Newman's closing paragraph in the *Essay on the Development of Christian Doctrine* was an entreaty to readers, but just as much to himself, to act courageously with the light of reason and faith in assent to revealed Truth; it was a description of the heavy state of his soul, suffused with an inner peace, which is the fruit of the Truth.

> Such were the thoughts concerning the "Blessed Vision of Peace," of one whose long-continued petition had been that the Most Merciful would not despise the work of His own Hands, nor leave him to himself;—while yet his eyes were dim, and his breast laden, and he could but employ Reason in the things of Faith. And now, dear Reader, time is short, eternity is long.
>
> Put not from you what you have here found; regard it not as mere matter of present controversy; set not out resolved to refute it, and looking about for the best way of doing so; seduce not yourself with the imagination that it comes of disappointment, or disgust, or restlessness, or wounded feeling, or undue sensibility, or other weakness. Wrap not

---

95 William Shakespeare, *Macbeth,* Scene 1, Act 1. The Complete Works of William Shakespeare, The Cambridge Edition Text, ed. William Aldis Wright, (Philadelphia: The Blakiston Co., 1944), 1027.

yourself round in the associations of years past, nor determine that to be truth which you wish to be so, nor make an idol of cherished anticipations. Time is short, eternity is long.[96]

NUNC DIMITTIS SERVUM TUUM DOMINE,
SECUNDUM VERBUM TUUM IN PACE
QUIA VIDERUNT OCULI MEI SALUTARE TUUM.[97]

---

96 *Dev.,* 445.

97 "Lord, now let your servant depart in peace, according to your word; for my eyes have seen your salvation . . ." Lk. 2:'29-30, quoted in *Dev.,* 445.

CHAPTER 34

FIRST YEARS AS A
ROMAN CATHOLIC

WHEN Newman was received into the Roman
Catholic Church, he was 44 years of age. He was
an accomplished writer and an important religious figure
in England. He had reached a high level of intellectual and
spiritual maturity. For the remaining 45 years of his life, he
was to play an important role in Roman Catholic intellectual life, which extends to this day.

The last day of October 1845, Newman went to St.
Mary's College in Oscott to meet with Dr. Wiseman, who
was President of the college and Apostolic Vicar for the
Central District of England. On the feast of All Saints,
Wiseman administered the sacrament of Confirmation to
Newman, who took the name of Mary as his Confirmation
name. Afterward, Wiseman asked Newman to carry out
an intellectual defense of the Catholic faith against growing agnosticism and unfaithfulness by means of an intense
preaching of Catholic doctrine. Wiseman also asked Newman to move with his community of friends to St. Mary's
College. At the end of December, Newman and his friends
left Littlemore and moved to Oscott. Newman related to
James Hope the thoughts of Wiseman: "He thinks such
a community, cultivating sacred literature, or acting in
missions and the like through England, according to

the calling of each [member of it], is the best chance for the conversion of our country."[1]

In the last weeks of 1845, others followed Newman's conversion to Rome: Albany Christie, John Walker, Frederick Oakeley, William Faber, Watts-Russell, Thomas Knox, Maria Giberne and Robert Coffin. He wrote to Lucy Ann the Marquise de Salvo: "I earnestly exhort you to join the Catholic Church. It is necessary for your salvation, considering your present state of mind."[2] Shortly afterwards in 1846 she was received into the Church and Newman expressed his joy to hear and gave thanks to God. Soon others from aristocratic families such as Lady Georgiana Fullerton, who was a novelist, followed. Many more, influenced by Newman's writings and life, were to follow in the years afterward. Other close friends, such as Charles Marriot and John Bloxam, his former curate, remained Anglican. Newman and Bloxam maintained friendly contact and Newman always hoped that he would become a Catholic.

In February of 1846, Newman spent some time gathering his belongings at Littlemore. Upon leaving, he wrote to Copeland about the melancholy he experienced: "I have been most happy there, though in a state of suspence [sic]. And there it has been, that I have both been taught my way and received an answer to my prayers."[3] Newman spent his forty-fifth birthday, February 21, alone at Littlemore. On Sunday, February 22, he spent his last night at Oxford, with his friend Manuel Johnson, Bowden's cousin, who

---

1 *LD*, Vol. XI. JHN to James Hope (December 19, 1845), 71-72, 71.

2 *LD*, Vol. XI. JHN to the Marquise de Salvo, (December 18, 1845), 71.

3 *LD*, Vol. XI, JHN to W. J. Copeland (March 10, 1846), 132-33.

was an astronomer and director of the Radcliffe Observatory.[4] Some of his Anglican friends: Lewis, Copeland, Church, G. Buckle, Pattison, and Pusey stopped to say farewell. Newman also called on James Ogle, his former private Tutor. A few days later Copeland wrote to Newman from Littlemore: "the poor old place seems indeed a strange place without you . . . and deeply did I think when I was with you on Sunday week [sic] what it must have cost you to have left it . . . ."[5]

Soon after Newman's farewells came the publication of his *Essay on the Development of Christian Doctrine.* People had anticipated the book, and the first edition was sold out within two weeks. The readers expected to find in the *Essay* the explanation for Newman's conversion, and many Anglicans criticized Newman for the book. At first English-speaking Catholics reacted to the book with certain reservations. In contrast to this, Pope Gregory XVI sent Newman a silver crucifix with a relic of the true cross, which Newman interpreted as an "indirect approval" of his book.[6] The date on the certificate of the sacred relic coincided with the same day *Tract 90* had been published.

The Oxford Movement had begun to unravel a few years before Newman's final step; now it received its greatest blow and the objectives of its founders clearly diverged. In retrospect Newman saw the Movement as leading men toward the Catholic Church. He began to pray for the conversion

---

4 *LD,* Vol. XI, Diary entry (Sunday, February 22), 1846, 125.

5 *LD,* Vol. XI, W. J. Copeland to JHN, (March 7, 1846), 132.

6 *LD,* Vol. XI, JHN to Miss M. R. Giberne (March 20, 1846), 139-40; 140.

of Keble, Pusey, Williams, and others. He could not understand why they would not convert. It soon became evident that neither Keble, nor Pusey, who together with himself and Froude had begun the Oxford Movement, would convert. Pusey tried to dissuade possible converts. He wished to part peaceably with Newman, but tension arose between the two when he realized that his friend planned to proselytize Anglicans.[7] Except for a short visit to Pusey, who was ill, many years passed before Newman met either Pusey or Keble again.

After Easter 1846, Wiseman encouraged Newman to study for some time at the Roman College of *Propaganda Fidei* in order to deepen his knowledge of Roman Catholic theology and to prepare for ordination as a Roman Catholic priest. *Propaganda Fidei* was a college founded in 1627 to house and educate theology students from mission countries. The Jesuits ran the college, and students went to classes at the Gregorian University. Newman made plans to study in Rome with Ambrose St. John, hoping that a stay in Rome would allow him (Newman) to find his place in the Catholic Church. At the same time, he was uneasy because he felt like a showcase for Wiseman's apostolic zeal. He also felt that Catholics were expecting too much from him and the new converts.

Newman traveled through Paris to Milan, where he prayed before the tombs of St. Ambrose and St. Charles Borromeo. Writing to his sister Jemima he said: "Milan is a most favored place, as having been blessed with that wonder Saint Charles. I have been reading a good deal of a

---

7 Morales, *Newman (1801-1890)*, 136-37.

very accurate life of him. A great Saint indeed . . . He died in the midst of a great career of reform at the early age of 46—but he lives still."[8] He arrived in Rome in late October 1846, two months after the death of Pope Gregory XVI, who was succeeded by (now beatified) Pope Pius IX. This was to be Newman's second of four visits to Rome. He was again impressed by Rome and went to a papal Mass at the Altar of Peter's Confession in St. Peter's Basilica. Newman and Ambrose St. John moved into the *Propaganda Fidei* College and within a few weeks they had an audience with Pope Pius IX, who received them in a jovial and affectionate manner. The Pope gave Newman a painting of the Virgin Mary.

Mid-nineteenth-century Rome had a relatively small population of 160,000 inhabitants.[9] The cultural level of Florence and Milan was higher than that of Rome, which had some artists but few philosophers and writers.[10] Newman was received kindly at *Propaganda Fidei* College and he was impressed that 32 languages were spoken, but he did not find a vibrant theological environment in which he could discuss theology and his *Essay on the Development of Christian Doctrine*. He discovered that in Rome the works of St. Augustine and St. Thomas Aquinas were not used, nor those of Aristotle. Newman transcribed the

---

8 *LD*, Vol XI, JHN to Mrs. John Mozley, (October 22, 1846), 264-266, 265.

9 Pope Pius IX brought about a reform of the administration of the Pontifical States, and introduced, for the first time in their history, laymen into their government. Despite his reform efforts, in 1848, the Roman Republic was proclaimed and the Pope fled to Gaeta.

10 Morales, *Newman (1801-1890)*, 143.

reply a Jesuit father made to the question on whether the youths learned Aristotle: "O no—he said—Aristotle is in no favor here—no, not in Rome:—not St. Thomas. I have read Aristotle and St. Thos [sic], and owe a great deal to them, but they are out of favor here and throughout Italy."[11]

In Rome, Carlo Passaglia, a leading dogmatic theologian, did not agree with the *Essay on Development*. Newman wrote Dalgairns that Passaglia "has certainly in lecture spoken against the view, and after lecture said he was speaking against me. I don't like to begin my career in the Catholic Church with a condemnation or retraction."[12] Newman worried a great deal about being misunderstood by others, in particular at the Holy See, and he prepared a summary of his thesis to show ecclesiastical authorities. In the spring of 1847, Newman sought advice and approval of his thesis from Giovanni Perrone, another leading Roman theologian with whom he had had prior correspondence. Perrone, who had contributed to the theological notion of Tradition and of the Church as the mystical Body of Christ, offered Newman some moderate and constructive criticism which reassured Newman, and laid the ground for an academic friendship between the two. St. John wrote to Dalgairns, "N. has struck up quite a close friendship with F. Perrone: they embrace each other."[13]

What concerned Newman most in Rome, however, was

---

11 *LD*, Vol. XI, JHN to John Dobrée Dalgairns (November 22, 1846), 279-82; 279.

12 *LD*, Vol. XII, JHN to J. D. Dalgairns (February, 14, 1847), 33-36, 36.

13 *LD*, Vol. XII, JHN to J. D. Dalgairns from Ambrose St. John (April, 1847), 40; Morales, *Newman (1801-1890),* 144-45.

discovering the spiritual calling that God had in store for him and for his friends. What were they to do as Catholics? What was their mission in the Church? As an Anglican, Newman had promoted the idea of colleges for the formation of celibate clergymen, dedicated to preaching in cities. He and his friends began to study the spiritual characteristics and apostolic activities of various religious congregations within the Catholic Church, for they wished to join one of the existing religious institutions.

One of the religious institutions that was investigated by Newman and his friends was the Oratory of St. Philip Neri. Newman first heard of the Oratory in a review of Froude's *Remains* by Wiseman. In this article, Wiseman had expressed the idea that the best way to spread the Catholic faith in England was through a community of priests who lived a common life such as the Oratory of St. Philip Neri. Newman and his friends visited the Oratorian houses of Milan, Rome, and Naples. Dalgairns favored joining the Dominicans and St. John the Jesuits. Newman admired both of these religious communities, but neither satisfied what he looked for. After visiting the rooms where St. Philip Neri had lived and died, he felt more inclined to the Oratorian way of life, especially to the Oratorian spirit of Christian love and mild ascetical practices. He was attracted by the libraries which the Oratorians had, and he thought that the way of life of the Oratorians provided continuity with the life that they had lived at Oxford.[14]

---

14 *LD*, Vol. XI, JHN to J. D. Dalgairns (December 31, 1846), 303-07; 305-06; Ian Ker, *John Henry Newman*, Oxford University Press, Oxford 1988, 328-30.

In January 1847, Newman made a novena of prayers at the Tomb of St. Peter, and shortly afterward he, Ambrose St. John, and Dalgairns agreed that they would become Oratorians.[15] He wrote to Fr. Dominic: "We are to be Oratorians. The Pope has been very kind to us—suggested that others of us had better come here and pass their novitiate with us all together under an Oratorian Father."[16] The Pope even offered them an Oratorian house in Malta which could be the novice house for the English mission, but not wishing to be separated, some in Rome and some in Malta, they politely declined the offer.

Newman was captivated by the life and example of St. Philip Neri and later wrote an essay describing the witness of this holy man, who was filled with a burning love for God and neighbor.[17] Philip Neri, called the apostle of Rome, was a diocesan priest who lived a long and fruitful life in sixteenth-century Rome. He was known for his wise counsel and the moderation with which he guided not only simple men, but also the clergy and aristocracy. He gathered young laymen to practice spiritual devotions and carry out works of charity with the infirm poor. The word "Oratory" described the devotional and ascetical practices of the youth under Philip Neri. Later the name Oratory was given to the houses established in various parts of Europe. Toward the end of Philip's life, urged by the ecclesiastical authorities of Rome, he wrote statutes for priests who would continue the work with laity in a stable manner.

---

15 *LD,* Vol. XII, Diary entry (January 17, 1847) and footnote n. 2, 19.

16 *LD,* Vol. XII, JHN to Fr. Dominic Barbieri (March 14, 1847), 62.

17 "The Mission of St. Philip," in *OS,* 218-42,

Drawn by St. Philip's life, Newman asked Pius IX permission to start an Oratory in England. The Pope granted the permission, but he asked Newman to make adaptations of the rule for England. In his adaptation, Newman added that English Oratorians could run preparatory schools to prepare Catholics for university studies. He also did away with the practice of public penance. Newman thus departed from the monastic idea that he had practiced for some time. He believed that monastic life was necessary for some, in certain periods of life, but he saw his future Christian vocation differently.[18]

The new convert considered the vocation of an Oratorian priest to be different from both the monastic and the Jesuit spirituality. As a model for the English Oratorians, Newman had in mind something akin to that of celibate Fellows in Oxford colleges who cultivated an intellectual life and, as clergymen, exercised pastoral care; this had been his way of life at Oriel, St. Mary's, and Littlemore.[19] In St. Philip Neri, Newman saw the model of a great saint who, faced with the Renaissance's exaltation of man, responded by presenting the Christian ideal of purity and truth.

On Trinity Sunday, May 30, 1847, Newman was ordained a Catholic priest by Cardinal Frasoni in the chapel of the college of *Propaganda Fidei,* and celebrated his first Mass at a private chapel of the Jesuits on June 3rd, which that day was the feast of Corpus Christi. Ambrose St. John (1815–1875), who had become Roman Catholic only a few days before Newman, was ordained on the same day with Newman.

---

18 Morales, *Newman (1801-1890),* 150-54.
19 *Ibid.,* 153.

St. John, fourteen years Newman's junior, had graduated from Christ Church College at Oxford. He was a clever and good-natured man despite moments of quick temper. He knew German and Spanish, and had knowledge of Semitic languages and exegesis. Unlike Newman, he had no interest in Patristics or Philosophy and did not have a good ear for music.[20] St. John would remain a very close lifelong friend of Newman for thirty-two years, taking the place that Richard Hurrell Froude (1803–1836) had occupied.

Like Froude and St. John, Henry William Wilberforce (1807–1873) was one of Newman's closest friends; it was he who had introduced St. John, once his curate, to Newman. When Newman became Roman Catholic, Wilberforce felt the pain of their separation, but their friendship was not hurt by Newman's change. Newman considered St. John to be a sign of their friendship, and encouraged Wilberforce to become Roman Catholic, which he eventually did in 1850.

In July 1847, Newman and six other converts gathered in Rome at the Church of the Santa Croce where they underwent a brief novitiate. The seven men were Newman, Ambrose St. John, John Dalgairns, William Penny, Richard Stanton, Frederick Bowles, and Robert Coffin. All, except for Penny, had become Roman Catholics in 1845; Penny had converted a year earlier. In August 1847, the Pope himself visited the Oratorians, and he formally established the Oratory. Newman was named the first superior of the English Oratory. He remained for some months in Rome, and in December, he and St. John returned to Maryvale,

---

20 Morales, *Newman (1801-1890),* 155.

stopping by the House of the Holy Family in Loreto, and Munich, where they visited Döllinger.

Renamed Maryvale out of Marian devotion, Old Oscott was the first home for the Oratorians when they returned to England. Old Oscott was situated on the outskirts of Birmingham. Soon William Faber and a group of young converts who had followed him expressed the desire to join the Oratory. Faber, a Fellow at Oxford, was a very intelligent and gifted preacher with an enthusiastic personality.[21] Newman, however, was worried by Faber's impulsive character and lack of prudence. He was concerned that Faber would not understand the spirit of the Oratory, but upon Faber's assurances of submissiveness, Newman decided to admit him and his friends, which included two priests and lay brothers, into the Oratory. That same year, Newman's friend, George Ryder, became Roman Catholic. One of Ryder's sons, Henry Ignatius, once a pupil to Newman, had already become Catholic and later joined the Oratory. Newman's spirits were high. Just a few days before closing the year he wrote to Henry Wilberforce:

"Lately several of our Fathers held a mission in this neighborhood. They heard between 700–800 confessions, and received 22 persons into the Church. Never surely were the words more strikingly exemplified, 'The Harvest is great, the labourers are few' than in England. We could convert England, humanly speaking, at least the lower classes, had we priests enough." In 1849, the Oratorians moved to Birmingham, where they set up a provisional house in a poor neighborhood on Alcester Street in an unused gin

---

21 Morales, *Newman (1801-1890)*, 159-60.

distillery. Soon, large numbers attended talks in the chapel, which accommodated as many as 600 people. In addition to running the Oratory, Newman made time to hear confessions and care for the sick; he also set aside time for study. Despite the good initial results, Newman thought that the Oratory should prepare students for university studies, as had been stipulated in the statutes for the English Oratory.

Faber did not understand Newman's vision for the Oratory, which involved exerting influence on the educated classes of society. He and Newman had very different backgrounds and temperaments; the former was charismatic and the latter shy in public. Faber disliked Newman's close friendship with Ambrose St. John, and he and the new arrivals to the Oratory found it awkward to deal with Newman because of his shyness. Faber was soon impatient to open a London house for the Oratory. Newman wished to remain in Birmingham, but in April, he rented a property for the London Oratory and in May decided that Faber should be the superior.[22] On May 31, 1850, the London Oratory was established, and according to the statutes, it was independent of Birmingham.

William Bernard Ullathorne, a Benedictine monk who was ordained a bishop in 1846 as Vicar Apostolic for the Western District of England, became the Bishop of Birmingham in 1850.[23] He was emblematic of "Old Catholic" families, who had remained faithful throughout three centuries of Protestant persecutions. Although at first Ullathorne

---

22 Brian Martin, *John Henry Newman, His Life & Work* (London: Continuum, 1982), 88-89.

23 Morales, *Newman (1801-1890),* 162-63.

did not understand the canonical rights of the Oratorians, he and Newman eventually developed a sincere friendship. Ullathorne, an intelligent and humble man, became Newman's strong defender and supporter. He was the bishop of the diocese in which Newman would work for the rest of his life.

In addition to Old Catholics, English Catholics consisted of immigrants and the new converts.[24] The immigrants were primarily poor Irish Catholics who had flocked in large numbers to the industrial cities. Some relatively new Italian religious congregations like the Passionists, Redemptorists, and Rosminians brought Italian devotions, and also a proselytic zeal that clashed with Old Catholics.[25] The converts proceeded for the most part from Oxford and Cambridge graduates and their families. Some came from wealthy families, such as the Phillipps, Wilberforce, or Bowden families. For instance, Elizabeth, Bowden's widow, and her children became Catholic. John, one of her sons, a student at Eaton, later joined the Oratory. Henry, Bowden's brother, married by Newman, became a Catholic with his wife and family in 1852.

---

24 Morales, *Newman (1801-1890)*, 165.
25 *Ibid.*, 166.

CHAPTER 35

PUBLIC DEFENSE OF CATHOLICS IN ENGLAND

IN 1849, Newman advised his friend, Henry Wilberforce, who was in a spiritual crisis over Anglicanism, not to delay his decision to become Roman Catholic. During this period, Newman spoke with severity about Anglicanism, and insisted that Anglicanism and Catholicism were two different religions. In November of that same year, he published a series of conferences titled: *Discourses to Mixed Congregations*. In one of these he wrote of Anglicanism: "It has then no internal consistency, or individuality, or soul, to give it the capacity of propagation. Methodism represents some sort of an idea, Congregationalism an idea; the Established Religion has in it no idea beyond establishment."[1] These conferences, which readily went through a first and second edition, were directed to winning the conversion of Anglicans to Catholicism or urging those who were Catholics to a more Christian life. In the first years after his own conversion, Father Newman spoke with such force because he saw the need to publicly defend the Church, and to give spiritual advice to those who sought this advice.[2]

In March 1850, only a few months after Newman's

---

1 John Henry Newman, *Discourses to Mixed Congregations,* "Prospects of the Catholic Missioner" (May 31, 1849), 251, available at: http://www. newmanreader.org/works/discourses/discourse12.html.

2 Morales, *Newman (1801-1890),* 186-87.

Discourses to Mixed Congregations, the Gorham case contributed to the conversion of some well-known Anglican clergy and laymen to Catholicism. The Bishop of Exeter had refused to install George C. Gorham, as vicar of a parish for his denial of baptismal regeneration. Gorham appealed to the Privy Council, which repealed the bishop's sentence. Among those received into the Catholic Church in the wake of the Gorham case were Edward Manning, future Archbishop of Westminster, and two distinguished lawyers, James Hope and Edward L. Badeley, all Newman's friends. Badeley had been the counsel for Henry Phillpotts, the Bishop of Exeter.

Between May and July 1850, at the request of Bishop Wiseman, Newman gave twelve conferences at the Brompton Oratory in London. In these conferences, later published as *Lectures on certain difficulties felt by Anglicans in submitting to the Catholic Church*, Newman made an energetic call to those who had been a part of the Oxford Movement to convert to Catholicism. He graciously admitted the spiritual gifts and graces among Anglicans, and recalled his past:

> Can I forget,—I never can forget,— the day when in my youth I first bound myself to the ministry of God in that old church of St. Frideswide, the patroness of Oxford? nor how I wept most abundant, and most sweet tears, when I thought what I had then become; though I looked on ordination as no sacramental rite, nor even to baptism ascribed any supernatural virtue? Can I wipe from my memory, or wish to wipe out, those happy Sunday mornings, light or dark, year after year, when I celebrated your communion-rite, in my own church of St. Mary's, and in the pleasantness and joy of it heard nothing of the strife of tongues which surrounded its walls?[3]

---

3 *Diff.*, I, 81-82.

Newman explained that the grace which they had received in the Movement was a preparation for the step that they should take; Catholicism was the natural end of the Movement. The influential Victorian writer and critic R. H. Hutton, described the lectures:

Never did a voice seem better adapted to persuade without irritating. Singularly sweet, perfectly free from any dictatorial note, and yet rich in all the cadences proper to the expression of pathos, of wonder, and of ridicule, there was still nothing in it that anyone could properly describe as insinuating, for its simplicity, and frankness, and freedom from the half-smothered notes which express indirect purpose, was as remarkable as its sweetness, its freshness and its gentle distinctness.[4]

The same year Pope Pius IX conferred on Newman the degree of Doctor of Divinity. Newman was moved by this honor, which was considered a recognition for his public defense of the Roman Catholic faith. He thanked the Pope for this kind gesture, although, with noteworthy humility, he did not consider himself a theologian.

In 1850, after some years of preparation, the Holy See restored the Catholic hierarchy of England with the creation of thirteen dioceses corresponding to locations and names different from existing Anglican dioceses. English Protestants received the news poorly. Their misunderstanding was fueled by a pastoral letter written by Wiseman, who was made Archbishop of the new Archdiocese of Westminster and a cardinal. *The Times* and *Punch* repeatedly attacked Catholics and especially Newman and Wiseman.

---

4 R. H. Hutton, *Cardinal Newman,* London, 1891, 207-208.

The Prime Minister, the Anglican bishops, and people at large also criticized the Pope. After his unfortunate pastoral letter, Wiseman made an eloquent appeal to the English people published in *The Times*. As on other occasions, Newman boldly stood up for the Catholic Church. He gave a series of masterful lectures later published as *Lectures on the Present Position of English Catholics*. With extraordinary wit and satire, he accused the Protestants of anti-Catholic bias. Newman pointed out:

> [T]here is a Protestant side, and there is a Catholic side—and if you have heard but one of them, you will think nothing at all can be said on the other. If, then, a person listens only to Protestantism, and does not give fair play to the Catholic reply to it, of course he thinks Protestantism very rational and straightforward, and Catholics very absurd; because he takes for granted the Protestant facts, which are commonly fictions, and opens his mind to Protestant arguments, which are always fallacies.[5]

Newman gave an example of people's unexamined and stubborn ideas which keep them from entering into the minds of strangers: "So it is especially between country and country: the Englishman thinks his beef and pudding worth all the resources of the French cuisine; and the Frenchman thought for certain, until the peace, that he had gained the battle of Trafalgar."[6]

Newman dedicated the lectures to Paul Cullen, then

---

5 John Henry Newman, *Lectures on the Present Positions of Catholics in England*, 5, available at: http://www.newmanreader.org/works/england/lecture1.html.

6 *Ibid.*, 6.

recently appointed Archbishop of Armagh, who only a few weeks earlier had invited Newman to establish a Catholic University in Ireland. In the lectures Newman urged the laity to cultivate learning and to exercise an active presence in the Catholic Church and in English society. Bishop Ullathorne and others expressed concern at Newman's novel ideas.[7]

In the fifth lecture Newman criticized Giacinto Achilli, an ex-Dominican priest, who became Protestant after the Roman Inquisition sentenced him to imprisonment on account of sexual immorality with women.[8] The Evangelical Alliance had brought Achilli to lecture and agitate throughout the country. Despite the veracity of Newman's denunciation, Achilli brought forth a libel suit which would drain Newman's time and energies.

Newman based his statements on a detailed account by Wiseman in the *Dublin Review,* but Wiseman did not make a real effort to provide legal evidence for Newman's defense, and Msgr. George Talbot, the English Chamberlain to Pius IX, who was antagonistic to Newman, procrastinated in obtaining documents from the Inquisition for Newman's defense. In 1852, Newman sent two Oratorians to obtain legal proofs in Italy against the ex-friar, but they failed in their mission. After great expense and effort, Maria Giberne was able to obtain testimony from some women against Achilli. Despite the testimony presented, the jury and the judges demonstrated their corrupt sense of justice and anti-Catholic hatred. Newman was found

---

7 Morales, *Newman (1801-1890),* 203.
8 Ian Ker, *John Henry Newman,* 372-75.

guilty and fined £100. The injustice was such that even *The Times* spoke of the harm done to the English character and administration of justice and censured the Chief Justice, Lord Campbell.[9]

Newman's friends raised over £14,000 in Europe and America to pay for the legal expenses and loyally stood by him during the Achilli trial. Of the amount raised, over £2000 were collected in Ireland and sent to Newman by Archbishop Cullen. Newman dedicated his book, *The Idea of a University*, discourses on university education, to all the benefactors who had raised the funds for his defense. Although the funds came from every social class, the support of Edward Badeley, James Hope, and other benefactors was an indication of the role that educated Catholics could play in the Church and in society.

In July 1852, the new Ecclesiastic Province of Westminster celebrated its first provincial synod, presided over by Wiseman. Newman and Manning were invited with other theologians; contrary to what Newman would have wished, laymen were not invited. Newman pronounced a memorable opening sermon, "The Second Spring." In the closing remarks of his address, he told the synod Fathers:

> Yes, my Fathers and Brothers, and if it be God's blessed will, not Saints alone, not Doctors only, not Preachers only, shall be ours—but Martyrs, too, shall reconsecrate the soil to God. We know not what is before us, ere we win our own; we are engaged in a great, a joyful work, but in proportion to God's grace is the fury of His enemies.[10]

---

9 Martin, *John Henry Newman, His Life & Work*, 94.
10 "The Second Spring," in *OS* (July 13, 1852), 178.

The year 1852 had been an exhausting one for Newman. In addition to the Achilli trial, the Birmingham Oratory moved to Edgbaston, another location in Birmingham; he traveled a number of times to Ireland to prepare for the future university; and he experienced the premature loss of his sister Harriet, whom he had not seen since 1843, and the death of his elderly Aunt Elizabeth Newman. On the advice of his physician, Newman spent two weeks' vacation at Abbotsford, the home of his friend, James Hope, who had inherited the property from the novelist Sir Walter Scott, one of Newman's favorite authors. Hope had become Roman Catholic in 1851. Incidentally, upon marrying a granddaughter of Walter Scott and then inheriting Abbotsford, Hope would change his name to Hope-Scott.

CHAPTER 36

FOUNDER OF THE CATHOLIC UNIVERSITY OF IRELAND

IN 1851, Archbishop Cullen offered Newman the presidency of a new Catholic University in Ireland. James Hope-Scott, who had suggested Newman's name, and the Oratorians convinced Newman to take this position. From the start, Newman faced numerous difficulties: finding capable professors, attracting Catholic students, and raising necessary funds. The primary difficulty, however, was Irish distrust for Englishmen, and the bishops' resistance to laymen playing roles in the administration of the new university. One of Newman's great accomplishments was the formulation of coherent ideas about university education, which Cullen asked Newman to present as public lectures to Dublin's educated Catholic laity. Newman spoke of the proper and necessary role of theology in every university, of the scientific character of theology, of the harmonic integration of human learning and theology, and of knowledge as its own reward.

Newman presented the ideal of a liberal education without rationalism or religious indifferentism. According to his educational ideal, profane science has its own autonomy, which freely accepts religion and theology. Newman repeated the idea expressed in *The Tamworth Reading Room Lectures* that knowledge is not a substitute, or cause, for virtue. By itself, knowledge does not make people good. This is the province of moral virtue: "Quarry the granite rock with razors, or moor the vessel with a thread of silk; then may you hope with such keen and delicate instruments as human knowledge and human reason to contend against those giants, the passion and the pride of man."[1]

In his third lecture, "Bearing of Theology on other Knowledge," Newman taught about the role of Natural Theology in university studies. Newman believed that each branch of knowledge has its proper domain and limits, which have bearing on all other branches of knowledge and which cannot be neglected without detriment to the rest. He taught that theology is not only necessary to complete the full range of studies at a university, but because it leads to the knowledge of man's ultimate end. Newman concluded the lecture as follows: "In a word, Religious Truth is not only a portion, but a condition of general knowledge. To blot it out is nothing short, if I may so speak, of unraveling the web of University Teaching."[2] The result of nine lectures, only four of them actually delivered, became the classic *Idea of a University*.

Newman wished to bring to the Catholic University of Ireland professors, known outside of Ireland, who would attract students. He also wished to have as Tutors some young single men whom he knew well, and he wished to pick a trusted Vice-Rector with whom he could work. Cullen, then Archbishop of Dublin, demurred and resisted

---

1 John Henry Newman, *The Idea of a University,* 121, available at: http://www.newmanreader.org/works/idea/index.html. After this it will be cited *Idea*.

2 *Ibid.,* 70.

Newman, who also found opposition among the university's board of bishops. To attempt to remedy Newman's inferior position in Ireland and possibly to make up for his failure in the Achilli case, Wiseman asked Pope Pius IX to name Newman bishop.[3] Newman realized that he did not have the talent to govern a diocese—his talents lay elsewhere—but an Episcopal appointment would increase his leadership capacity in establishing the Catholic University of Ireland. The Pope made known his desire to make Newman a bishop, and the news became semi-public; but at the last moment Archbishop Cullen, who wished to retain control over the university, stopped Newman's nomination.[4] It was a blow to Newman, who never received an explanation about the affair from Wiseman, but Newman accepted the change in plans without holding any resentments.

Despite the bishops' lack of cooperation, Newman was able to establish the Catholic University of Ireland. Classes at the university began in 1854, with a school of liberal arts. Soon afterward a school of medicine was incorporated. With the money left over from the funds raised for the Achilli trial Newman built a church for the university. He began a school newspaper, *The Catholic University Gazette*, a newspaper not only to communicate with professors and students but to make the university known in and outside of Ireland. He dreamed of a distinguished Catholic university for all the English-speaking countries, and he crafted on paper its curricula, ways of examining, and other administrative plans. Newman thought that laymen

---

3 Morales, *Newman (1801-1890)*, 218.
4 *Ibid.*, 220.

should have the day-to-day management of the university, and that under ordinary circumstances the president and the teaching faculty should be able to run the university. The Irish Episcopate, however, was not ready for these ideas and resented having an English convert in charge of an institution in their country. Only one Irish prelate, David Moriarty, Bishop of Kerry, who befriended Newman, understood Newman's arguments concerning the role of the laity in the governance of the university, and helped him to establish contacts in Dublin.[5]

Even with all the turmoil caused by the situation with the University, Newman found time to finish a novel that he had begun a number of years earlier. Writing seemed to be what kept him anchored and perhaps gave a needed mental respite from the stressful situation. It is not surprising that he chose to write a novel during this period—he could, at least while he wrote, immerse himself in a world over which he had control. And so it was that in 1855, during his Long Vacation, that he completed his second novel, *Callista: A Tale of the Third Century*, a moving story of a young woman in Northern Africa in the third century, during the times of the persecution of Christians. The novel depicts the love of Christians and their courage under Roman torture. The narrative describes their belief in eternal life as well as eternal punishment, and their celebration of the Mass. Newman's love for the Church Fathers is evident in his portrayal of St. Cyprian, Bishop of Carthage.

Upon his return to Dublin, Newman encountered one difficulty after another; he had his hands tied because the

---

5 Morales, *Newman, 1801-1890,* 221.

board of bishops would not allow him to run the university. Newman had judged incorrectly that he could establish a Catholic university for the English-speaking world. There was no interest for the university in England. Only a few English graduates from St. Cuthbert's College in Ushaw near Durham had enrolled. And the Catholic Irish society did not have sufficient middle-class families to send students to the university. By the end of the academic year, 1855 to 1856, the number of students enrolled did not surpass a hundred. In 1857, Newman, who wished to resign, suggested a compromise to the board whereby he would spend two or three weeks each term in Dublin with a resident Vice-Rector whom he could trust. Until then, Patrick Leahy, Archbishop of Cashel, had been the Vice-Rector and generally absent. For a year Newman continued to work as Rector. In a draft of a letter to Leahy he wrote: "For myself all I can say is, that my time has been absolutely occupied with correspondence and other matters of the University ever since I left it in the beginning of the winter, and, that I have taken no salary since I ceased to reside. But I know perfectly that a resident Rector is indispensable."[6] Discouraged by the delay and opposition of the board, Newman resigned his position as Rector of the university at the end of 1858.

During the seven years Newman worked to start the Catholic University of Ireland, he traveled back and forth between Dublin and Birmingham; he crossed St. George's Channel fifty-six times. Newman was relieved to be able

---

6 LD, JHN to Patrick Leahy, Archbishop of Cahel (October 5, 1858), 476-477, 476.

to dedicate his full attention to the needs of the community at Birmingham. During his frequent absences, the relation between the Birmingham Oratory and the London Oratory had worsened and reached a painful crisis. In 1855, Faber and the London Oratory asked the Holy See to change their statutes to allow the community to hear the confessions of religious women and undertake their spiritual care. The London Oratory did not consult, or inform Newman, the founder of the Oratory in England, of the proceedings.[7] As soon as Newman, who was in Dublin, found out he protested to the *Sacred Congregation of Propaganda Fidei*, which was unaware that Newman had not been consulted. He also protested to Cardinal Wiseman, about this plot and about the compromise of a far wider principle: "If our Rule may be relaxed in one point without our having cognisance of it, before the event, the same misfortune may happen in any other; and what is to hinder its being swept away altogether without our knowing it?"[8]

In a letter to Newman, Fr. John Stanislaus Flanagan of the Birmingham Oratory acknowledged the gravity of the matter:

> The real point at issue, my dear Father, in my mind, is not—whether we may direct Nuns or take charge of Convents or not, but whether the Brimm [sic] Oratory is to be ruled by, and fashioned after the model of the London one—whether *that* house has it in its powers to force its views, its interpretations and developments of the Rule upon *this* or not. I cannot

---

7 Ronald Chapman, *Father Faber* (London: Burns & Oates, 1961), "An Unhappy Quarrel," 261-90; 270, 278.

8 *LD*, Vol. XVII, JHN to Cardinal Wiseman, (October 19, 1855), 13-14, 13.

express how strongly I feel this, because as you yourself say, it positively strikes at the root of one's vocation.[9]

Newman considered that a modification of the rule was so vital that he traveled to Rome along with Ambrose St. John, visiting on the way the Oratories of Northern Italy to consult on the matter that took them to Rome. In these visits it became clearer that in addition to the question regarding changing the Rule, there was a long tradition of complete independence between Oratories. In January 1856, they met with Alessandro Banabó, head of the Congregation for *Propaganda Fidei* and Pope Pius IX, who nevertheless did not wish to limit Newman's powers and in fact wished to extend his power to setting up an Oratory in Ireland, even though each Oratory was to be independent.[10] Newman spoke charitably of the London Oratorians, but asked for a more complete separation of the two houses, the Birmingham Oratory and the London Oratory. From the start Newman had enjoined his brothers at Birmingham to treat those at the Brompton or London Oratory with only kindness and respect, imitating St. Philip, who "scarcely ever had this sentence of St. Bernard out of his mouth, 'to despise the world, to despise no one, to despise self, to despise being despised.' "[11]

After a long silence, the London Oratorians asked Newman's forgiveness, but years later Fr. Faber still told

---

9 *LD*, Vol. XVII, John Stanislas Flanagan to JHN (October 22, 1855), 14-15.

10 *LD*, Vol. XVII, JHN to Edward Caswall (January 29, 1856), 138-139, 139.

11 *LD*, Vol. XVII, JHN to Fr. Ambrose St. John and all the Fathers at Birmingham (November 9, 1855), 40-51, 49.

others that quarrel had arisen because Newman wanted to be superior of both houses. In the end, the Holy See established complete independence between the Birmingham Oratory and the London Oratory. Newman had responded energetically because of the weight of the matter at hand, but the difference of temperament between him and Faber, and their vision of the Oratory, as well as the one-sided support of Archbishop Wiseman for Faber contributed to the final separation of the two houses.[12] The conflict with Faber and the London Oratory damaged Newman's reputation among ecclesiastical circles in London.

The canonical separation of the London Oratory and later the end of his office at the Catholic University of Ireland brought some calm again to Newman. Life at the Birmingham Oratory suited Newman well. He was not cut out for the government of a university or a diocese. In the midst of this painful period there was, however, an important satisfaction at the university. He wrote Lord Henry Kerr, father of one of the students at the Oratory School: "We have opened our Medical School with great success."[13] To Mrs. Bowden, he was more spontaneous and candid: "We have opened the Medical School with great eclat, and in spite of much croking [sic] beforehand."[14]

Newman had many friends and many visitors, but he was a timid and quiet person, and to those who did not know him, he gave the impression of being distant.[15] Newman, however, was busy and happy at Birmingham. He

---

12 Morales, *Newman (1801-1890)*, 235-36.

13 *LD*, Vol. XVII, JHN to Lord Henry Kerr (November 15, 1855), 62.

14 *LD*, Vol. XVII, JHN to Mrs. J. W. Bowden (November 18, 1855), 68.

15 *Ibid.,* 241-43.

supervised the enlargement of the church, took care of order in the library, did bookkeeping, helped in the sacristy, and dedicated much time to the pastoral care of the poor. He heard confessions regularly, preached every Sunday, and helped with children's catechesis. Newman spent a lot of time writing letters as well as ordering and classifying his extensive correspondence according to dates.

CHAPTER 37

ADVOCATE OF AN EDUCATED CATHOLIC LAITY

ONCE settled in Birmingham, Newman was free to put into action what he had long hoped for: the Oratory School, a school for laymen from the upper classes that would equal the education imparted at the prestigious "public schools" of Eton and Winchester. Till then, Catholic laymen were obliged to study with future priests at Prior Park (1830), Oscott (1794), Ushaw (1808) and St. Edmund's (1793) in Ware, and were barred entrance into England's universities.[1] Newman had appealed to the Catholic laity in his *Lectures on the Present Position of Catholics in England:*

> Your strength lies in your God and your conscience; therefore it lies not in your number. It lies not in your number any more than in intrigue, or combination or worldly wisdom . . . What I desiderate in Catholics is the gift of bringing out what their religion is . . . I want a laity, not arrogant, not rash in speech, not disputatious, but men who know their religion, who enter into it, who know just where they stand, who know what they hold and what they do not, who know their creed so well that they can give an account of it, who know so much of history that they can defend it. I want an intelligent, well-instructed laity; I am not denying

---

1 The Jesuits had established Stonyhurst College in Lancashire (1794), and the Benedictines had schools at Ampleforth Abbey (1802) and Downside Abbey (1814).

you are such already; but I mean to be severe, and, as some
would say, exorbitant in my demands, I wish you to enlarge
your knowledge, to cultivate your reason, to get an insight
into the relation of truth to truth, to learn to view things as they
are, to understand how faith and reason stand to each other,
what are the bases and principles of Catholicism, and where
lie the main inconsistencies and absurdities of the Protestant
theory.[2]

A group of laymen, led by Edward Bellasis, Thomas
Allies and Francis Ward, promoted the plan. . . . Among the
latter were James Hope-Scott, Lord John Acton, Edward
Badeley, Henry Wilberforce and the Duke of Norfolk.[3]
Newman wrote to Bellasis: "We have decided to commence the School. . . . We have come to this decision in
consequence of the wish expressed by the noblemen and
gentlemen, whose names you sent me. We do not think
it any presumption in us to undertake it with the sanction
of such friends."[4] Bishop Ullathorne initially supported
Newman's plans. Soon, however, under the influence of
Archbishop Wiseman, who had been persuaded by Faber
and the London Oratorians that a school was contrary to
the spirit of the Oratory of St. Philip Neri, he entertained
doubts about Newman's plans. Newman feared that Fr.
Faber would oppose the plans by proposing a rival school
in London. Bellasis assured him "that no attempt at a rival
school is likely to be made by Faber without the con-

---

2 John Henry Newman, *Lectures on the Present Position of Catholics
in England*, 388-391.

3 Paul Shrimpton, *A Catholic Eton? Newman's Oratory School*
(Leominster: Gracewing, 2005), 40-41; 60.

4 *LD*, Vol. XVIII, JHN to Edward Bellasis (April 23, 1858), 330-332,
331.

currence and aid of the Duke, and we do not think that, under the circumstances, and considering the Duke knows of your plan and even promised to aid pecuniarily [sic] towards it, he would be likely to get encouragement from that quarter."[5]

Overcoming Cardinal Wiseman's opposition, in May 1859, Newman was able to begin the Oratory School at Birmingham with seven boys, all of them sons of converts. Wiseman, however, was the cause of much suffering for Newman on other projects too; a notable one was the project for a new English translation of the Bible.[6] In 1857, Wiseman informed Newman that the second Provincial Synod of Westminster celebrated in 1855 had decided to entrust him with a new English translation of the Bible. Since the Douay-Rheims translation with modifications by Bishop Challoner in the seventeenth century, there had not been another English translation. After asking Wiseman for a copy of the synod's decree and reading it himself, Newman undertook this major project.[7] He sought advice from many scholars for the undertaking, chose three Oratorians to work on it, and prepared a detailed budget and work plan, which he sent to the Archbishop of Westminster.

Wiseman, who before the synod had wished that his friends at the London Oratory would undertake the translation, delayed in replying to Newman's letters. In the

---

5 *LD*, Vol. XVIII, Edward Bellasis to JHN (December 25, 1858), 554.

6 *AW,* 256-60.

7 *LD*, Vol. XVIII, JHN to P. N. Lynch, Bishop of Charleston, (December 7, 1858), 531-534.

summer of 1858, Newman learned from his good friend William Clifford, Bishop of Clifton, that Wiseman had blocked the project.[8] In 1859, Newman felt obliged to abandon the undertaking, for which he had made plans with great interest. Newman had used a large sum of his own money to begin the translation, but he realized that without the support of Cardinal Wiseman, the project was doomed.

Dropping the translation of the Bible engendered great disappointment in Newman, yet he reacted with respect and charity toward the English bishops, as he had done earlier toward the Irish bishops. His obedience and love for the Church was also tested in 1859, when he reluctantly agreed to take up the editorship of *The Rambler*. This journal had been started ten years earlier by John M. Capes, an Oxford convert. It was a publication for Catholic intellectuals that was critical of the two most circulated Catholic periodicals, the *Dublin Review* and *The Tablet*.[9] *The Rambler* had acquired an anti-Roman tone and it challenged the Catholic bishops on subjects of public policy, such as education. At the end of 1858, Lord Acton had stirred opposition when he described St. Augustine as "the father of Jansenism." Newman wrote to Acton, proprietor of the *Rambler*: "Power, to be powerful, and strength, to be strong and effective, must be exerted only now and then—I then would be strong and effective, and affect public opinion without offending piety or good sense."[10] At the behest of Archbishop Ullathorne,

---

8 Morales, *Newman (1801-1890)*, 253.

9 *Ibid.*, 255.

10 *LD*, Vol. XVIII, JHN to Sir John Acton, (December 31, 1858), 559-562, 562.

Newman acted as intermediary between Simpson Capes, the editor, and the bishops. Simpson agreed to relinquish the editorship, and Newman reluctantly became the editor of *The Rambler*.

Newman wished to support a publication of high intellectual level for Catholic laypersons, which was moderate and open to liberal opinions.[11] In the May issue of the journal, he ran into trouble when he voiced the idea that if laypersons had been consulted in the preparation of the dogmatic definition of the Immaculate Conception (1854), it would be logical that they could be consulted in important practical matters such as education. The bishops were then discussing the proposal of a royal commission on education and feared pressure from laymen. Soon negative criticism against Newman arose from a professor in dogmatic theology at Ushaw and on the part of bishops. Wiseman, who had established the *Dublin Review*, also did not like to see Newman at the head of a competing publication.[12] As a result of all this, Ullathorne asked Newman to step down as editor, and Newman immediately followed the order of his superior. Writing to Henry Wilberforce, Newman explained that upon being asked to resign he had prayed to see God's will. Newman thought he was writing what needed to be said, but told his friend, "I have always preached that things which are *really* useful, still are done, according to God's will, at one time or another—and that, if you attempt at a wrong time, what in itself is right, you perhaps become a heretic or schismatic. . . . Of course it is

---

11 Morales, *Newman (1801-1890)*, 258.
12 *Ibid.*, 259.

discouraging to be out of joint with time, and to be snubbed and stopped as soon as I begin to act."[13]

Upon resignation and by indication of his bishop, Newman wrote a lengthy article titled "On Consulting the Faithful in Matters of Doctrine," which was published in the July issue of the magazine.[14] In the article Newman explained the doctrine later called *sensus fidelium*. Newman distinguished between consultation on practical matters and matters of Catholic faith; in the former, the hierarchy sought advice for their decisions, whereas in the latter they only sought the verification of the existence of a given doctrine. Consultation by the Holy See or bishops did not mean submission to the laity. Newman explained, "Doubtless their advice, their opinion, their judgment on the question of definition is not asked; but the matter of fact, viz. their belief, is sought for, as a testimony to that apostolical Tradition, on which alone any doctrine whatsoever can be defined."[15] But for Newman, the consent of the faithful was more than a witness to the truth. The faithful, guided by the Holy Spirit, understood the content of the faith instinctively and were very sensitive to error or scandal. Newman offered an example from his book, *The Arians of the Fourth Century* in which he showed how this was a period when "the divine tradition committed to the infallible Church was

---

13 *LD*, Vol. XIX, JHN to Henry Wilberforce, (July 17, 1859), 179-180; 179.

14 John Henry Newman, "On Consulting the Faithful in Matters of Doctrine," *The Rambler* (July 1859):198-230, available at: http://www.newmanreader.org/works/rambler/consulting.html.

15 *Ibid.,* 199.

proclaimed and maintained far more by the faithful than by the Episcopate . . ."[16]

Newman's insightful article, however, only awakened more misunderstanding, and Bishop Thomas J. Brown of Newport accused Newman of heresy before the Holy See.[17] Newman wished to find out what propositions were objectionable, and he wrote to Ullathorne, who was in Rome. Informed by Ullathorne of the accusation, Wiseman expressed sadness and notified Newman that he would take care of the matter. The Congregation for *Propaganda Fidei* sent Wiseman a list of passages in the article that might be objectionable, or require certain qualification, but Wiseman dropped the matter and thus Newman never received this important information. The Prefect of *Propaganda*, Alessandro Barnabó, mistakenly interpreted Newman's silence as disobedience.

Some years later he confided to Emily Bowles regarding the *Rambler*:

I not only made the best of it, but I really determined to make it *my work.* All those questions of the day which make so much noise now, Faith and Reason, Inspiration, etc etc would have been, according to my ability, worked out or fairly opened. Of course I required elbow room—but this was *impossible.* Our good Bishop, who has ever acted as a true friend, came after the publication of the first number, and advised me to give up the Editorship. He said I had caused dissatisfaction. I only edited two numbers; but I wrote enough to cause one of our Bishops formally to denounce one of the articles to Propaganda.[18]

---

16 *Ibid*, 213.

17 Morales, *Newman (1801-1890)*, 261.

18 *LD,* Vol. XX, JHN to Emily Bowles, (May 19, 1863), 445-448; 447.

Newman explained that *Propaganda* did not know of "the niceties of the English language." It was a "quasi-military power, extraordinary, for missionary countries" but did not understand an intellectual movement.[19]

This episode saddened Newman and made him retire from public life. He was more cautious with projects that involved Cardinal Wiseman and Rome, and wished to be left alone. From 1859 to 1864, he did not publish any works. Newman felt *Propaganda Fidei* was on top of him or with "a chain on my arm."[20] He wrote Emily that in earlier times in history, the Holy See was a court of ultimate appeal, but now he felt that there was no freedom of opinion. Instead of having his bishop judge, someone would denounce him directly to Rome. It was a time of interior suffering for Newman. He felt he was not using his talents and was thwarted from doing so. This injustice and others, which he experienced years later, helped to purify his intentions and took him to a new height of spiritual life in which he became more detached from others' opinions. He accepted these injustices as the spiritual Cross that he was asked to bear.[21]

In 1860, the year following the publication of Darwin's *The Origin of Species,* a volume of seven essays with a critical rationalist approach to Sacred Scripture and Revelation, titled *Essays and Reviews,* was published.[22] In light of this publication, Newman began to write once more

---

19 *Ibid,* 446.
20 *Ibid,* 446.
21 *AW,* 275.
22 Morales, *Newman (1801-1890),* 266.

on Faith and Reason and on the certitude obtained through Faith. His writing, culminating ten years later with the publication of *A Grammar of Assent*, was a continuation of the *University Sermons*.[23] Newman thought that the German theories of biblical criticism influencing Anglican writers should be criticized; this would, however, first require serious study on the part of Catholics. In 1861, Newman studied the nature of Biblical Inspiration in response to the ideas put forth in *Essays and Reviews*. That same year, Cardinal Wiseman began the Academy of the Catholic Religion to introduce Catholic thought into the intellectual debate. Newman excused himself from forming part of this academy, which Wiseman inaugurated with a discourse having a triumphal tone.[24]

In 1861, the Oratory School at Birmingham faced a grave crisis under Fr. Nicholas Darnell, assigned to this post by Newman. Without consulting Newman, Fr. Darnell threatened to dismiss Mrs. Wooten, the woman in charge of the motherly attention of the boys, over serious disagreements.[25] Mrs. Wooten, who was loyal to Newman, would not allow Darnell to take complete control of the school.[26] Under Darnell the school faced serious disciplinary problems and a neglect of the religious formation of the boys. After a great deal of tension, Darnell, who left the Oratory, resigned with all the staff of Masters, and then resisted entreaties to come back. Newman managed to overcome the crisis

---

23 *Ibid.*, 266.

24 *Ibid.*, 267; Robert Gray, *Cardinal Manning, A Biography* (New York: St. Martin's Press, 1985), 183.

25 Shrimpton, *A Catholic Eton? Newman's Oratory School*, 116-124.

26 Morales, *Newman (1801-1890)*, 272.

by regaining the confidence of parents, which he did by hiring new teachers and placing the reliable Ambrose St. John as headmaster. Fortunately the school did not lose any boys and even increased in numbers. Newman felt that this had been the gravest crisis experienced by the Birmingham community. He wrote an Oxford friend and convert, "But the real affliction has been the blow to the Congregation, the severance of such long and intimate ties—and the enormous scandal."[27]

Newman's health was seriously affected by the events at the Oratory School (he was unable to sleep) and he was obliged by doctors to take long periods of rest and to go away for some time. To Sister Mary Gabriel Du Boulay, who sent him a consoling letter he said: "I have not the faith, patience, and resignation which I ought to have—but this is another matter. My ailment is a physical effect, I may call it, on my mind. It is said that in a naval engagement, while the vessels near, and the men are standing quite still, the knees of the bravest shake."[28] But Newman was suffering also from many other slights and gestures of ungratefulness that had surfaced in his mind. He confided a few days later to Maria Giberne: "As for me, my writing days are for the present day over. The long cares I have had, the disappointments of religious hopes, and the sense of cruelty in word and deed on the part of those from whom I deserved other things,—a penance which I have had in one shape or another for thirty years,—at length have fallen

---

27 *LD,* Vol XX, JHN to John Hungerford Pollen, (January 21, 1862), 131-132; 131.

28 *Ibid,* JHN to Sister Mary Gabriel Du Boulay, (August 18, 1861), 29-31, 29.

on my nerves . . ."[29] Newman had other reasons for sorrow: Frederick Bowles, who had lived at Littlemore and converted in 1845, unexpectedly left the Oratory in 1860, and joined the diocesan clergy. He did, however, maintain contact with Newman and remained his friend.[30] In 1862, John Stanislas Flanagan, who together with Bowles had been part of the Oratory since 1848, also left the Oratory. Returning to Ireland, Flanagan joined the diocesan clergy of a diocese in his homeland.

29 *Ibid*, JHN to Maria Giberne (Miss M. R. Giberne), (August 28, 1861), 37-38, 37.

30 Morales, *Newman (1801-1890)*, 273.

CHAPTER 38

APOLOGIA PRO VITA SUA

I N 1864, Newman broke his long public silence to respond to false accusations and the ridicule of Roman Catholic priests by Charles Kingsley, a novelist, Chaplain to the Queen, and professor of Modern History at Cambridge. In the January 1864 issue of Macmillan's Magazine, which Newman received in late December 1863, Kingsley accused Newman of having stated as an Anglican that the Roman clergy did not consider truthfulness a virtue. Kingsley wrote, "Truth, for its own sake, had never been a virtue with the Roman clergy. Father Newman informs us that it need not, and on the whole ought not to be . . ."[1]

After an unsatisfactory apology by Kingsley in the following issue of *Macmillan's Magazine*, Newman began to write a pamphlet which eventually evolved into his famous autobiography. For some time, Newman had been seeking an opportunity to explain and defend his religious opinions and certain steps in his life. In this attack, he had found the occasion. He gathered old correspondence from Anglican friends and worked with remarkable intensity to relate the history of his religious beliefs. From late April to early June, he worked an average of over fifteen hours each day,

---

1 Charles Kingsley, *Macmillan's Magazine* (January 1864), quoted by Ian Ker, *John Henry Newman*, 533.

writing in standing position at his desk at the library of the Birmingham Oratory. The result was a powerful autobiography that reflected Newman's passion for the truth and the evolution of his religious beliefs. Newman wrote his friend Richard Church about Kingsley's accusation: "Thus, publicly challenged, I must speak—and, unless I speak strongly, men won't believe me in earnest."[2] He asked his friend, a witness of Newman's last years as an Anglican, to "correct any fault of fact" in his statement. The *Apologia Pro Vita Sua* was read throughout the country by people of every religious creed. It was a vindication of Newman's intellectual honesty and of the validity of the Catholic Creed.

The *Apologia* signaled a new beginning in Newman's public life. His name and reputation were restored in England, in particular among Protestants. He gained the respect not only of many of his opponents but also gained respect for Roman Catholic theologians from Anglicans and others. Newman thanked God that after twenty years, his conduct had been cleared in the sight of Protestants.[3] He had unsuccessfully tried to clear his name in Rome, but had little further desire or hope of doing so in his lifetime. A large number of English Catholics wrote Newman to thank him and to congratulate him. Newman paid tribute in this book to his brother priests at the Birmingham Oratory and dedicated it to Ambrose St. John, who was the link between Newman's old and new life. For the span of twenty-two years, St. John had been very generous and loyal to Newman.

---

2 *LD*, Vol. XXI, JHN to R. W. Church (April 23, 1964), 100-101, 100.
3 *AW* (October 30, 1867), 262.

The publication of the *Apologia* helped to revive Newman's former friendships. During the decade of the sixties,
he renewed his contact with old Anglican friends. In 1861,
Newman reestablished correspondence with Isaac Williams, one of the early members of the Oxford Movement.
Newman wrote to Williams: "There is no pleasure of this
world which to me would be so great in itself, as to see you
and other of my old friends. Before I became what I am, the
loss of them was the great trouble which lay before me; and
it has not ceased to be, up to this hour, the special sacrifice
which I offer up to my Lord . . ."[4] That same year Newman
met in London with William Copeland, who had been his
curate at St. Mary's, and would later edit his Anglican sermons in 1868.

Frederic Rogers, Newman's pupil and a Fellow at Oriel
in 1833, visited Newman at Birmingham, and from then
on they remained in close contact the rest of their lives. In
July 1865, Rogers and William Church, who later wrote
a very favorable history of the Oxford Movement, gave
Newman the gift of a fine violin. Newman still loved to
play the violin, and even feared he indulged when playing
it, but he claimed that he wrote more and slept better after
playing music.[5] Once when Jemima visited her brother at
Birmingham, she played Beethoven's sonatas on a piano
while he accompanied her on the violin. Classical music
delighted Newman, and Beethoven's *Sonata in A minor* in
particular filled him with emotion.[6] It was also in 1865 that

---

4 *LD,* Vol. XX, JHN to Isaac Williams (October 21, 1861), 59-61; 59-60.

5 *LD,* Vol. XXII, JHN to R. W. Church (July 11, 1865), 9.

6 *LD,* Vol. XXIII, JHN to Mrs. John Mozley (June 19, 1867), 255.

Newman made the memorable visit to his old friend John Keble, and met with his other close friend, Edward Pusey, at Keble's home.

One of Newman's friends, Henry Manning, a convert to Catholicism and secretary to Cardinal Wiseman, became successor to the See of Westminster when Wiseman died in 1865. In the letter congratulating Manning for his appointment Newman asked him not to do anything to have him made bishop. Manning admitted: "I have for more than two years done my part to accomplish it . . . but your wish must be final with me."[7] Newman and Manning were men of very different temperaments. Their opinions on many ecclesiastical matters varied greatly. On a number of occasions, as had happened with Wiseman, Newman was unjustly treated by Manning.[8] The latter actually maintained that he had tried to set things right with Newman but that Newman was oversensitive.[9] The relationship between these two important English Catholics sadly worsened over the years, albeit remaining civil.

In 1865, Archbishop Ullathorne asked Newman to establish an Oratory in Oxford. Newman was worried about the dangers of interconfessional education, but due to Ullathorne's insistence, he acquiesced. At this time the English bishops debated the issue of Catholic youth studying at Protestant universities. Under Manning's pressure the bishops decided against Catholics studying at the public

---

7 LD, Vol. XXI, Archbishop Manning to JHN (June 4, 1865), 479.

8 *AW* (February 20, 1865), 260-61.

9 Leslie Shane, *Henry Edward Manning, His Life and Labours* (London: Burns, Oates and Washbourne Limited, 1921), "The Case of Dr. Newman," 269-87; 279, 283.

universities.[10] The bishops feared that Catholic youth attending public universities would lose their faith, and Manning
worried that by having an Oratory at Oxford, Newman's
prestige would attract Catholic youth to Oxford University.
In December 1866, *Propaganda Fidei* gave permission for
an Oratory in Oxford attached to the Birmingham Oratory,
but gave a secret instruction to Bishop Ullathorne prohibit-
ing Newman from residing in Oxford. The following year
Newman found out about this. Against his better instinct
that a project for an Oxford Oratory would fail, Newman
raised money from wealthy Catholics and bought a property in Oxford for that purpose.[11] He had an optimistic
view of the Christian spirit and was inimical to being on
the defensive. He argued that although Oxford was dangerous, every place was dangerous; the world was dangerous,
and yet "you cannot keep young men under glass cases."[12]
Only a few months earlier, while the bishops were on the
defensive against Protestant errors at Oxford, Newman's
influence at Oxford was raising new giants for the Catholic Church: Gerard Manley Hopkins wrote Newman that
along with three friends he had had a conversion, yet they
had all been received into the Church earlier. He wished to
be received by Newman, who was pleased to do so. Hopkins signed his letter to Newman, "your affectionate son in
Christ."[13]

---

10 James Pereiro, *Cardinal Manning, An Intellectual Biography*
(Oxford: Clarendon University Press, 1998), 235-45.

11 Morales, *Newman (1801-1890)*, 289-94.

12 *LD*, Vol. XXIII, JHN to Sir Justin Sheil (March 22, 1867), 100-102;
101.

13 *LD*, Vol. XXII, Gerard Manley Hopkins to JHN (October 18,1866),

At stake was not only a future Oratory at Oxford but the Oratory School already established at Birmingham. Archbishop Manning sent Herbert Vaughan, his future successor as Archbishop of Westminster, to Rome to persuade Alessandro Barnabó, Prefect of the office of *Propaganda Fidei,* and the Pope that the Oratory School's real objective was to prepare students for the public English universities, and that Newman's presence at Oxford would only encourage Catholic youth to study there.[14] In March 1867, Ullathorne wrote Newman of the opposition against the Oratory by Cardinal Manning and others: "Dr. Herbert Vaughan, who is at Rome, and has considerable weight there speaks openly of you as having established a school to train youths for Oxford."[15]

Ullathorne urged Newman to go to Rome to defend himself, but Newman sent Ambrose St. John and Henry Bittleson to clarify misunderstandings. St. John was able to find out that some of the misunderstandings dated back to Newman's article on "Consulting the Lay Faithful," and to Wiseman's failure to notify Newman of Barnabó's list of objections. Matters came to a head when a Roman correspondent questioning Newman's orthodoxy in an

302.

14 *LD,* Vol. XXIII, JHN to James Hope-Scott (March 29, 1867), 112-13; Instructions for Ambrose St. John (April 2, 1867), 120-21. Periero, *Cardinal Manning, An Intellectual Biography,* 244. Manning, who doubted Newman's orthodoxy, told Vaughan that Newman did not have the right "Catholic spirit."

15 *LD,* Vol. XXIII, from Bishop Ullathorne to JHN, (March 28), 1867, 111.

article for the *Weekly Register* revealed what was common knowledge in Vatican circles, namely the secret instruction to keep Newman from going to Oxford. When Newman heard of the condition he wrote a letter to his bishop. In a draft which was not approved by the fathers of the Oratory, he wrote,

> And now, on at length knowing it, I am obliged to say at once I cannot accept the mission with that condition. Nor am I likely to change my mind on this point. If I am a missioner at Oxford, I claim to be there, as much as or as little as I please . . . Not that I have ever intended to leave residence in Birmingham; but such a condition would be a snare to my conscience, and if I stopped at Oxford for a few days in Term time, it would easily be construed by Propaganda into residence. No compromise is possible here. [16]

Newman added that he could no longer trust Propaganda. Newman had an overwhelming support of the educated English laity who were very upset about the claims of the *Weekly Register*. In April, Newman's friend William Monsell drew up a lay address in support of Newman which was signed by the Catholic members of the House of Commons, nearly all the Catholic peers and a great majority of prominent laymen. Newman wrote to Cardinal Barnabó that he was unjustly being singled out. In August 1867, the Holy See sent an instruction to the English bishops which categorically declared that sending a Catholic youth to study at Oxford or Cambridge constituted a proximate occasion of grave sin that would not allow exceptions. Upon hearing of

---

16 *LD,* Vol.. XXIII, JHN to Bishop Ullathorne,(April 6, 1867), 130-131; 131.

this indication by Rome, Newman wrote his bishop, asking permission to withdraw from the Oxford project. Already before the rescript from Rome, Newman had decided not to go on with the Oxford mission.

Despite Newman's renewed prestige in England, some Catholics questioned Newman's orthodoxy, tarnishing his reputation both in England and Rome. Herbert Vaughan, Manning's envoy to Rome, went as far as to accuse Newman of being the greatest exponent of liberal thought.[17] This was far from true; Newman understood and respected Tradition and authority in the Church. Since Newman believed that theologians should help the hierarchy to formulate dogmatic definitions, he distanced himself from Ignaz Döllinger, a German Church historian. Döllinger had opposed the dogma of the Immaculate Conception based on a fixed notion of Tradition that was the opposite of Newman's Theory of Development. In 1858, Newman did not attend some conferences that Lord John Acton held for liberal Catholics at his country home; Döllinger, under whom Acton had studied in Germany, participated. Later, in 1864, when the Holy See issued a Syllabus of Errors, Newman defended Rome's decision from the theological point of view.

The failure of the Oxford project and accusations of heterodoxy, even heresy, were very painful for a man as obedient to his bishop and steeped in Tradition as Newman was. Surprisingly, after Manning's own opposition to Newman, he wrote to Newman to profess his friendship and decry the public's views of their differences. Manning

---

17 Gray, *Cardinal Manning, A Biography*, 214-15.

expressed a desire to clarify matters with Newman and to heal their friendship. Newman replied that the sentiments of their past friendship could not be erased but that their trust had been broken and it would be very difficult to mend: "I should rejoice indeed, if it were so easy to set matters right. It is only as time goes on, that new deeds can reverse the old. There is no short cut to a restoration of confidence, when confidence has been seriously damaged."[18]

The damage done to the friendship with Manning did not keep Newman from recognizing the good intentions of Manning and the achievements of Wiseman and Faber. These good men had acted unjustly toward Newman out of human frailty. They had also surrounded themselves with advisers who were antagonistic to Newman and misrepresented him with other ecclesiastics and the Holy See. Initially, Newman defended himself, but he later accepted this suffering and decided not to worry about pleasing anyone other than God.[19] He recorded the wrongs done to him only in private letters to a few friends and in his personal notes. However, to the credit of Cardinal Manning, it should be noted that on one occasion after Newman's *Letter to the Duke of Norfolk,* he wrote to the Holy See to ward off any hasty judgment of Newman's *Letter.*[20]

---

18 *LD,* Vol. XXIII, JHN to Archbishop Manning (August 10, 1867), 290-291, 290.

19 *AW* (February 22), 1865, 260-261.

20 Shane, *Henry Edward Manning, His Life and Labours,* 269-87; 281.

CHAPTER 39

NEWMAN, THE PHILOSOPHER

AFTER this difficult period in his life, during which he tried to defend his intentions and actions, as well as those of Catholic priests, and Catholic intellectual thought in general, came one of Newman's greatest works: *An Essay in Aid of a Grammar of Assent,* published in March of 1870. It was a heavily philosophical book, and the one on which he worked for the longest time. Newman wrote it in response to the difficulties of William Froude, a Protestant friend who was losing his faith. The book, which was a culmination of his thinking about the philosophical nature of belief and certitude in the *University Sermons,* interrupted Newman's writing on metaphysics.

Newman had a philosophical mind and read widely on philosophy. At the end of 1858 he began a course of reading on metaphysics to write a book for a projected *magnum opus* on philosophy of religion. Some years later he abandoned this work, titled *Discursive Enquiries on Metaphysical Subjects,* but his notes were compiled into a book and published posthumously as his *Philosophical Notebook.* He had studied in detail Aristotle's *Logic, Rhetoric* and *Nichomachean Ethics,* which had a major influence on his thinking about knowledge as a personal possession and about knowledge as the grasping of existent realities, rather than abstractions. In the *Grammar of Assent* he acknowledged deriving from Aristotle ideas on moral duty and φρόνησις (phronesis), or the personal prudential judgment. Regarding his own doctrine of the Illative sense, he wrote: "As to the intellectual position from which I have contemplated the subject (of human knowledge), Aristotle has been my master."[1]

The study of Joseph Butler's *Analogy of Religion* helped him to overcome a nominalist and rationalist reading of Aristotle, predominant at Oriel College. He was influenced by Butler's notion of probability, without accepting the way Butler left it, and thus avoided the mistaken claim of falling into skepticism. In the *Grammar of Assent* he says: "My aim is of a practical character, such as that of Butler in his *Analogy*, with this difference, that he treats of probability, doubt, expediency and duty, whereas in these pages, without excluding, from it, the question of duty, I would confine myself to the truth of things, and to the mind's certitude of that truth."[2]

From the Alexandrian Fathers, especially Clement and Origen, he was acquainted and influenced by the Neo-Platonic philosophy about the unseen world. He greatly admired Francis Bacon and his distinction between physics and natural theology, and had studied Isaac Newton's *Principia*. He read English and Scottish philosophers, in particular John Locke, whom he considered a "highly respected adversary with whom he liked to discuss (figuratively) his

---

1 John Henry Newman, *An Essay in Aid of a Grammar of Assent*, University of Notre Dame Press (1979), p. 334. After this it will be cited *GA*.
2 *GA*, 271.

own ideas."[3] On the surface it would seem that Newman had a few ideas in common with Locke, such as making the individual, or self, the starting point of his whole philosophy; but the self and the God of Locke were completely rationalist and alien to the thought of Newman, who opposed British Empiricism, of which he considered Locke to be the founder.

A minor source of his philosophical thought was St. Thomas Aquinas. At Oxford he had a 28-volume set of St. Thomas's works, which he read in part, and while residing in Rome he attempted to study Aquinas's philosophy and theology. He was disappointed to find that Aquinas and Aristotle were both in disregard, but this may have actually helped Newman to further his development of a type of personalism relying at once on both Ancient and Patristic sources and on modern empirical thought, particularly on associationist theories in psychology. From Abraham Tucker and Joshua Reynolds, representatives of this theory of knowledge, Newman may have taken the notion of the imagination as a cognitive power capable of giving us direct apprehension of individual objects with which we come into experiential contact.[4] Through the imagination particular things can absorb the attention of the knowing subject, and the cognition is a personal and living relationship between the knower and the object. Knowledge is therefore more than reasoning; rather, it is a real possession of the things we know. This was a key point for Newman's

---

3 John Henry Newman, *The Philosophical Notebook,* Ed. Edward J. Sillem, Nauwelaerts Publishing House, Louvain, 1969, Vol. II, 203.

4 *Ibid,* 207.

argument for the existence of God, as well as his explanation of a person's understanding of the teaching of Scripture and the articles of the Creed about the Blessed Trinity. Today his philosophical approach would be described as phenomenology, or more specifically, Christian personalism, with elements of Aristotelian philosophy of the human mind and ethics.

The *Grammar of Assent* is a philosophy of knowledge and a philosophy of religion or natural theology. It was a criticism of the natural theology of deists such as William Paley and skeptics such as David Hume, and an exposition of a Christian approach to belief in God and the Catholic Church. The book has two parts; the first is an explanation of how the mind assents to God and other religious truths, and the second, of how the mind arrives at certitude. Newman began with the assent of the mind to truths in general, since according to him we assent to God's existence and attributes in the same way that we assent to other truths. Newman explained that a person knows real objects as well as notions or concepts. Faith or religion consists in the knowledge of the real objects, whereas theology consists in the knowledge of propositions or notions, which are judged to be true.

In this first part of the book, Newman developed his argument for the existence of God from the moral conscience. It is an argument which he often had referred to in his sermons and also in the *Apologia*. There, Newman explained that for a child, God is a real being. A child perceives the existence of God as a Sovereign Law Giver and Judge, someone outside of himself. God is not a notion or a conclusion. By means of his moral conscience a child has an image of God which, although nascent and capable of being dimmed or obliterated, is nevertheless real. "It is an image of the good God, good in Himself, good relatively to the child, with whatever incompleteness; an image, before it has been reflected on, and before it is recognized as a notion. Though he cannot explain or define the word 'God,' when told to use it, his acts show that to him it is far more than a word."[5] Something similar can be said for many adults: they cannot explain religious truths, but they know them because they have a moral conscience that speaks to them of right and wrong, and of a Law Giver and Judge.

In the same way, all men can have this real knowledge of God—that is, faith—in God and in the fact that He creates, provides, judges, rewards and punishes. The question of the certainty of this faith soon arises. Over the years Newman had discussed with William Froude, younger brother of Hurrell, the subject of the certainty of propositions and certitude of the mind. Froude claimed the right to skepticism of any truth: "Our doubts in fact, appear to me as *sacred,* and I think deserve to be cherished as *sacredly* as our beliefs."[6] In a reply to Froude, Newman distinguished between religion and science: "Much lies in the meaning of the words certainty and doubt—much again in our duties to a *person,* as e.g. a friend—Religion is not merely a *science,* but a *devotion.*"[7]

In the second part of the *Grammar of Assent*, Newman tried to give an account of the certitude of faith. He argued

5 *GA*, 105.

6 *LD,* Vol XIX, William Froude to JHN (December 29, 1859), 270.

7 *Ibid,* 273.

that the mind reaches certitude through informal inference and formal inference and that religious faith is based on the former. In it he made the well-known observation: "Many a man will live and die upon a dogma: no man will be a martyr for a conclusion,"[8] the result of a logical syllogism. He insisted, "No one, I say, will die for his calculations: he dies for realities."[9] Newman explained that informal inference is attained by means of what he called the illative faculty or sense. This is a natural mode of reasoning which is unconscious and implicit; it goes from concrete things to universal principles, not from propositions to conclusions, as in formal inference or logic.

For Newman, a man reaches certitude through this illative sense. A skeptic might reply that this is tantamount to a leap of faith, but there is no such leap because the assent of faith has a cumulative and pains-taking dimension. It is something of a process, and we grow into a conviction, rather than leap into it.[10] Newman used the example of a polygon inscribed in a circle. As its sides become smaller it tends to become the circle. It never becomes the circle but the mind closes the gap.[11]

On this subject Newman shared a number of ideas with Blaise Pascal (1623–1662), whom he quoted in various places, especially in the *Grammar of Assent.* Newman's understanding of implicit (or instinctual) reasoning and the illative sense has common elements with Pascal's notion of the heart and the intuitive mind. Like Pascal, Newman

---

8 *GA*, 89.

9 *Ibid.*

10 *Ibid.* 18 (introduction).

11 *Ibid.* 253-254.

thought that external proofs of religion as grounds of faith were insufficient for most ordinary people. Instead he pointed out that the assent of faith depends on a person's moral character and openness to believe. Newman explained that the inquirer is "guided by the implicit process of the reasoning faculty, not by any manufacture of arguments forcing their way to an irrefragable conclusion.

Faith is a two-dimensional personal act. It is subjective in so far as it is different for me than it would be for anyone else, and yet objective as well, since through it a person apprehends religious truths from the Church. For Newman, humility, or a childlike spirit, is a necessary condition for belief. Without humility one is incapable of believing in God; a person establishes his own universe and banishes any supernatural reality. Pride closes a person in a limited sphere of rationality.

The second part of the *Grammar of Assent* ends with a long section on natural and revealed religion. It presents arguments on how Catholicism fulfills what would be expected of a true revealed religion and how it corresponds to the fulfillment and completion of the promises God made to the Jewish people.

Newman considered the *Grammar of Assent*, together with the *Prophetic Office of the Church, Lectures on Justification,* the *Development of Christian Doctrine,* and *Idea of a University* to be one of the books that gathered the central themes of his thought on fundamental subjects. He hoped that it would show the harmony of faith and reason, and renew Christian apologetics. Although Newman discontinued his projected work on metaphysics, his philosophical notes and sermons reveal an original philosopher who made a lasting contribution to philosophy of religion through his *University Sermons* and his *Grammar of Assent.* William Froude died in 1878 while engaged in a continued correspondence with Newman on religion and certainty. His wife, Mrs. William Froude, had long since, in 1857, become a Roman Catholic with the help of Newman's lengthy correspondence.

CHAPTER 40

PAPAL INFALLIBILITY AND LETTER TO THE DUKE OF NORFOLK

DOUBTS concerning Newman's orthodoxy would arise when some of his writings were taken out of context. As a Roman Catholic, Newman fully accepted Papal Infallibility in doctrinal matters. This is shown in his *Essay on the Development of Christian Doctrine*, in which he examined the subject of papal authority and illustrated its historical reach. When in 1867 Pope Pius IX announced the intention of convoking an ecumenical council, it became evident that the council would deal with the question of Papal Infallibility. Dupanloup, the French Bishop of Orleans, invited Newman to accompany him to the Convocation as his theologian, but Newman declined. Next the Pope asked Newman through Archbishop Ullathorne to be a consultant for one of the preparatory committees. Newman again declined. Strangely, Bishop Thomas J. Brown, who had denounced him to the Holy See, also invited Newman, and Bishop Dupanloup sent a second invitation. Newman excused himself, alleging delicate health. To Maria Giberne, Newman described the capacity of a theologian, which he denied that he possessed, although history has shown that he surely fit this description well. The once proud Oxford don had become a humble theologian who shunned personal controversy.

The subject of infallibility, however, was destined to become a heated debate which created division among English Catholics. Newman did not publicly take part in the controversy, but he assisted the Oratorian, Ignatius Ryder, who wrote an article in response to W. G. Ward's extreme views of papal authority. Ward sustained in the *Dublin Review* the belief that everything the Pope said was infallible. Newman wrote to Pusey, "As to the Infallibility of the Pope, I see nothing against it, or to dread in it—for I am confident that it *must* be so limited practically that it will leave things as they are."[1] When Catholic periodicals in Europe began to debate a truth, which in practice was peacefully received, Newman expressed his sorrow in a confidential letter to Ullathorne. But Newman's letter was mysteriously made public in the *London Standard*, resulting in embarrassment to Newman.

In July 1870, the Church's bishops met in Rome for the ecumenical council Vatican I, which defined the dogma of Papal Infallibility before the council was interrupted by the Franco-Prussian War. The definition was a measured pronouncement of the authority of the successor of St. Peter. Newman, who had expected this prudent tone, was very pleased.[2] Even so, he wrote Ambrose St. John that "this

---

1 *LD.,* Vol. XXII, JHN to E. B. Pusey (November 17, 1865), 103-105; 103.

2 The definition holds that it is a divinely revealed truth that "when the Roman Pontiff speaks EX CATHEDRA, that is, when, in the exercise of his office as shepherd and teacher of all Christians, in virtue of his supreme apostolic authority, he defines a doctrine concerning faith or morals to be held by the whole Church, he possesses, by the divine assistance promised to him in blessed Peter, that infallibility which the divine Redeemer

definition, while it gives the Pope power, creates for him, in the very act of doing so, a precedent and a suggestion to use his power without necessity, when ever he will, when not called to do so."[3] Newman worried that "the tyrant majority is still aiming at enlarging the *province* of infallibility."[4] At the same time Newman wrote Georges Darboy, Archbishop of Paris, that "when Rome spoke on this subject every misgiving vanished; for, if by some fiction those who love me will have it that I am a teacher of the faithful, I am above all a disciple of the Church, *doctor fidelium discipulis ecclesiae.*"[5] He reasoned that the definition would put an end to the ideas which gave rise to Jansenism and Gallicanism in France, and the Branch Theory in England. The same council texts had the opposite effect on Döllinger, an opponent of Papal Infallibility, who shortly thereafter separated himself from the Catholic Church.

Church doctrine and history occupied Newman's thoughts as a theologian and Church historian, yet he was a man of great humanity who was still concerned with his friends and those around him. Newman, who lived a long life, outlived his Oxford friends and felt their loss. In 1873, Edward Bellasis, to whom years later he dedicated the

---

willed his Church to enjoy in defining doctrine concerning faith or morals." Vatican Council, session IV, chapter IV (July 18, 1870), available at: http://www.ewtn.com/library/COUNCILS/V1.HTM#6.

3 *LD*, Vol. XXV, JHN to Ambrose St. John (August 21, 1870), 191-193, 192.

4 *Ibid.*

5 *LD*, Vol. XXV, JHN to Georges Darboy, Archbishop of Paris (end of 1870), 259.

Grammar of Assent, died. Bellasis had been a loyal friend and a trusted legal adviser. He had become a Catholic in 1850, and two of his sons joined the Birmingham Oratory. In 1872, Newman lost two other close friends, Henry William Wilberforce and James Hope-Scott. At the funeral Mass for Wilberforce, a priest took Newman to the pulpit. After being unable to say anything for some minutes, Newman spoke of his friend whom he had met fifty years before and who became "a fool for Christ's sake."[6] A week later, Newman preached a beautiful homily, "In the World, but not of the World," at the funeral Mass for James Hope-Scott in London.[7] Newman praised his friend, a distinguished lawyer, who, despite great prestige and numerous professional contacts and social relations, had been able to keep himself from worldliness.

These men embodied Newman's vision of a Christian gentleman, which differed from the worldly and utilitarian vision espoused by Lord Shaftesbury. Newman's friends were men of faith and virtue. They were much more than men polished by the fine arts, proper taste, or useful knowledge.[8] These were the type of men that Newman had wished to form at the Catholic University of Ireland and at an Oratory in Oxford. Denied the possibility of effectively carrying out his work in Dublin or of establishing an Oratory at Oxford, he and the Birmingham Oratorians formed

---

6 *The Weekly Register* (May 10, 1873), 295, cited in *LD,* Vol. XXVI, footnote n. 1, 300.

7 "In the World, but not of the World," in *OS*, 263-80.

8 M. Katherine Tillman, "A Rhetoric in Conduct: The Gentleman of the University and the Gentleman of the Oratory," *Newman Studies Journal* (Fall 2008), Vol. 5, No. 2, 6-25.

younger men at the Oratory School. They hoped that these men would one day carry their faith and virtues into the university and professional occupations. Both Wilberforce and Hope-Scott owed a great deal to Newman, who recognized and fostered the unique and vital role that Catholic laymen should play in the intellectual spheres of society and government.

Newman's was not the only attempt at starting a Catholic university. In 1874, a plan by Archbishop Manning to establish a Catholic university in Kensington, just south of London, failed for lack of sufficient Catholic youth prepared for university studies and of families who could afford the costs. Newman did not oppose Manning's plans for a Catholic university, but he had become convinced that the presence of Catholic students at public universities was inevitable.[9]

Even as Newman's public profile receded, still there came a time when he had to make another public defense. He had chosen not to accept invitations to serve as an expert at Vatican Council I, but soon he was called upon to publicly defend the council's dogma of Papal Infallibility. It was another important service rendered to the Church, as had been the case with his *Lectures on the Present Position of Catholics in England* and his *Apologia Pro Vita Sua*. The occasion arose when his friend, William E. Gladstone, a religious man with a good sense of justice, surprisingly wrote an article in which he criticized some of the council decrees. Gladstone argued that Catholic convictions would lead men to relinquish their moral and intellectual freedom

---

9 Morales, *Newman (1801-1890)*, 312.

and to abandon their civil responsibilities on the basis of a foreign authority.

As a rebuttal to this nonsense, and urged on by Henry Fitzalan Howard (the Duke of Norfolk), and other Catholic nobles such as William Monsell (1st Baron Emly), and George Robinson (Marquis of Ripon), himself a recent convert to Catholicism, Newman published on January 14, 1875, the soon famous *Letter to the Duke of Norfolk*. It was a brilliant defense of Catholic citizens in which Newman asserted that they are loyal citizens of any just state. He explained that the Catholic religion does not keep Catholics from fulfilling their obligations as loyal citizens and that the Holy See does not have the custom of interfering in their civic duties. Newman repeated the teaching of the Constitution *Pastor Aeternus* of Vatican Council I, which asks Catholics for obedience to the Pope only in matters of faith and morals, and in matters of discipline and ecclesiastical government. From this qualification regarding the obedience asked of Catholics by the Pope, Newman offered a masterful explanation of the moral conscience, which is neither eliminated, nor substituted by authority. Proper authority strengthens the judgment of conscience, making it possible for the person to act with true freedom.

Newman explained that together with the external witness to God which comes to us through the teaching of the Pope and the *Magisterium*, we have conscience, an internal witness which commands man to fulfill his duty. He described conscience as a messenger from God, an internal witness of God's Revelation which like a high priest is able to command, to judge and to bless:

The rule and measure of duty is not utility, nor expedience, nor the happiness of the greatest number, nor State convenience, nor fitness, order, and the *pulchrum*. Conscience is not a long-sighted selfishness, nor a desire to be consistent with oneself; but it is a messenger from Him, who, both in nature and in grace, speaks to us behind a veil, and teaches and rules us by His representatives. Conscience is the aboriginal Vicar of Christ, a prophet in its informations, a monarch in its peremptoriness, a priest in its blessings and anathemas, and, even though the eternal priesthood throughout the Church could cease to be, in it the sacerdotal principle would remain and would have a sway.[10]

In this same passage and others in the *Letter to the Duke of Norfolk* Newman argued against the arbitrary usurpation of conscience as a license for one's own utility or pleasure. Conscience is always bound to the truth. It should never be used as a justification for a self-referential interpretation of goods and events which cuts man off from God and His Revelation.

Newman received numerous congratulations for his Letter, including those of Paul Cullen, Archbishop of Dublin.[11] Cullen had issued a pastoral letter about Gladstone's claims. In it he wrote: "The grounds on which this statesman founded his expostulation have been admirably answered by the venerable Dr. Newman, for many years the great and pious and learned rector of the Catholic University, whom Ireland will revere. . . ."[12]

Newman and Gladstone remained friends. In January 1875 Newman wrote him a friendly letter expressing his

10 "A Letter Addressed to the Duke of Norfolk on Occasion of Mr. Gladstone's Recent Expostulation," in *Diff.*, II, 248–249.

11 Morales, *Newman (1801-1890),* 317.

12 *LD.,* Vol 27, xvi.

grief at having had to write the *Letter to the Duke of Norfolk*. He explained, "I could not help writing it. I was called upon from such various quarters; and my conscience told me, that I, who had been in great measure the cause of so many becoming Catholics, had no right to leave them in the lurch, when charges were made against them as serious and unexpected."[13] Gladstone replied that he had intended the remarks for "Vaticanismus" only, that is, Ultramontane Catholics.

A few months later, in May of 1875, Ambrose St. John, Newman's close friend and disciple, died a premature death. Newman told David Moriarty, Bishop of Kerry, that this was the greatest affliction that he had suffered in his life.[14] And he told another friend that this severe blow was a necessary preparation for his own death.[15] It was only natural that as his intimate friends died, Newman thought more and more about the reality of death and eternal life.

More than just considering the last things, in 1864, while writing the *Apologia,* he had a presentiment of an imminent death. In this situation, Newman wrote a final testament, which revealed a deep Trinitarian faith. Newman's will expressed his lively sense of the communion of the saints and his devotion to the Fathers of the Church. A few months later, in 1865, Newman composed and published his longest poem, *The Dream of Gerontius.* The poem conveys

---

13 *LD,* Vol. XXVII, JHN to William Ewart Gladstone, (January 16, 1875), 193.

14 *LD,* Vol. XXVII, JHN to David Moriarty, Bishop of Kerry (June 5, 1875), 313.

15 *LD,* Vol. XXVII, JHN to John Hungerford Pollen (September 5, 1875), 350.

important Christian truths about the soul's immortality, personal judgment at the moment of death, the intercession of the saints and angels, Christ's Majesty, and the merciful nature of Purgatory. Most of the ideas were already present in his Anglican sermons. The poem was well received, and later became famous when, in 1900, Edward Elgar turned it into a musical oratorio.

CHAPTER 41

CARDINAL OF THE ROMAN CATHOLIC CHURCH

IN addition to the *Dream of Gerontius* and the *Apologia*, the *Letter to the Duke of Norfolk* consolidated Newman's national prestige. People honored Newman; one of the honors that was most moving to him came from his first college at Oxford. In 1878, Samuel William Wayte, President of Trinity College, conferred on Newman the position of Honorary Fellow of Trinity. Newman traveled to Oxford as Wayte's guest. There he saw Short, his old Tutor, and called on Pusey. It was an emotionally charged visit, since it was the first after a very long lapse in years, filled with powerful memories of his youth, the Oxford Movement, and his later conversion to Roman Catholicism.

Toward the end of Newman's life came an even more important event that was the crowning achievement of his human career and re-vindication of the orthodoxy of his writings as a Roman Catholic. For years, Newman had hoped to have his conduct and writings cleared by the Holy See.[1] This finally happened when Pope Leo XIII, who in 1878 succeeded Pope Pius IX, decided to create

---

1 *AW*, 262.

Newman a cardinal of the Roman Catholic Church.[2] In the summer of 1878, Henry, the fourteenth Duke of Norfolk, had asked his cousin, Cardinal Edward Henry Howard, to obtain a complete rehabilitation of Newman's good name in England and ask the Pope to create him cardinal. Henry had studied as a boy at the Oratory School, and when he reached an adult age. he worked to advance the Catholic cause in his country. The Duke also asked Manning, then a cardinal, to present the petition to the Pope. Leo XIII, who knew about Newman and the Oxford Movement from the time he had been *nuncio* in Belgium, agreed to the petition, but wished to know Newman's opinion beforehand. In December of 1878, a friend of Newman working at the French Embassy in Rome was able to greet the Pope whose secretary Msgr. Macchi asked the Pope for an Apostolic blessing for Newman. Pope Leo XIII took a picture of Our Lady of Lourdes from his breviary and wrote a dedication to Newman with his own hand.[3]

Upon notification by Bishop Ullathorne of the Pope's wishes, Newman wrote a letter to Ullathorne thanking the Pope and pleading to be excused from moving to Rome, for cardinals without a See were obliged to live in Rome. This letter, which could be interpreted as a rejection of the Pope's offer, was to be accompanied by a letter from Ullathorne to Manning plainly stating that Newman accepted but wished to be excused from living in Rome. An unsympathetic Cardinal Manning misinformed the Vatican's Secretary of State that Newman declined the honor. When the

---

2 Morales, *Newman (1801-1890)*, 323-29.

3 See *LD*, Vol. XXVIII, note (December 27, 1878), 435.

press found out of Newman's alleged rejection of the cardinalate, Manning was obliged to convey to Pope Leo XIII Newman's acceptance.

Newman's friends and admirers asked Newman about the rumors and pleaded with him to accept. In a letter John Patrick Crichton-Stuart, Marquis of Bute, wrote: "My object is to implore you not to decline—I know that St. Philip declined, and that you will have a tendency to do the same."[4] Bute proceeded to enumerate various reasons. The first was for the sake "of the labours and principles, which would thus be sanctioned, and of your disciples, who have admired the one and received the other, and of the general world, to whom they would thus be made more useful . . ."[5] Newman candidly complained: "if the facts be as the Papers give them and private correspondence confirms, it would seem that, when I send to Rome a confidential letter to be interpreted necessarily by the Pope, it is intercepted, read, interpreted and that interpretation given to the world, when it gets no further than London!"[6] When Newman wrote to Cardinal Howard in Rome that the impression that he had declined the Holy Father's wishes was unfounded, Howard replied to congratulate Newman and told him: "At first a report gained some credence that in your humility for various reasons you had been disposed to decline this honour, but it immediately became known that the Holy Father very decidedly wished to confer the hat upon you,

---

4 *LD*, Vol. XXIX, Lord Bute to JHN (February 19, 1879), 33.

5 *Ibid.*

6 *LD*, Vol. XXIX, JHN to the Marquis of Bute (February 21, 1879), 33.

and thus all doubt ceased to exist upon the subject."[7] Pope Leo XIII quickly informed Newman that he would not need to move permanently to Rome. Due to Manning's inexcusable action, Newman was almost denied the honor of the cardinalate, as he had been denied the episcopacy by Cullen's and Wiseman's actions.[8] After this course of events, a wearied Newman had more reason to maintain his distant relation with Cardinal Manning.

In April 1879, Newman traveled for his fourth and last time to Rome. A few days after his arrival he had a very warm meeting with the Holy Father, who affectionately asked him about the Birmingham Oratory. On May 12, Newman delivered an address known as the *Biglietto Speech*, named thus for the Italian word for ticket, officially notifying him of his elevation to the cardinalate. In this memorable address, Newman described his life's ambition and work: "For thirty, forty, fifty years I have resisted to the best of my powers the spirit of liberalism in religion . . . it will not, I hope, be considered out of place, if I renew the protest against it which I have made so often."[9] On May 15, at a consistory, the Pope conferred on Newman the red hat worn by cardinals. Papal authority had figured prominently in Newman's conversion, and from the time of his conversion he had received signs of recognition and kindness from Pope Gregory XVI and Pius IX. This gracious act by

---

7 *LD*, Vol. XXIX, Cardinal Howard to JHN (March 10, 1879), 59.

8 Gray, *Cardinal Manning, A Biography*, 266-67.

9 John Henry Newman, *Addresses to Cardinal Newman and His Replies,* "Biglietto Speech" (May 12, 1879), 64, available at: http://www.newman-reader.org/works/addresses/file2.html#biglietto.

Pope Leo XIII recognized Newman's orthodoxy and service to the Church. The Pope asked Manning to tell Newman " that in elevating you to the Sacred College he intends to bestow on you a testimony to your virtues and learning: and to do an act grateful to the Catholics of England, and to England itself for which he feels an affectionate interest."[10]

In June 1879, Newman returned to England as a national figure. Many groups wished to honor him, and he again visited Trinity College. His Anglican friends: Frederic Rogers, who had become Lord Blachford, William Church, William Copeland, and Lord Coleridge gave him the gift of a carriage. Newman's joy was mingled with sorrow, for that year, on Christmas Day, Jemima, his only remaining sister, died at the age of seventy-two. And Pusey, whose conversion Newman prayed for, did not advance toward Catholicism. In 1878, hearing that Pusey was gravely ill, Newman had sent him a note through Henry P. Liddon, Pusey's close friend and biographer. It was an invitation to die as a Roman Catholic. Pusey recovered, and for his birthday in 1880, Newman wrote to him: "You know the prayer your birthday raises in my mind. I don't like to say it out, yet I don't like it unsaid,"[11] but Edward B. Pusey died an Anglican in 1882.

Newman continued to prepare and publish a standard edition of his works which he had begun in 1876. He finished the edition in 1881 with the publication of his translation of the *Treatises of St. Athanasius*. Newman's

---

10 *LD*, Vol. XXIX, Cardinal Manning to JHN (March 8, 1879), 60.

11 *LD*, Vol. XXIX, JHN to E. B. Pusey (August 22, 1880), 296-297, 297.

body had aged, but his intellectual capacity remained intact. He was interested in Leo XIII's encyclical *Aeterni Patris*, the question of Biblical Inspiration, and especially the growing problem of the secularism of English society.

In addition to preparing the standard edition of his works, Newman prepared materials and letters for someone to write a biography of his Anglican years. Earlier, Newman had expressed the opposite desire, since he had already written an autobiography. He changed his mind, considering that without adequate materials and his letters, a biography would be incomplete and contain errors. He wished for an Anglican to write the biography of the first period of his life and to publish his correspondence as an Anglican. Newman found in Anne Mozley, his sister-in-law, the right person and corresponded a great deal with her to assist her. One year after Newman's death, she published his correspondence up to 1845. In a memorandum for a future biography Newman had written: "I don't want a panegyric written of me, which would be sickening, but a real fair downright account of me according to the best ability and judgment of the writer."[12]

In the last decade of his life, Newman's activity was significantly curtailed by poor eyesight and difficulty in hearing. Fr. William Neville, a convert, ordained a priest in 1861, cared for Newman with great dedication. Newman still had visitors, but his correspondence was reduced to the minimum and he usually dictated his letters, for he could hardly write. The Cardinal celebrated Holy Mass in a small chapel set up next to his room in the Birmingham

---

12 *LD*, Vol XXVIII, Memorandum (July 24, 1876), 92.

Oratory. The chapel was dedicated to St. Philip Neri and had a large painting of the saint made by Maria Giberne. It also had many photos of his deceased friends, whom he remembered daily during the Mass. Newman kept a calendar with the anniversary of significant dates in the lives of his friends, and particularly the date of their death. He offered Mass for their souls on the anniversary of their deaths.[13] Newman found great comfort in the practice of prayer for the deceased. His deceased family members and friends lived on not only in his memory, but also in his prayers.

Newman no longer traveled much, but in 1886, he went to the Brompton Oratory in London for the funeral Mass of the Duchess of Norfolk, Henry's mother. There he met Cardinal Manning, whom he had not seen for some years. In 1887, he went to London again, this time to see his physician, Dr. Ogle. Newman was aware that he was gradually declining in health even though his doctor denied it. That same year, Newman had a visit from Archbishop Ullathorne. The Archbishop later recounted that after a long and lively conversation, Newman asked him in a soft and humble manner to please give him a blessing, and then knelt down to receive it. Ullathorne could not refuse to bless him, despite the protocol that ranks a cardinal above an Archbishop. After the visit, the latter wrote, "I felt annihilated in his presence, there is a saint in the man."[14]

---

13 James Tolhurst, "A Blessed and Ever enduring Fellowship: The development of John Henry Newman's Thought on Death and Life Beyond," *Recusant History*, XXII (1994-1995): 439-40.

14 William Ullathorne cited by Martin, *John Henry Newman, His Life & Work*, 138.

Along with testimonials like this one by Ullathorne and descriptions of Newman by William Church, various portraits were made of Newman in his old age. In 1888, Newman sat for a second portrait by Emmeline Deanes; she had painted another one of him in 1844. Lady Coleridge (1874), Walter William Ouless (1879), and John Millais (1881) had also done portraits of Newman. One of Newman's friends commented on Millais's portrait of Newman as a cardinal: "It is magnificent; it gives the dignity, gentleness and strength of his face; a most powerful portrait."[15] The painter's daughter, Miss Millais, said the Cardinal is a "beautiful old man."[16] Newman also had a number of photographs taken of him alone, or with his Oratory brothers.

In June 1888, Newman traveled to London to make out his will. He chose as his executors three members of the Birmingham Oratory: William Neville, Henry Bellasis, and Anthony Pollen, and through them left his property to the Oratory. He entrusted the copyright of all his works, and his letters and documents, exclusively to Fr. Neville.

The following year, Newman went to Wales for a short vacation. In October, he had a fall which made the Oratorians fear for his life, and he was administered the Last Sacraments. Newman recovered, but he felt closer to his final home. The last of his old friends, Frederic Rogers, died in November. On Christmas Day of that year, 1889, Newman celebrated his last Mass.

In July of the following year, he was able to give the prizes at the Oratory School and to attend the performance

---

15 Anne Pollen cited, *ibid.*, 136.
16 Miss Millais cited, *ibid.*, 137.

of *Andria*, a Latin play. Newman had arranged the text for the students. A few weeks later, on the night of August 9, he developed pneumonia and received the Last Sacraments. Then, on the evening of August 11, 1890, in his ninetieth year, John Henry Cardinal Newman died.

The whole country mourned Newman's death. Every newspaper carried the news of his death and praised his accomplishments. According to the contemporary writer, Richard H. Hutton, there was "an almost unanimous outburst of admiration and reverence from all the English churches and all the English sects for the man who had certainly caused the defection of a larger number of cultivated Protestants from their Protestant faith than any other English writer or preacher since the Reformation."[17] Newman's funeral Mass was held at the Brompton Oratory in London, and Cardinal Manning preached the homily, giving tribute to the greatness of Newman.

Newman was buried on August 19 at Rednal, a country home for the Oratorians just outside Birmingham, and according to his instructions, his remains were placed in the grave of his dear friend Ambrose St. John.[18] Newman chose for himself the epitaph *Ex Umbris et Imaginibus in Veritatem* (From the shadows and reflections into the truth). His cardinal's motto, *Cor ad cor loquitur* (The heart speaks to the heart) was embroidered on the pall. Both

---

17 Richard H. Hutton, *Cardinal Newman* (London: Methuen and Co., 1891), 250.

18 Newman had chosen this existing, yet uncommon practice of friends sharing tombs as a sign of his special bond of friendship with Ambrose St. John.

the epitaph and the pall made reference to seeking and speaking the truth. All his life, from a very young age, Newman had sought the truth in religious matters. Newman had embraced what he called a "doctrinal principle," the belief that religion is based on set truths that hold a claim on people's reason and heart.

Newman had summed up his life's pursuit of truth when he defined relativism in religion at the ceremony where he accepted his appointment as cardinal:

> Liberalism in religion is the doctrine that there is no positive truth in religion, but that one creed is as good as another, and this is the teaching which is gaining substance and force daily. It is inconsistent with any recognition of any religion, as true. It teaches that all are to be tolerated, for all are matters of opinion. Revealed religion is not a truth, but a sentiment and a taste; not an objective fact, not miraculous; and it is the right of each individual to make it say just what strikes his fancy.[19]

From his youth, Newman had embraced the maxim, "Holiness rather than peace,"[20] almost synonymous with "Truth rather than peace." He maintained this principle to the end of his life. And he employed his intellect and energies in fighting Liberalism in religion, the idea which is with us still, that there are no fixed principles and that there is no one truth in religion. After a very long and careful examination of religious truths, together with daily prayer and frequent fasting, he became convinced that the Roman Catholic Church was the one and only Church founded by Christ and God's chosen instrument of salvation.

---

19 Newman, *Addresses to Cardinal Newman and His Replies,* 64.
20 *Apo.,* 5.

The pursuit of truth overcame his natural desire to remain within the comfort of his Anglican parish and Oxford College.

The Oxford don, Anglican clergyman, and finally Roman Catholic priest of the Oratory of St. Philip Neri dedicated his life to explaining and defending religious truths, and to uncovering and correcting errors. He did so with the force of logical reasoning, deep knowledge of Scripture, and with the aid of historical facts. Sometimes he employed satire, which made him a formidable opponent. But at all times, like his patron, St. Philip Neri, he defended religious truths with patience tempered with understanding, and with a forgiving spirit bolstered by cheerfulness. And like St. Francis de Sales, from whom Newman took the motto *Cor ad cor loquitur*, he sought to win others by gentle persuasion to the truth.

Newman leaves a rich intellectual and spiritual legacy. His long life and extensive writings continue to inspire and teach numerous Christians. New editions of his works are published every year, as well as many scholarly and popular articles. Theology continues to be enriched by his ideas and arguments. People find in his sermons reasons to live their Christian vocation more earnestly. Many, guided by Newman, overcome prejudices toward Roman Catholicism, and still many Christians, also under his inspiration, are received into full communion with the Catholic Church.

No biography of Newman would be complete without a mention of his prayer life, which sustained him throughout the whole of his lifetime. As a Catholic priest, Newman continued to dedicate much time to daily prayer. In addition to praying the Liturgy of the Hours, he offered the Sacrifice of the Mass daily. Newman also spent time meditating on the liturgical feasts and seasons of the year. Some of the reflections and prayers that he composed were compiled (after his death) under the title *Meditations and Devotions*.[21] We can fathom a little bit of his relationship with God by looking at the choice of words in the prayers that he composed and the subjects of his reflections. For instance, for visits to the Blessed Sacrament he composed meditations on Christian doctrine. Newman considered often the Passion and Death of Jesus Christ, as reflected in his meditations for the practice of the Stations of the Cross. In them, Newman expressed a constant awareness of man's sinfulness and fall from grace, yet a childlike trust in God's forgiveness, as well as our need to take part in Christ's suffering. For the fifth station he wrote:

> JESUS could bear His Cross alone, did He so will; but He permits Simon to help Him, in order to remind us that we must take part in His sufferings, and have a fellowship in His work . . . He saves us by His blood, but it is through and with ourselves that He saves us. Dear Lord, teach us to suffer with Thee, make it pleasant to us to suffer for Thy sake, and sanctify all our sufferings by the merits of Thy own.[22]

He wrote in a simple and profound way, and used a familiar style for children and for people who went to the Oratory parish in Birmingham. The Oratorian's devotion

---

21 John Henry Newman, *Meditations and Devotions*, available at: http://www.newmanreader.org/works/meditations/index.html. After this it will be cited *MD*.

22 *MD*, 159.

to the Blessed Virgin Mary was a tender one, rooted in the biblical texts. He composed beautiful Marian reflections for each day of May, traditionally dedicated to Mary. In these reflections he explained the richness of Christian Tradition, as when he comments on the litanies of the Rosary:

> She is called the *Tower* of David because she had so signally fulfilled the office of defending her Divine Son from the assaults of His foes. It is customary with those who are not Catholics to fancy that the honours we pay to her interfere with the supreme worship which we pay to Him; that in Catholic teaching she eclipses Him. But this is the very reverse of the truth.[23]

Newman's prayer was centered on a humble praise to the Blessed Trinity, and a constant petition to God for the necessary graces to live a holy life. As a Catholic, the angels and the saints, especially the Blessed Virgin Mary, St. Joseph, the Apostles, St. Philip, and St. Athanasius were frequently on his mind. Also, as a Catholic, his interior life was marked by intercessory prayer, especially for the conversion of friends. The fruits of his relationship with God were charity toward his neighbors, forbearance, perseverance, and hope.

In England, the Oratory of St. Philip Neri established by Newman continues to fulfill its mission and to bear new fruits. In 1990, Maurice Couve de Murville, Archbishop of Birmingham, asked the Birmingham Oratory to run the Church of St. Aloysius in Oxford, formerly under the care of the Jesuits. In 1993, the Oxford Oratory was established as an independent congregation. Thus the desire of both

---

23 *MD,* 68.

Archbishop Ullathorne and Newman was in the end realized: an Oratory was founded in Oxford to serve the human,
intellectual, and spiritual needs of Catholics at Oxford.

The distinguished Oratorian was greatly admired by Pope
Pius XII and Pope Paul VI, but due to delays in gathering
necessary documentary proofs for the diocesan process, his
Cause for beatification moved slowly. Once the diocesan
process was completed, the findings were sent to Rome for
the apostolic process. In January 1991, the happy outcome
of the latter led Blessed Pope John Paul II to declare that
John Henry Newman had lived all of the Christian virtues
in a heroic degree and was thus henceforth to be called by
the title "Venerable."

The results of this theological and canonical process
were confirmed by divine intervention in 2001. In that year,
John Sullivan, a 62-year-old Boston man, who had asked
Venerable Newman for his intercession, was miraculously
cured from lumbar disc disease that had produced severe
pain and incapacity to walk. A study by physicians concluded that there was no medical explanation for the man's
instantaneous cure, and in 2009, the Holy See approved the
cure as a miracle attributed to the intercession of Venerable
Newman.

This miraculous cure opened the way for the Roman
Catholic Church's formal recognition of Newman's sanctity. On September 19, 2010, Pope Benedict XVI, a longtime admirer of Newman, beatified John Henry Newman
in the city of Birmingham. The Pope, who earlier had spoken of Newman's "passion for the truth" and called him a
"champion of the laity," included Newman in the "tradition
of gentle scholarship, deep human wisdom and profound

love for the Lord" of men and women such as Saint Bede, Saint Hilda, Saint Aelred, and Blessed Duns Scotus.[24] Like Pope Leo XIII's elevation of Newman to the dignity of cardinal—and even more, this national event has undoubtedly filled the English people with joy. It is the hope of many that it will awaken in people a desire to read Newman's life and works and that it will usher in a new spring in the re-evangelization of the English-speaking world, and in particular, of Great Britain.

---

24 Benedict XVI, Papal Homily at the Beatification of John Henry Newman, September 19, 2010, available at: http://www.zenit.org/article-30411?1=english.

ABOUT THE AUTHOR

THOUGH born in Venezuela, Fr. Juan R. Vélez grew up in Colombia, where his family traces its roots for many generations. He studied for some years in London and Philadelphia, then obtained a degree in medicine at the University of Navarre, Spain and trained in Internal Medicine in Pittsburgh. Afterwards he studied theology at the Pontifical University Santa Croce in Rome and obtained a doctorate in theology at the University of Navarre. In 1998 he was ordained a priest for the Prelature of Opus Dei, and since then has served as a university chaplain in Boston, Princeton, and Los Angeles. At present he resides in Chicago. He has published a number of academic articles on Cardinal John Henry Newman and co-authored a short anthology of texts titled *Take Five, Meditations on John Henry Newman*. He has also written a number of journal articles on Medical Ethics. Most recently he has published *A University Education for the 21st Century: the Opening of the American Mind* (Createspace, 2015).

GLOSSARY OF TERMS

Anglo-Catholics. Anglicans who adhere to many of the liturgical practices, devotions, traditions and doctrines of the Roman Catholic Church. Anglo-Catholics are also known as High Church Anglicans.

B.A. Bachelor of Arts. The undergraduate degree gained after passing final examinations once completing 3 to 4 years at Oxford.

B.D. Bachelor of Divinity. At Oxford, unlike other universities, this is a postgraduate degree.

Chancellor. The ceremonial head of the university appointed by Convocation.

Class. The level of award of a degree, for example, first, second or simply pass.

Collections. Exams at the beginning of the term.

Colleges. The institutions which make up the University. Each has its own governing body, Fellows, and Tutors. The senior office of each college is often referred to as the Head of House.

Common Room. A meeting place for students that was the center of the college life. Fellows had a Senior Common Room.

Conditional Baptism. Baptism in case of doubt as to whether a person has already been validly baptized. The priest baptizes using the words, "If you are not baptized, N., I baptize you . . . "

Convocation at Oxford. Meeting of the Oxford M.A.s to elect the university officers and vote on proposed measures and the revision of statutes.

Convocation. An assembly or synod of Anglican bishops and representatives of the clergy. Convocation was suspended in England at the beginning of the eighteenth century.

Curate. Clergyman who assists a rector in the spiritual care of a parish. He may have in his charge a curacy, which is a small chapel within a parish.

Dean. Title of the head of some colleges, "for example, the Dean of Christ Church College. Also a Fellow responsible for supervising the conduct of Junior Members of the College."

Dissenters. The name given in 19th-century England to Christians who were not members of the Anglican Church, such as Puritans and Roman Catholics.

Don. A professor, a lecturer or a Fellow. The name derives from the Latin *dominus,* meaning master.

Evangelical. The group in the Anglican Church that emphasized piety, biblical teaching, and morality, while minimalizing the role of the hierarchy, Tradition, and doctrine.

Exhibition. A financial grant or award to a student. The student awarded this scholarship is an exhibitioner.

Fellow. An elected member of a college. Fellows are members of the governing body of the college.

Gentleman-Commoner. A student who does not have a scholarship.

Hall. Like a college, a residence for students that has its own teaching staff. Also the dining hall of a college.

Hebdomadal Council. Administrative council of the University.

High Church Anglicans. Another name for Anglo-Catholics or for the party of Anglo-Catholics within the Anglican Church.

Hilary term. Spring term. (See Michaelmas and Trinity.)

Latitudinarian. See Low Church Anglicans.

Living. A benefice or salary and housing for a clergyman.

Long Vacation. Summer holidays.

Low Church Anglicans. Initially a pejorative term for Anglicans who espoused Protestant and Puritan beliefs and practices, in contradistinction to High Church Anglicans. "Low Church" is synonymous with "Broad Church" and "Latitudinarian" because these Anglicans provided much latitude in church doctrine and discipline.

M.A. Master of Arts. A degree obtained after 21 terms (7 years) as a Fellow.

Master. Another name for the principal of a college. For example, the Master at Balliol College or Pembroke College.

Michaelmas term. Autumn term. (See Hilary and Trinity.)

Non-Conformists. Another name for Dissenters from the Established Anglican Church.

Oriel. The fifth oldest college, founded at Oxford in the early fourteenth century. Newman was a Fellow and Tutor at Oriel.

President. Another name for principal of a college. For example, the President at Corpus Christi College.

Proctors. Two proctors (senior and junior proctors), university officers, elected each year by colleges in rotation to serve for one year. They ensure the statutes, regulations and customs are observed.

Provost. Head of a college, for example, Provost of Oriel.

Rector. Head of a college, for example, Rector of Lincoln College, or the head of an Anglican parish.

Thirty-Nine Articles. The statements defining Anglican doctrine established in 1563 by a Convocation of the Church of England.

Trinity term. Summer term. (See Hilary and Michaelmas.) Trinity is the name of a college founded in the sixteenth century. Newman did his undergraduate studies at Trinity College.

Tutor. A college Fellow assigned students on an individual basis and serves as both a teacher and academic guide. Tuition is the teaching provided at the college.

Vicar. A clergyman who works at a parish. A vicar was often called a curate from the Latin word *cura,* meaning spiritual charge.

Vice-Chancellor. The senior officer of the University.

BIBLIOGRAPHY

Primary Sources

Newman, John Henry. *Letters and Diaries*. Edited by Charles Stephen Dessain, Ian Ker, Thomas Gornall, Edward E. Kelly, Gerard Tracey, and Francis J. McGrath. Oxford: Clarendon Press, 1978–2009.

Newman, John Henry. Uniform Edition. http://www.newmanreader.org/works/index.html.

Newman, John Henry. *Autobiographical Writings*. Edited by Henry Tristram. New York: Sheed & Ward, 1957.

Newman, John Henry. *Mary, the Virgin Mary in the Life and Writings of John Henry Newman*. Edited by Philip Boyce. Leominster, England: Gracewing Publishing, 2001.

Newman, John Henry. *The Philosophical Notebook of John Henry Newman*. Edited by Edward Sillem, 2 vols. New York: Humanities Press, 1969–1970.

Newman, John Henry. *Sermon Notes of John Henry Newman, 1849–1878*. Edited by Fathers of the Birmingham Oratory. London: Longmans & Green Co., 1913.

595

Newman, John Henry. *John Henry Newman and the Abbé Jager: A Controversy on Scripture and Tradition, 1834–1835.* Edited by Louis Allen. London: Oxford University Press, 1975.

Secondary Sources

Abbott, Edwin A. *The Anglican Career of Cardinal Newman.* Vol. II. London: Macmillan and Co., 1892.

Blehl, Vincent. *The White Stone: The Spiritual Theology of John Henry Newman.* Petersham: St. Bede's Publications, 1999.

Culler, Dwight. *The Imperial Intellect: A Study of Newman's Educational Ideal.* New Haven: Yale University Press, 1955.

Dessain, Charles S. *John Henry Newman.* Oxford: Oxford University Press, 1980.

Ker, Ian. *John Henry Newman.* Oxford: Oxford University Press, 1988.

Lockhart, William. *Cardinal Newman.* London: Burns & Oates, 1891.

Martin, Brian. *John Henry Newman.* London: Continuum, 1982.

Morales, José. *Newman 1801–1890*. Madrid: Ediciones Rialp, 1990.

Trevor, Meriol. *Newman, The Pillar of the Cloud; Newman, Light in Winter.* Garden City, New York: Doubleday & Company, Inc., 1962.

Ward, Maisie. *Young Mr. Newman.* New York: Sheed & Ward, 1948.

OTHER

Bowden, John Edward. *The Life and Letters of Frederick William Faber, D.D.* Philadelphia: John Murphy & Co., 1869.

Church, Richard William. *The Oxford Movement: Twelve Years, 1833–1845.* London, Macmillan & Co, 1904.

Chapman, Ronald. *Father Faber.* London: Burns & Oates, 1961.

Dawson, Christopher. *The Spirit of the Oxford Movement.* London: Sheed & Ward, 1933.

Finch, Michael. *Newman, Towards the Second Spring.* San Francisco: Ignatius Press, 1991.

Gray, Robert. *Cardinal Manning, A Biography.* New York: St. Martin's Press, 1985.

Hulsman, John. *The Rule of Our Warfare, A Reader.* New York: Scepter Publishers, 2003.

Hutton, Richard H. *Cardinal Newman.* London: Methuen and Co., 1891.

Jaki, Stanley L. *Newman to Converts, An Existential Ecclesiology.* New Hope, Kentucky, 2001.

Liddon, Henry Parry. *Life of Edward Bouverie Pusey.* London: Longmans, Green, and Co., 1894.

Mann, Stephanie A. *Supremacy and Survival: How Catholics Endured the English Reformation.* New York, Scepter Publishing, 2007.

Newman Studies Journal. National Institute for Newman Studies, 2004–2011.

Newman Studies Institute webpage: http://www.newmanworks.org.

Newsome, David. *The Parting of Friends: The Wilberforces and Henry Manning.* Grand Rapids: Wm. B. Eerdmans Publishing Co., 1993.

Nichols, Aidan. *The Panther and the Hind.* Edinburgh: T & T Clark, 1993.

Periero, James. *Cardinal Manning, An Intellectual Biography.* Oxford: Clarendon University Press, 1998.

Shane, Leslie. *Henry Edward Manning, His Life and Labours*. London: Burns, Oats, & Washbourne, Ltd., 1921.

Ratzinger, Joseph. *God Is Near Us*. San Francisco: Ignatius Press, 2003.

Shrimpton, Paul. *A Catholic Eton? Newman's Oratory School*. Leominster: Gracewing, 2005.

Wilson, Alfred. *Blessed Dominic Barbieri, Supernaturalized Briton*. London: Sands & Co. Ltd., 1967.

Ward, Wilfrid. *The Life and Times of Cardinal Wiseman*. London: Longmans, Green and Co., 1897.

INDEX

Achilli, Giacinto, 525, 526, 527, 530

Acton, Lord John Emerich Edward Dalberg, 538, 540, 555

Adams, John Quincy, 8

Aeterni Patris, 579

Allies, Thomas William, 430, 483, 538

St. Ambrose, 18, 297, 551

Anglo-Catholic Theology, 220–244

Antiquity of the Catholic Church, 37, 170, 202, 208–210 222, 269, 274, 275, 332, 359, 375

St. Anselm, 428

Apologia Pro Vita Sua, 2, 36, 46, 117, 158, 229, 240, 320, 347, 485, 548–556, 560, 569, 572, 574

Apostolicity ("note"), 472

Apostolic Fathers, 52

Apostolic Succession, Doctrine of, 32, 52, 54, 168, 173, 175, 176, 180, 183, 185, 193, 274, 276, 280, 286, 295, 298, 302, 408, 477, 481

Aquinas, St. Thomas, 229, 256, 512, 559

Arian Heresy, 129, 132, 134, 136, 181, 249, 340, 342

Arians of the Fourth Century, The, 130–136, 186, 542

Aristotle, 45, 512, 513, 557–559

Arnold, Thomas, 88, 101, 182, 310, 342, 360

St. Athanasius, 135, 142, 181, 297, 340, 348, 356, 358, 359, 360, 367, 411, 436, 470, 586

Athanasian Creed, 17, 45

St. Augustine, xi, 18, 225, 226, 275, 276, 291, 297, 396, 481, 499, 512, 540

Autobiographical Writings, 63, 65

Dr. Babington, 430

Bacon, Francis, 558

Badeley, Edward, 364, 385, 418, 429, 440, 522, 526, 538

Bagot, Bishop of Oxford, 243, 248, 263, 267, 270, 324–326, 339, 340, 344, 362–365, 371, 390, 394

Baptism, 37, 38, 40, 43, 44, 177, 194–196, 204, 215, 221, 224, 227, 228, 238–240, 245, 261, 267, 295, 298, 300, 318, 360, 414, 481, 482, 503, 590; Regeneration, 37–40, 54, 58, 108, 180, 198, 218, 321, 522

Baptists, 195, 345

Barbieri, Fr. Dominic, 329, 376, 377, 381, 436, 498

Barnabó, Alessandro, 543, 553, 554

St. Basil, 135, 142, 181, 291, 297

Venerable Bede, 428

Becket, St. Thomas, 150, 182

Beethoven, 26, 97, 550

St. Bellarmine, Robert, 203, 229, 256

Bellasis, Edward, 285, 364, 392, 445, 446, 538, 567, 568

Beveridge, William, 174, 232; *Private Thoughts Upon Religion,* 18

Biglietto Speech, 577

Birmingham Oratory, xvi, xviii, 67, 285, 527, 533–535, 549, 550, 552, 568, 577, 579, 581, 582, 586; Edgbaston, 241, 527; Rednal, 241, 582

Bishop of Jerusalem, 344

Bittleson, Henry, 553

Blanco White, Joseph, 31, 44, 45, 51, 97, 207, 461 467

Blomfield, Charles James, Bishop of London, 103, 198, 343, 344, 432, 447, 470

Bloxam, J.R., 242, 278, 281, 288–290, 309, 328, 329, 330, 374, 509

Book of Common Prayer, 46, 111, 113, 116, 161, 162, 175, 176, 180, 210, 269, 316, 363, 434

Borromeo, St. Charles, 296, 511

Bowden, Elizabeth, 75, 311, 415, 419, 432, 442, 463, 464, 488, 490, 500, 501, 504, 520, 535

Bowden, Henry, 52, 520

Bowden, John (son of John William Bowden), 520

Bowden, John William, 22, 25, 28, 75, 98, 144, 172, 174, 181, 189, 199–201, 216, 223, 234–236, 247, 257, 262, 264, 269, 278, 284, 291, 292, 303, 304, 321, 344, 414, 415, 416, 429, 463, 471, 509

Bowden, Marianne, 75, 98, 487

Bowles, Emily, 455, 543

Bowles, Frederick Sellwood, 370, 389, 453, 454, 502, 504, 517, 547

Bowles, Mrs. Frederick, 390, 454, 455

Branch Theory, 29, 222, 275, 343, 567

Breviary (Liturgy of the Hours), 216, 219, 230, 231, 244, 267–269, 362, 368, 369, 575

Bridges, Charles B., 387, 389, 436

British Critic, 208, 220, 246, 247, 249, 270–272, 280, 281, 286, 287, 302–305, 333, 348, 354, 355, 360, 364, 366, 367, 379, 393, 397

British Magazine, 130, 137, 138, 140, 180, 183, 184, 186, 199, 311, 439

Brompton Oratory (London Oratory), 519, 522, 533–535, 539, 580, 582

Lord Brougham, 100, 103, 349–352

Bull, John (*Defensio Fidei Nicenae*), 131

Bunsen, Christian J., 147, 342

Butler, Joseph, 34, 40–43, 46, 558; *Analogy of Religion, Natural and Revealed, to the Constitution and Course of Nature,* 40, 558

Callista: A Tale of the Third Century, 531

Calvinism, Calvinist, 3, 12, 15, 17, 19, 31, 39, 58, 107, 161–163, 298, 363, 434

Campion, St. Edmund, 163

Capes, John Moore, 456, 457, 498, 540

Capes, Simpson, 541

Caroline Divines, 115, 116, 163, 164

Catholic Emancipation, 91, 101, 102, 109, 188; Irish Temporalities Bill, 102, 103, 180

Catholic University Gazette, The, 530

Catholic University of Ireland, 67, 525–536, 568

Catholicity, 222, 298, 343, 359, 406, 472, 478, 479

Celibacy, 19, 49, 63, 64, 72, 76, 77, 150, 300

Chricton-Stuart, John Patrick, Marquis of Bute, 576

Christian Missionary Society, 100, 106, 198

Christian Observer (Evangelical), 176, 223, 224

Christian Remembrancer, 441

Christian Year, 46, 86, 415

Christie, Albany J., 366, 451, 486, 500, 509

Christie, John Frederic, 240, 241, 263, 265, 284, 304, 326, 356, 423, 451

Church Architecture (cross reference Pugin), 52, 281, 306, 307, 309, 372

Church Fathers, 18, 52, 79, 129, 131, 134, 136, 151, 174, 178, 210, 222, 233, 243, 245, 257, 260, 262, 271, 273, 276, 356, 477, 479, 531

Church, Richard W. "Dean", 41, 117, 165, 260, 386, 549

Churton, Edward, 246–248, 305

Clapham Sect, 15, 167

Clifford, William, Bishop of Clifton, 540

Coffin, Robert, 509, 517

Coleridge, Edward, 421–423

Lady Coleridge, 581

Communion (Sacrament of), 23, 57, 77, 116, 124, 160, 240, 253, 257, 344, 371, 392, 415, 416, 427, 429, 448, 465, 466, 488, 498, 503

Communion Service, 77, 162, 231, 232, 244, 284, 299, 433, 482, 496

Confession (Sacrament of), 29, 164, 239, 299, 300, 430, 479, 483, 498

Confirmation (Sacrament of), 23, 81, 215, 238, 239, 284, 344, 482, 498, 508

Constantine, Emperor, 135

Convocation, Oxford, 101, 102, 160, 189, 190, 193, 199, 212, 338, 432–435, 439–441, 443, 444, 446, 466, 468, 471, 565

Copeland, William, 119, 172, 233, 305, 357, 509, 510, 550, 578

Copleston, Edward, 47, 211

Councils, 130, 131, 134, 205, 206, 273, 274, 316, 323, 386, 389, 410, 411, 445, 478, 522, 565–567, 569, 570; Chalcedon, 274, 410, 478; Constantinople, 135, 478; Nicaea, 135, 411; Trent, 203, 204, 215, 228–230, 243, 253, 316, 323, 377, 389; Vatican I, 566

Cranmer, Thomas, Archbishop of Canterbury, 160, 161, 266

Cullen, Paul, Archbishop of Armagh, Later Archbishop of Dublin, 524, 526, 528–530, 571, 577

St. Cyprian, 481, 531

Dalgairns, John Dobrée, 259, 357, 369, 376, 377, 389, 396, 405, 436, 448, 450, 452, 453, 498, 499, 500, 502, 504, 513–515, 517

Darnell, Fr. Nicholas, 545

Davison, John, 367

Dawson, Christopher, 105

De Maistre, Joseph, 474

Deanes, Emmeline, 581

Deism, 41, 105

Development of Christian Doctrine, Theory of, xi, 204, 205, 413, 436, 470–485

Discourses to Mixed Congregations, 521, 522

Dissenters, 21, 166, 176, 179, 187, 188, 189, 192, 194–197, 199, 240, 254, 310, 330; Dissenter's Marriage Bill, 193, 194, 196, 197, 241; Dissenters University Relief Bill, 188; Jubber Affair, 195, 196

Döllinger, Johann Joseph Ignaz, 229, 518, 555, 567

Donatist Heresy, 274–276, 411, 462, 477

Dream of Gerontius, The, 574, 575

Dublin Review, 274, 291, 381, 497, 525, 540, 541, 565, 566

Eden, Charles, 383, 429

Editorship of the British Critic, 270, 271, 280, 303, 354–356, 360, 393

Elgar, Edward, 573

English Churchman, 380, 420, 433, 441

English Reformation, 113, 158, 187, 201, 267

Erastianism, Thomas Erastus, 53, 100, 173

Essay in Aid of a Grammar of Assent, An, xii, 13, 285, 400, 545, 557, 558, 560–564, 568

Essay on Apollonius of Tyana, 33

Essay on the Development of Christian Doctrine, An (cross reference Development of Christian Doctrine, Theory of), 42, 210, 272, 398, 470–507

Essay on Miracles (*Two Essays on Biblical and on Ecclesiastical Miracles*), 33, 97

Eucharist, Holy, 29, 49, 57, 116, 149, 162, 176, 207, 216, 232, 239, 245–270, 298, 299, 318, 320, 332, 335, 341, 346, 347, 384, 386, 415, 466, 482, 483, 485; Real Presence, 49, 116, 160, 162, 163, 255–257, 269, 299, 335, 384, 386, 425, 466, 482

Evangelical Movement (The Society for Promoting Christian Knowledge and The Society for the Propagation of the Gospel), 14, 30, 32, 106, 165

Faber, Frederick William, 259, 300, 396, 402, 426, 427, 438, 502, 509, 518, 519, 533–535, 538, 556

Faber, George S., 200, 261, 262

Fasting, 177, 231, 244, 278, 282, 288, 295, 312, 363, 367, 368, 369, 379, 583

Fausset, Godfrey, 252–256, 269, 354, 355, 384, 386

Fisher, St. John, 160

Flanagan, Fr. John Stanislas, 533, 547

Fortescue, Edward B., 455

Froude, Richard Hurrell, 19, 45, 47–49, 74, 76, 98, 102, 105, 109, 111–120, 125, 126, 128, 137, 138, 144, 146, 150, 169, 171–174, 179, 181, 182, 184, 207, 211, 215, 216, 218, 219, 220, 230, 231, 233–235, 247, 248, 251, 252, 253, 255, 263, 267, 301; *Remains of the Late Rev. Richard Hurrell Froude*, 113, 234, 235, 248, 251, 252, 266, 267, 269, 302, 514

Froude, Mrs. William, 408, 409, 413, 418, 500, 564

Froude, William, 247, 557, 561, 564

Fullerton, Lady Georgiana, 495, 509

Garbett, James, 338, 339

Gentili, Fr. Luigi, 377, 378, 390, 429

Gibbon, Edward, 131

Giberne, Maria, 75, 86, 90, 92, 221, 235, 249, 265, 291, 299, 307, 310, 325, 397, 420, 438, 449, 463, 465, 481, 493, 509, 525, 546, 565, 580

Gladstone, Helen, 373, 374

Gladstone, William Ewart, 78, 97, 339, 343, 373, 395, 405, 406, 422, 423, 441, 444, 489, 569, 571, 572

Golightly, Charles, 83, 266, 267, 302, 321, 381, 419, 420, 467; Memorial to the English Reformers, 266, 302

Good, Elizabeth, 2, 11

Gorham, George C., 179, 522

Gregorian University, 511

Haddan, Arthur, 305

Hampden, Renn Dickson, 184, 190, 191, 193, 211–214, 238, 310, 360, 365, 366, 385, 432; "Elucidations of Dr. Hampden's theological statements," 212

Harrison, Benjamin, 172, 202, 265, 310

Hawkins, Edward, 31, 36, 39, 44, 47, 48, 58, 77, 102, 103, 109, 115, 121, 124, 126–128, 136, 191, 321, 341, 365, 366, 383, 384, 387, 419, 467, 500

Hobbes, Thomas, 123

Holmes, Miss Mary, 299, 305, 306, 312, 334–336, 346, 372, 373, 382, 387, 388, 424–429, 449, 451, 458

Homilies, 161, 224, 227, 228, 244, 257, 316, 317, 323, 434

Hooker, Richard, 105, 342

Hope, James R. (Hope-Scott), 284, 285, 302, 303, 310, 327, 341, 344, 364, 405, 406, 440, 445, 508, 522, 526–528, 538, 568, 569

Hopkins, Gerard Manley, 552

Howard, Cardinal Edward Henry, 575, 576

Howley, Archbishop of Canterbury, 342–344, 444

Hume, David, 34, 560

Hutton, Richard H., 523, 582

The Idea of a University, 349, 353, 526, 529, 563

St. Ignatius of Antioch, 52, 174, 271, 272, 366, 413

The Imitation of Christ, 306, 390

Inglis, Sir Robert, 102

St. Irenaeus, 43, 174, 233, 413, 484

Jager, Abbé Jean-Nicholas, 202, 204–207, 219, 224, 232, 261

Jelf, Richard, 59, 321, 322, 357

Jenkyns, Henry, 124, 341, 432

Jerusalem Bishopric, 103, 316, 342, 344, 345, 347, 359, 468

Jesuits, 327, 511, 514, 516, 586

Johnson, Manuel, 509

Justification, Doctrine of, 15, 30, 37, 53, 224–229, 237, 238, 243, 248, 250, 317, 318, 341, 360, 565

Keble, John, 45–48, 73, 86, 98, 101, 105, 111–113, 117–119, 137–139, 169, 171, 172, 178, 179, 191, 196, 199, 211–213, 216, 221, 233, 235, 247, 248, 259, 263, 264, 267–269, 284, 286, 287, 305, 308, 322, 326, 338, 341, 342, 355, 363, 380, 383, 385, 391, 394, 397, 398, 400, 401, 409, 410, 413, 415, 416, 420, 422, 423, 424, 438, 459, 489, 499, 501, 505, 511, 551

Keble, Thomas, 118, 172, 241

Ker, Ian, xii, xiii

King, 160, 179, 183, 199, 212, 342; Charles I, 163; Charles II, 163; Edward VI, 29, 161; George III, 100; Henry II, 150; Henry VIII, 20, 21, 159, 161, 180, 183, 208, 222; James I, 89

Kingsley, Charles, 548, 549

Knox, Thomas Francis, 302, 449, 509

Laud, William, Archbishop of Canterbury, 78, 105, 164, 210, 385

Law, William (*Serious Call to Holiness and Devotion*), 17

"Lead Kindly Light," 156, 467

Leahy, Patrick, Archbishop of Cashel, 532

LeBas, Charles Web, 249

Lectures on certain difficulties felt by Anglicans in submitting to the Catholic Church, 522

Lectures on Justification, 40, 229, 243, 248, 563

Lectures on the Present Position of Catholics in England, 457, 524, 537, 569

Lectures on the Prophetical Office of the Church, 219, 223, 563; *Viewed Relatively to Romanism and Popular Protestantism*, 208, 220, 222, 408

Legge, Edward, Bishop of Oxford, 56, 72

Lenthall, Elizabeth, 416, 488

Letter to the Duke of Norfolk, 556, 565–574

Lewis, David, 357, 510

Library of the Church Fathers, 233, 266, 356

Liddon, Henry P., 578

Lifford, Lord James H., 236–238

Liguori, St. Alphonse, 327, 340, 375

Littlemore, 81, 88, 99, 108, 109, 155, 216, 218, 219, 241, 242, 257, 265, 267, 275, 278, 281, 284, 288–290, 305, 308, 311, 356–361, 367–372, 377, 378, 380, 383, 387, 389–391, 396, 397, 402, 404, 428, 429, 430, 436, 438, 448–454, 458, 463, 484, 487, 488, 490, 491, 494, 496, 498, 499, 500, 502–505, 508–510, 516, 547; Church of St. Mary and St. Nicholas, 219

Lives of English Saints, The, 384, 396

Lloyd, Charles, 32, 113

Locke, John, 558, 559

Lockhart, William, 79, 370, 390, 397, 454

Lockhart, Mrs. (mother of William Lockhart), 390, 454

Lollards (John Wycliffe), 158, 159

Loss and Gain, 482, 503

Luther, Martin, 30, 37, 159, 160, 225, 226, 257

Lutheranism, Lutheran, 103, 106, 158, 159, 160, 161, 208, 224, 225, 226, 257, 269, 298, 316, 342, 344, 347, 359, 434, 468

Lyall, William R., 130, 131

Lyra Apostolica, 138, 221

Lythgoe, Fr. Randal, 496

Maclaurin, William Cowper, 292–295

Maitland, Samuel, 246, 247

Manning, Henry Edward, Cardinal, 78, 221, 235, 236, 246–248, 259, 260, 276, 277, 283, 310, 394, 410, 421, 422, 442, 443, 489, 522, 526, 551–553, 555, 556, 569, 575, 576, 577, 578, 579, 580, 582

Mansell, Willliam, 538

Mant, R., Bishop of Down, Connor and Dromore, 361, 362

Manzoni, Alessandro (*Promesi Sposi*), 282, 327

Marriot, Charles, 290, 438, 441, 509

Mayers, Walter, 12, 16, 18, 51, 55, 121

Maynooth (St. Patrick's College), 375

Meditations and Devotions, 585

Mediterranean Travel, 125, 131, 137–151, 152–157, 176, 291; Corfu, 141–142, 146, 151; Ithaca, 141; Malta, 137, 140, 141, 143, 144, 146, 304, 515; Naples, 145, 146, 150–152, 514; Sicily, xiii, 141, 144–146, 150–157

Methodism, Methodist revival, 30, 78, 108, 165, 175, 345, 521

Meyrick, Thomas, 396, 451

Millais, John, 581

Milner, Joseph (*History of the Church of Christ*), 14, 17, 103

Miracles, 33–35, 43, 45, 47, 93, 94, 133, 405

Miraculous Medal, 452, 453

Mohler, Johannes, 474

Monk, 21, 72, 122, 160, 262, 327, 367, 396, 405, 519; monastery, 219, 289, 291, 327, 357, 358

Monophysitism, Monophysite, 274, 275, 344, 410, 411, 424, 478

Monsell, William (1st Baron Emly), 554, 570

Montgomery, George, 447, 448, 453, 498

Morales Marín, José, xv

More, Hannah, 51, 237

More, St. Thomas, xi, 160

Moriarty, David, Bishop of Kerry, 531, 572

Morris, Thomas Edward, 259, 277, 278, 285

Mozley, Anne, 75, 76, 443, 579

Mozley, James Bowling, 265, 266, 281, 304, 441, 442, 467

Mozley, John, 218, 247, 395

Mozley, Thomas, 73, 76, 98, 145, 174, 218, 263, 266, 280, 284, 290, 303, 304, 307, 308, 313, 355, 364, 366, 379, 393, 397, 402, 407; *Reminiscences Chiefly of Oriel College and the Oxford Movement,* 98

Neri, St. Philip, 514–516, 580, 584

Neville, William, 579, 581

Newman, Charles Robert, 4, 43, 66, 70, 91, 93–96, 99, 132, 217, 313, 314, 485, 486

Newman, Elizabeth, 11, 216, 219, 282, 423, 463, 486, 492, 527

Newman, Frank (Francis), 4, 23, 25, 43, 44, 61, 66, 69, 70, 73, 75, 83, 91–93, 96, 108, 218, 314, 485, 486, 493, 497

Newman, Harriet, 4, 9, 33, 88, 90, 98, 122, 142, 196, 218, 266, 308, 311, 314, 322, 373, 393, 394, 485, 527

Newman, Jemima (sister), 4, 8, 52, 77, 84, 86, 88, 89, 90, 145, 149,

200, 215, 218, 223, 238, 240, 258, 266, 288, 301, 302, 309, 313, 314, 343, 390, 394, 395, 418, 423, 438, 442, 443, 461, 463, 485, 492, 500, 511, 550, 578

Newman, Jemima Fourdrinier (mother of John Henry), 2, 3, 4, 23, 25, 55, 60, 62, 63, 73, 83, 84, 88, 89, 90, 91, 96, 216, 217, 258

Newman, John (father of John Henry) 2–5, 10, 11, 20, 25, 28, 55, 59, 60–64, 66, 69, 86, 91, 199

Newman, Mary, 4, 45, 77, 84–88, 99, 240, 260

Newton, Isaac, 17, 18, 42, 558

Nicholas, George, 6, 10, 28

Non-Jurors, 115

Norfolk, Duke Henry Fitzalan-Howard, 15th Duke of Norfolk, 538, 570

Oakeley, Frederick, 259, 311, 324, 355, 379, 388, 395, 396, 416, 436, 445, 446, 451, 455, 465, 468, 509

Oath of Supremacy, 160, 162, 383

Ogle, Dr. James A., 125, 266, 510, 580

Ogle, Octavius, 487

Old Catholics, 520

"On Consulting the Faithful in Matters of Doctrine", 184, 542

Oratorians, 514–518, 520, 525, 528, 534, 538, 539, 545, 566, 568, 581, 582, 585, 587; Oratory of St. Philip Neri, xviii, 514, 538, 584, 586

Oratory School, 535, 537, 539, 545, 546, 553, 569, 575, 581

Oriel College (Tutor), 25–37, 41, 45, 48, 52, 53, 54, 59, 64, 67, 77, 89, 97, 99, 110, 111, 112, 115, 118, 121–129, 130, 171, 184, 188, 189, 198, 200, 245, 266, 289, 291, 301, 357, 365, 367, 415, 470, 558

Oscott (St. Mary's College Oscott), 328, 337, 374, 450, 458, 498, 500, 504, 508, 518, 537

Ouless, Walter William, 581

Oxford Conservative Journal, 38, 376

Oxford Movement, 79, 111, 117, 118, 119, 129, 138, 139, 157–186, 193, 200, 201, 207, 217, 219, 221, 240, 242, 246, 266, 267, 272, 273, 281, 286, 306, 355, 357, 361, 363, 379, 397, 402, 450, 467, 503, 510, 511, 522, 523, 550, 574, 575

Oxford Oratory, 552, 553, 568, 586

Oxford Society for Promoting the Study of Gothic Architecture, 281

Oxford University, 19, 20, 55, 102, 107, 165, 166, 187, 190, 193, 310, 316, 496, 552; Religious tests or Subscription, 188, 190, 192, 193, 194, 211, 212, 214, 439

Oxford University Sermons, 399, 400

Paine, Thomas, 12

Palgrave, Sir Francis, 407

Palmer, Roundel, 385, 397

Palmer, William, 171–173, 183, 281, 305, 322

Papacy, 52, 158, 159, 193, 287, 294, 295, 413, 479, 512, 565, 566, 567; Pope as Antichrist, 18, 295, 296, 491

Papal Infallibility, 202, 205, 206, 211, 386, 436, 542, 565–573

Parker, Jane, 483

Parochial and Plain Sermons, 50, 81, 282, 312, 315

Pascal, Blaise, 117, 306, 330, 562; *Pensées*, 306

Passaglia, Carlo, 513

Passionist, 329, 376, 377, 436, 499, 504, 520

Peel, Robert, 101, 102, 110, 126, 348–350, 352, 353

Penny, Charles, 420

Perceval, Arthur, 171, 172, 176, 214, 215, 242, 322; *The Churchman's Manual*, 176

Perrone, Giovanni, 513

Phillipps, Ambrose, 328–332, 337, 377, 378, 381, 520

Phillpotts, Henry, Bishop of Exeter, 179, 250, 522

Philosophical Notebook, 557

Pole, Cardinal Reginald, 161

Pollen, Anthony, 581

Pope, 18, 146, 159, 160, 162, 164, 180, 183, 185, 200, 223, 224, 253, 274, 295–297, 320, 405 , 413, 481, 490, 491, 566, 567, 569, 570, 577; Benedict XVI, xi, 587; Gregory XVI, 505, 510, 512, 577; Leo the Great, 274, 410, 411, 478; Leo XIII, 574, 575, 576, 577, 578, 588; Bl. Pope Pius IX, 512, 515, 516, 517, 523, 524, 530, 534, 553, 565, 574, 577; Ven. Pope Pius XII, 587; Pope Paul VI, 587; Bl. John Paul II, 587; Julius, 411

Pope, Simeon Lloyd, 70, 98, 120, 199, 281, 497

Prayer, intercession, 11, 17, 18, 22, 23, 51, 56, 57, 61, 69, 113, 114, 139, 144, 156, 175, 218, 230–232, 238, 243, 261, 268, 278, 282, 283, 287, 288, 289, 310, 311, 313, 322, 327, 332, 333, 334, 347, 355, 356, 357, 367, 369, 371, 373, 374, 375, 379, 387, 389, 392, 397, 401, 429, 432, 462, 482, 488, 506, 515, 580, 583, 584, 585, 586; Invocation to the saints and the Blessed Virgin Mary, 389, 472, 479, 484, 515; Prayer for the deceased, 245, 260, 261, 362, 437, 580

Predestination, Doctrine of, 15, 17, 19, 39, 40, 50

Primitive Christianity, 34, 209, 210, 243, 269, 472, 473, 473

Private Judgment, 51, 202, 222, 261, 269, 272, 292–294, 333, 335, 426, 435, 455, 469

"Private Judgment" (essay), 354, 358, 359, 360

"Private Judgment" (poem), 138

Propaganda Fidei, Roman College of, Sacred Congregation of, 511, 512, 516, 533, 534, 543, 544, 552, 553

Protestant Reformation, 113, 158, 163, 206, 219, 231, 245, 248, 263, 267, 269, 307, 361, 366, 384, 411, 422, 475

Pugin, Augustus Welby, 307, 374, 407

Purgatory, doctrine, 37, 52, 149, 176, 201, 203, 320, 321, 386, 472, 479, 573

Puritanism, Puritan, 163, 164, 363

Pusey, Edward Bouverie, 31, 32, 47, 52, 55, 56, 73, 81, 90, 108, 111, 119, 172, 177, 178, 191, 196, 211, 212, 216, 221, 228, 232, 233, 235, 242, 243, 247, 248, 258, 259, 262, 263, 264, 267, 269, 279, 283, 284, 287, 288, 289, 290, 291, 292, 300, 302, 304, 305, 307, 315, 319, 321, 322, 324, 325, 326, 330, 341, 353, 355, 366, 373,

382, 384–386, 390, 392, 394, 397, 406, 409, 410, 414, 417, 428, 432, 433, 442, 444, 445, 446, 448, 449, 452, 453, 456, 459, 460, 461, 463, 468, 473, 481, 488, 489, 500, 502, 505, 510, 511, 551, 566, 574, 578;

Pusey, Maria (wife of Edward), 90, 240, 262, 279

Pusey, Lucy, 280, 414

Queen, 2, 160, 162, 439, 548; Catherine of Aragon, 159, 160; Elizabeth I, 160–163, 180, 183; Mary, 159, 160–162, 267

Record, The, 176, 185, 186, 338, 341, 371

Rambler, The, 540, 541, 543

Reform Bill, 101, 349

Revelation, xviii, 14, 16, 30, 34, 41, 47, 52, 94, 132, 170, 212, 214, 226, 351, 461, 473, 498, 544, 570, 571

Reynolds, Joshua, 559

Richmond, George, 488

Rickards, Samuel, 83, 98, 102, 120, 148, 191, 218, 240

Rivington, Francis, 174, 221, 405–407

Robinson, George, Marquess of Ripon, 570

Rogers, Frederic, Lord Blachford, 97, 128, 152, 155, 156, 182, 199, 233, 235, 241, 247, 275, 282, 284, 287, 297, 305, 309, 327, 440, 456, 467, 550, 578, 581

Rome, xvii, 119, 144–148, 150, 151, 158, 161, 167, 185, 200–202, 204, 207, 209, 239, 245, 252, 254, 255, 259, 273, 274, 276, 277, 282, 289, 292–298, 300, 310, 311, 315, 317, 324, 327–330, 333, 334, 336, 337, 340, 357, 359, 373, 375, 383, 384, 387–389, 394, 395, 397, 405, 408–410, 418, 426, 431, 435–438, 443, 449–451, 454, 455, 458, 464–466, 468, 469, 472, 477–479, 486, 488, 493, 494, 501–504, 509, 511, 513–515, 517, 534, 543, 544, 549, 553, 554, 559, 566, 575–577, 587

Rose, Hugh James, 130, 131, 137, 170, 171, 172, 177, 181, 182, 186, 213, 251, 266, 273

Rosmini, Antonio, 377

Ross, Sir William, 488

Routh, Martin Joseph, 208, 213, 223, 356, 446, 447

Russell, Lord John, 100, 193, 197, 365

Russell, Fr. Charles W., 299, 320, 328, 340, 376, 376, 429

Ryder, George, 74, 166, 518

Ryder, Henry Ignatius, 566

Sacred Scripture, canonicity, 11, 14, 15, 43, 53, 58, 68, 79, 80, 93, 132, 203, 208, 222, 226, 261, 387, 407, 437, 544; "Lectures on the Scripture Proof of the Doctrines of the Church," 262

de Sales, St. Francis, 296, 330, 337, 584

Schism, 20, 30, 139, 159, 177, 182, 222, 274, 293, 331, 336, 358, 360, 363, 374, 398, 411, 412, 456, 457, 466, 478, 479, 481–483, 493

Scott, Thomas, 14, 16, 17, 40, 103, 166, 454

Scott, Walter 7, 88, 370, 527

Seager, Charles, 39

Select Treatises of St. Athanasius in Controversy with the Arians, 359

Semi-Arians, 131, 340, 359

Sermons on Subjects of the Day, 313, 345, 400, 402

Short, Mr. Thomas, 23, 28

Shuttleworth, Philip, Bishop of Chichester, 310

Sibthorp, Richard Waldo, 337, 388

Smedley, Edward, 33

Smith, Bernard, 374, 375, 494, 495, 498

Socinianism, 238

Sparrow, Anthony, *A Rationale upon the Book of Common Prayer of the Church of England*, 243, 305

Spencer, Fr. George, 283, 284, 288, 327, 331, 458, 498

Spiritual Combat, The, 387

Spiritual direction, 152, 425–428, 449, 458

Standard, The, 189, 338, 420, 566

Stanton, Richard, 448, 449, 500, 502, 504, 517

St. Alban's Hall, 35, 59, 66, 67, 77

St. Clement's Church, 54, 55–59, 64, 77, 81, 395, 504

St. Margaret Chapel, 395, 445, 446

St. Mary the Virgin, University Church, 2, 31, 77–79, 81, 82, 109, 118, 126, 129, 311, 362, 380–403, 516

Sullivan, John, 587

Sumner, John Bird, *Apostolic Preaching Considered In An Examination Of St. Paul's Epistles*, 39

Tablet, The, 498, 540

Talbot, John, Sixteenth Earl of Shrewsbury, 307, 498

Talbot, Msgr. George, 525

Tamworth Reading Room, 123, 348, 352, 528

Times, The, 343, 348, 349, 350, 352, 420, 432, 523, 524, 526

"The Parting of Friends," 391, 402

Thirty-Nine Articles, 29, 92, 130, 162, 179, 188, 193, 201, 213, 214, 219, 224, 315–317, 321, 333, 377, 383, 388, 433, 440

Thucydides, 142, 153

Tickell, George, 436, 451–453

Tract 90, 270, 315–348, 354, 357, 359, 360, 361–379, 383, 384, 431, 434, 440–445, 466, 468, 510

Tracts of the Times, 118, 172–178, 185, 200–202, 223, 224, 228, 242, 243, 258, 263, 264, 267, 281, 285, 315, 324–327, 360, 361, 472

Tradition, 49, 52, 54, 58, 131, 132, 155, 165, 168, 202–208, 214–216, 219, 221, 261, 269, 277, 361, 412, 434, 446, 513, 542, 555, 586

Transubstantiation, 201, 203, 252, 253, 256, 257, 258, 269, 318–320, 332, 335, 384, 388, 389, 472

Trevor, Meriol, xiii, 74, 76

Trinity College, 20–27, 45, 70, 77, 98, 108, 117, 118, 121, 172, 181, 199, 232, 266, 301, 305, 339, 353, 366, 449, 574, 578

Tucker, Abraham, 559

Ullathorne, William Bernard, Bishop of Birmingham, 519, 520, 525, 538, 540, 541, 543, 551–553, 565, 566, 575, 580, 581, 587

Unitarianism, Unitarian, 16, 51, 100, 105, 386

University Sermons, 313, 466, 473, 545, 557, 564

Vaughan, Herbert, 339, 553, 555

Verses on Various Occasions, 140

Via Media, 200–219, 222, 229, 243, 378, 411

St. Vincent of Lerins (*Commonitorium*), 202, 205

Virgil, 6, 150, 153

Virgin Mary, 49, 52, 230, 327, 332, 359, 389, 426, 452, 472, 478, 483, 484, 512, 586

Wackerbath, Francis D., 328, 337

Ward, Maisie, 9, 72, 208

Ward, Wilfred, xiii, 208, 346

Ward, William G., 207, 259, 328, 341, 431–435, 439–447, 468, 496, 498, 566

Watts-Russell, Michael, 457, 458, 509

Weltch, Henry William, 487

Wesley, John, 14, 30, 78

Westamacott, Richard, 265, 337, 491

Whately, Richard, 31, 32, 35, 36, 44, 101, 102, 110, 116, 118, 211, 467

Wilberforce, Henry, 73, 83, 85, 89, 191, 195, 196, 231, 247, 280, 300, 303, 332, 334, 381, 388, 418, 446, 453–456, 463, 467, 488, 500, 517, 518, 521, 538, 541, 568, 569

Wilberforce, Robert Isaac, 47, 48, 74, 85, 86, 109, 112, 115, 120, 125, 126, 128, 247, 431, 489

Wilberforce, Samuel, 85, 236, 260

Wilberforce, William, *Practical Christianity*, 70, 147, 166, 167, 235, 284

Williams, Isaac, 108, 112, 117–120, 144, 172, 195, 218, 240, 258,

273, 281, 326, 338, 339, 366, 419, 420, 442, 511, 550

Williams, Robert, 258, 262, 267, 268, 275, 292, 293, 316, 336, 416

Wilson, Robert Francis, 128, 147, 198, 214, 247, 454, 499

Wiseman, Cardinal Nicholas, 147, 208, 274–276, 291, 320, 330, 332, 373, 374, 382, 424, 494–496, 498, 508, 511, 514, 522–526, 530, 533, 535, 538–541, 543–545, 551, 553, 556, 577

Wood, Charlotte, 464, 465, 488

Wood, Samuel Francis, 128, 224, 233, 258, 260, 267, 268, 293, 336, 337, 346, 397

Woodgate, Henry Arthur, 235, 240, 241, 258, 285, 291, 345, 358, 402

Wooten, Mrs., 545

Wynter, Philip, Vice-Chancellor of Oxford University, 321, 384, 432, 439

Young, Isabella, 373, 375

Young, Peter, 341

Saint Benedict Press publishes books, Bibles, and multimedia that explore and defend the Catholic intellectual tradition. Our mission is to present the truths of the Catholic faith in an attractive and accessible manner.

Founded in 2006, our name pays homage to the guiding influence of the Rule of Saint Benedict and the Benedictine monks of Belmont Abbey, just a short distance from our headquarters in Charlotte, NC.

Saint Benedict Press publishes under several imprints. Our TAN Books imprint (TANBooks.com), publishes over 500 titles in theology, spirituality, devotions, Church doctrine, history, and the Lives of the Saints. Our Catholic Courses imprint (CatholicCourses.com) publishes audio and video lectures from the world's best professors in Theology, Philosophy, Scripture, Literature and more.

For a free catalog, visit us online at
SaintBenedictPress.com

Or call us toll-free at
(800) 437-5876

Printed in August 2019
by Rotomail Italia S.p.A., Vignate (MI) - Italy